COSMOLOGY AND BIOLOGY IN ANCIENT PHILOSOPHY

In antiquity, living beings are inextricably linked to the cosmos as a whole. Ancient biology and cosmology depend upon one another, and therefore a complete understanding of one requires a full account of the other. This volume addresses many philosophical issues that arise from this double relation. Does the cosmos have a soul of its own? Why? Is either of these two disciplines more basic than the other, or are they at the same explanatory level? What is the relationship between living things and the cosmos as a whole? If the cosmos is an animate intelligent being, what is the nature of its thoughts and actions? How do these relate to our own thoughts and actions? Do they pose a threat to our autonomy as subjects and agents? And what is the place of zoogony in cosmogony? A distinguished international team of contributors provides original essays discussing these questions.

Ricardo Salles is a researcher at the Instituto de Investigaciones Filosóficas of the Universidad Nacional Autónoma de México. His recent books include *Los Filósofos Estoicos: Ontología, Lógica, Física y Ética* (with Marcelo Boeri, 2014) and *Alejandro de Afrodisias: De la Mixtura y el Crecimiento* (with José Molina, 2020). He is the editor of *Metaphysics, Soul and Ethics: Themes from the Work of Richard Sorabji* (2005) and of *God and Cosmos in Stoicism* (2009).

T0382273

COSMOLOGY AND BIOLOGY IN ANCIENT PHILOSOPHY

From Thales to Avicenna

EDITED BY

RICARDO SALLES

Universidad Nacional Autónoma de México

CAMBRIDGE UNIVERSITY PRESS

Shaftesbury Road, Cambridge CB2 8EA, United Kingdom

One Liberty Plaza, 20th Floor, New York, NY 10006, USA

477 Williamstown Road, Port Melbourne, VIC 3207, Australia

314–321, 3rd Floor, Plot 3, Splendor Forum, Jasola District Centre, New Delhi – 110025, India

103 Penang Road, #05–06/07, Visioncrest Commercial, Singapore 238467

Cambridge University Press is part of Cambridge University Press & Assessment,
a department of the University of Cambridge.

We share the University's mission to contribute to society through the pursuit of
education, learning and research at the highest international levels of excellence.

www.cambridge.org
Information on this title: www.cambridge.org/9781108812597

DOI: 10.1017/9781108873970

First published 2021
First paperback edition 2023

A catalogue record for this publication is available from the British Library

ISBN   978-1-108-83657-9   Hardback
ISBN   978-1-108-81259-7   Paperback

Contents

Contributors

TOMMASO ALPINA is Wissenschaftlicher Mitarbeiter at the Munich School of Ancient Philosophy of the Ludwig-Maximilians-Universität in Munich. He received his PhD in Islamic Philosophy from the Scuola Normale Superiore of Pisa. His main areas of research are the reception of Aristotelian philosophical psychology and zoology in Arabic philosophy, notably in Avicenna, and the connections between natural philosophy and medicine. He is the author of *Subject, Definition, Activity: Framing Avicenna's Science of the Soul* (2021).

GEORGE BOYS-STONES is Professor of Classics and Philosophy at the University of Toronto. His published work has focussed on the schools of the Hellenistic period and subsequent philosophical developments in the Roman Mediterranean. Books include *Post-Hellenistic Philosophy* (2001), *Platonist Philosophy 80 BC to AD 250* (2018) and the first complete edition of the Stoic Cornutus (2018).

JOHN M. COOPER (AB magna cum laude, Harvard, 1961; BPhil, Oxford, 1963; PhD, Harvard, 1967) was a faculty member at Princeton 1981–2016, until his retirement to emeritus status in July 2016. He taught previously at Harvard and the University of Pittsburgh. He works on Greek philosophy and is the author of *Reason and Human Good in Aristotle* (1975), *Reason and Emotion* (1999), *Knowledge, Nature, and the Good* (2004) and *Pursuits of Wisdom: Six Ways of Life in Ancient Philosophy from Socrates to Plotinus* (2012) and the editor of *Seneca: Moral and Political Essays* (1995) and *Plato: Complete Works* (1997).

JOHN DILLON, born 15 September 1939 in Madison, Wisconsin, USA, was educated at Oxford (BA, MA) and the University of California, Berkeley (PhD, 'The Fragments of Iamblichus' Commentary on the

Timaeus of Plato'). He was on the faculty of the Department of Classics, UC Berkeley, 1969–1980 (Chair of Department, 1977–1980) and was Regius Professor of Greek, Trinity College, Dublin, 1980–2006. Main focus of research is Plato and the Platonic tradition. Chief works include *The Middle Platonists* (1977, 2nd ed. 1996), *Iamblichus, De Anima* (with John Finamore, 2000), *Alcinous: The Handbook of Platonism* (1993), *The Heirs of Plato* (2003), *The Roots of Platonism* (2018) and three volumes of collected essays.

DIMITRI EL MURR is Professor of Ancient Philosophy (and Chair) at the Department of Philosophy, Ecole Normale Supérieure–Université PSL, and a member of the Centre Jean Pépin (UMR 8230, CNRS). His research area is ancient philosophy, especially Socrates, Plato and political Platonism in antiquity and beyond. He has published many articles on different aspects of Plato's thought. He is the author of *L'Amitié*, a collection of texts on the philosophy of friendship, with introduction and commentaries (2001; repr. with corrections, 2018). He co-edited, with A. Brancacci and D. P. Taormina, *Aglaïa: Autour de Platon* (2010); with G. Boys-Stones and C. Gill, *The Platonic Art of Philosophy* (Cambridge, 2013); and with M. Dixsaut et al., *Platon. Le Politique* (texte grec, introduction, traduction et commentaire, 2018). He also edited a volume on the *Theaetetus*: *La Mesure du savoir : Études sur le Théétète* (2013). His latest book is *Savoir et gouverner: Essai sur la science politique platonicienne* (2014).

LLOYD P. GERSON is Professor of Philosophy in the University of Toronto. He is the author of many monographs, articles and reviews on ancient philosophy, including the forthcoming *Platonism and Naturalism: The Possibility of Philosophy*. He is the editor and translator (with five others) of *Plotinus: The Enneads* (2017) and the editor of *The Cambridge History of Philosophy in Late Antiquity* (Cambridge, 2010).

R. J. HANKINSON grew up in London and was educated at Oxford and Cambridge Universities. Since 1986 he has lived and taught in North America. He has written several monographs and numerous articles on various aspects of ancient philosophy and science, in particular medicine.

ANDRÉ LAKS, born in 1950, was taught at the École Normale Supérieure in Paris, at the University of Paris-Sorbonne and the University of Lille, where he studied with Jean Bollack. He taught as a Professor of Greek and Ancient Philosophy at the University of Lille, at Princeton

University and at the University of Paris-Sorbonne, from which he retired in 2011. He has been teaching at the Universidad Panamericana in Mexico City since then. He was a member of the Wissenschaftskolleg in Berlin in 1999–2000 and of the Institut Universitaire de France from 1998 to 2008, and he spent 2017–2019 as a visiting scholar and professor at Princeton.

JAMES G. LENNOX is Professor Emeritus of History and Philosophy of Science at the University of Pittsburgh. He has translated Aristotle's *On the Parts of Animals* for the Clarendon Aristotle Series (2001) and is the author of *Aristotle's Philosophy of Biology: Essays in the Origins of Life Science* (Cambridge, 2001). He is co-editor of *Philosophical Issues in Aristotle's Biology* (Cambridge, 1987), *Self-Motion from Aristotle to Newton* (1994), *Concepts, Theories and Rationality in the Biological Sciences* (1995) and *Being, Nature, and Life in Aristotle* (Cambridge, 2010). He has also published widely on the importance of teleology in the history of biology, in particular in the writings of Robert Boyle, William Harvey, Asa Gray and Charles Darwin, and he is the author of the entries on 'Aristotle's Biology' and 'Darwinism' in the *Stanford Encyclopedia of Philosophy*.

RICARDO SALLES (BA Universidad Nacional Autónoma de México 1990; MPhil-PhD King's College London 1992–1997) is a Researcher at the UNAM, and was Junior Fellow of Center for Hellenic Studies in Washington, DC (2002–2003), Member of the Institute for Advanced Study in Princeton (2010–2011), Senior Fellow of the National Humanities Center in North Carolina (2018) and Visiting Scholar at Wolfson College in Oxford (2019). He is the author (with Marcelo Boeri) of *Los Filósofos Estoicos: Ontología, Lógica, Física y Ética. Traducción, comentario filosófico y edición anotada de los principales textos griegos y latinos* (2014). His latest works in English include 'Why Is the Cosmos Intelligent? (1) Stoic Cosmology and Plato, *Philebus* 29a9–30a8', *Rhizomata* 6.1 (2018), and 'Two Classic Problems in the Stoic Theory of Time', *Oxford Studies in Ancient Philosophy* 55 (2018).

BARBARA M. SATTLER is Professor for Ancient and Medieval Philosophy at the Ruhr-Universtät Bochum. She has previously taught at the University of Illinois at Urbana-Champaign, at Yale University and at St. Andrews University. Her main area of research is metaphysics and natural philosophy in the ancient Greek world, especially with the Presocratics, Plato and Aristotle. She is the author of *The Concept of*

Motion in Ancient Greek Thought (Cambridge, 2020) and is currently working on two book projects: one on the development of spatial notions in early Greek thought up to Aristotle and one on ancient notions of time, which connects ancient understandings of time with contemporary debates.

EMMANUELE VIMERCATI is Professor of History of Ancient Philosophy at the Pontifical Lateran University (Rome), where he has served as Dean of the Faculty of Philosophy (2014–2020). He is also invited Professor at the Patristic Institute 'Augustinianum' (Rome). He specialises in Stoicism and Imperial Platonism, with research interests also in the relation between philosophy and early Christianity and in the influences of ancient philosophy on later thought. His publications include *Il Mediostoicismo di Panezio* (2004), *Medioplatonici, Opere, frammenti e testimonianze* (2015), *Fate, Providence, and Free Will: Philosophy and Religion in Dialogue in the Early Imperial Age* (edited with René Brouwer, 2020), *Nicholas of Cusa and the Aristotelian Tradition: A Philosophical and Theological Survey* (edited with Valentina Zaffino, 2020) and several articles on peer-reviewed journals and edited collections.

KATJA MARIA VOGT (Columbia University) specialises in ancient philosophy, ethics and normative epistemology. In her books and papers, she focusses on questions that figure both in ancient and contemporary discussions: What are values? What kinds of values are knowledge and truth? What does it mean to want one's life to go well? She has published widely on ancient skepticism and its interlocutors as well as related themes in philosophy today. Her most recent book – *Desiring the Good: Ancient Proposals and Contemporary Theory* (2017) – focusses on questions about human motivation and agency. Currently, she is working on papers on Stoic logic and physics, as well as Plato's *Euthyphro* and *Philebus*. She is an editor of *Nous* and serves on the editorial boards of the *Journal of Philosophy, Apeiron*, and *Rhizomata* and as Associate Editor for philosophy of language, epistemology and logic of *Dialogoi: Ancient Philosophy Today*.

JAMES WILBERDING is Professor of Ancient and Contemporary Philosophy at the Humboldt-Universität zu Berlin. He is the author of *Plotinus' Cosmology* (2006), *Porphyry on How Embryos Are Ensouled and On What Is in Our Power* (2011) and *Souls, Forms and Embryos: Neoplatonists on Human Reproduction* (2016) and co-editor of *Neoplatonism and Natural Philosophy* (2011) and *Philosophical Themes in Galen* (2014), as well as having authored numerous articles and chapters on ancient philosophy.

Acknowledgements

The project behind the present volume involved three conferences held in Mexico City, when academic travel was still possible, from May 2016 to February 2017. I wish to thank the speakers for their participation as much as all the authors of chapters for joining the project. I am also thankful to David Sedley, Christopher Gill, Verity Harte, and André Laks for advice at the early stages; to Michael Sharp at Cambridge University Press for his interest and guidance; and to Sarah Starkey for taking the book forward through to publication. The three conferences took place at the Universidad Nacional Autónoma de México, and I am grateful to two research grants for their generous support, PAPIIT UNAM IN400517 and IN403620, as well as to the PAEP program, also from the UNAM, for its ongoing support. Important steps were completed while I was a GlaxoSmithKline Senior Fellow at the National Humanities Center in North Carolina and a Visiting Fellow at Wolfson College, Oxford, in 2018 and 2019, to which I am greatly indebted. Antonio Domínguez and Mayra Huerta helped me to revise the Index Locorum and I thank them for this. All remaining errors are my own.

The Intersection of Biology and Cosmology in Ancient Philosophy

Ricardo Salles

Ancient philosophers believed that biology and cosmology are two sciences that intersect one another insofar as biological concepts explain crucial features of the cosmos and, conversely, cosmological concepts account for important biological properties and events. 'Cosmobiology' is the term that I shall use to refer to this view. The aim of this introduction is to present some central cosmobiological theses in antiquity, to describe how the present volume is organised, and to offer a brief overview of the chapters.

The single most notorious expression of ancient cosmobiology is the idea, first fully developed by Plato, of a cosmic soul. The cosmos as a whole – understood as the ordered system composed of the Earth, the planets, the sun and the so-called fixed stars – is a single living animate being, comparable in many fundamental respects to an animal and, especially, to an intelligent animal, i.e. a living being that is capable of thinking and of displaying the characteristic motions unique to intelligent beings. In one of the strongest versions of this idea, the Stoic one, the different species of living beings constitute the organic parts of the cosmos in the sense that they have a specific function within the whole in much the same way as the different parts of an ordinary animal (its fins or its eyes, for instance) have a specific function in the life and the behaviour of the animal as a whole.[1] Cosmobiology, however, is not limited to the idea of a cosmic soul. The thesis that defines it – that biology and cosmology intersect one another – is very broad and does not necessarily imply the concept of a cosmic soul. In fact, some ancient philosophers accepted the thesis but rejected the concept. One case in point, as we shall see, is Aristotle. Moreover, philosophers who did accept the concept, often treat

---

[1] As is noted in Sedley 2016, the notion of organisms whose functional parts are also organisms, or 'superorganisms', is already present in Empedocles though not specifically applied to the cosmos as a whole as in Plato and the Stoics.

cosmobiological issues that are independent from it. One example is the
discussion of 'recapitulation' in Plato and Plotinus, i.e. of whether the
generation of individual living beings reproduces in small scale the generation, or logical design, of their species as distinct from other species in
the cosmic order. The chapters collected in this volume address ancient
cosmobiology in all its generality, including the concept of cosmic soul but
other cosmobiological themes as well.

Nowadays, ancient cosmobiology is frequently deemed the forerunner
of influential ideas in the philosophy of science and in metaphysics.
Modern panpsychism, for instance, is the view that at least some mental
powers are fundamental and ubiquitous in the cosmos.[2] One particular
variety of modern panpsychism, cosmopsychism, may be singled out for
attention.[3] Cosmopsychism is the combination of two metaphysical views:
priority monism, according to which all things ultimately exist and have
the powers they actually possess in virtue of certain facts about the cosmos
as a whole, and *constitutive panpsychism*, according to which facts about
the mental powers of animals are constituted by facts about the mental
powers of more fundamental entities. It follows from the combination of
these two views that all facts about the mental powers of animals are
constituted by facts about the mental powers of the cosmos as a whole.
Although modern cosmopsychists are not necessarily committed to the
ancient cosmobiological thesis that the cosmos is a single agent and the
subject of complex mental activities such as thought – '[i]t could be that
the consciousness of the universe is a gigantic mess that doesn't add up to
anything coherent enough to ground cognition'[4] – the general idea that
the cosmos as a whole possesses mental powers is no doubt present
in cosmopsychism.

In the field of philosophy of science, a theory that claims to be indebted
to ancient cosmobiology is the Gaia Hypothesis by James Lovelock and
Lynn Margulis.[5] This theory, opposed to the conception that life on Earth
exists only because the material conditions needed for its survival happen
by chance to be adequate, argues that the set of all living beings, or 'biota',
define and secure the endurance of these material conditions. One example

---

[2] See Russell 1927 and also Eddington 1928. For a recent collection on Russellian monism see Alter-
Nagasama 2015. See Nagel 1979 and, more recently, Nagel 2012: 35–70.
[3] For cosmopsychism see Mathews 2011, Jaskolla & Buck 2012, Shani 2015, Nagasawa & Wager
2016 and the collection of essays Brüntrup-Jaskolla 2017. See also Chapter 15 of this volume.
[4] Goff-Seagar-Hermanson 2017.
[5] For the earliest version of the Gaia Hypothesis, see Lovelock 1972, Lovelock-Margulis 1974, and
Lovelock 1976. See more recently Margulis 1999, Lovelock 2001 and Harding 2006.

given by the proponents of the Gaia Hypothesis is that of atmospheric temperature: although the energy provided by the sun has steadily increased since life began on Earth, the Earth atmospheric temperature has remained within the levels needed for the continued existence of life, and this regulation was supposedly achieved by the co-operative work of all biota through the performance of certain control functions, which vary from one species to the other. A similar explanation is given of the stability of oceanic salinity, of the overall amount of oxygen in the atmosphere, of the acidity of the soil, which are all crucial conditions for life. The idea that all living organisms work cooperatively to achieve the survival at the level of species led Gaia theorists to claim that the biosphere is itself a large single living organism. In the face of several scientific criticisms, the Gaia Hypothesis has evolved in many respects since it was first formulated, and has become an increasingly complex and sophisticated theory that cannot be adequately described in this introduction.[6] But the basic idea that all living beings taken together constitute a single living organism is obviously something that may be traced back, at least in general terms, to antiquity.

Leaving aside the question of whether all, or even some, of these modern ideas are present in detail in ancient cosmobiology – an issue that is not addressed systematically in this volume[7] – the key philosophical themes discussed in the present volume may be divided as follows. (a) Why would the cosmos have a soul of its own? What is the analogy, if any, between the psychic powers of the living beings and those of the cosmos? (b) Although biology and cosmology depend on one another by the use of biological concepts in cosmology and of cosmological concepts in biology, is either of these two disciplines *more basic* than the other or are they at exactly the same explanatory level? (c) What is the teleological relation between living things and the cosmos as a whole? In particular: do the former serve a higher cosmological purpose or is the cosmos teleologically ordered for their sake? What is the place of human beings within this complex structure? (d) If the cosmos is an animate intelligent being, what is the nature of its thoughts and actions? How do these relate to our own thoughts and actions? And do they pose a threat to our autonomy as subjects and agents? (e) What is the place of zoogony in cosmogony? No account of the generation of the cosmos could be complete without an account of the origin of living species, but how exactly do these evolve

---

[6] See for instance Tyrrell 2013.
[7] Chapter 15 discusses in detail modern panpsychism in connection with Plotinus.

from lower species or, in the case of non-evolutionary theories, how does their design involve features of lower species?

Despite their importance, most of these themes are still under-investigated in scholarship on ancient philosophy, and the sixteen essays that compose this volume will help to set the ground for the discussion of the issues. The chapters are divided by ancient authors ranging from key Preplatonic thinkers to Plato himself and the Middleplatonists (Chapters 1–5), and from Aristotle (Chapters 6 and 7) to the Stoics (Chapters 9–12) and to later Platonists (Chapters 13 and 14) and their reception in Avicenna (Chapter 15). Chapter 8 pursues the theme of biological recapitulation across the history of ancient philosophy, from early Preplatonic to late Platonic philosophy.

In most ancient Greek philosophies, 'soul' (ψυχή) is the principle of life. Any living being has a soul in virtue of which it is a living being as opposed to a non-living one. Thus even plants, insofar as they are living, have a soul. Higher mental capacities such as intellection or cognition, in the form in which they exist in human beings, are also accounted for by the possession of soul. Its explanatory connection to life and mental capacities is what *defines* soul.[8] This accounts for why ancient conceptions of the cosmos as a living being need to postulate a cosmic soul. The cosmos is supposed to have a soul of its own, distinct from the soul of the individual living beings that inhabit the cosmos, that explains why it is in itself a living intelligent being. This idea began to occupy a prominent place in ancient cosmobiology with Plato. But it is commonly assumed that it is an idea that Plato largely inherited from earlier thinkers, who should be regarded, therefore, as the first Greek cosmobiologists. The actual evidence for this, however, is extremely weak as is demonstrated by André Laks in Chapter 1 'Souls and Cosmos before Plato: Five Short Doxographical Studies') in connection with Thales, Anaximenes, Heraclitus, Pythagoras and Alcmeon. As is argued by Laks, the attribution to these authors of the concept of a cosmic soul is to a large extent the result of a Platonising and Stoicising exegesis.

Chapter 2, 'The Ensouled Cosmos in Plato's *Timaeus*: Biological Science as a Guide to Cosmology?' by Barbara Sattler, addresses the concept of cosmic soul in this central cosmobiological text, and explains

---

[8] The only notorious exception to this view is Stoicism, see below. The issue is addressed in connection with Plato in Carpenter 2010. Which powers, exactly, are involved in the possession of life is still a matter of dispute in modern science and philosophy of science. See Tirard-Morange-Lazcano 2010 discussed by Sattler in this volume.

how this concept is essentially biological and, in more general terms, how Platonic cosmobiology is indeed a part of biology. The Platonic cosmic soul resides in what Plato, followed by the Platonic tradition, postulates as the outermost sphere of the cosmos, the sphere that constitutes the surface of the cosmic body. The cosmic body is the focus of Dimitri El Murr in Chapter 3, 'Platonic "Desmology" and the Body of the World Animal (*Tim.* 30c–34a)'. The cosmic body is the subject of *Timaeus* 30c–34a. One of the main arguments in this difficult passage seeks to demonstrate that the physical cohesion of the whole cosmos is effected by the divine Demiurge through the action of four, and only four, basic elements or 'bonds' (δεσμοί): fire, air, water and earth. El Murr analyses this passage thoroughly and evinces its close connection to the philosophical project outlined by Plato in *Phaedo* 99b-c. The transmission of the Platonic concept of cosmic soul in the Academy is extremely complex. In Chapter 4, 'The World Soul Takes Command: The Doctrine of the World Soul in the *Epinomis* of Philip of Opus and in the Academy of Polemon', John Dillon explores the reception of this concept in the Old Academy by exploring its development from the late Plato of *Laws* X to Polemon, the last Head of the Old Academy and a crucial link in the transmission of Platonic cosmology to the Stoics and to later Platonism. In fact, cosmobiology and the concept of a cosmic soul are particularly prominent in Middle Platonism. Thus in Chapter 5, 'Begotten and Made: Creation as Cosmogony in Middle Platonism', George Boys-Stones brings out that according to key Middle Platonists the cosmos is indeed a living (and therefore ensouled) being, whose creation is explained in biological terms and whose soul is responsible for its biological functions.

Chapter 6, 'The *De Motu Animalium* on the Movement of the Heavens' by John M. Cooper, also explores Aristotle's criticism to the Platonic idea of cosmic soul. Cooper, however, concentrates on the *De Motu Animalium* and how Aristotle's reflection of animal locomotion led to him to posit in chapters 6–10 of *Metaphysics*, Book Lambda, a soul for each of the moved heavenly bodies, one that thinks the unmoved mover that it desires through a form of rational desire. Thus, Aristotle departs sharply from Plato and the subsequent Platonic, Stoic and Neoplatonic traditions, according to whom celestial motion is not be explained by individual souls in each of the celestial bodies, but by a single cosmic soul. Thus these two chapters complement each other well. The former presents a negative argument that proves indirectly that the cosmic prime mover cannot be a soul. The latter, by contrast, discusses the positive argument that even though the prime mover of the cosmos is not itself a soul, each of the

heavenly bodies must possess a soul by which they desire the primer
mover. Chapter 7, 'Biology and Cosmology in Aristotle' by James
G. Lennox, is devoted to the strong interrelation between biology and
cosmology in the actual practice of these two disciplines according to
Aristotle. As Lennox demonstrates, there are substantive borrowings in
both directions that evince how much each of them relies on facts established by the other. Before turning to the Stoics, one last chapter deals with
a cosmobiological theme running through the whole of ancient science, but
especially important in Plato and Aristotle. In Chapter 8, 'Recapitulation
Theory and Transcendental Morphology in Antiquity', James Wilberding
addresses the question of whether modern recapitulation theory and transcendental morphology may be traced back, at least in general terms, to
ancient philosophers and scientists. The key idea in recapitulation is that
ontogeny morphologically reproduces phylogeny: the morphology of an
embryo must correspond to the morphology of the animal at some point in
the evolution of its species or, in the case of non-evolutionary theories, at
some lower level in the scale of nature. The answer given by Wilberding
to the question of whether recapitulations theories, either evolutionary or
non-evolutionary, may be found in antiquity is largely negative.

The Stoics, following Plato, maintain that the cosmos has psychic
powers and, therefore, a soul. Chapters 9 and 10 concentrate on one
particular mental power that they attribute to the cosmos: rationality or
intellection. Chapter 9, 'The Stoics' Empiricist Model of Divine Thought'
by George Boys-Stones, examines the nature of Stoic divine intellection
which is, in some respects, analogous to cosmic intellection. An empiricist
explanation of divine intellection in terms of concept-acquisition faces two
basic challenges: god does not have sense-organs and, even if he did, there
is no appropriate object of empirical experience for him to have. Boys-
Stones offers a detailed discussion of these two challenges in the case of
god and argues that they can be adequately met if we look closely at the
(2) Stoic theory of perception and, in particular, Hierocles' discussion of
animal self-perception. Chapter 10, 'Why Is the Cosmos Intelligent? (2)
Stoic Cosmology and Plato, *Timaeus* 30a2–c1', offers a reconstruction of
one of the arguments given by the Stoics to prove that the cosmos is an
intelligent being, and explores its connection to the influential Platonic
proof at *Tim.* 30a2–c1. Chapter 11, 'Cardiology and Cosmology in Post-
Chrysippean Stoicism' by Emmanuele Vimercati, concentrates on another
feature of Stoic cosmobiology: the use by post-Chrysippean Stoics of
physiological concepts to describe the structure of the cosmos. Some
Roman Stoics – especially Seneca and Manilius – argued that cosmic

breath pervades the cosmos in the same way as the blood pumped by the heart circulates throughout animals. This cardiological conception of cosmic breath has important antecedents in earlier post-Chrysippean Stoics, especially in Diogenes of Babylon and Posidonius, in whom Vimercati points out an Aristotelian influence that may have played a significant role in the development of post-Chrysippean cosmobiology. In Chapter 12, 'The Agency of the World', the last of the chapters in this volume devoted to Stoicism, Katja Vogt tackles the general philosophical question of how the Stoics account for the totality of movement in the cosmos. Although the cosmos is a single unified whole, it is inhabited by an extremely large number of different entities that often seem to conflict and compete with one another. So is the totality of the movement in the cosmos the mere sum of the movements of all these entities or is it, rather, a complex action performed by a single entity, the active principle of the cosmos? Vogt does not aim at presenting how the Stoics solve this problem but at clarifying its nature. She does so by comparing it, and carefully distinguishing it from, the modern problem of free will and determinism.

The last three chapters of the volume – Chapter 13, 'God and the Material World: Biology and Cosmology in Galen's Physiology' by R. J. Hankinson; Chapter 14, 'At the Intersection of Cosmology and Biology: Plotinus on Nature' by Lloyd P. Gerson; and Chapter 15, 'Is the Heaven an Animal? Avicenna's Celestial Psychology between Cosmology and Biology' by Tommaso Alpina – address late cosmobiological theories in the ancient Greek philosophical tradition: Chapter 13 explores the teleological biology of Galen in his treatise *The Functionality of Parts* and its relation to cosmic teleology; Chapter 14 studies Plotinus' conception of nature as the lowest part of the cosmic soul and the extent to which this conception led him to adopt panpsychism, the view that beings other than ordinary living beings may have mental powers and, in particular, intellection or cognition; and Chapter 15 takes up an issue already addressed in Chapter 6, the attribution of soul to heavenly bodies in Aristotle, and explores its reception and development in Avicenna's cosmology.

CHAPTER I

Souls and Cosmos before Plato
Five Short Doxographical Studies

André Laks*

The five short case studies that I present here invite us to exercise caution when we try to reconstruct what early cosmo-philosophers, to coin a term, might have thought about the relationship between world and soul. My question is a limited one. It does not bear on Preplatonic theories of the soul in general, although it does affect the way we would have to deal with the question. But even within these limits, the review of the evidence is not complete, not so much because taking into account some thinkers such as Diogenes of Apollonia or certain Hippocratic treatises such as *On Breath* would exceed the limits of this chapter,[1] but above all because my point is methodological: it is meant to illustrate the general difficulty of raising questions of philosophico-doxographical nature ('What did they think about the soul?')[2] when we have good reasons to think that a certain notion of soul, broadly speaking the Platonic or quasi-Platonic notion that is still with us, was not available to them.[3] What I want to show is how two basic and interrelated meanings of *psukhē* – namely 'breath' and 'life'– which are pervasive in the archaic period, may have helped Platonizing, or for that matter Stoicizing, interpreters to justify their distorted reading of the evidence. The upshot is in a sense negative. I do suggest, however, that framing it in terms of 'breath' and 'life' helps us in getting a more adequate understanding both of the authentic evidence and of the history of its reception.

---

* This piece is a shortened version of Laks 2018. Many thanks to my various audiences at the UNAM, Mexico (Ricardo Salles), Columbia University (William V. Harris), Toronto (Rachel Barney), and especially to Brad Inwood, who commented on the chapter in Toronto and to Charles Brittain and Steven Menn for their stimulating questions and suggestions. Solveig Gold (Cambridge University) and the OSAP team did a wonderful job at improving the English of the chapter.

[1] The interested reader can find the relevant material in Laks 2008 (cf. also Section 1.3 on Heraclitus T6 and n. 60.) Karfik 2014 deals with Anaxagoras and Empedocles, but from an angle that does not concern me here (cf. Laks 2018: 2 n.1).

[2] On the 'doxographical' nature of many contemporary philosophical approaches of ancient material, see Frede 1992.

[3] For an approach based on premises radically opposed to those adopted here, see Finkelberg 2017.

The representative cases I shall consider are those of Thales, Anaximenes, Heraclitus, as well as some Pythagoreans and Alcmeon, but it will be helpful to begin with a chapter in Aëtius's doxographical handbook (Book 2, chapter 3) promisingly entitled 'Whether the world (*kosmos*) is ensouled (*empsukhos*) and administered by providence':[4]

1. All the others: the world is ensouled and administered by providence.
2. But Leucippus, Democritus and Epicurus and all those who introduce the atoms and the void: it is neither ensouled nor administered by providence, but by some unreasoning natural entity.
3. Ecphantus: the world is constituted of atoms, but administered by providence.
4. Aristotle: it is neither ensouled through and through nor endowed with sense-perception nor rational nor intellective nor governed by providence. For the heavenly region shares in all these [sc. features] because it contains ensouled and living spheres, while the region around the earth does not share in any of them but participates in good order by accident and not in a primary way.[5]

As Mansfeld and Runia have shown in their pathbreaking work, the chapters in Aëtius' handbook are structured according to a recurring pattern (which they call 'dialectical').[6] In the present case, the first two entries exhibit two opposing views on the pair of questions featured in the title: the Atomists, ancient and recent, reject the ensoulment of the cosmos as well as the notion that it is governed by providence; 'all the others', on the other hand, accept both tenets. This 'main *diairesis*' is followed by two particular cases – those of Ecphantus and Aristotle – which do not fall under either of the two broad options.[7]

The first lemma, which is anonymous, is the one in the present context that interests us most, not *in spite of* the fact that the position Aëtius reports is anonymous, but *because* of its very anonymity. It is highly probable that the formula 'all the others' is the result of the progressive abridgement of a list of names featuring in previous versions of the handbook.[8] Who the

---

[4] The translation is from Mansfeld and Runia 2009: 344, with some modifications. The second entry follows Ps.-Plutarch's version, rather than Stobaeus 1.21.3c.

[5] Unless otherwise noted, translations are from Laks and Most 2016 (henceforth, 'LM') with occasional slight modifications. The translations of the few passages not from LM (indicated by '≠ LM') are my own unless otherwise indicated.

[6] See e.g. Mansfeld 1990.

[7] For a detailed reconstruction and analysis of the chapter, see Mansfeld 1990: 337–46. Some details in Laks 2018: 4f.

[8] On this well-attested doxographical process of reduction, see Mansfeld and Runia 1997: 192.

authors concerned? Plato, as represented by his *Timaeus*, is certainly the first one that comes to mind. But the mention of Leucippus and Democritus in the second entry, as well as of Ecphantus in the third, is enough to remind us not merely that the authors mentioned in Aëtius's handbook extends from the first Greek thinkers to the Stoics, but also that those we call 'Presocratics' often constitute the bulk of the authors considered. As a matter of fact, there is little doubt that a number of these 'first philosophers', if not all of them, lurk behind the formula 'all the others'.

In what follows, I reproduce and comment on a representative sample, for each of the five authors I have selected, of the evidence for the notion of 'ensouled world'. To the extent that it is possible or relevant, the passages appear in *reverse* chronological order, i.e. from the most recent to the older ones,[9] so as to highlight the process by which, to put is crisply, Presocratic worlds became ensouled. In the clearest cases, the words that triggered the appropriation, Platonic or otherwise, can be identified. I have italicised those; the main terms or formula that I take to be the result of this appropriation, on the other hand, are printed in bold.

1.1   Thales

The evidence concerning Thales may be conveniently broken down into three sub-topics: cosmic soul, immortality of the soul and divinity of the principle.

Cosmic Soul
T1 Diogenes Laertius 1.27 (= A1 DK = R34b LM)
     [. . . he, Thales, thought] that **the world is animate** and *full of divinities*.
T2 Aëtius 1.7.11, 'On god' (= A23 DK = R35 LM)
     Thales: **god is the intelligence** [*noun*] **of the world**, but **the whole is ensouled** [*empsykhon*] and at the same time *full of divinities*; and **a divine power passes** also **through** the elementary moisture **and moves it**.
T3 Aristotle, *On the soul*, 1.5, 411a7–8 (= A22, R34a LM)
     Some people say that it [i.e. the soul] is mixed in the whole, which is perhaps also the reason why Thales thought that *all things are full of gods*.

Immortality of the Soul
T4 Diogenes Laertius 1.24 (= A1 DK = R37 LM)
     Some people also say that he was the first to say that **souls are immortal**; one of them is Choerilus the poet.

---

[9] There are some exceptions, due to some complications, see *infra*, nn. 22 and 49.

T5 Aëtius 4.2.1, 'On the soul' (= A22a DK = R36 LM)
Thales was the first to state that the soul is **a nature which is always in motion or which moves itself.**

Divinity of the Principle[10]

T6 (Ps.-?) Hippolytus, *Refutation of all the heresies*, 1.1 (= Th 210 Wöhrle = R39 LM)
[Thales said] . . . and all things are borne along and flow, carried along by the nature of the first principle [*arkhēgos*] of their becoming. **This is god,** that which has neither beginning nor ending.

T7 Cicero, *On the nature of the gods*, 1.10.25 (= A23 DK = R38LM)
For Thales of Miletus, who was the first to investigate these matters, said that water is the beginning of things, **but that god is the intelligence** capable of making all things out of water.

The idea that 'all is full of gods' is one of the most famous sayings attributed to Thales.[11] It is not only difficult, but also vain, to try to settle its original meaning; statements of this sort are by nature open-ended. Hesiodic gods are so numerous that the world could be said to be full of them; and the formula may be a rewording of a passage in Hesiod's *Works and days* that presents the deceased members of the golden race as 'fine divinities' now taking care of humans 'everywhere upon the earth'.[12] Aristotle, who knows the dictum – as with everything else he knows about Thales – by hearsay, may not have been the first to link it to the notion of soul (in T3): according to Diogenes Laertius's testimony (T4), the poet Choerilus (end of the fifth century BC, if this is the one in question)[13] had already attributed to Thales the idea that souls are immortal (the implicit argument for the assertion being that they are divinities). Indeed, Diogenes Laertius' phrasing suggests that Choerilus was only one among those who made this interpretive move. If so, this is the tradition that Aristotle is taking up in T3 and adapting with characteristic caution ('perhaps') to the specific perspective of his doxographical presentation. Immortality of the soul is not at stake for him. The view that interests Aristotle in the present context is the one according to which soul (apparently taken as a mass noun) is mixed in the whole, that is, I suggest, dispersed throughout it. Aristotle's formula 'in the whole', which paraphrases Thales' 'all things' in the formula 'all things are full of . . . ', is here combined with the idea that

[10] See also above, T1 and T2.
[11] Plato alludes to it without naming Thales at *Laws* 10, 899b9. Besides T3, Aristotle mentions it in *Generation of animals* 3.11, 762a21. Cf. also Cicero, *On the laws*, 2.26, Stobaeus, *Anthology* 1.1.29b.
[12] vv. 122–25. 'By the plans of great Zeus they are fine spirits upon the earth [. . .] clad in invisibility, walking everywhere upon the earth [. . .]'. (trans. G. W. Most).
[13] The identity of this Choerilus is uncertain.

Thales' 'divinities' or *daimones*, which Aristotle calls 'gods', thereby relaxing the connection between *daimones* and souls, fill the world. This double move opens avenues to later interpretations, for it allows Thales' statement to be read in terms of a cosmos animated by a world soul. To be sure, this is not yet the view Aristotle has in mind, since 'to be mixed with' is not the same as 'to be ensouled'. Still, we are making our way towards the formulas we find in T1 ('ensouled world') and in T2 ('the whole is ensouled'). At a more restricted level, T5 also testifies to the Platonization of Thales' saying, since the disjunction 'always moving or self-moving' reflects a celebrated textual problem in Plato, *Phaedrus* 245c.[14] T2 contains one further interpretative step, whereby soul is now specified as intelligence or mind (cf. T7). Taken by itself, this identification could point to an even stronger Platonized reading of Thales' dictum, with the integration of the demiurge, itself identified with the intellect, into the world soul. But the use of the verb 'to pass through' strongly suggests a Stoicization, rather than a simple Platonization, not only of this particular saying, but of Thales' position in general. Thales' water is animated by a force equivalent to that of the Stoic *pneuma*. Thales' primary element has now become a living, organising intelligence (cf. T6 and T7).

2. Anaximenes
    T1 Aëtius 1.3.4, 'On principles' (= B2 DK = D31 and R5 LM)
    Anaximenes, son of Eurystratos, asserted that the principle of beings is air. For it is out of this that all things come about and it is into this that they are dissolved in turn. He says, 'Just as our soul, which is air [*aēr*], holds us together, so too breath [*pneuma*] and air surround the whole world'. ('Air' and 'breath' are being used synonymously). But he too [sc. like Anaximander] is mistaken in that he thinks that animals are composed out of simple and uniform air and breath. For it is impossible to posit the matter of the beings from which all things come as the sole principle: it is also necessary to posit the efficient cause – for example, the silver is not enough for the cup to come about, if there is not what makes it, that is the silversmith; and so too for bronze, wood, and all other kinds of matter.
    T2 Aëtius 4.3.2, 'On soul' (= A23 DK = D30 LM)
    Anaximenes [. . .]: [sc. the soul is] of air.
    T3 Aëtius 1.7.13, 'On god' (= A10 DK = D5 LM)
    Anaximenes: air [sc. is god] [. . .].
    T4 Cicero, *On the nature of the gods*, 1.10.26 (= A10 DK = D6 LM)
    [. . .] Anaximenes declared that air is god, that it is born, and that it is immense and unlimited and always in motion [. . .].

[14] On this issue, see Section 1.5.

The apparent quotation at the beginning of T1 ('Just as ... the whole world', introduced by 'he says') plays a crucial role in the assessment of Anaximenes' thought.[15] Almost all interpreters agree that the wording of the sentence does not go back to Anaximenes. The main arguments against literal authenticity are (1) that the verb *sunkratei* is not otherwise attested before the first century AD at best and (2) that the mention of *pneuma* besides *aēr* looks like a paraphrase (Stoicizing or otherwise). There are further concerns about the use of *kosmos* in the sense of 'a well-ordered world' at an early period and about the use of *hoion* in a comparison. As for the initial 'he says', it does not necessarily signal a literal quotation and may well introduce an interpretation ('he says' = 'what he says, in substance, is...').[16] But whereas some interpreters think that the terminology points to later, non-Anaximenean *views*, others maintain that the sentence, if not its literal wording, does reflect Anaximenes' original thought. On this latter option, the next step is to decide between a strong interpretation, according to which air (or *pneuma*) not only 'surrounds' the whole cosmos but also 'dominates' it (*kratei*, here represented by the dubious compound *sunkratei*)[17] – i.e. governs it in the way that human soul governs us – and a weaker interpretation, whereby air dominates or governs the world just as a soul dominates or governs human beings, that is, not in the sense that the surrounding air is actually a soul, but only that it is soul-*like*, whatever we think that likeness entails.

Two preliminary remarks are in order here. First, given that the verb 'surround' is associated with 'govern' in a passage of Aristotle's *Physics* certainly referring to Anaximander,[18] there should be no objection to taking the surrounding air as representing the governing force of the world. Second, there is nothing problematic in attributing to Anaximenes a notion of all-embracing governance, if only because it is already present in Anaximander. But what about the soul and its cosmic role? The problem here is that whereas the dubious sentence does not *imply* the notion of a world soul, it does *lend itself* to being read that way. Taken by itself, the analogical scheme a/b = c/d posits a certain relation between

---

[15] Cf. Alt 1973: 129: 'whether the comparison microcosmos/macrocosmos is to be dated to the sixth century and whether we can show that there was already an interest in the human soul among the Milesians' (my translation).

[16] Cf. Kerschensteiner 1962: 82f., and subsequently Alt 1973: 129f. and 131 n. 15. See also Mansfeld and Runia 2009: 217f.

[17] Problematic, because the verb really means 'hold together', cf. LSJ *s.v.*

[18] Aristotle, *Physics*, 3.4, 203b11–12 = 12A15 DK = Anaximander D9 LM.

four different terms, namely a, b, c, d, which would usually be substantially different. But as far as Anaximenes is concerned, the notion that a (= 'the soul in us') is really, i.e. substantially, different from c (= 'the surrounding breath') is made less pregnant by the fact that an Anaximenean soul is itself made of air, or at least of an airy nature (see T2). One might consequently be tempted to say that the difference implied by the analogy is not between the soul in us and some other governing power, but between two kinds of soul, one human and one cosmic, and then address the further question whether the notion of a cosmic soul should be attributed to Anaximenes himself or to some of his interested readers (Diogenes of Apollonia and the Stoics in the first place, but there are also other candidates), which is a related, but nevertheless separate matter. But if we think, as I do, that (1) we should not erase the difference between human soul and cosmic breath and that (2) the analogy, if not its wording, goes back to Anaximenes himself, we should still recognise that denying to Anaximenes the notion of a world soul does not imply that the world for him is not 'alive' in some sense. If air is taken to be the source of life for us and in us, one understands why Anaximenes might have inferred that it is also the source of life in the world and for the world. And in *this* sense, one could even say that that the world is 'ensouled', meaning simply that it is 'living'.

Whatever position we adopt in the tricky case of Anaximenes, it is obvious that the link between air and soul is crucial for the question of the relationship between world, soul and life not only for him, but also for other Presocratic thinkers – whether they take air as principle (Diogenes of Apollonia and the author of the Hippocratic treatise *On Breath*) or not (some Pythagoreans, according to Aristotle's testimony,[19] and the Atomists). It is also at the centre of a controversial report of Sextus Empiricus about Heraclitus, which I now want to consider.[20]

3. Heraclitus

T1 Sextus Empiricus, *Against the logicians* 1 (= *Adv. Math.* 7) 127–34 (= A16 DK = R59 LM)

<A1> [127] [. . .] this natural philosopher [i.e. Heraclitus] holds the view that **what surrounds us** is **rational** and **endowed with thought** [φρενῆρες]. . . . [129] So according to Heraclitus, it is **by inhaling this divine reason when we breathe that we become intelligent** [*noêroi*], and

---

[19] See Section 1.4, T4–T6.
[20] For an analysis about the possible relationship between Heraclitus and Anaximenes on this issue, cf. Betegh 2013: 225–61, in Appendix 2, 254–7.

whereas we forget it when we sleep, we become intelligent [*emphrones*] again when we are awake. <A2> For when we sleep, **the channels of perception are closed** and **the mind within us is separated from its natural connection with what surrounds, and only the point of attachment, respiration, subsists like a kind of root, and when it is separated it loses the faculty of memory that it had before;** [130] but then when it awakens, **leaning towards the channels of perception as though towards windows and encountering what surrounds, it takes on the faculty of reason once again.** In the same way as pieces of charcoal brought near to a fire are kindled according to a transformation but are extinguished when they are removed from it, so too **the portion coming from what surrounds, which resides with our bodies, in the state of separation becomes almost unreasoning, but in the state of union by most of the channels it is restored to its affinity with the whole.** <B1> [131] Heraclitus says that this reason, which is in common and divine, and by participation in which we become rational, is the criterion of the truth; <B2> this is why what appears to all in common is reliable (for it is apprehended by the reason that is common and divine), while what is evident to one man alone is unreliable, for the opposite reason. <C> [132] For this is what the above mentioned man says at the beginning of his book *On Nature* [or: of his remarks about nature], when in a certain way he is indicating **what surrounds**: '*Of this reason that is* humans are uncomprehending, both before they hear it and once they have first heard it. For, although all things come about according to this reason, they resemble people without experience of them, when they have experience both of words and of things of the sort I explain when I analyse each [scil. of them] in conformity with its nature and indicate how it is. But other men *are unaware of all they do when they are awake, just as they forget all they do while they are asleep*' [= B1 DK = D1 LM]. [133] After he has indicated explicitly in these words that it is **by participation in divine reason** that we do and think everything, a little later he adds that we ought to follow the reason that is in common (for *xunos* [i.e. the Ionic term] means 'in common'): 'But although the reason is in common, most people live as though they had their own *thought*' [= B2 DK = D2 LM]. This is nothing other than an explanation of **the way in which the whole is organized**.

T2 Aëtius 4.3.12, 'Whether the soul is a body and what is its essence' (= A15 DK = R48a LM)

Heraclitus: **the soul of the world** is an *exhalation* of the moisture it contains, and the one that is in animals, which derives from the external exhalation and from the one that is in them, is of the same kind.

T3 Aëtius 4.7.2, 'On the indestructibility of the soul' (= A17 DK = R48b LM)

Heraclitus said that the souls that leave the body return to **the soul of the whole**, since their genus and substance are of the same nature.

T4 Aëtius 2.17.4, 'What is the source of the illumination of the stars'
(= A11DK = R65 LM = SVF 2.690)

Heraclitus and the Stoics: the stars are nourished by the exhalation
coming from the earth.

T5 Macrobius, *Commentary on Cicero's 'Dream of Scipio'*, 1.14.19
(= T 782 Mouraviev = R48c LM)[21]

Heraclitus, the natural philosopher, [sc. calls the soul] **a spark of the
stars' substance**.

T6 Aristotle, *On the soul,* 1.2, 405a21–8 (= A15 DK = R43 LM)

Diogenes similarly to some others too [sc. says that it, i.e. soul, is] air,
thinking that this is of all things the one that is most rarefied and that it is a
principle. And it is for this reason that the soul both knows and moves:
because it is first and everything else comes from it, it knows, and because it
is the most rarefied, it is able to impart motion. Heraclitus too says that the
principle is the soul, since it is an *exhalation*, from which he constitutes the
other things. And surely it [sc. the soul] is most incorporeal and continually
flowing; and what is moved is known by what is moved.

The Heraclitean material on the topic at hand is richer than that available
for other Presocratics. In spite of the many obscurities and uncertainties
that beset the evidence – obscurities and uncertainties that, given the state
of our knowledge, are not likely to be removed by scholarly acumen – it
gives us a good sense of the interpretive processes that lead to the ensoulment of his world (as well as of other Preplatonic worlds). This is because
in this case we can, up to a certain point, confront the doxographical
evidence with some of Heraclitus's original fragments.

The two most important doxographical reports are, at the beginning of
the story, Aristotle's lines in the first book of *On the soul* (T6), which are
seminal for all later interpretations, and, at a much later stage, Sextus
Empiricus's long exposition of Heraclitus's alleged 'psycho-atmospheric'
doctrine (T1). As far as Heraclitus is concerned, the fragments in question
are essentially 22 B1, B2 (quoted in T1), and, among others, B12 and B36
DK. The key notion, which features in Aristotle's passage, is that of
'exhalation' (ἀναθυμίασις), which makes the link between Heraclitean
souls (B12), a number of physiological and cosmic processes or realities,
and the cosmos itself.

Sextus's passage clearly breaks down into three sections, with a further
subdivision for the first two:

---

[21] Macrobius T5 comes after Aëtius T2–T4 for thematic, not chronological reasons.

A. *Exposition* of Heraclitus's 'psycho-atmospheric' thesis about the relationship between human reason and divine reason
  A1 Statement of Heraclitus's psycho-atmospheric thesis
  A2 Explanation of the physiological mechanism presupposed by the thesis
B. *Identification* of Heraclitus's (alleged) criterion of truth
  B1 Identification of the criterion with atmospheric 'reason'
  B2 Short epistemological commentary
C. *Justification* of the initial statement concerning Heraclitus's psycho-atmospheric thesis (A) on the basis of two original quotations (B1, B2 DK).

Heraclitus's alleged psycho-atmospheric thesis is plain enough. Reason is up there, literally in the air; as we breathe, we inhale reason in quantities that differ depending on our physiological states. That such quantitative variations occur while we are aware might be implied, but the most significant difference (which may be paradigmatic of other possible ones) is between the state of being awake, during which we are 'intelligent', i.e. participating in reason, and the state of sleep, during which we lose this intelligence or, as Sextus says, using the Heraclitean term that will appear in the fragments quoted in section (C), 'forget' it. There is a physiological basis for this alternation, which the report mentions through a somewhat elliptical description that can be expanded in the following way: as we sleep, we keep breathing and thus inhaling reason, but reason is prevented from reaching the places in us where it could be active, the centre or centres of perception. This is because the channels through which these places could be reached, namely the 'channels of perception', are blocked during sleep, with the result that our internal reason becomes isolated from the source that is able to activate it when we are awake. Two metaphors, one taken from the domain of plants, the other from everyday experience, illustrate the two-sided nature of sleep. On the one hand, we keep breathing during sleep, which means that our contact with the surrounding atmosphere is not lost – the 'roots' of life are not broken off; on the other hand, life during sleep is deprived of intelligence, because inhaled atmospheric reason cannot connect with internal reason. There is an effective break with our surroundings, even though we can reestablish connection, just as fire can reanimate extinguished charcoal.

The picture of Heraclitus's theory that emerges from Sextus's report is surprising on more than one count, compared with what we otherwise know about Heraclitus's thought and especially about his principle.

Although Heraclitean fire can still be faintly spotted, with some charity, in
the metaphorical charcoal representing the state of sleep, the mechanism
described may remind us, as far as the Presocratics are concerned, of
Diogenes of Apollonia. Diogenes' principle is air: this air is divine, or
more exactly, it is the god;[22] a small part of this divinity dwells inside us;[23]
channels go through the whole human (and most animals') body,[24]
allowing air to diffuse, thus endowing living beings not only with sensation, but also with intelligence – thanks, in particular, to a strong continuity between sensation and intelligence, both of which fall under the
term *noēseis* or 'apprehensions'.[25] The animals that lacks those channels –
e.g. birds – range from less intelligent to entirely stupid.[26] Other, more
recent models, dependent on or close in inspiration to the one provided by
Diogenes but possessing a greater topicality in the Hellenistic period and
derived from texts both philosophical and medical,[27] may lurk behind the
picture conveyed by Sextus. It seems fairly obvious that what we have to
deal with here is a rather forceful interpretation of Heraclitus, related to a
Hellenistic debate about the relationship between reason and the senses.
Heraclitus himself is no doubt implicated in this debate at some level. But
at what level and to what degree exactly? Some interpreters think that
the report contains at least one important idea going back to Heraclitus
himself, namely that of a continuous process of transformation from
watery stuffs (which individual souls are said by Heraclitus in B12 to
exhale) to fire – a stage of which is represented by the mass noun 'soul'
referring to a stuff like any other.[28] That might be true to some extent, as
we shall see shortly – after all, soul and air are closely related. But what is
clear is that Sextus's presentation relies on a physiological interpretation
of the phenomenon of sleep, which is mentioned in fragment B1 DK only
by way of analogy – a clear-cut one that does not present the ambiguities
of Anaximenes' analogy – and in a context that evidently is neither
physiological nor cosmological.

The properly doxographical (Aëtian) tradition on Heraclitus's ensouled
cosmos – of which Sextus's report is, I take it, a version, adapted for specific
purposes[29] – has been characterised by Mansfeld in the following terms:

---

[22] B5 DK = D10 LM.   [23] A19 §42 DK = D13 LM.   [24] B6 DK = D27 LM.
[25] Cf. B4 DK = D9 LM and the last sentence of B5 DK= D44 LM.
[26] On birds' stupidity, see A19 §44 DK = D44 LM.
[27] Philosophical: Reinhardt 1926: 201f. and Burkhard 1973; medical: Polito 2004: 137f.
[28] See especially Betegh 2007 and 2013.
[29] Most probably related to the way in which Aenesidemus read and used Heraclitus. On this complex
and much discussed question, see Burkhard 1973; Polito 2004; Pérez-Jean 2005.

'Though according to the verbatim fragments of Heraclitus there is something out there that is both dominant and rational (22 B32, B64 DK), the
uninhibited use of the concept of a world soul, of which the souls of
human are parts, shows the mark of a later *interpretatio*'.[30] I fully agree
with this assessment (which *mutatis mutandis* would apply, too, in
Anaximenes' case), and I also think that Mansfeld is right to consider T2
and T3 as 'two not entirely but still sufficiently different attempts to make
sense of Heraclitus' utterances about the relation of the human soul to
the Fire that, as he claims, dominates the cosmos'.[31] The interpretation in
question, which clearly fits a Stoic picture of the world (cf. the notion that
'soul that leaves the body returns to the soul of the whole' in T3), also
rings, more generally, Platonic bells (cf. Macrobius's phrasing in T5).[32]

Of course, the situation here is in some respect similar to the one we
faced in the case of Anaximenes' alleged quotation. We might be inclined
to believe that the formula 'Heraclitus and the Stoics' (in T4) indicates that
the Stoics took their doctrine from Heraclitus, rather than that they read it
into some of Heraclitus's fragments; or, alternatively, that the content of
the doxographical reports about Heraclitus's world soul is authentically
Heraclitean, although its wording might be late. However, we are in a
somewhat better position to assess the evidence in the present case, both
because we are reasonably well informed about Stoic resolutely appropri-
ative practices, especially when it comes to Heraclitus,[33] and because we
are able to confront the relevant doxographical reports about Heraclitus
with some of his authentic fragments. Since we must elicit the meaning
and implications of these fragments on the basis of elaborate interpretation – a practice no less necessary for the ancients than for us – we can be
fairly confident that our doxographical reports reflect assimilative interpretation rather than containing direct information to be taken at face value.[34]

At the beginning of the story stands Aristotle's intriguing testimony on
Heraclitus in chapter 1.2 of *On the soul* (T6). The lengthy and complex
doxography occupying this chapter aims at establishing that previous
theories about the nature of the soul depend on a double assumption,
namely (1) that soul is an entity endowed with a capacity for both moving

---

[30] Mansfeld 2015: 63. Mansfeld also stresses the overall rarity of the concept of the world soul in
Aëtius's doxographical handbook.
[31] Mansfeld 2015: 64.   [32] Cf. also Diogenes Laertius 9.9 = R46 LM.
[33] The technical term is *sunoikeioun* ('to assimilate'), cf. Philodemus' testimony about Chrysippus'
interpretive practice in *On piety*, col 7.12–8.13 (= *SVF* 2.636).
[34] For the question of the relationship between Heraclitus's original fragments on sleep and the
doxographical tradition, see further Laks 2015: 29–50.

(the animated being) and knowing, and (2) that these two capacities belong to the principle (*arkhê*).[35] Aristotle looks to previous thinkers for declarations that can support his own assumptions about their reasons for asserting what they said concerning the nature of the soul.

As far as we can see on the basis of independent information – essentially, a few original fragments from the authors in question – Aristotle's doxographical scheme does not apply with equal facility to all of them. Things are simple in the case of Diogenes of Apollonia, for example, who on the one hand certainly thought of soul as being (a kind of) air[36] and on the other hand made air the principle.[37] Even if we cannot be certain that Diogenes used the word 'most subtle' to qualify air, nor that he related air's subtleness to its moving capacity, Aristotle's report about Diogenes is no doubt closer to Diogenes' actual pronouncements than what he says about Heraclitus.

This is especially clear in the final lines of T6, which explain that the Heraclitean soul's cognitive capacities exist because the soul is 'most incorporeal' and therefore 'continuously flowing', i.e. in movement, which enables it to apprehend a world that is itself continuously flowing – for 'the same knows the same'.[38] That this argument is a construct based on Plato's treatment of Heraclitus in the *Cratylus* and the *Theaetetus*[39] is obvious.

The main problem with Aristotle's report, however, is to understand whether *psykhê* can really be claimed to be Heraclitus's principle, an assertion that Aristotle needs for the sake of his argument. In the first book of the *Metaphysics*, Heraclitus's principle is said, unsurprisingly, to be fire.[40] In the passage from *On the soul*, the phrase 'exhalation, from which he constitutes the other things' refers not to a material principle, but to the effect that fire has on watery stuff.[41] The function of the clause introduced

---

[35] On the complicated construction of Aristotle's doxography, cf. Laks 2007: 145. For a detailed analysis of Aristotle's reception of Presocratic theories about the soul, see Sánchez Castro 2016.

[36] Cf. B5 DK = D10 LM, on which Aristotle is obviously relying.   [37] Cf. 13 A4 DK = D7 LM.

[38] The beginning of the report illustrates Aristotle's other hermeneutical assumption, which is that knowledge must belong to the *principle*, because the principle is, of all things, in the best position to know what it itself is the origin of.

[39] *Cratylus*, 401d–402d; *Theatetus*, 152d-e.

[40] Cf. Aristotle, *Metaphysics* 1.3.984a7 (= 18 [Hippasus] 7 DK = Hippasus D3 LM). Aristotle probably relies mainly on Heraclitus' B31 DK (= D86 LM): 'Turnings of fire: first sea; then half of the sea, earth; the other half, lightning storm [. . .]'.

[41] The verb *thumiaō* that Heraclitus uses means 'to burn so as to produce smoke', especially as happens in incense offerings. The secondary substantive *anathumiasis* specifies that the smoke in question goes upwards.

by 'since' (with the nuance of 'if it is true that') is to justify Aristotle's unexpected assertion, prompted by his argument.[42]

Is Aristotle relying on original Heraclitean material that is no longer at our disposal? His explanation assumes the following two propositions: according to Heraclitus: (1) the source of (other) things is the exhalation, *anathumiasis*, and (2) soul is not only an exhalation among others but the exhalation *par excellence*, and hence the principle. Now the word *anathumiasis*, which features in later doxographical reports, especially in Diogenes Laertius's uniquely detailed exposition of Heraclitus's cosmology in Book 9.7–11 of his *Lives of Eminent Philosophers*, does not appear in the fragments of Heraclitus and is unlikely to have occurred in his book (the word is not attested before Aristotle).[43] On the other hand, a passage from Arius Didymus's Stoic doxography,[44] which reports Cleanthes' exposition of Zeno's views about the soul, contains a sentence that constitutes a clear parallel to Aristotle's *On the soul* 1.2: 'and souls are exhaled from moist things'.[45] Although some interpreters refuse to consider these words as constituting an authentic fragment of Heraclitus,[46] the words could be an echo of the Heraclitean utterance on which Aristotle is himself relying in T6 when he equates 'soul' and 'exhalation'. If so, Aristotle will have extracted the idea that soul in Heraclitus is an exhalation (Aristotle talks of *the* exhalation) from the Heraclitean sentence that Zeno the Stoic was also to quote later in favour of his own definition of the soul as 'an exhalation endowed with perception'.

Taken by itself, this sentence only says something about souls (in the plural), not about any large-scale cosmic process of the kind that is implied, on the one hand, by Aristotle's statement about exhalation being the origin of everything else, and on the other hand by Heraclitus's fragment B36 DK, where *psukhē* is mentioned as the first and the last stage (the first time in the plural, the second time in the singular) in a cycle of transformation: 'For souls it is death to become water, for water it is death to become earth; but out of earth, water comes to be, and out of water, soul'.[47]

---

[42] Sánchez Castro (2021) talks rightly of the 'hypothetical hue' implied by the use of this 'since' (*eiper*).

[43] *Contra* Finkelberg 2016, p. 70. Diogenes Laertius's report is usually considered to ultimately go back to Theophrastus (whose name appears in 9.6), but its reliability is open to serious doubts, especially although by far not only because of its mentioning not one, but two exhalations, which injects Heraclitus's (alleged) cosmology with a typically Aristotelian doctrine.

[44] In Eusebius, *Evangelical preparation* 15.20.2 (SVF 1.141 = Arius Didymus, Fr. 39 Diels in *Doxographi Graeci*, p. 471f.).

[45] Cf. B12 DK *sub fine* = Heraclitus D102 LM.

[46] References in Marcovich 2001: 213 n. 1 ad fr. 40 M.   [47] B36 DK = D100 LM.

Just how the entity called *psukhē,* which we translate as 'soul', can be named on par with water and fire in B36 DK and how it can be said to proceed from water and be associated with *anathumiasis* on the basis of B12 DK becomes much clearer if we recall that the first meaning of *psukhē* is 'breath': a certain kind of 'breath', namely a vapour, that is 'exhaled' from water when it is heated. Indeed, one might consider simply translating *psukhē* in Heraclitus's B12 and B36 not as 'soul', but as 'breath'. In any case, we can now see better how Aristotle's *ad hoc* interpretation of Heraclitus in the doxographical section of *On the soul* contains *in nuce* a reading of Heraclitus's principle as being not fire, but 'air' ('breathing', 'soul'), which is at the basis of Sextus's report.

4. Pythagoras and Pythagoreans

T1 Sextus Empiricus, *Against the natural philosophers* 1.127 (= *Adv. Math.* 9.127 = Empedocles R39 LM = 31 B136.1–5 DK)

Pythagoras, Empedocles, and most of the other Italians say that there exists for us a community not only with regard to one another and with regard to the gods, but also with regard to the irrational animals. For there exists **a single breath that extends through the whole world like a soul**, which also unifies us with them.

T2 Ps.-Philolaus, *On the soul* (Stobaeus, *Anth.* 1.20.2 = 44 B21 DK; cf. Pythagorean Reception R51 LM)[48]

... But the world, which is one, continuous, **by nature traversed by the breath** [*pneuma*] and rotating from the beginning, also possesses the principle of movement and change. ... The unchanging part reaches from the soul that embraces the whole to the moon.

T3 Cicero, *On the nature of the gods,* 1.11.27 (≠ DK, ≠ LM)'

For Pythagoras, who thought that **the soul** [*animus*] was **extending and circulating through the whole nature**, and that **our souls were taken from there** [...]

T4 Aristotle, *Metaphysics* N3 1091a13–18 (58B.26 DK, Pythagorean Doctrines D28 LM)

There can be no disagreement about whether the Pythagoreans do or do not accept a generation. For they say clearly that once the One had been formed, whether out of planes, out of a surface, out of a seed, or out of something that they have difficulty in naming, the nearest part of the unlimited was immediately *drawn in* and limited by the limit.

---

[48] Translation (slightly modified) from Huffman 1993: 341f. This pseudo-Pythagorean forgery and Cicero's testimony (T3) reflect material that is either earlier than or more or less contemporaneous with Sextus's source.

T5 Aristotle, *Physics* 4.6, 213b22–7 (= 58 B30 DK = Pythagorean Doctrines D29 LM)

The Pythagoreans also said that there is a void, and that it is introduced into the heavens from *the unlimited breath as though it* [i.e. the heavens] *were inhaling* the void too, which produces a distinction in the natures of things, on the idea that the void is some kind of separation between the elements of a series and a distinction. And this happens first of all in numbers. For the void produces a distinction in their nature.

T6 Aristotle fr. 201 Rose = Aëtius 1.18.6, 'On void' (= 58 B30 DK = Pythagorean Doctrines D30 LM)

In the first book of his *On the Philosophy of Pythagoras*, he [i.e. Aristotle] writes that the heavens are one, but that into them, coming from the unlimited, were introduced time, *breath*, and also the void, which always produces a distinction in [or: defines] the places of each thing.

T1 and T3 are unanimously recognised as Hellenistic projections of Platonic and Stoic tenets onto the founder Pythagoras, and T2 as a Neopythagorean forgery.[49] The comparison with Aristotle's testimonies about 'the Pythagoreans', who in all probability represent Philolaus's doctrine, speaks for itself. None of the three relevant passages by Aristotle mentions the soul, nor its extending throughout the world. What they speak about is the origin of the world and how breath first penetrated it from the outside.[50] The model is clearly that of respiration, and interpreters have rightly pointed to the parallelism existing in Philolaus's thought between the generation of the world and that of human beings: just as a newborn begins to breathe in order to cool the hot embryo, so the formation of the central fire is followed by the inhalation of the 'unlimiteds', which include *pneuma* – breath.[51] Given Philolaus's views about the world's primeval breathing, Platonists wishing to argue that the world soul was already known by the ancient Pythagoreans would have had an easier task than those interpreters who had to deal with Heraclitus's pronouncements. But as T1–T3 show, the association between world, soul, and breath could be even more easily be implemented by reference to the Pythagorean doctrine of transmigration: both soul and air circulate throughout the whole world.

[49] On B21 DK, cf. Burkert 1972: 242 with n. 21; Huffman 1993: 212ff.

[50] Cf. also Aristotle's famous testimony about the 'the view one finds in the so-called Orphic verses' in *On the soul* 1.2. 410b27–30: 'the soul penetrates from the whole when they inhale, carried by the winds' (fr. 421 Bernabé, ≠ LM).

[51] Huffman 1993: 213.

5. Alcmaeon

T1 Diogenes Laertius 8.83 (B1 DK = Alcmaeon D10 LM)

He said that the soul is immortal and that it moves continually like the sun.

T2 Clement of Alexandria, *Protrepticus* 66.2 (A12 DK = Alcmaeon R4 LM)

Alcmaeon of Croton thought that the heavenly bodies are gods **endowed with a soul**.

T3 Boethus in Porphyry in Eusebius, *Evangelical Preparation* 11.28.8–9 Mras (= Porph. 243F Smith = A12 DK, ≠ LM)

But that nothing of what is ours becomes more similar to god than the soul, one would trust it without needing to treat the matter at length, not only because of the continuity and the uninterrupted character of the movement that it [i.e. the soul] produces in us, but also of that of the mind which is in it. It was with this in view that the natural philosopher from Croton too said that it is immortal and because of its nature avoids every form of rest, just as those bodies which are divine.[52]

T4 Aëtius 4.2.2, 'On the soul' (A12 DK = Alcmaeon R3 LM) ÷

Alcmaeon: [*scil.* the soul is] a nature **that moves itself (*autokinētos*)** with an eternal motion, and it is for this reason that he thinks that it is immortal and similar to divine things.

T5 Cicero, *On the nature of the gods* 1.27 (A12 DK = Alcmaeon R5 LM)

Alcmaeon of Croton, who attributed **divinity** to the sun, the moon, and all the other heavenly bodies, and besides those to the soul, did not understand that he was attributing immortality to things that are mortal.

T6 Aristotle, *On the soul* 1.2, 405a29–b1 (A12 DK = Alcmaeon D9 LM)

Alcmaeon too seems to have had a conception about the soul similar to these [sc. those who explain the nature of the soul with reference to its mobility, namely, Thales, Diogenes of Apollonia, and Heraclitus]. For he says that it is immortal because it resembles the immortals. This belongs to it because it is always in motion. For everything that is divine always moves continually: the moon, the sun, the heavenly bodies, and the whole heavens.

Mansfeld has shown beyond any doubt[53] that later interpretations are in play in Aëtius's 'self-moved' soul, Cicero's 'divine' soul, and Clement's 'ensouled' stars; moreover, the only reliable evidence about Alcmaeon's views on the soul (and the stars) is to be found in Aristotle's testimony, of which the testimonies of Boethus (of Sidon) and Diogenes Laertius are close variations without independent value.

---

[52] Translation is mine (the last sentence is taken with slight modifications from Mansfeld 2014: 3).
[53] Mansfeld 2014: 1–9.

Alcmaeon's case illustrates clearly the mechanism by which an originally analogical scheme is stripped of its analogical dimension and turned into a substantive determination.

What can be extracted from Aristotle's testimony are the following three indications:

a. Soul in general – this certainly means individual soul[54] – is immortal.
b. This is because soul bears a resemblance to the stars.
c. This resemblance consists in that soul, like the stars, is always in movement.

On this basis, we may easily reconstruct the Platonization of Alcmaeon's views, once we are aware of the mediating role played by a famous development in Plato's *Phaedrus*. At 245c, Plato argues that the soul is immortal (*athanatos*) because it is always in movement (*aeikinêtos*) and that it is always in movement because it is something that moves itself (*to hauto kinoun*): it is the principle of movement, its 'source and beginning'. The word *autokinêtos* that occurs in Aëtius T4 is not Platonic. It occurs for the first time in Aristotle's *Physics* 8.5, 258a2 in an argument, *pace* Plato, that the principle of movement must be immobile and not self-moving. The word *autokinêtos*, a *hapax* in the whole Aristotelian corpus, clearly takes the participial phrase occurring in Plato's *Phaedrus* to a higher conceptual level. There has been ongoing discussion about whether the argument in the *Phaedrus* is meant to pertain to the individual soul or the soul in general, i.e. the celestial soul (or world soul) of which individual souls are fragments. This question does not affect the matter at stake here. The relevant consideration is that, since Alcmaeon had, on the one hand, declared soul to be immortal and, on the other hand, compared it on this basis to the (immortal) stars, his views could easily be harmonised with Plato's in the *Phaedrus* (and in a more systematic way in the *Timaeus*): it is not only that both soul and stars are, because of their continuous motion, immortal, but that (1) soul is self-moving, (2) self-moving stars have souls, and (3) since to be immortal is what it is to be a divinity, soul itself is a 'divinity'.

There is abundant evidence, in the rest of the chapter in Aëtius's handbook from which the notice on Alcmaeon is extracted, that the process of Platonization and more generally Academization affected other pre-Platonic thinkers as well. We have already met the first entry of this chapter, Thales (cf. *supra*, Thales T5, p. 11).[55] After Thales and Alcmaeon

---

[54] Cf. Mansfeld 2014: 5.   [55] Section 1.1.

comes Pythagoras (closely associated with Xenocrates), then Plato, before Aristotle, Dichaearchus and Asclepiades. Although the order of the chapter is chronological up to a certain point,[56] it is also co-determined by a conceptual progression that goes in part from the less determinate position to the more determinate one and, in part, from a more 'idealistic' stance to a 'materialistic' one. The section that interests us here is restricted to the first five entries (up to Plato), before Aristotle introduces the problem of the relation between soul and matter through his doctrine of the soul as 'the first entelechy of a natural, organic *body*'. (The doxographer refers to Aristotle, *On the soul*, 2.1.412a27f.) Whereas Thales anticipates Plato (cf. Thales T5 above) at the most possible general level, both on the question of the substance of the soul and in the question of its relation to movement, Alcmaeon is already more specific: soul is still a simple 'natural substance', but its resemblance to the gods (referring to the stars, as we know from Aristotle's testimony) provides it with an incipient determination. It is only in the third and fourth entries (as Diels prints them), respectively devoted to Pythagoras and Xenocrates, that the nature of the soul is fully determined, namely as 'a number which moves itself' – more exactly, the additional exegesis wants us to believe, as a (self-moving) intellect:

> Aëtius. 4.2.3–4, 'On the soul' (= Pythagorean Reception R30 LM, ≠ DK).
> Pythagoras: it [i.e. the soul] is a number that moves itself; he understands number instead of the mind.
> So too Xenocrates.[57]

Obviously, Pythagoras's alleged doctrine is in reality Xenocrates' – a condensation of Plato's views on the mathematical structure of the world soul in the *Timaeus* projected back on to Pythagoras.

Plato is – remarkably – introduced as a correction of Xenocrates' overdetermined reading of his own doctrine: soul is not a number that moves itself, still less an intellect, but only an *intelligible substance*. This characterisation, which of course is much clearer than the underdetermined 'nature' of Thales with which we began, opens the way to Aristotle's definition of the soul as the form or actuality of a body. There would be more to say about the overall structure of this chapter.[58] In the present

---

[56] See next note.

[57] Xenocrates fr. 60 Heinze. The entry on Pythagoras would represent the first chronological reversal of the chapter, if Pythagoras were really himself here and not another name for Xenocrates. In reality, what Diels prints as two separate entries (and now Mansfeld and Runia 2020: 1393) can be considered as building a unity.

[58] Cf. Manfeld and Runia 2020: 1402.

context, however, the important point is to clarify the condition under which the Platonization of Alcmaeon is possible. If the *analogical* relationship implied by Alcmaeon's comparison between the soul and the divine stars – i.e. both are immortal and eternally moving – is set aside in favour of substantial determination, stars become part of a psychic system paradigmatically represented by the doctrine of the world soul that is adumbrated in the *Phaedrus* and elaborated in the *Timaeus*.

1.2   Conclusion

Bremmer 1983, p. 5, wrote that 'the fact that *psyche* once had a connection with breath does not necessarily means that it has this meaning in Homer' and recommended: 'our point of departure must always be the assumption that the meaning of a word can only be derived from its use in the language'. The application of this principle to three of the thinkers we have considered here (Anaximenes, Heraclitus, and Philolaus), however, confirms the force of this very association, so far as early Greek philosophers are concerned. The fact that the Greek word usually translated with 'soul' – namely *psukhē* – means 'life' and was felt to be closely associated with 'breath'[59] illuminates the way in which a pre-Platonic world could become ensouled, in a sense that was neither meant nor anticipated by the original authors. Another, related but different scheme leading to the same result is provided in Thales' and Alcmaeon's cases, where the mediating terms are not 'air' and 'breathing', but rather 'divinities' – either indeterminate ones (Thales' gods), or specific ones (Alcmaeon's stars). Moreover, the evidence concerning Anaximenes, Heraclitus and above all Alcmaeon illustrates how easily what may have been only an analogy for Anaximenes and was certainly only one for Heraclitus and Alcmaeon (although analogy had a very different purpose in each case) was read as an assertion of substantial identity between the terms implied. In spite of the scarcity of source material, we are still in a position to see how a heavy reading of the Platonic tradition homogenised the views of a number of Presocratic thinkers up to a point where most of them could become 'all the others'.[60]

---

[59] 'It is also well known that the feminine substantive *psukhē*, despite its already diverse uses in Homer, originally signifies the 'breath' that is present in a human while alive and departs temporarily during fainting and permanently in death'. Jouanna 1987: 203, my translation). Philolaus's analogy between the birth of the cosmos and that of the embryo (see Section 1.4) is also relevant here.

[60] For a few further observations about the 'others' I have deliberately left aside here, see Laks 2018: 32 n. 80.

Interpreters are generally aware that using the doxographical material available to us in order to reconstruct the theories of ancient philosophers requires a fair amount of caution and critical acumen. This is true in general, but particularly true in the case of early Greek philosophers, who represent an extreme and for that reason paradigmatic case because they do not share the conceptual world that Plato devised for the entire history of philosophy after him. The analysis I have developed here of course confirms this trivial and basically negative point. But there is a positive side to it too. For the doxographical material, which is heterogeneous in its form as well as in its substance (Aëtius is not Aristotle, nor Sextus Empiricus) offers, at least in the most favourable cases, traces of the process by which a view, generally encapsulated in a certain formula or term, has been interpreted, sometimes in a legitimate way, sometimes interestingly, sometimes flatly. To reconstruct this process is not only interesting in itself, because it teaches us a great deal about reading practices, in this case philosophical reading practices, in antiquity and more generally about the history of the ancient reception of early Greek philosophy. It is also the unique way which is open to us when we care to identify not only what our own interpretations but perhaps also and more importantly ancient interpretations could rely on when they assessed those texts – for example phrases such as Thales' 'everything is full of gods' or Heraclitus' use of the verb 'exhale' in a certain context. I hope to have shown in the five cases here presented how we can to various degree (depending of the material available), work our way back to the points where interpretation, on which so much of what we say depends, starts and in some cases see or fathom why they go in a certain direction.

The Ensouled Cosmos in Plato's Timaeus
Biological Science as a Guide to Cosmology?

Barbara M. Sattler*

2.1 Introduction

Plato's cosmology in the *Timaeus* is not only an account of the universe as a whole, its structure and origin, but also an account of the genesis of life: on the micro level – the development of human beings, animals, and plants – and on the macro level – for the whole universe is a living being. Plato's cosmology thus not only includes biology, but seems to be essentially framed in what we could call biological terms.

For us cosmology and biology may be mainly linked by the attempt to find life on other planets in the universe and perhaps, in connection with this, by what in contemporary metaphysics and philosophy of science are called 'fine-tuning arguments': given that so many parameters have to be very finely tuned in order to allow for life on our planet, how can we explain the extremely unlikely fact that all these parameters are indeed in place on earth? Do we want to see in this some mark of intelligent design? Or do we assume something like the so-called multiverse theory, i.e. that there is not just one universe, but rather that all possible universes have been actualised, even our own, highly unlikely universe containing life on earth?

But in these cases, in which we may get exposed to the combination of biology and cosmology in contemporary philosophy, the universe is not itself assumed to be a living being – so pursuing cosmology does not in itself imply being engaged in some form of biology. Thinking of the universe itself as a living being may be a very peculiar thought for us, but one not necessarily unfamiliar in the ancient world.[1]

---

* I want to thank Sarah Broadie for helpful comments on the chapter.
[1] We may see some precursors to this idea in Xenophanes's characterisation of his unantropomorphic god, in Empedocles's sphere and Anaxagoras's *Nous*. A close connection between what we would call biology and cosmology can also be found with Anaximander; cf. Gregory 2016.

In Plato's account, the world is not only a living being, but also a very special living being – a god. Associations with some form of pantheism may arise here, where there is some form of identity between god and the universe this god brings about. But again this is not what we find in Plato. In the *Timaeus* the universe is a god and there is indeed a 'creator' god. But the universe is a god that is different from the creator god. The creator god, whom Plato calls the demiurge,[2] is an *eternal* god. He is responsible for the coming into being and the continuous existence of the universe, which is only a *never ending* god.[3] As the world is made by the demiurge, it has a beginning, in contrast to the demiurge; but thanks to the demiurge's promise, it will not have an end.

In this chapter I want to argue that the central assumption that leads Plato to understand the created cosmos as a living being is the idea that the world is as good as possible. In a second step I want to show that this very same assumption of the world being as good as possible is also responsible for two important twists to the biological framing Plato uses:

First, being as good as possible also implies that the world is self-sufficient, which in turn means that a lot of our common biological notions are of no relevance for an account of the cosmos as a living being. Most importantly, the idea of organs is explicitly denied of this living being, as organs come into play predominantly if there is some lack, or if a living being wants to interact with something outside itself – both points do not hold of the cosmos as a whole.[4]

Secondly, I will show that while Plato gives an account of all kinds of living beings, his assumption of the bestness of the world means that he is ultimately focusing on rational living beings. Accordingly, what starts out

---

[2] Menn 1995: 66, n.1 claims that 'demiurge' is not really the god's proper name or title that expresses his nature, but a placeholder. A lot of the arguments about the creator god's doing, however, rely on the idea of a craftsman, for example, the claim that in order to produce something he works with a model.

[3] Cornford 1937 has argued for identifying the World Soul and the demiurge and thus in effect the two gods. If they were identified, however, it would be hard to see why Plato, at least on a literal reading of the text, has the world come into being, but not the demiurge and why the demiurge is explicitly mentioned as the agent creating the World Soul in the earlier part of the dialogue. Broadie 2012 has shown that the World Soul and the demiurge are two rather different kinds of causes: while the demiurge is a 'one-many principle', so a principle that has many effects (it produces the World Soul, the World Body, gods etc.), the World Soul is a one-one principle (its function is to animate the cosmos). Finally, according to Broadie, if the demiurge and the World Soul were not clearly distinguished, it would be much harder to explain how we human beings can be simultaneously akin to the cosmos and yet relatively autonomous.

[4] This also seems to hold true of Empedocles's sphere.

in biological terms turns into a form of rational psychology and rational theology.[5]

There is in fact a good deal more that we may see as a kind of biological research in the *Timaeus* in the third part of the work (in the part that connects the work of reason and necessity), where Plato gives us not only an extensive account of the human body and its functioning, but also some account of animals and plants. But this account is not connected with his cosmology and thus will not be in the foreground of this chapter. I will, however, look briefly at life in (and indeed also beyond) the cosmos in order to discuss whether these accounts can be integrated with Plato's notion of life and living beings as exemplified by merely rational beings.

2.2   The Cosmos as a Living Being

2.2.1   *Bestness of the World*

While biology had not yet been established as a separate science in the time of Plato,[6] in contrast to medicine or mathematics, what we would call the core biological notions of 'life' and 'living beings' are at the heart of Plato's cosmology. His cosmology deals with the set-up of the universe as a whole, its structure and development. It attempts to understand the whole of the cosmos, and since the cosmos as a whole is a living being for Plato, cosmology can be understood as a form of biology. But why does Plato think that the cosmos is a living being?

In accordance with most of the Presocratic cosmologies, cosmology is done by way of a cosmo*gony* in the *Timaeus*, by explaining how the cosmos as a whole came into being.[7] Since the cosmos can (at least in part) be perceived, it is a sensible thing, and all sensible things at one point came into being according to Plato (28b-c). In order for something to come into

[5] This is a modern way of capturing what Plato does, but arguably for both Plato and Aristotle intellectual activity is literally a vital activity, not just analogous to one. We will see that the cosmos's intellectual activity (which is all the vital activity it possesses as a living being) is what animates its body.

[6] Roughly speaking, by biology I understand here the study of life and living organisms, including their structure, function, growth, evolution, distribution, identification, and taxonomy. The word 'biology', used in order to refer to a science, seems to be mentioned for the first time in Latin in 1736 by Carl von Linné in his *Bibliotheca botanica* (pointed out by Gregory 2016). For the English word 'biology' the OED refers to '1766, in the title of a work by M. C. Hanov, or earlier'.

[7] Cosmologies are given in terms of cosmogonies from Anaximander onwards, and cosmogonies that more specifically also include the generation of human beings are familiar at least from Parmenides onwards. On Parmenides's account, however, the world is not itself a living being.

being, there has to be a cause for this process, and Plato translates this cause immediately into a maker, an agent (28a-c); more specifically, it is a divine demiurge who brings about the cosmos.[8]

And this divine maker is good and thus makes the world as good as possible. This means, for Plato, making it a living being:

> Now it wasn't permitted (nor is it now) that one who is supremely good should do anything but what is best. Accordingly, the god reasoned and concluded that in the realm of things naturally visible no unintelligent thing could as a whole be better than anything which does possess intelligence as a whole, and he further concluded that it is impossible for anything to come to possess intelligence apart from soul. Guided by this reasoning, he put intelligence in soul, and soul in body, and so he constructed the universe. He wanted to produce a piece of work that would be as excellent and supreme as its nature would allow. This, then, in keeping with our likely account, is how we must say divine providence brought our world into being as a truly living thing, endowed with soul and intelligence. (30a6–c1)[9]

Since whatever has intelligence (*nous*) is more excellent than what does not have intelligence, the cosmos is given intelligence in order to make it as excellent as possible.[10] Being given intelligence does not simply mean that something with intelligence is made part of the cosmos – as we could claim it to be the case for a solely materially determined world into which intelligent living beings are put. Rather the whole world itself is given intelligence so that intelligence can be all-pervading.

Within the sensible world, intelligence does not float around freely, but rather is a feature of souls, so the cosmos must have a soul.[11] And souls in the sensible world are in bodies, so that we get a perfect embodied soul,

---

[8] For possible explanations of why Timaeus takes the cause of the universe to be a craftsman, see Broadie 2012: 31–8 and Johansen 2014. It presupposes that there is some intelligence already at the beginning of the formation of the universe.

[9] Translations are by Zeyl, with alterations.

[10] There is no further explanation for why having intelligence is better than not having intelligence in the *Timaeus* (though see p. 97 below), but we seem to find one in the Stoics, cf. Salles in this volume.

[11] The world itself is (at least in part) perceptible and as such needs to have a body and has come into being. Given this condition, intelligence can only belong to it by its having a soul. By contrast, the demiurge, while to some degree interacting with the sensible world (or at least with its necessary conditions, like the receptacle and the traces in the receptacle), is not himself perceptible and has not come into being, thus does not need a soul to have (or even be) intelligence. Some scholars have read Timaeus's claim in 30b3 that 'nothing can possess intelligence apart from soul' as requiring that the demiurge and the World Soul have to be identified, so Cornford 1937, Cherniss 1944: 425, and Carone 2005: 42–51. However, this statement of Timaeus is explicitly made with respect to visible, i.e. sensible things; since the demiurge is not one of the sensible things, this does not apply to him (cf. also Menn 1995: 19–21). Some of the problems such an identification raises are mentioned in footnote 3.

a perfect living being. We see that the reason why Plato frames his cosmology in terms that we may call biological is his assumption that the world is as good as possible.

The perfection of the living being is guaranteed by its going on living for ever and by having nothing outside it:

> Now each of the four constituents was entirely used up in the process of building the world. The builder built it from all the fire, water, air and earth there was, and left no part or power of any of them out. His intentions in doing so were these: First, that as a living thing it should be as whole and complete as possible and made up of complete parts. Second, that it should be just one universe in that nothing would be left over from which another one just like it could be made. Third, that it should not get old and diseased. He realized that when heat or cold or anything else that possesses strong powers surrounds a composite body from outside and attacks it, it destroys this body prematurely, brings disease and old age upon it and so causes it to waste away. That is why he concluded that he should fashion the world as a single whole, composed of all wholes, complete and free of old age and disease, and why he fashioned it that way. (32c5–33b1)

The demiurge uses all of the available material, all there is of the four elements, in order to make the World Body. Accordingly, there is nothing left outside the one body, and thus there can be no sickness or ageing, which would be based on some interaction with an outside. Thus, the cosmos is perfect, not only because it is complete, but also because this form of completeness saves it from external destruction, and it allows the cosmos, together with the promise from the demiurge not to destroy it,[12] to go on without end. The cosmos is thus immortal and hence divine – accordingly, the world is not only a living being, but a god.

2.2.2   Self-Sufficiency of the World

As the world is as good as possible and thus complete, it is also fully self-sufficient in the sense that it is independent of anything physical outside it.[13]

---

[12] As Betegh 2018: 9 puts it, who looks at the cosmic and human soul together, given that they are the best possible, 'it is good that they remain in existence, and the demiurge will therefore not let them disintegrate'.

[13] It still depends, however, on the 'good-will' of the demiurge for its continued existence.

Completeness and self-sufficiency[14] express themselves in its particular shape – a shape appropriate to the world's status:

> And he gave it a shape appropriate to the kind of thing it is. The appropriate shape for that living thing that is to contain within itself all the living things would be the one which embraces within itself all the shapes there are. Hence he gave it a round shape, the form of a sphere, with its centre equidistant from its extremes in all directions. This of all shapes is the most complete and most like itself, which he gave to it because he believed that likeness is incalculably more excellent than unlikeness. And he gave it a smooth round finish all over on the outside for many reasons. It needed no eyes, since there was nothing visible left outside it; nor did it need ears, since there was nothing audible there, either. There was no air enveloping it that it might need for breathing, nor did it need any organ by which to take in food or, again, expel it when it had been digested. For since there wasn't anything else, there would be nothing to leave it or come to it from anywhere. It supplies its own wasting for its food. Anything that it did or experienced it was designed to do or experience within itself and by itself. For the builder thought that if it were self-sufficient (αὔταρκες), it would be a better thing than if it required other things. And since it had no need to catch hold of or fend off anything, the god thought it would be pointless to attach hands to it. Nor would it need feet or any support to stand on. (33b1–34a1)

The cosmos is given the sphere as a shape so that it is the same distance from each of its points on its surface to the middle – a body as self-similar as possible. And it encompasses all the other shapes, as may be best seen in Kepler's well-known study of the sphere into which the other Platonic bodies are inscribed.[15] Accordingly, this spherical god is bestowed with a perfect shape.

The world can be given such a perfect and simple form, because the completeness of the cosmos also implies its self-sufficiency, which in turn means it does not need any bodily tools to supply itself with anything from outside.[16] A consequence of its self-sufficiency is that many of our common biological notions are not applicable to this special living being. Most importantly, what we may understand as the idea of organs and limbs is

---

[14] John Dillon pointed out to me that the word '*autarkês*' is hardly used in Plato, but it occurs twice in the *Timaeus* to characterize the cosmos: in 33d2 the world body is described as *autarkes* (see quotation below), and in 68e3–4 we read that the demiurge has created the self-sufficient and most perfect god, τὸν αὐτάρκη τε καὶ τὸν τελεώτατον θεὸν ἐγέννα). In 34b7 we are also told that the world body does not need anything else (οὐδενὸς ἑτέρου προσδεόμενον).

[15] Kepler 1596.

[16] El Murr in this volume, Section 3.4, points out that not having any limbs and organs is also what allows the cosmos, in contrast to all other animals, to be perfectly symmetrical.

explicitly denied of this living being.[17] Organs and limbs, it seems, come into play if there is some lack or some requirement to interact with an outside world. Of all such needs the cosmos is, however, free. No limbs are required, since there is nothing outside for hands to get in contact with, nor is the cosmos in need of feet to walk around or to stand on. Similarly, there is no want that would require any organs: the cosmos as a whole does not need eyes or ears because there is nothing visible or audible left outside. And since there is no inflow or outflow, no organ (*organon*, 33c) is required to process food from outside or again to excrete what has been processed. Accordingly, the cosmos is not in need of any organs, it does not require them to sustain itself or to perceive anything outside.[18]

But what about organs for two activities that we do indeed find within the cosmos as a whole – organs for thought and for maintaining itself internally? Given that the World Soul is constantly thinking, we may assume that it should have an organ for thought. Thinking is, however, not ascribed to one particular organ; rather the whole of the World Soul just is the circles of the Same and the Different whose motions are its thinking.

While there is nothing outside the world to interact with and so no external inflow for the cosmos to maintain itself, we may still think that organs are important for a living being to sustain itself internally – for some form of what we would call metabolism.[19] The heart, for example, seems to perform such a function, distributing the blood everywhere in the body.[20] As a living being the cosmos indeed nourishes and thus maintains itself. But it does so completely from within: while a heart distributes to all the cells oxygen, that the lungs have gained from the outside as well as

[17] By organs I understand here any bodily unit that serves a particular physiological task or function (such as the sense-organs, the lung, or liver).

[18] By contrast, there is, a detailed description of organs in the case of human beings who need to interact with an outside world. While the Stoic god is also self-sufficient, not experiencing any need, and without sense-organs, it nevertheless seems to have perception as a basic form of self-awareness; since god is everywhere, this implies also that it can perceive everything there is, cf. Boys-Stones on Stoicism in this volume. Also Plato's World Soul may be seen to possess some form of self-awareness; not through perception, however, but through thought.

[19] While today we often think of metabolism as the (or at least including) *chemical* processes that occur within a living organism in order to maintain life, I still think it makes sense to use the notion of metabolism for a discussion of the *Timaeus* in order to look at the processes that maintain a particular living being, even if this is not done on what we may call the chemical level. (Plato's account of how the triangles that form the basis of the four elements get added, cut up, transformed into parts of other elements, and expelled in the body of human beings may, however, be seen as a predecessor also to ideas about such chemical processes).

[20] In the case of human beings we are explicitly told about their metabolism as they take in food from outside and excrete what they have digested.

nutrients gained from external food, there is no need of food or air from outside for the cosmos, since it is fully self-sufficient. The cosmos lives of its own wasting or consumption (φθίσις), as we are told in, 33c. And there is no need to distribute stuff within the World Body – while the elements are in constant transformation and thus moving to different parts of the cosmos, this is not a motion that needs to be maintained by an organ of the world.

We see that the cosmos as a living being lives a perfect life, but that in order to explain this life, only a very limit arsenal of biological notions is required.[21] Thus we may think that the notion of biology needed in the case of the cosmos as a whole is rather narrow. The notion of biology is, however, also quite broad, for with the cosmos it includes a merely rational being – an idea that we will see further supported below.

2.2.3   Astronomy and the Cognition of the Word Soul

What does the fact that the whole cosmos is a thinking living being mean for cosmology and astronomy? Perhaps the most striking point is that for Plato doing astronomy means being engaged in something like rational psychology or epistemology: when we look at the motions of the planets and stars, what we see is the cognition of the World Soul – the heavenly motions are manifestations of its cognition. In this way Plato tries to establish a surprisingly tight connection between rational psychology and astronomy. But what does it mean that when we look at the heavenly bodies we look at the cognition of the World Soul? In order to understand this idea we should look at the set-up of the World Soul:

The World Soul is composed out of two bands that intersect at two points so as to define a sphere. Both bands are mixed out of three ingredients, Being, Difference and Sameness, each of which is composed of indivisible and divisible components (35a). The whole mixture of Being, Difference, and Sameness is split into two bands that are put into one encompassing motion (36c). The motion of the outer band is called the

---

[21] The notion of semen or seed does pop up in the *Timaeus* – in biological and non-biological contexts. Understood in a biological way, we find semen, for example, in 73c, where we are told that the marrow is meant to carry the seed in it, and in 91bff. it is described how in the case of human beings the male semen (*sperma*) is linked to the desire of giving life and procreation and is put into the female womb as onto a field; see also 74a and 77a. In a non-biological way, we find Timaeus talk about the tetrahedron as *stoicheion* and *sperma* of fire (56b). But the notion of semen plays no role for the account of the cosmos as a living being, nor does the cosmos need sexual organs, since the cosmos does not reproduce.

movement of the Same, the one of the inner band the movement of the Different, even though both are mixed from Sameness and Difference alike. While the Circle of the Same is undivided, the Circle of the Different is split up into seven circles. The motions of the Same and the Different are first and foremost understood as cognitive motions of the World Soul.[22] Cognition of what is indivisible, i.e. of objects of reasoning, is performed by the Circle of the Same, which is itself undivided.[23] Cognition of what is divisible, i.e. of what pertains to the realm of becoming and is perceptible, is performed by the Circle of the Different and brings about true opinion. The Circle of the Different is suited for cognition of what is divisible since it is itself divided into seven circles.[24]

The cognitive motions are made visible by the heavenly bodies. The fixed stars move in the Circle of the Same (40a), whereas the sun, the moon, and the five then known planets are set into the seven circles of the Different in such a way that each Circle of the Different accommodates one heavenly body (38c-d). And these seven heavenly bodies move according to both circles, the Circle of the Different specific to them and the Circle of the Same, which affects them all (38c–39b). The sideways motion of the Circle of the Same to the right is usually understood by commentators as motion along the Equator from East to West,[25] while the diagonal motion of the Circle of the Different to the left is taken to be motion along the Ecliptic.

In Plato's account, the motions of the heavenly bodies are thus nothing other than the visible manifestations of the intellectual motions of the World Soul.[26] Since the motions of the World Soul are regular, also the motions of the planets and the fixed stars are regular,[27] and in this way show on a physical level the rationality of the motions of the World Soul's reasoning. Being visible everywhere, these motions of the heavenly bodies and their rational structure are accessible for whoever perceives them with her senses.

Astronomy thus investigates the phenomenal level of the motions of the World Soul, as it deals with the heavenly motions that make visible the

---

[22] For a detailed discussion of how we can understand the cognition of the World Soul, see Sattler in preparation.

[23] While being undivided is, of course, not the same as being indivisible, it seems to be at least similar to it, which is all that is required for cognition that is based on the like-to-like principle.

[24] While the World Soul itself possesses only reasoning, it thus also has opinions about sensible things.

[25] See e.g. Proclus, *Commentary on Plato's* Timaeus, Book III, 237–8, Cornford 1937:74–86, and Taylor 1928: 147–52.

[26] Cf. also Sedley 1997b: 329.   [27] See e.g. 39b–d and below.

rational motions of the World Soul. Investigating the heavenly motions is important for us not only to understand the regularity in the natural world around us, but also, and more importantly, in order to gain access to the cognitions of the World Soul.

Thus what seems to start out as a cosmological biology – investigating the cosmos as one big living being – turns into a form of theology, as well as rational psychology or epistemology. Investigating the cosmos means in some sense doing rational psychology, since we are investigating the visible manifestations of the cognitions of the World Soul. But it can also be seen as a form of theology: if we do cosmology, what we do is investigate the created God and try to understand the intentions of the creator god in order to understand the way he set up the universe.[28]

2.3   Life in and beyond the Cosmos

Plato's account of the whole cosmos as a living being may be one of the most puzzling ideas in the *Timaeus*, but the cosmos is certainly not the only living being discussed. Rather, Plato also introduces a familiar diversity of life-forms *in* the cosmos, and, probably less familiar, *beyond* the cosmos. Let us start with the first one.

In the third part of his speech, Timaeus gives an account of animals and plants. But while Plato's cosmology has a place for all kinds of living beings – gods (prominently the gods which are the heavenly bodies), human beings, animals and plants – he is not interested in a biological taxonomy of living beings in the way we are used to from the biological sciences and as it starts to be developed with Aristotle and his school. Plato does give a kind of taxonomy of all living beings, but it is an abstract deductive taxonomy, not a taxonomy based on inductive investigation of individual species: in 39e we learn that the number and kinds of living beings in the model determines the number and kinds of living beings in the sensible cosmos. The basic kinds of living beings correspond to the four elements, earth, water, air, and fire: there is the fiery kind of the gods, the heavenly bodies, and three mortal kinds that live in the air, in water, and on earth, respectively.[29] This taxonomy derives from an idea of completeness – in order for the cosmos to be complete, it needs all four kinds of living beings.

---

[28] Interestingly, it is the universe as a created god who is an object of worship, but not the creator god, who may seem to be the more natural deity to worship for us.
[29] This suggests a close connection between the model and the Form of Fire, etc., but we are not told any details about this connection.

While this taxonomy gives us a kind of overview of the different types of living beings to be expected in the cosmos, what Plato is really interested in is not the totality of living beings, but rather *rational* living beings, that is, gods and human beings. This raises the question whether Plato's cosmological project in the *Timaeus* is thus not a different explanatory enterprise than what we usually think ancient cosmologies to be.

The Presocratic thinkers are often seen as starting philosophy by replacing gods as causes with naturalistic explanations – for example, the phenomenon of the rainbow is famously explained by Xenophanes as a combination of clouds, rather than as a messenger of the gods.[30] Given that Plato's cosmology showed itself as a kind of theology, is Plato in the *Timaeus* thus failing to achieve this form of explanation in naturalistic terms that we have come to consider as scientific or proto-scientific? I do not think so, not even if we were to reduce our understanding of 'naturalistic' to 'mechanistic'. It is true that Plato does not bother to spell out why we get lunar and solar eclipses or similar phenomena. But he gives a basic set-up of all the planets in the universe, their motions, and mutual relations which is meant to enable 'those who are schooled in these matters' to figure out any details themselves.[31] And Plato discusses several phenomena, such as respiration, in quite some detail in mechanistic terms – in terms of elemental locomotion and transformation. Such an interplay between elements can be seen as a well-known part of cosmologies at least since Empedocles. Plato takes up this traditional cosmological approach in his *Timaeus*, while at the same time attempting to show that it had not been done properly: what were seen as elements so far – earth, water, air and fire – are not even so much as syllables of the book of the world, let alone *stoicheia*. But this form of explanation, that we may call mechanistic, is only one specific part of Plato's cosmological story.[32] It does not play a role with the set-up of the World Soul and the heavenly bodies in the first part, where we find teleological reasoning. While bound to a creator god and his intentions, this teleological reasoning is, however, also not an unscientific theistic explanation in the sense that a god intervenes in nature due to his personal fancy.[33]

---

[30] Xenophanes, Scholium BLT on *Iliad* 11.27.   [31] 53c.

[32] Precursors to a combination of mechanistic and non-mechanistic explanations may be seen in Anaximander's divine *apeiron*, in Heraclitus' *logos*, and in Xenophanes's combination of theology and mechanistic explanations.

[33] In the way that, for example, a storm at sea arises because Poseidon is angry about Odysseus. We may want to call the teleological reasoning we find in Plato naturalistic, because it does not work with a god who is brought in to explain exceptional or otherwise unexplained phenomena, but rather with a god who establishes regularities in nature that then seem to work without him interfering. But the label does not matter in the end.

Both kinds of explanation, mechanistic and teleological, are needed in order to give a full explanation of one central kind of living being, namely us human beings. Furthermore, we as embodied souls cannot be accounted for simply by having our body explained in mechanistic terms and our soul in teleological terms. Rather, also our body, which follows mechanistic causation, is made so as to be teleologically satisfying.

Accordingly, it is with the explanation of human organs where we turn from the reason part to the necessity part of the *Timaeus* – in order to explain not only to what end they are created but also how they work, we need necessity as well as reason. Human beings are only explainable with the help of both, and biology as the science of living beings has to connect mechanistic and teleological reasoning.

The introduction of a god as the craftsman of the world allows Plato to bring in teleological reasoning fairly naturally on the cosmic level, and thus ultimately to combine mechanistic explanations with explanations connected with intentions. And, as we have seen, these are not the mixed intentions of the Olympic gods, which may in part be driven by jealousy and immoral desires. Plato's creator god is not just a primus inter pares, in the way Zeus may be understood. Rather, as the all good creator, he is more like Xenophanes's God, who is free of all human baseness and possesses the 'human features' he has (like thinking) in the most eminent way. While there are other gods apart from the creator god in the *Timaeus*, the demiurge is on a different metaphysical level, as he, together with the model and the receptacle, forms what is eternally there 'before' the world comes into being, and he generates all the other gods.

Human beings – the case where the combination of mechanistic and teleological explanation is most clearly required – are first introduced, it seems, merely for completeness purposes. But their real prominence is based on the fact that they are a part of the world that can itself reflect about the world and make themselves more like the whole world, by adapting their reasoning to the reasoning of the World Soul.

There is a clear hierarchy of living beings in the cosmos: human beings are introduced immediately after the set-up of the World Soul and the World Body and thus seem to be part of the attempt to ensure that the universe is made as similar as possible to the model. Animals, while also introduced for completeness purposes, are shown to be fallen human souls.[34] Plants, finally, are there as food for human beings to eat.

So far we have dealt with the cosmos as a living being, and living beings in the cosmos. However, for Plato there is also life 'beyond' the cosmos, for the model of the cosmos is also a living being. Let us briefly turn to this even more special living being:

Connected with the figure of the demiurge, who makes the cosmos, is the idea that the maker of the world looks at a model according to which he creates. And in order to make a good world the demiurge has to look at an unchanging eternal model and make the world as a likeness of it. This unchanging eternal model, of which the cosmos is a copy, is itself called a living being:

> When the maker made our world, what living thing did he make it resemble? Let us not stoop to think that it was any of those that have the natural character of a part, for nothing that is a likeness of anything incomplete could ever turn out beautiful. Rather, let us lay it down that the universe resembles more closely than anything else that Living Thing of which all other living things are parts, both individually and by kinds. For that Living Thing comprehends within itself all intelligible living things, just as our world is made up of us and all visible creatures. Since the god wanted nothing more than to make the world like the best of the intelligible things, complete in every way, he made a single visible living thing, which contains within itself all the living things whose nature it is to share its kind. (30c2–31a1)

The model according to which our cosmos is formed is a living being; a living being, however, that is not perceptible, but only accessible by reason.[35] I will have to put to the side the question of how to think about the model in relation to the Platonic Forms.[36] But we will briefly look at

---

[34] On the one hand we are told that all the mortal animals on earth, in water, and in the air are needed in order to have all the living beings in the intelligible model also mirrored in the created cosmos. On the other hand we learn that all the animals that exist are souls that originally were human beings, but, because of their bad behaviour, were reborn as animals (exemplifying a particular aspect of their badness). Thus we are given two different and, it seems, competing explanations of the creation of mortal animals without them being explicitly connected with each other.

[35] Plato does not call the model an *empsuchon*, however, presumably because this would imply that it has its own body and it may also imply change.

[36] It has been understood either as (a) the whole intelligible realm (so Zeyl 2000: xxxvii n.66) or as (b) a particular Form (most prominently by Cornford 1937: 40 and Sedley 2007: 108 n.36 who understand the model as 'the Form of the Genus "Animal"') or (c) a group of Forms (for example in Thein 2006, who understands it as the sum of four Forms, one for each type of life).

the relationship between the model and the cosmos and at the question what it may mean for the model to be a living being.

With both the model and the cosmos we get the idea that they are somehow the whole of all living beings: the model comprises all intelligible living beings, the cosmos all the perceptible living beings.[37] Thus, we are dealing with the same kind of part-whole relationship. But why is the intelligible model itself a living being? Do we have a self-predication move here – as the Form of Beauty seems to be a paradigm of beauty and thus, at least on some interpretations, to be beautiful itself, so the Form or Model for the cosmos as a living being has to be itself a living being?[38] And what does it mean for the model to be a living being? Usually, Plato seems to understand soul as a principle of life,[39] but does this mean that also the model would need a soul? Aristotle gives us a biological account of life (*zôe*) in his *De anima* as 'possessing the capacity for self-sustenance, growth and decay' (412a14–15) – an account which would not square very well with the idea of a Form or something merely intelligible possessing life. But for Plato, growth and decay do not necessarily seem to be part of life – the world as a whole also does not grow nor undergo decay, even if we are told about its sustenance. However, also Aristotle allows for another understanding of life, it seems, when in his *Metaphysics* Book XII, chapter 7, he claims that the unmoved mover, who is pure thinking, has to be alive 'for the actuality of thought is life'. It is this kind of life, a life itself independent of the sensible world (though of utmost importance for this world), and only related to thought, that also seems to fit Plato's idea of the model as a living Being – we are not dealing with any old form of life here, but with intelligent life that is nothing but intelligent life.[40]

---

[37] Parry 1991: 20–25 claims that the way in which the model contains all the other intelligible animals (as individuals and as kinds) and is thus complete is the reason it functions as a model for our cosmos. And indeed the quotation just given stresses the particular part-whole relationship as an important point in which our cosmos resemble the model.

[38] Both Sedley and Cornford have inferred from their interpretation of the model as the Form of the Genus 'Animal' that the model is thus not a living being itself. And it is true that a *zôon* need not indicate a living being in Greek, but can also mean an image. However, given that Plato wants to account for the model of the whole cosmos, it seems unlikely to me that he would use the word '*zôon*' as meaning 'image' here. The parallel that Sedley provides – the Form of the couch in the *Republic* which is also called a couch (*klinê*) – seems to me unconvincing. It is unclear what it would mean for the Form of the couch to be itself a couch, while it seems reasonable for Plato to understand the Form of Beauty as a paradigm of beauty and thus as itself beautiful. And the model in the *Timaeus* seems to be more like the Form of Beauty than the Form of a couch (the latter being an oddity among Plato's set of Forms in any case).

[39] See e.g. *Phaedo* 105b–c.

[40] Both Plato and Aristotle share the idea, foreign to a contemporary notion of life in biology, that intellectual activity could be the sole vital activity something has as a living being.

2.4   Plato's Notion of Life in the *Timaeus*

We have seen different forms of life in Plato's *Timaeus*. The first one we discussed is the cosmos as a living being. It has a body and a soul, and thus may seem to be alive in the same way human beings are (just more perfect and on a grander scale). However, the World Soul is in fact more of a World *Nous*, since the World Soul consists only of the intellect. We do not hear anything about the other two soul parts we are familiar with from Plato's psychology, *thumos* and *epithumia*, even though in the case of human beings these two mortal parts of the soul come about once the immortal rational soul is embodied, and also the World Soul is embodied. Cornford has tried to argue for some irrational part of the World Soul.[41] Following the *Phaedrus*, Cornford claims that only souls can be causes for motions. Rational souls, however, would bring about orderly motion. In order to explain the irregular motion of the traces and the receptacle 'before' creation then, Cornford assumes we need an irrational soul part. I do not see, however, that we have any basis for such an assumption, if we follow the Platonic text; the motions before creation are said to stem from the differences in the *dunameis* of the traces of the elements in the receptacle.[42] Lower soul parts seem to be required only if a soul is embodied into a body that is itself only a part and in which the rational soul is housed only in a part of that body.[43] By contrast, the World Body is the whole of all bodily stuff, and the World Soul pervades the World Body throughout.

Hence the soul of the cosmos possesses only the reason part of the soul. And the eternal model, after which the cosmos is formed and which is thus in some sense the paradigmatic form of life, is also tied to reason alone. But what does this mean for other forms of life, especially non-intelligent ones? Does Plato in fact have a consistent account of life that can encompass all the life-forms discussed in the *Timaeus*?[44]

Given that the World Soul and the eternal model are characterised only by reason, it seems that life for Plato has to be tied exclusively to reason. We saw that human beings and animals (qua fallen human souls) also have

---

[41] See Cornford 1937: 203–10; and also Vlastos's 1939 criticism of it.   [42] Cf. Sattler 2012.

[43] Given that our human body is just a part, it has to interact with an outside and maintain itself (through appetites and so forth). And due to the insular location of the rational soul in the head, the spirited soul part has to help it keep control over its whole body.

[44] Thein 2006: 247–8 claims that the four created life-forms and their corresponding parts of the model only have the name 'living thing' in common, but not the definitions, since the latter do not move and are objects, not subjects of thought.

at their core a rational soul and thus can be seen as fitting an understanding of living beings that is tied to reason alone. However, Plato also calls plants *zôa*, living beings, in the *Timaeus*, in 77b-c. But plants participate in life solely because they partake in the lowest part of the soul, they have desires and some *aisthêsis* of what is pleasant and unpleasant. They do not, however, in any way partake in the rational part (they possess no *nous*, *logismos*, or *doxa*). This raises a problem, since so far the two lower parts of the soul only seemed to come about if the rational soul gets embodied. Thus these two soul parts seemed to depend on the existence first of a rational soul – an account which does not work with plants. More importantly, the introduction of plants also means that Plato's notion of life seems to fall apart into two independent notions: one notion is tied solely to reason and intellect, as with the model and the cosmos as a whole, whereas the other notion refers to any form of desire and *aisthêsis* and thus includes plants. Part of the linguistic background for these two different understandings of living beings is the fact that the Greek word *zôon* can be used either to refer to animals, thus excluding plants,[45] or, indeed, to living beings, and thus including them.

Both notions of life that we find in Plato cover human beings and animals, but the second one excludes the cosmos and the model, while the first one excludes plants. It is the understanding of life tied to reason that is central for Plato.

2.5 Conclusion

The main focus of Plato's cosmology is not the explanation of the set of phenomena that cosmologies in the Presocratic tradition attempt to explain, such as solar and lunar eclipses, the phases of the moon, the changes of the seasons, or meteorological phenomena. Rather, the focus of his cosmology is to understand the world as the best possible ordered whole[46]– as a divine living being. For Plato the world we experience is not only intelligible, i.e. it is capable of being understood by rational beings, but also itself a thinking being, a being given the power of reasoning, whose reasoning is the basis for processes in the natural and human realm. We may think Plato is going too far here – does he really have to understand the

---

[45] A meaning we find, for example, in Plato's *Phaedo*, 70d, when in his argument from opposites Socrates considers the question whether the living are born from the dead not only with regard to human beings but also to all animals as well as plants (κατὰ ζῴων πάντων καὶ φυτῶν).

[46] Within the constraints of necessity, that is.

cosmos as a living being for it to be the best possible whole? Could Plato not obtain the intelligibility of the cosmos with some weaker assumption? Accessibility to reason does not imply that what is accessed has itself to possess reason. But a cosmos that is not a living being would not be the *best* possible for Plato, since what possesses reason is better than what lacks reason. And understanding the world as itself a rational living being gives us human beings an intimate connection to the world: like ourselves, it is an embodied soul, and, even more, it is an embodied soul that deals in a paradigmatic way with its embodiment, where the circles of the Same and the Difference are in perfect harmony. Thus also for moral reasons we should be engaged in cosmology – because it will help us to set our thinking straight.[47]

Plato's account also implies that the biology in terms of which his cosmology is captured, should be described more accurately in terms of rational theology and psychology. Today biology is not especially tied to an investigation of rationality; rational living beings are not the pinnacle of biological investigations and often not even part of what biology deals with – certainly gods are not standard objects of investigation for biologists, and human beings only to a limited degree. Biology rather concentrates on a notion of life that makes sure it also captures plants and amoebia.[48] In the history of thought, the notion of life captures a broad spectrum, ranging in its focus from mere rationality to mere self-reproduction and metabolism. While contemporary biology has settled on one end of the spectrum of what has been understood by life,[49] Plato is mainly interested in the other end.

---

[47] The *Timaeus* says nothing, however, about how the circling intelligence in us is supposed to control our limbs in situations in which we act according to practical reason (unless the story about marrow is the beginning of such an account), as Sarah Broadie pointed out to me in oral communication.

[48] Contemporary definitions of life include the capacity to grow, metabolize, respond to stimuli, adapt, transform energy (displaying oxidation-reduction reactions to provide energy for themselves), and reproduce (cf. e.g. the entry in the *Encyclopedia Britannica*); even if there does not seem to be a commonly agreed definition of life among biological scientists, cf. Tirard, Morange, and Lazcano 2010.

[49] Also the so-called Gaia theory, which may be the modern project closest to Plato's combination of cosmology and biology, seems situated on that end of the spectrum.

CHAPTER 3

Platonic 'Desmology' and the Body of the World Animal (Tim. 30c–34a)

*Dimitri El Murr**

3.1 Introduction

In the intellectual biography he offers of Socrates in the *Phaedo*, Plato takes us back to the days of Socrates' youth, to his optimism with physical speculation, and most importantly, to his subsequent disillusionment.

> Imagine not being able to distinguish the real cause from that without which the cause would not be able to act as a cause. It is what the majority appear to do, like people groping in the dark; they call it a cause, thus giving it a name that does not belong to it. That is why one man surrounds the earth with a vortex to make the heavens keep it in place, another makes the air support it like a wide lid. As for their capacity of being in the best place they could possibly be put, this they do not look for, nor do they believe it to have any divine force, but they believe that they will some time discover a stronger and more immortal Atlas to hold everything together more, and they do not believe that the truly good and 'binding' binds and holds them together. I would gladly become the disciple of any man who taught the workings of that kind of cause. (*Phd.* 99b-c, trans. Grube)

As the end of the passage makes clear, Socrates' disillusionment concerns the physical speculation of his time, not physical enquiry as such. To be sure, it has long been acknowledged that in this passage and in the broader section of the *Phaedo* it belongs to, Plato presents a scientific manifesto in

* Predecessors of this chapter greatly benefitted from discussion at the December 2014 Conference 'Conformity with nature in ancient philosophy' held at the university of Roma La Sapienza; at the April 2017 Conference 'Myth, Creation, and Science in the *Timaeus*', Brown University; at the December 2018 Workshop in ancient philosophy, University of Geneva; and at the UCLA Department of philosophy in March 2019. I am particularly grateful to Paolo Crivelli, Michel Crubellier, Francesco Fronterrota, Mary Louise Gill, Pierre-Marie Morel, for very helpful suggestions, and to Ricardo Salles and the anonymous referee at CUP, for written comments. My utmost gratitude goes to David Sedley who read the final version of this chapter and made decisive suggestions for improving it.

favour of a teleological programme in natural philosophy.[1] It is well-worn territory as well that the intellectualised and theologised physics Plato develops in the *Timaeus* is the kind of programme Plato's Socrates confessed in the *Phaedo* to never having learnt, but would for sure have welcomed.[2] The divine cosmic craftsmanship of the *Timaeus* indeed provides the kind of teleological explanation Socrates is eager to find in the *Phaedo*, for the *Timaeus* shows that the Demiurge made the world the kind of being it is and endowed it with specific properties because these were *for the best*. Hence the Demiurge is not yet another 'stronger and more immortal Atlas' (*Phd.* 99c3–4). Because explanations according to divine cosmic craftsmanship show that 'the good and 'binding' truly binds and holds together' the world (*Phd.* 99c5–6: ὡς ἀληθῶς τὸ ἀγαθὸν καὶ δέον συνδεῖν καὶ συνέχειν), the teleological programme of the *Timaeus* expressly meets the challenge spelt out in the *Phaedo*.

To elucidate in more detail what this challenge consists in, the wording of Socrates' sentence at *Phaedo*, 99c5–6 deserves attention: the true cause Socrates longs to see at work in physical enquiry is τὸ ἀγαθὸν καὶ δέον, 'the good and binding'. The presence of a single article for both adjectives prompts us to read them as referring to the same thing and understand the καί as epexegetical, not as purely connective. If this is correct, Socrates is then using the clause καὶ δέον to elucidate an aspect of the good.[3] That this elucidation is no minor specification but something crucial to his point is expressed by the adverbial clause preceding τὸ ἀγαθὸν, namely ὡς ἀληθῶς ('truly, in fact'). Just as, earlier on, Socrates played on the word Ἅδης (Hades) understood as etymologically connected to ἀιδής, 'the unseen', while making a serious philosophical point signalled by his use of the phrase ὡς ἀληθῶς (*Phd.* 80d5: εἰς Ἅιδου ὡς ἀληθῶς, 'to Hades, in fact'), here too, he alludes to a conceptual connection[4] between the good and the binding so as to defend a crucial philosophical truth, namely that the good and binding (viz. 'what is good and ought to be done',

---

[1] See e.g. Graham 1991 who convincingly argues that the teleological programme of the *Timaeus* has roots in Socratic ethics and in particular in Socrates' understanding of the crafts.

[2] See Sedley 2007: 91.

[3] Such seems to be the understanding of the Greek in several French translations of the *Phaedo*: see Robin 1950: 828. ('le bien, l'obligatoire'), Vicaire 1983 *ad loc.* ('le bien, qui est aussi lien'), Dixsaut 1991: 277 ('le bien – l'exigeant').

[4] When in the *Cratylus* (418e–419a), Socrates contrasts the (only apparent) etymological connection between δέον and δεσμός, with the alternative (archaic) etymology connecting δέον to διόν, he claims that 'obligation is an aspect of the good' (*Cra.* 418e7: ἀγαθοῦ ἰδέα οὖσα τὸ δέον).

τὸ ἀγαθὸν καὶ δέον), is, *in truth*, i.e. according to its real meaning what binds and holds together.[5]

In Greek, τὸ δέον refers to what should be done as well as to what is literally binding one thing to another. This shows that according to Socrates, the good is the true cause, required for any real explanation, inasmuch as it explains why things *should* be what they are in themselves. But providing a true explanation also consists in showing why things should be what they are not only in themselves but also in relation to one another, how they cohere and fit with one another, so as to form a unified whole. Just like Atlas, the titan holding the *kosmos*, non-teleological explanations might be thought to 'hold everything together' (99c4–5: ἅπαντα συνέχοντα). Yet, because they do not take the good into account, they cannot explain why things cohere or why indeed there is such thing as a unified *kosmos*. When Socrates mentions τὸ ἀγαθὸν καὶ δέον at *Phaedo*, 99c, I claim he insists on both aspects of teleological explanations: obligation and cohesiveness. For a true cause explains why things should be what they are but also why they cohere with one another, why they are bound to one another.

To the best of my knowledge, Socrates' precise wording of the true cause at *Phd.* 99c has not attracted much attention from commentators and translators alike. Some do point out that Socrates is here reiterating an etymological account already given in the *Cratylus* (418b–e),[6] others that he might anticipate the *Republic* and the analogy between the good and the sun, where light is analogous to being and truth and also said to be a 'bond', a *desmos* (*R.* 507e, 508e–509a).[7] Neither of these options seems to do justice to the specific context of the *Phaedo* passage, focussed on the need for teleological explanation in natural philosophy. There is, however, another dialogue that makes a significant philosophical use of *desmos*-related terms in the context of providing a teleological account of the world,

---

[5] I depart from Grube, in the translation of the *Phaedo* quoted above (Grube in Cooper 1997), in understanding, ὡς ἀληθῶς as modifying τὸ ἀγαθὸν καὶ δέον. Grube's construal ('the truly good and binding') seems unlikely Greek for Plato should then have written τὸ ὡς ἀληθῶς ἀγαθὸν καὶ δέον. It is also perfectly possible to understand the adverbial clause as modifying the two verbs συνδεῖν καὶ συνέχειν: see e.g. Rowe 2010: 145. and Sedley-Long 2011: 94. In the earlier version of his French translation of the *Phaedo*, Robin understands ὡς ἀληθῶς as modifying συνδεῖν καὶ συνέχειν (Robin 1926: 72: 'ce n'est pas lui qui relie et supporte *en vérité* quoi que ce soit'), but in the later version, understands the clause as modifying οὐδὲν οἴονται (Robin 1950: 828: 'voilà une chose dont ils n'ont *véritablement* aucune idée').

[6] E.g. Robin 1950: 1376–7, who understands *Phd.* 99c as making the 'same joke' ('même calembour') as *Cra.* 418e.

[7] E.g. Dixsaut 1991: 370–71.

and this is the *Timaeus*. Readers of this dialogue cannot but notice how frequently *desmos*-related terms are mentioned to describe the cosmogonical and zoogonical processes undertaken by the Demiurge and the lesser gods.[8] Hence the main claim of this chapter that the bond theory of the *Timaeus* – this is the 'desmology' of my title – is key to understanding how the *Timaeus* meets the teleological programme set by Socrates in the *Phaedo*.

To establish this claim properly and spell out the principles and main applications of this Platonic 'desmology', a systematic analysis of all relevant passages in the *Timaeus* would be needed. Such comprehensive analysis extends obviously far beyond the scope of this chapter. For present purposes, I shall content myself with examining one of the most detailed passages of the *Timaeus* on bond theory (31b–32c), where Timaeus provides arguments to show why and how the body of the world was made from four primary elements, thereby initiating a wider investigation, carried throughout the *Timaeus*, into the rational principles underlying the process of binding and its limitations. The broader context of *Tim.* 31b–32c should not, however, be overlooked, for this passage is part of a larger discussion (30c–34a) where the main properties attributed to the body of the World Animal are being explored. Making full sense of Platonic desmology thus requires to clarify how these 'desmological' principles are put to use within the wider cosmological context of the passage. For that very reason, this chapter, although mostly concerned with one property of the body of the World Animal (its composition out of four elements), also considers the other properties attributed to it at *Tim.* 30c–34a and, to that extent, examines arguments which attest to the influence of biological concepts on cosmology.

---

[8] For passages using δεσμός / δέσις and δέω to describe cosmogonical or zoogonical processes, see *Tim.* 31c1–2 (the making of World Body) 36a7 (the making of the World Soul), 41b1–5 (the Demiurge's will), 43a2 (the making of the human body), 73b3, d6 (the bone marrow of the human body), 74d7 (bones and sinews), 77e3 (the head and the body), 81d6–7 (body and soul), 84a3 (flesh and bone). For passages using συνδέω and συνδέσις, see 31c2, b1 (the proportion of the elements involved in the World Body), 32c4 (the Demiurge), 37a4 (the proportions involved in the making of the World Soul), 41b6 (the making of the lesser gods), 43d6 (the World Soul), d7 (the Demiurge), 73b4 (body and soul), 74b5 (sinews and limbs), 84a1 (flesh and bone). For passages using ἐνδέω, see 43a6, 44b1, d5 (introduction of the soul into the body), 45a7 (implantation of the sensory organs on the face), b4 (implantation of the eyes), 69e4 (implantation of the mortal part of the soul in the diaphragm). For passages using καταδέω, see 70e3 (the mortal part of the soul is tied like a beast) and 73c3 (implantation of the various types of soul in the marrow).

3.2 'Intellectualizing Physics'

The section of the *Timaeus* devoted to the body of the world belongs to a wider portion of the dialogue that Léon Robin, in his French translation of the dialogue, aptly describes as 'the teleological deduction of the world's properties'.[9] For this part of the *Timaeus* is indeed a fantastic stretch of *a priori* reasoning attempting to reconstruct how a good divinity would build the world. That the Demiurge is good is nowhere demonstrated but stated as obvious, a truth so obvious that it would be impious to think otherwise (see *Tim.* 30a).[10]

Timaeus starts with two important points: first, he establishes that the universe is an image of an intelligible Model; second, that it is a *zoon*, an animal, endowed with soul and intelligence, and with a body.[11] Taken together, these two points raise an immediate question, which, as Timaeus puts it, 'comes next' (30c2: ἐφεξῆς): given that the universe is framed by being modelled on something, and that it is a *zoon*, what is that thing it is modelled on? Presumably, that thing will be a *zoon* too, but of what kind? This is the crucial question that opens the passage this chapter is concerned with.

From the nature of the Model the world has been modelled on, it follows, Timaeus argues, that the world is 'a single visible animal' (30d3: ζῷον ἓν ὁρατόν) (30c2–31a1). This brings Timaeus to the second question he explicitly addresses (31a2–b3): 'Have we been correct in speaking of *one* heaven/universe, or would it have been more correct to say that there are many, in fact infinitely many?'[12] Having provided arguments showing that the world is a *visible* animal and that it is unique, Timaeus then considers what kind of body belongs to the World Animal. He argues, first, that it is made of a perfect arrangement of four primary elements (31b4–32c4), and second, that is has a spherical shape and circular movement (32c5–34a7).

As we shall see in more detail below, the properties that are being attributed to the body of the World Animal in this section of the

---

[9] Robin 1950: 445: '*la déduction finaliste des propriétés du monde*'. See also the first chapter of Robin's marvellous but seldom read booklet on the *Timaeus*: Robin 1919: 7–12.

[10] On this passage, see Sattler's contribution to this volume (Chapter 2).

[11] On *Tim.* 30a-c as the background to Stoic proofs of the intelligence of the cosmos, see Salles' contribution to this volume (Chapter 11).

[12] *Tim.* 31a2–3: πότερον οὖν ὀρθῶς ἕνα οὐρανὸν προσειρήκαμεν, ἢ πολλοὺς καὶ ἀπείρους λέγειν ἦν ὀρθότερον; Throughout this chapter, translations of the *Timaeus* are borrowed from Zeyl 2000, sometime slightly modified.

Timaeus are: (1) completeness; (2) uniqueness; (3) composition out of four elements; (4) sphericity and circular movement. As David Sedley rightly argued, some of these properties were widely accepted as empirical facts in antiquity, and this is particularly true of properties (3) and (4).[13] Yet, in our passage, no empirical argument is provided in favour of them. This neatly corresponds to what Sedley has labelled 'the project of intellectualizing physics', which he sees as distinctive of the *Timaeus*. That it is indeed an *intellectualisation* is particularly clear in the passage we are concerned with where Timaeus makes frequent use of verbs referring to the Demiurge's *reasoning*.[14] This does not mean, of course, that one should downplay the efficient role of the Demiurge in the actual making of the world. For the passage also uses a wide variety of verbs (and some of them repeatedly) to describe the Demiurgic activity of the god.[15] The very structure of the passage signals nonetheless that emphasis is constantly placed on the intellectual activity of the Demiurge, i.e. on the rational principles that determine his practical decisions and actions.

Analytical summary of the passage:

Section A (30c2–31a1): The World Is Modelled on the Intelligible Animal

- 30c2–4: Question (What animal did the Demiurge choose to model the world on?)
- 30c4–7: Wrong answer (any of those that have the natural character of a part)
- 30c7–d1: Correct answer (the Animal of which all other animals are part)
- 30d1–31a1: The Demiurge's decision and action: he made the world a single complete visible Animal

Section B (31a2–b3): There Is Just One World

- 31a2–3: Question (Should we say there is just one world, or more?)
- 31a3–b1: Answer (There is just one world)

---

[13] Sedley 2007: 110.
[14] Verbs such as 'to have in mind' (32c8: διανοηθείς), 'to realise' (33a3: κατανοῶν), 'to think' (33b7: νομίσας), 'to hold' (33d1: ἡγήσατο), 'to think' (33d4: ᾤετο), and 'to reason' (34b1: λογισθείς). See also 33a6 (where 'reasoning', λογισμός, is used twice) and 34a8 ('the god's reasoning', λογισμὸς θεοῦ).
[15] The Demiurge 'made' (30c3: συνέστησεν; see also 31a1, b7, b8, 32b7, c7), 'crafted' (31a4: δεδημιουργημένος), 'set' (32b4: θείς), 'bound' (32b7: συνέδησεν), 'framed' (33b1: ἐτεκτήνατο), 'turned' (33b5: ἐτορνεύσατο), 'finished off' (33c1: ἀπηκριβοῦτο). Similarly, the Demiurge is described as a 'maker' (30c3: ὁ συνιστάς), a 'producer' (31b3: ὁ ποιῶν), and a 'builder' (33d2: ὁ συνθείς).

- 31b1–3: ('for these reasons' διὰ ταῦτα) The Demiurge's decision and action: he made just one world.

Section C (31b4–32c4): The Body of the World Is Made of the Four Elements
- 31b4–6: For the world to have a 'bodily form' (σωματοειδές) requires fire and earth
- 31b6–7: ('that is why' ὅθεν) The Demiurge's decision and action: he began his work with fire and earth
- 31b8–32b3: Why two further elements are needed.
- 32b3–c4: ('thus' οὕτω) The Demiurge's decision and action: he set water and air between fire and earth

Section D (32c5–34a7): The Body of the World Has the Shape of a Perfect Sphere and Circular Movement
- 32c5–8: The Demiurge's decision and action: the Demiurge used up the entire elemental material
- 32c8–33b1: The reasons for this decision
- 33b1–34a1: Why the Demiurge chose to confer sphericity to the world
- 34a1–7: Why the Demiurge gave (merely) circular movement to the world.

As this analytical summary makes clear, it is indeed one distinctive feature of this passage to provide first the rationale, then the decision and action taken by the Demiurge according to those arguments. This method clearly indicates that Plato's intention is to emphasise the rationality of the world by drawing attention to the actual reasoning of the Demiurge, which is in turn responsible for his practical decisions of bestowing specific properties upon the world. In doing so, Plato shows how the good is effective in the world and how it explains some of its essential properties. Because this passage constantly emphasises that the Demiurge took any given action because he saw that it is best, it provides the kind of teleological account praised by Socrates in the *Phaedo*.

3.3   Completeness and Uniqueness of the World Animal

Let us now consider in more detail the properties bestowed upon the world by the Demiurge.

At *Tim.* 29d7–31c1, Timaeus explained why the Demiurge, aiming for the best, created an intelligent world that could only be a *zoon*, an animal.[16]

---

[16] For compelling arguments in favour of this translation, see Sedley 2007: 108 n. 36.

Since any good craftsman looks at a model to create his product (28a-b), the question that now needs to be answered is: what is that Form of a *zoon* that the Demiurge contemplated to create the world? Timaeus begins with distinguishing two types of animals: on the one hand, 'those that have the natural character of a part' (30c4: τῶν μὲν ἐν μέρους εἴδει πεφυκότων), and on the other hand, 'that Animal of which all other animals are parts, both individually and by kinds' (c5–6: οὗ δ' ἔστιν τἆλλα ζῷα καθ' ἓν καὶ κατὰ γένη μόρια). Timaeus thus draws a sharp contrast between 1) any *particular* species of animal, and 2) the genus Animal as such, to which partake every individual animal as well as every animal species. The reason why the Demiurge chose to model the world on the latter, and not on any of its parts (particular species) is that completeness is more beautiful, therefore better, than incompleteness.

But what is this Intelligible Animal that our world is an image of? This much debated question[17] amounts to examining whether this Model is a) the intelligible realm as such, inclusive of any Form there is, and understood as some kind of living organism, or b) the very Form of the Genus Animal. The second option has received a powerful defence by Cornford, and more recently, by Sedley.[18] One reason, among many, for favouring it is that when Timaeus, at the end of our passage, considers how the body of the World Animal was shaped, he is eager to emphasise, for reasons we shall consider later, that the Demiurge did not impose any biological specification upon it, indicating thereby that its model is understood not only as an animal, but also as a *generic* animal. Timaeus then concludes section A:

> 'Since the god wanted nothing more than to make the world like the best of the intelligible things, complete in every way, he made it a single visible living thing, which contains within itself all the living things whose nature it is to share its kind'.[19]

Why did the Demiurge make the world 'a *single* visible animal' (30d3: ζῷον ἓν ὁρατόν)? Timaeus devotes the whole of section B to answering this question, and rightly so, for this question is an important one. His answer is straightforward: 'There is but one, if it is to have been crafted after its model' (31a3–4). This indicates that according to Timaeus, the

---

[17] The issue is very well summarized by Zeyl 2000: xxxvii–xxxviii.
[18] See Cornford 1937: 40–41, and Sedley 2007: 108.
[19] *Tim.* 30d1–31a1: τῷ γὰρ τῶν νοουμένων καλλίστῳ καὶ κατὰ πάντα τελέῳ μάλιστα αὐτὸν ὁ θεὸς ὁμοιῶσαι βουληθεὶς ζῷον ἓν ὁρατόν, πάνθ' ὅσα αὐτοῦ κατὰ φύσιν συγγενῆ ζῷα ἐντὸς ἔχον ἑαυτοῦ [...].

uniqueness of the Model entails the uniqueness of its created image, the world. On the face of it, this is a surprising claim, for the very fact that the model a craftsman looks to is unique surely does not imply that there will be *only one* sensible image of that model. Is it not, after all, usual practice for craftsmen to make multiple copies of a given model?

Two related issues are at stake here. First, why is there a unique Model? Second, why should the uniqueness of this Model entail that of its image?[20] Lines 31a4–b1 are devoted to answering the first question. To prove that the Model is unique, Timaeus relies on a point repeatedly made in the previous section of the passage (section A), namely that the Model includes *all* intelligible animals. He then proposes the following *reductio*. The Model cannot be one of a pair (or one of any larger number), because if it were, the second Intelligible Animal of the pair would not be contained in the first, therefore the first Intelligible Animal would not be an *all-inclusive* Model. The only true Intelligible Animal would then be the one and only one containing these two. In other words, the requirement of completeness implies the uniqueness of the Model.[21]

But how does one move from here to proving that the Demiurge has created *just one world*? Timaeus says that the Demiurge created just one world, 'in order that this animal should be like the complete animal *in respect of uniqueness*' (31a8–b1: ἵνα οὖν τόδε κατὰ τὴν μόνωσιν ὅμοιον ᾖ τῷ παντελεῖ ζῴῳ): uniqueness is understood here as a property of the Model that should be imitated in the same way and to the same extent as its other properties. Therefore, from the point of view of the Demiurge, making a single copy of a *single* Model is in fact making a *better* copy of it than copying it twice or more. In being only one of its kind, the world thus imitates more perfectly the singularity of its Model. Although this has sometimes been understood as a strange argument,[22] I think the main point is that the uniqueness of the created world depends on the Demiurge's will to make the closest image of the Model, and that the will of the Demiurge is, in turn, entirely governed by its intrinsic goodness (see 29e3–4).

---

[20] There is a vast literature on this *Timaeus* passage and both issues. To the best of my knowledge, the most helpful contributions are Parry 1979 and Patterson 1981. See also the brief but insightful analysis in Broadie 2012: 72 n. 19.

[21] I agree with Patterson 1981: 107 that the argument, thus understood, does not resort to any form of regress and to a Platonic 'One over many' principle.

[22] See the classic discussion of this argument by Keyt 1971.

3.4 How the Demiurge Made the Body of the World Animal

The central part of the passage (section C) is then devoted to the actual making of the body of the World Animal from the four primary elements. Obviously, there is nothing original in turning to air, water, fire and earth to explain the making of the world's body, as these four elements were widely acknowledged as the primary constituents of the universe before Plato. Yet, the specific account Timaeus provides of how these elements are combined so as to form one body is deeply original.

The first question that launched Timaeus' inquiry into the origin of the universe was raised at 28b and consisted in asking whether the world had been generated. The answer was again straightforward: it has been generated (28b7: γέγονεν). And the reason for this was simply the *empirical* fact that '[the world] is both visible and tangible, and it has a body' (b7–8: ὁρατὸς γὰρ ἁπτός τέ ἐστιν καὶ σῶμα ἔχων). In section C, Timaeus examines these properties further and what is indeed *required*[23] for the world to be σωματοειδές ('have a bodily form').

The properties of being visible and tangible require that the world be made of specific components that correspond to the perception of these properties. In more detail, being visible (ὁρατόν) involves that the object seen be partly made of fire,[24] and being tangible (ἁπτόν) requires it to be a solid, i.e. requires resistance, hence implies that it is made of earth.[25] Interestingly Timaeus tells us that 'that is why' (31b6: ὅθεν) the Demiurge made the body of the world, 'starting' (31b7: ἀρχόμενος) from fire and earth. One should not put too much weight on this verb and suggest that it entails some kind of erring on the Demiurge's part, as if he had started with two elements and then realised this could not work. More interestingly, the subtly chronological narrative helps emphasise, once again, that the Demiurge obeys rational principles that are external to, and independent of, his *boulèsis*.[26]

Let us now consider one of these principles.

---

[23] Note the use of δεῖ at 31b4: 'Now that which comes to be *must* have bodily form' (σωματοειδὲς δὲ δὴ καὶ ὁρατὸν ἁπτόν τε δεῖ τὸ γενόμενον εἶναι).

[24] The reason for this is given later in the dialogue, when the phenomenon of sight is explained: see *Tim.* 45b-d)

[25] See the explanation provided at 55d-e and 62b-c.

[26] On this very passage and the seemingly chronological sequence, there is an interesting discussion in Proclus who argues against those who read the cosmogony of the *Timaeus* chronologically: see *in Tim.* 2.12.29–13.3.

'But it isn't possible to combine two things well all by themselves, without a third; there has to be some bond between the two that unites them. Now the best bond is one that really and truly makes a unity of itself together with the things bonded by it, and this in the nature of things is best accomplished by proportion'.[27]

Timaeus' wording is strikingly general and highly abstract. Note the use of δύο and τρίτου ('two things' and 'a third') at 31b8, which refer to any given thing. Note the verb chosen to express the process of combination, συνίστασθαι ('to combine'), which is one of the most frequent, and most general verbs used by Timaeus to describe the action of the Demiurge. Timaeus is here spelling out an abstract principle that he considers key to the understanding of the Demiurge's practical decisions concerning the making of the body of the World Animal. This passage is thus more than a mere description of what will turn out to be the specific bond of *proportion*: it is part, or so I claim, of a wider Platonic reflection on bond theory.

There are indeed many ways of combining two things. Think of two objects glued together, or think of a faggot of sticks of wood kept together by a string: both are examples of the very process of συναγωγὸν γίγνεσθαι ('to unite') in that both are combined and form a σύστασις, a 'composition' (and sometimes a σύστημα, a 'whole', too), at least to some extent. These two examples are used by Aristotle in *Metaph.* Δ.6.1016a, to illustrate things that are said to be *one by themselves* (ἓν καθ'αὑτό), although they are less one than other things, because they are one *by continuity only*. Among things that are one by continuity, Aristotle adds, some are more *one* than others. For, if continuity is achieved by *tekhnè*, artificially, the thing will be less *one* than if the continuity is natural, as it is in the case of a limb, e.g. an arm or a leg, which are bent and made of two distinct parts, yet continuous.

Interestingly, none of the combinations illustrated by these examples borrowed from Aristotle corresponds to what the Demiurge is doing when he combines the primary elements. So when Timaeus emphasises the need for a third term, acting as a *desmos* between two elements so as to form a combination, he is not thinking of the type of unity that e.g. the *desmos* imposes on two sticks of wood so as to form a faggot. The type of bond he is considering is, as he puts it, ἐν μέσῳ, 'in between' (31c1), not superimposed on the two elements, but mediating them.

[27] *Tim.* 31b8–c5: δύο δὲ μόνω καλῶς συνίστασθαι τρίτου χωρὶς οὐ δυνατόν· δεσμὸν γὰρ ἐν μέσῳ δεῖ τινα ἀμφοῖν συναγωγὸν γίγνεσθαι. δεσμῶν δὲ κάλλιστος ὃς ἂν αὑτὸν καὶ τὰ συνδούμενα ὅτι μάλιστα ἓν ποιῇ, τοῦτο δὲ πέφυκεν ἀναλογία κάλλιστα ἀποτελεῖν.

Yet, this is still insufficient to make clear what type of bond the Demiurge has in mind. In fact, what the Demiurge is seeking is not only a specific type of bond, but 'the most beautiful of bonds' (31c2: δεσμῶν κάλλιστος). This appeal to practical and/or aesthetic considerations coheres with the idea that the Demiurge is the best of causes and can thereby only bestow goodness upon what he makes. It would thus be absurd to consider that the body of the most beautiful of all generated things, i.e. the World Animal, would not be bound by the best of bonds. What is less clear, however, is the clause that follows, explaining what the supreme beauty of this bond consists in: 'it really and truly makes a unity of itself together with the things bonded by it, and this in the nature of things is best accomplished by proportion' (31c2–4). Timaeus' formulation deserves notice: the most beautiful bond confers unity on what is bound (τὰ συνδούμενα) *and on itself* (αὐτὸν). But in what sense does a bond confer unity *on itself* in binding together different elements? This formulation sheds light on the precise bond the Demiurge has in mind, namely *analogia*. For introducing proportionality between several elements amounts to adding something to them (a mathematical ratio), but without, I take it, adding anything purely external to them. This, I think, is the key point.

Among the many commentators on Plato's *Timaeus*, no one has paid more attention to this passage than Proclus. The emphasis I lay on the concept of *desmos* in the passage owes a lot to Proclus, who devotes a whole section of his commentary to its elucidation.[28] Proclus' approach to Platonic bond theory starts from the Neoplatonic general principle according to which 'each entity in fact exists in a triple manner, either causally (*kat' aitian*) or existentially (*kath' huparxin*) or by participation (*kata methexin*)'.[29] To elucidate what Timaeus means by *desmos* in our passage, Proclus applies this tripartite scheme.

> 'Now a bond is spoken of in three ways. One kind (1) is the pre-existing bond in the *cause* of the things that have come together. Another (2) is the immanent bond in the things that have been bound together, which has the same rank as them and is connate with them. The third sense of bond

---

[28] See Proclus, *in Tim.* 2.13.15–28.7. For a detailed reading of this section of Proclus' commentary on the *Timaeus*, see Lernould 2000.

[29] Proclus, *in Tim.* 1.234.23–4 Diehl (= Diehl 1903–6): τριχῶς γάρ ἐστιν ἕκαστον, ἢ κατ' αἰτίαν, ἢ καθ' ὕπαρξιν, ἢ κατὰ μέθεξιν. Translations from Runia and Share 2008.

(3) is intermediate between these. On the one hand, it proceeds from the cause, but on the other it is also manifested in the things that have been bound.[30]

A bond can exist either (1) *kat' aitian* inasmuch as it pre-exists in the cause of the things bound, or (2) *kath' huparxin*, i.e. within the things bound, or (3) *kata methexin*, i.e. by being intermediate between the cause and the things bound, in that it proceeds from the cause but is manifested in the things bound. To clarify this very abstract triad of bonds, Proclus then provides three examples. Consider an animal and how as a whole it relates to its parts. 'The one rational forming principle (*logos*) that has been pre-established in the very cause of the animal'[31] is (1) the first bond between the animal and its parts. This bond is the true cause of the animal, understood as distinct from its effects. The second bond (2) is in turn 'the nerves and the muscles [which] come to be a bond of the things in the animal'.[32] This is the organic bond that holds the different parts of the animal together and consists in nerves, sinews and muscles. Proclus sees this second bond as an instrumental bond, whose rationality is purely external to the bond itself.[33] The third bond (3) is 'the single physical rational forming principle that proceeds from the cause and uses the nerves and all the material organic bonds for the composition of the animal'.[34] In contrast with the first bond, the third bond is not separate from the things bound, but in contrast with the second, it is connected to the very cause of the animal since it proceeds from it: 'for this third thing is neither transcendent in relation to what has been composed nor is it excluded from the class of true causes, since it has the status of "that without which"'.[35]

Proclus then concludes that the *desmos* mentioned at *Timaeus* 31b9–c4, a *desmos* ἐν μέσῳ, 'in between', playing a mediating role between two elements, can only be the bond of the third kind.

---

[30] Proclus, *in Tim.* 2.15.12–17 Diehl: ἀλλὰ ὁ δεσμὸς λέγεται τριχῶς· ἄλλος μὲν γὰρ δεσμὸς <ὁ> ἐν τῇ αἰτίᾳ τῶν συνελθόντων προϋπάρχων, ἄλλος δὲ ὁ ἐν αὐτοῖς τοῖς δεδεμένοις ἐνυπάρχων ὁμόστοιχος αὐτοῖς καὶ συμφυής, τρίτος δὲ ἄλλος ἐν μέσῳ τούτων, προϊὼν μὲν ἀπὸ τῆς αἰτίας, ἐν δὲ τοῖς συνδεομένοις ἐμφαινόμενος. All translations from Baltzly 2007. The numerals in the translations have been introduced for the sake of clarity.

[31] Proclus, *in Tim.* 2.15.18–19 Diehl: ὁ εἷς λόγος, ὁ ἐν αὐτῇ τῇ αἰτίᾳ τοῦ ζῴου προϊδρυμένος.

[32] Proclus, *in Tim.* 2.15.19–20 Diehl: ἄλλος δὲ γίγνεται τῶν ἐν αὐτῷ, τὰ νεῦρα καὶ αἱ ἶνες, δεσμός.

[33] Proclus explains, a few lines below, that this bond 'is not master of itself' (2.15.31–2: οὐκ ἔστιν ἑαυτοῦ κύριος).

[34] Proclus, *in Tim.* 2.15.21–3 Diehl: ὁ ἀπὸ τῆς αἰτίας προελθὼν φυσικὸς εἷς λόγος καὶ χρώμενος τοῖς τε νεύροις καὶ τοῖς ὑλικοῖς πᾶσιν ὀργανικοῖς δεσμοῖς πρὸς τὴν τοῦ ζῴου σύνδεσιν.

[35] Proclus, *in Tim.* 2.15.23–5 Diehl: οὗτος γὰρ οὔτε ἐξῄρηται τῶν συνδεδεμένων οὔτε τὸν ὢν οὐκ ἄνευ λόγον ἐπέχων ἄμοιρός ἐστι τῆς ἀληθινῆς αἰτίας.

But remember that Plato said 'that which makes both itself and the composite to be one'. It is possible to arrange this in the middle and for it to have this power through proportion, which is the most beautiful bond, and it is possible to give to this bond the power of making all things one and the same. Therefore, this too is a bond which is inseparable from the things that it binds, and the proportion (too) is a bond, which is both different from all the things that have been bound, and at the same time immanent in them, and the Demiurgic will is a bond that transcends the things bound.[36]

I have significantly modified Baltzly's translation of this passage. His translation of the last sentence reads: 'Therefore this bond is inseparable from the things that it binds (ἔστιν οὖν καὶ οὗτος δεσμὸς ἀχώριστος τῶν συνδεθέντων) and the proportion is the bond (καὶ ἡ ἀναλογία δεσμός). It is both different from all the things that have been bound, and at the same time immanent in them (ἄλλη μὲν οὖσα τῶν δεδεμένων πάντων, ἐν αὐτοῖς δὲ ὑφεστηκυῖα). The Demiurgic will is a transcendent bond of the things bound (καὶ ἡ βούλησις ἡ δημιουργικὴ δεσμὸς ἐξηρημένος τῶν δεδεμένων.)'. Following Festugière,[37] Baltzly understands οὗτος as referring to the bond Proclus describes in the first part of the passage (namely proportion). But this is problematic, for the proportion introduced by the Demiurge between the elements is indeed *separable* from the things bound, inasmuch as it is a mathematical ratio distinct from them. I therefore make the alternative suggestion[38] that before moving to a new point,[39] Proclus is in this passage recapitulating the triad of bonds he has previously mentioned, as I think the sequence καί ... καί ... καί ... introduced by οὖν ('therefore') clearly indicates. According to that reading, οὗτος (at 2.16.5) should be understood as referring not to proportion but to the organic bond mentioned in the lines immediately preceding our passage (*in Tim.* 2.15.32–4). If this is correct, what this passage finally makes clear is that 'the bond inseparable from the things it binds' is the organic bond (2), that the first bond and true cause (1) is the Demiurgic will, and that the bond introduced between the elements by the Demiurge

---

[36] Proclus, *in Tim.* 2.15.32–16.8 Diehl: ὁ δὲ αὖ Πλάτων προσέθηκεν, <ὃς ἂν αὐτόν τε καὶ τὰ συνδούμενα ἐν ποιῇ>· τοῦτον γὰρ καὶ ἐν τῷ μέσῳ τετάχθαι δυνατόν, ἔχειν δὲ τὴν τοιαύτην δύναμιν διὰ τῆς ἀναλογίας, ἣν κάλλιστον οὖσαν δεσμὸν καὶ τούτῳ διδόναι τὴν ταυτοποιὸν καὶ ἑνοποιὸν τῶν πάντων δύναμιν. ἔστιν οὖν καὶ οὗτος δεσμὸς ἀχώριστος τῶν συνδεθέντων, καὶ ἡ ἀναλογία δεσμός, ἄλλη μὲν οὖσα τῶν δεδεμένων πάντων, ἐν αὐτοῖς δὲ ὑφεστηκυῖα, καὶ ἡ βούλησις ἡ δημιουργικὴ δεσμὸς ἐξηρημένος τῶν δεδεμένων.
[37] Festugière 1966–8, vol. 3, n. 1, 39.   [38] Following Lernould 2000: 132.
[39] The new point begins at 2.16.13 with a question: 'From whence do we get the conception of such a bond, and of what is it a symbol?' (πόθεν οὖν ὁ τοιοῦτος ἐπινοεῖται δεσμός, καὶ τίνος ἐστὶ σύμβολον;)

is proportion, an intermediate bond (3) 'both different from all the things that have been bound, and at the same time immanent in them'.

One need not adhere to the systematic Neoplatonic interpretative principles and metaphysical background that govern Proclus' reading to recognise the depth of his view on Plato's notion of *desmos* in this *Timaeus* passage. What Proclus makes clear is that the bond mentioned by Timaeus is neither the Demiurge's will (βούλησις),[40] nor the physical bond binding the parts of an organism. In Proclus' highly metaphysical vocabulary, the *desmos* at *Tim.* 31b9–c4 is both immanent and transcendent in relation to its terms: indeed, proportion is different from the individual elements (hence it is not ἀχώριστος, 'inseparable'), but it stems from the combination of the elements themselves, not from anything external, superimposed on them.

This is why, Proclus argues, Plato has aptly written that this '*in the nature of things* (πέφυκεν) is best accomplished by proportion' (31c3).

> For this reason Plato appropriately adds that bonding is 'by nature' best accomplished by proportion. Because all proportions and middle terms have such a quality innately, they do not impose a bond in a contrived manner nor through some ability foreign to them. Rather their capacity to accomplish this is made manifest in the very essences and the powers of objects.[41]

Proclus' comments finally help understand why Timaeus points out that *proportion*, when binding the elements, confers unity upon them *and upon itself.* Proportion imposes order and structure on the elements by using the elements themselves, and nothing more. This also explains why *analogia* is the most beautiful of bonds. It does not require anything else than the four elements and a mathematical ratio ordering them.

Let us now consider in more detail the specific proportion introduced between the primary elements so as to make the body of the World Animal.

> 'For whenever of three numbers (or bulks or powers)[42] the middle term between any two of them is such that what the first term is to it, it is to the

---

[40] On the will (βούλησις) of the Demiurge and bond theory in the *Timaeus*, see *infra*.

[41] Proclus, *in Tim.* 2.20.5–9 Diehl: διὸ καὶ τὸ πέφυκεν οἰκείως προσέθηκεν ὁ Πλάτων, ὅτι τὸ αὐτοφυὲς ἔχουσιν αἱ ἀναλογίαι καὶ πᾶσαι αἱ μεσότητες καὶ οὐ μεμηχανημένον ἐπάγουσι τὸν δεσμὸν οὐδ' ἐπείσακτον, ἀλλ' ἐν αὐταῖς ταῖς οὐσίαις καὶ ταῖς δυνάμεσιν ἀναφαίνονται τῶν πραγμάτων.

[42] The interpretation of this clause (31c4: ἀριθμῶν τριῶν εἴτε ὄγκων εἴτε δυνάμεων ὡντινωνοῦν) has been much disputed and given rise to two alternative solutions. According e.g. to Cornford 1937: 45–52, the clause εἴτε ὄγκων εἴτε δυνάμεων (ἀριθμῶν) refers to cube and square *numbers* respectively, whereas, according e.g. to Pritchard 1990, it refers to bulks and powers. For a good discussion of the grammatical and mathematical issues involved, see, in addition to Cornford, Caveing 1965-1966, and Harte 2002: 228, n. 379.

last, and, conversely, what the last term is to the middle, it is to the first, then, since the middle term turns out to be both first and last, and the last and the first likewise both turn out to be middle terms, they will all of necessity turn out to have the same relationship to each other, and, given this, will all be unified'.[43]

What is the specific type of mathematical proportion here introduced by the Demiurge? Introducing a *desmos* between two terms (the two terms being here fire and earth) requires introducing a middle term between them that will stand in a certain relation to each of the other two. This specific relation is that of geometric progression. Take two numbers, e.g. 2 and 8. Introducing a middle term between them and ordering them according to a geometrical progression amounts to introducing the number 4, because 4 is to 2 what 8 is to 4, i.e. the double. In other words, in a geometric progression, the ratio between each term and the next remains constant (unlike an arithmetical progression, where the *number* between each term and the next is the same). The interesting property, singled out by Timaeus, of such a progression is that every term can play the role of the middle term, every term being then a bond between all the other terms. Take our basic geometric progression with 4 acting as a middle term: 2:4=4:8. As Timaeus notes, 'the middle term [. . .] is such that what the first term is to it, it is to the last'; but it is also true that 'what the last term is to the middle, it is to the first'. Moreover, according to the same geometric proportion, it is true to say that 4:2=8:4, where the middle term (i.e. 4) turns out to be first and last and the first and last terms (i.e. 2 and 8) turn out to be middle terms.

Since the world has a body, it is a *solid*, which implies, as Timaeus argues, that not only one but two middle terms are introduced between fire and earth. Hence the introduction of water and air at 32b6–7. Once again, the gist of Timaeus' approach to the doctrine of the four elements is to show that the Demiurge's productive actions[44] in the making of the world's body comply with rational (and indeed mathematical) principles and requirements. The consequence of this approach is notably that the (classic) doctrine of the *four* elements is justified[45] rationally from a

---

[43] *Tim.* 31c4–32a7: ὁπόταν γὰρ ἀριθμῶν τριῶν εἴτε ὄγκων εἴτε δυνάμεων ὡντινωνοῦν ᾖ τὸ μέσον, ὅτιπερ τὸ πρῶτον πρὸς αὐτό, τοῦτο αὐτὸ πρὸς τὸ ἔσχατον, καὶ πάλιν αὖθις, ὅτι τὸ ἔσχατον πρὸς τὸ μέσον, τὸ μέσον πρὸς τὸ πρῶτον, τότε τὸ μέσον μὲν πρῶτον καὶ ἔσχατον γιγνόμενον, τὸ δ' ἔσχατον καὶ τὸ πρῶτον αὖ μέσα ἀμφότερα, πάνθ' οὕτως ἐξ ἀνάγκης τὰ αὐτὰ εἶναι συμβήσεται, τὰ αὐτὰ δὲ γενόμενα ἀλλήλοις ἓν πάντα ἔσται.

[44] See *Tim.* 32b7: συνέδησεν καὶ συνεστήσατο ('he bound and constructed. . .')

[45] See καὶ διὰ ταῦτα ('this is the reason why') at 32b8.

partially non-empirical basis. The role and existence of the first two elements (fire and earth) were inferred from sensible properties of the world (visibility and tangibility), but such is not the case for the remaining two elements: the rational need for these is deduced from the property of being *somatoeidès*, that is, from the property of being a *solid*. This being said, it is true that one is at pains to find here an argument in the text explaining why these two remaining elements are *water* and *air*. Timaeus justifies rationally why the Demiurge makes use of two additional elements but not why these two elements are what they are: they seem to be chosen only because they are the remaining two in the classic list of four elements provided, notably, by Empedocles.

That Empedocles stands in the background to Timaeus' rationalising of the doctrine of the four primary elements is nowhere clearer that in the following passage, which concludes section C:

> 'This is the reason why these four particular constituents were used to beget the body of the world, making it a symphony of proportion. They bestowed friendship upon it, so that, having come together into a unity with itself, it could not be undone by anyone but the one who had bound it together'.[46]

The solemn and slightly pompous tone of this passage echoes the 'curiously archaic' character of the entire description of the World Body, well noted by Cornford[47] who remarks on how much it owes to earlier traditions, in particular to Empedocles.

Timaeus' mention of *philia* ('friendship') bestowed upon the elements is indeed a direct allusion to Empedocles' cosmology based upon four elements and two fundamental forces, *Philotēs* and *Neikos*,[48] whose interactions explain how the elements mix into compounds and how compounds dissolve into elements. Interestingly, the passage quoted above shows that, according to Timaeus, *philia* has nothing to do with an external force of attraction between elements that would explain their combination into compounds: friendship is a *consequence* of the geometric proportion introduced by the Demiurge between the elements. By the very nature of the *desmos*, which, or so I claim, is not external to, although

---

[46] *Tim.* 32b8–c4: καὶ διὰ ταῦτα ἔκ τε δὴ τούτων τοιούτων καὶ τὸν ἀριθμὸν τεττάρων τὸ τοῦ κόσμου σῶμα ἐγεννήθη δι' ἀναλογίας ὁμολογῆσαν, φιλίαν τε ἔσχεν ἐκ τούτων, ὥστε εἰς ταὐτὸν αὑτῷ συνελθὸν ἄλυτον ὑπό του ἄλλου πλὴν ὑπὸ τοῦ συνδήσαντος γενέσθαι.

[47] Cornford 1937: 57.

[48] See Taylor 1928: 99, and Cornford 1937: 44, n. 4 who reads the mention of friendship in the passage as 'a reference to the *Philia* of Empedocles' system' and translates φιλία as 'Amity', presumably to render Timaeus' archaic tone here.

different from the elements, it is from these very elements themselves that *philia* is bestowed upon the World Body (cf. 32c2: φιλίαν τε ἔσχεν ἐκ τούτων).[49] *Philia* is therefore another property of the body of the world that can be explained by resorting to mere rational principles. What's more, contrary to what Empedocles thought, *philia* does not correspond to a phase in the cycle of the world, where it would be predominant over *Neikos*: *philia* is a property of the world as such, because, as Timaeus makes clear, it is a *consequence* of its expert making. From the rational principles involved in the making of the world, it is clear, then, that Timaeus draws consequences subverting the need for *philia* as understood by Empedocles.[50]

Understood as a property belonging the world, friendship also signals that a great unity is conferred to the World Body by the Demiurge, which, in turn, implies that the world's unity and integrity are dependent upon the Demiurge. Notice Timaeus' peculiar phrasing: the world is 'indissoluble' (32c3: ἄλυτον) 'except by who bound it' (32c3–4: πλὴν ὑπὸ τοῦ συνδήσαντος). Indissolubility is not therefore a property that belongs to the world in the same sense as, say, its uniqueness. The *desmos* introduced by the Demiurge – who is significantly referred to here by the periphrasis τοῦ συνδήσαντος (32c3–4), 'the one who bound [the world] together'– is not indissoluble *per se*. Its indissolubility and everlastingness are dependent on another principle, which Plato also describes as a *desmos*: the Demiurge's *boulèsis*, on which more anon.

3.5   Sphericity and Movement of the World Animal

The last section (section D, 32c5–34a7) of the passage is devoted to exposing the Demiurge's reasons for conferring upon the body of the

---

[49] I follow Cornford 1937: 44 and Zeyl 2000: 17 in understanding ἐκ τούτων at 32c3 as referring to the same thing as the preceding clause at b8–c1 (ἐκ τούτων τοιούτων καὶ τὸν ἀριθμὸν τεττάρων), i.e. the four elements. Other translators translate ἐκ τούτων more loosely, as 'these conditions' (e.g. Rivaud 1925: 145, Robin 1950: 447). Brisson 1995: 121 has 'les rapports instaurés par cette proportion' for ἐκ τούτων, which says more than the Greek does.

[50] This critical move in the conclusion of section C may well echo a similar one in the conclusion of the preceding section. Timaeus notes therein that 'our heaven came to be as the one and only thing of its kind, is so now, and will continue to be so in the future' (31b3: εἷς ὅδε μονογενὴς οὐρανὸς γεγονὼς ἔστιν καὶ ἔτ' ἔσται). Harte 2002: 234 n. 390, suggests that the word μονογενής might be read here as an allusion to Parmenides (DK B8, 4). If so, Plato would then be using a Parmenidean concept to make a very un-Parmenidean point, for Parmenides denied the pertinence of past and future to his μονογενής Being. Yet, the textual influence could be the other way round: see O'Brien 1987: 318–22 who argues vigorously that the *Timaeus* passage has interfered with the transmission of Parmenides's Poem.

World Animal a perfectly spherical shape and a perfectly regular circular movement. But the results of the previous sections are not forgotten, for section D begins with a complex argument (32c5–33b1) designed to show that further reflections on the Demiurge's thoughts involved in the actual making of the body of the world (C) can help guarantee what was already established in sections A and B, namely that the world is complete and unique. Thus, what we have at 32c5–33b1 are additional reasons for the Demiurge's choice of a single world, stemming from the previous arguments that have shown why four elements (no more, no less) were needed.

Now that it is clear that the body of the world was made from four elements, Timaeus claims that the *whole* of each of the four constituents was used in that making: 'Now, each one of the four constituents was entirely used up in the process of building the world'.[51] As a consequence, nothing is left 'outside' (32c8: ἔξωθεν) the world. Within the first part of the dialogue dedicated to the works of reason (27d–47e), there are no less than six references to an 'outside' of the universe, four of which belong to our passage (32c8, 33a4, c1, c2) and prove to be negative.[52] This emphasis is no accident, for it signals the importance of the claim that there is nothing outside the world, which will turn out to be key for the arguments to come.

Timaeus provides three reasons why the Demiurge thought best to use the entire stock of matter in the making of the world.[53] As the conclusion of the argument shows,[54] these three reasons explain why he thought he should frame the world as a single, whole, and everlasting animal[55] The first reason concerns the *completeness* of the world: as an animal, the world is indeed more complete if it is made of complete parts, therefore it is a whole composed of all wholes. The second reason concerns its *uniqueness* and brings in the earlier claim that there is nothing outside the world: indeed, if there is nothing outside the world, there is no material left from which another similar world could be made, therefore the world is unique.

---

[51] *Tim.* 32c5–6: τῶν δὲ δὴ τεττάρων ἓν ὅλον ἕκαστον εἴληφεν ἡ τοῦ κόσμου σύστασις.

[52] The last two mentions of ἔξωθεν 'from outside' (34b4 and 36e3) belong to the next section of the *Timaeus* on the World Soul and are more difficult to interpret. O'Brien 1997: 395–6, suggests they both refer to Empedocles' cosmological system and indicate that Plato sees the World Soul as occupying the positions of Love *and* Strife.

[53] See *Tim.* 32c9: πρῶτον μὲν ('first'); 33a1: πρὸς δὲ τούτοις ('second'); 33a2: ἔτι δέ ('third').

[54] See *Tim.* 33a6–b1.

[55] Commentators have rightly pointed out that in this passage Plato rejects earlier Ionian as well as atomistic accounts of the cosmos: see e.g. Cornford 1937: 52–3.

The last property of the world, its everlastingness, is the one Timaeus explores the most (33a1–6). In doing so, he examines further one essential feature of the World Animal that was pointed out in the previous section: its indissolubility.

> 'Third, [the Demiurge's intention was] that it should not get old and diseased. He realized that when hot or cold things or anything else that possesses strong powers surrounds a composite body from outside and attacks it, it destroys that body prematurely, brings disease and old age upon it and so causes it to waste away'.[56]

Just as a body can be destroyed by *external* strong powers,[57] dissolubility could occur because of an external intervention. Consider, for instance, the description Timaeus provides later on, at 43a-c, of the consequences of the introduction of the soul into individual bodies: all animals (humans beings included of course) experience great confusion when their bodies (created by the lesser gods) are disturbed by their first perception of the outside world. In the case of the World Animal, Timaeus claims that if there were hot and cold primary bodies outside the cosmos, they could act as 'powers' damaging its health. But if no element is left outside the world from which such powers could act as causes of sickness or decay, no such trouble can occur. Being immune to any trouble caused from the outside, the body of the World Animal is immune to external attacks, and therefore indissoluble. This argument, however, is perplexing in the light of the conclusion of section C. For it seems to assume that a collision from outside *could* have destroyed the world. But, if this is so, how are we then to understand Timaeus' very strong point at 32c that the maker of the World Animal is the *only* cause that could in principle dissolve it, the body of the world being indissoluble 'by anyone but the one who had bound it together' (32c3–4: ὑπό του ἄλλου πλὴν ὑπὸ τοῦ συνδήσαντος)? My view is that Timaeus' point at 33c on the indissolubility of the World Animal immune to disease and old age helps understand his previous point at 32c. In the earlier passage, Timaeus is considering internal causes of dissolution and the possibility of the dissolution of the bond of proportion unifying the elements, while at 33a, he is examining in turn the possibility that the World Animal could suffer from external causes of dissolution. At

---

[56] *Tim.* 33a2–6: ἔτι δὲ ἵν' ἀγήρων καὶ ἄνοσον ᾖ, κατανοῶν ὡς συστάτῳ σώματι θερμὰ καὶ ψυχρὰ καὶ πάνθ' ὅσα δυνάμεις ἰσχυρὰς ἔχει περιιστάμενα ἔξωθεν καὶ προσπίπτοντα ἀκαίρως λύει καὶ νόσους γήράς τε ἐπάγοντα φθίνειν ποιεῖ.

[57] Note the use of the adverb ἔξωθεν ('from outside') at 33a4.

33a are then provided the reasons why the Demiurge chose to use the whole stock of the four constituents to make the body of the World Animal: in doing so, he left no possibility that a cause independent of his will (e.g. some kind of mechanical cause) could affect the World Animal. Although the body of World Animal is a composite body and, as such, could theoretically suffer from dissolution, the perfect unification of the elements within the body of the World Animal and their immunity to external affection as a result of the Demiurge's decisions manifest that the World Animal is indissoluble 'by anyone but the one who had bound it together'.

Having explained that the Demiurge used the whole of the four primary elements so as to build a World Animal endowed with the crucial properties of uniqueness, wholeness and everlastingness, Timaeus then explores the type of shape and movement that should be attributed to the body of the World Animal, and also singles out interesting biological properties that the World is granted, which make it a very peculiar Animal. At 33b1–7, Timaeus considers why the Demiurge chose the sphere as the best possible form of the World Animal and, at 33b7–d3, why this sphere can only be, as it were, *a perfectly polished sphere*, whose surface is perfectly regular, when it is looked from the outside (again ἔξωθεν at 33c1), that is, from a point of view only accessible to the Demiurge. The difference between these two points is well expressed by the two verbs used by Timaeus to refer to the actual making of the sphere: at 33b5, the Demiurge is said to 'turn <the World Animal> into a circle' (κυκλοτερὲς αὐτὸ ἐτορνεύσατο), whereas at 33b7–c1, he is said to 'give it a smooth, round finish, all over on the outside' (λεῖον δὲ δὴ κύκλῳ πᾶν ἔξωθεν αὐτὸ ἀπηκριβοῦτο). Both verbs belong to the vocabulary of pottery or sculpture,[58] but refer to two different phases in the process: the former verb (τορνεύω) to the actual making of the spherical shape, the latter (ἀπακριβόομαι) to its bringing into perfection. The third and last part of the passage (33d3–34a7) then considers the movement of the sphere, which can only be circular.

Timaeus provides an interesting mixture of reasons accounting for the Demiurge's decision to confer upon the world the property of being 'in the form of a sphere' (33b4: σφαιροειδές):

> 'The appropriate shape for that living thing that is to contain within itself all the living things would be the one which embraces within itself all the

---

[58] At *Tim.* 73e6–74a1, τορνεύω ('to turn, round off') is used to explain the fabrication of the skull.

shapes there are. Hence he gave it a round shape, the form of a sphere, with its centre equidistant from its extremes in all directions. This of all shapes is the most complete and most like itself, which he gave to it because he believed that likeness is incalculably more excellent than unlikeness'.[59]

Although he sums up in a single phrase the properties of the sphere by saying that it is 'of all shapes the most complete and most like itself' (πάντων τελεώτατον ὁμοιότατόν τε αὐτὸ ἑαυτῷ σχημάτων), Timaeus makes two different points here. He says (1) that the sphere is a mathematical *skhèma* that embraces all other *skhèmata*, being thereby the most complete of all *skhèmata*, and matching perfectly the World Animal, which contains all living beings. But he also claims (2) that the sphere is 'most like itself'. The first point refers presumably to a mathematical property,[60] whereas the second points out to a quasi-aesthetic feature, as Timaeus seems to acknowledge when he notes the Demiurge 'believed that likeness is *incalculably more excellent* (μυρίῳ κάλλιον) than unlikeness'. This discrepancy is worthy of note because, in the present case, Timaeus could have contented himself with mere 'scientific' reasons. For, when Timaeus elucidates what similarity consists in as far as the sphere is concerned, he argues that the sphere is most similar to itself because 'its centre [is] equidistant from its extremes in all directions' (33b4–5: ἐκ μέσου πάντη πρὸς τὰς τελευτὰς ἴσον ἀπέχον). This implies that the similarity of the sphere lies in the perfect equality of its radii, and not e.g. in the perfect homogeneity of its parts.[61] Such understanding of self-similarity is perfectly adequate to another property conferred upon the world by the Demiurge, later on in the passage (34a1–7), i.e. axial rotation.[62] All this shows that Plato could have developed his view on the likeness of the sphere so as to make it *explicitly* coherent with its specific (and only) movement. Rather, he chose to underline the Demiurge's preference of likeness over unlikeness on aesthetic and/or moral terms, and this again coheres with his insistence on the complexity of the set of considerations that are involved in the Demiurge's decisions.

---

[59] *Tim.* 33b2–7: τῷ δὲ τὰ πάντα ἐν αὑτῷ ζῷα περιέχειν μέλλοντι ζῴῳ πρέπον ἂν εἴη σχῆμα τὸ περιειληφὸς ἐν αὑτῷ πάντα ὁπόσα σχήματα· διὸ καὶ σφαιροειδές, ἐκ μέσου πάντη πρὸς τὰς τελευτὰς ἴσον ἀπέχον, κυκλοτερὲς αὐτὸ ἐτορνεύσατο, πάντων τελεώτατον ὁμοιότατόν τε αὐτὸ ἑαυτῷ σχημάτων, νομίσας μυρίῳ κάλλιον ὅμοιον ἀνομοίου.

[60] On which see Proclus (*in Tim.* 2.71.7–23) who suggests that the sphere is the only shape where all regular polyhedrons can be inscribed (see Baltzly 2007: 128).

[61] See Mortley 1969.

[62] Timaeus adds that axial rotation is the form of movement most suited to understanding and intelligence. See *Tim.* 34a2–3, with *Plt.* 269b, a parallel passage well-noted by Robin 1919: 10.

The next lines of the passage (33b7–d3) provide an amazing negative description of the Demiurge's craft when he puts the finishing touch to the spherical body of the World Animal. Since the world is a *zoon*, it is expected that it should be equipped with the usual components of a living organism, and be attributed vital functions and organs. Yet, Timaeus explains why the world has been deprived[63] of all organs and limbs and why it is thus 'smooth' (33b7: λεῖον), why, in other words, it is a perfectly regular sphere. The basic argument in favour of the Demiurge's choice clearly stems from his earlier decision of leaving nothing outside the world: indeed, if there is nothing outside, why would the World Animal need *external* perception? It would not. Hence it has no need for eyes and ears. Similarly, where would it stand? Where would it need to go? What would it need to grab? The answer is invariably the same: nothing and nowhere. Hence the World Animal has no need for legs, hands and feet. But does the same hold for its vital functions? One is indeed entitled to ask about them, since the World Animal is a *living* creature. Following the same pattern as before, Timaeus shows that the World Animal has no need for lungs because there is no external air to breathe, and no need for a digestive system because there is no food to take in. The world is therefore a perfectly efficient recycling animal, feeding off its own waste.[64]

This negative description, as a whole, is intended to emphasise the perfect self-sufficiency of the world chosen by the Demiurge, because it is 'better' (33d2: ἄμεινον) to be self-sufficient than require other things. There is nothing surprising, surely, in the attribution of self-sufficiency to the World Animal: being *autarkes* is after all a standard attribute of gods in Greek theology and of goodness in Greek ethics.[65] But the perfect spherical surface of the world also signals an aesthetic property, namely its perfect symmetry. In contrast with all other animals, which have limbs and external organs, and therefore are not perfectly symmetrical, the World Animal is endowed with perfect symmetry in the form of perfect sphericity (in spite of having internal asymmetries). This last feature takes us back to the first section of our passage and the issue about the nature of the World Animal. The lack of external organs and other biological marks that would have inevitably specified the nature of the World Animal

---

[63] Notice the constant repetition of οὐδείς, οὐκ and οὐδέ over no more than ten lines of text.

[64] *Tim.* 33c7–8: 'It supplied its own waste for its food' (αὐτὸ γὰρ ἑαυτῷ τροφὴν τὴν ἑαυτοῦ φθίσιν παρέχον).

[65] On the self-sufficiency of the world, see Sattler's contribution to this volume (Chapter 2).

shows that the World Animal is understood as a generic animal, modelled on the generic Form of Animal, and not as a particular species of *zoon*.[66]

3.6 Conclusion: Platonic 'Desmology'

The very fact that Proclus devoted to the Platonic *desmos* a whole section of his commentary amply shows that he has absolutely no doubt that the *Timaeus* demonstrates a rich understanding of the notion of bond. Yet, should we follow Proclus' hint and argue that Plato's approach to the notion of bond is theoretically structured so as to form what I have labelled so far a 'desmology'?

Let us consider how the Demiurge achieves the different tasks that fall upon him. The Demiurge is not directly in charge of the making of each and every part of the universe, although he does of course supervise everything. Being the perfect craftsman he is, the Demiurge, as craftsmen usually do, delegates some crucial tasks to others.[67] These are the lesser gods he has himself created. Some of these lesser gods are indeed responsible for the making of important parts of the universe, and notably for the making of the mortal parts of human beings. Before setting this agenda to the lesser gods, the Demiurge addresses them as follows:

> 'O gods, works divine whose maker and father I am, whatever has come to be by my hands cannot be undone but by my own consent. Now while it is true that anything that is bound is liable to being undone, still, only one who is evil would consent to the undoing of what has been well fitted together and is in fine condition. This is the reason why you, as creatures that have come to be, are neither completely immortal nor exempt from being undone. Still, you will not be undone nor will death be your portion,

---

[66] As convincingly argued by Sedley 2007: 112.

[67] For a good discussion whether the Demiurge actually supervises the tasks left to the lesser gods, see Boys-Stones in this volume (Chapter 5). I agree with Boys-Stones that Timaeus does not mention 'supervision' or 'delegation' at 41a-b, but one need not understand supervision here as entailing lack of autonomy on the part of the lesser gods. Indeed, it is vital to recognise that the Demiurge is debarred from undertaking the creation of the human and lower animals capable of badness, for that very reason that he can only be responsible for the creation of *good* things. Hence the need for the secondary gods: see *Tim.* 42d2–e4. The important point, I think, is that the Demiurge is *prescribing* specific tasks to the lesser gods, which they then accomplish by imitation of their father's own work. See *Tim.* 69c3–5: 'but he assigned his own progeny the task of fashioning the generation of those that were mortal. They imitated him' (τῶν δὲ θνητῶν τὴν γένεσιν τοῖς ἑαυτοῦ γεννήμασιν δημιουργεῖν προσέταξεν. οἱ δὲ μιμούμενοι [. . .]).

since you have received the guarantee of my will – a greater, more sovereign
bond than those with which you were bound when you came to be'.[68]

This is a crucial passage for understanding Platonic 'desmology' for two
reasons at least. First, it spells out some key principles underlying Plato's
use of the notion of *desmos* in teleological contexts. Second, it illuminates
how these principles account for a systematic approach to bonds in some
of the cosmogonical and zoogonical processes described in the *Timaeus*.

That everything that has been composed or bound is liable to be
decomposed or unbound forms one of these principles. This principle of
dissolubility, as I propose to label it, shows that the eternity conferred
upon the lesser gods is similar to the one conferred upon the world, to
which Timaeus alluded to in a passage quoted previously. For, just like the
lesser gods, the body of the world could not be undone 'by anyone but the
one who had bound it together' (*Tim.* 32c4). The principle of dissolubility
is here granted the status of an axiomatic truth in favour of which no direct
argument needs to be given because, presumably, it is self-evident, and
relies wholly on the core Platonic dualism between being and becoming.[69]
Because, according to this principle, the very fact of having been generated
implies the possibility of degeneration and ultimately destruction, the only
true immortal beings, apart from the Demiurge, are the intelligible Forms.
This shows that the kind of immortality that is conferred upon the body of
the world and the lesser gods is, as it were, second-order.[70] As the speech
of the Demiurge makes clear, the body of the World Animal and the lesser
gods are not immortal, but will not perish. Why is that so?

The Demiurge's answer is that the lesser gods are bound by yet another
bond, the *desmos* of his *boulèsis*. Now, the nature and conditions of this bond
are explained by the Demiurge himself. The Demiurge could destroy the
lesser gods who have been harmoniously bound, but the reason why he shall
not is that if he were to destroy them, he would then be *kakos*, hence would

---

[68] *Tim.* 41a7–b6: "Θεοί, θεῶν ὧν ἐγὼ δημιουργὸς πατήρ τε ἔργων, <τὰ> δι' ἐμοῦ γενόμενα ἄλυτα
ἐμοῦ γε μὴ ἐθέλοντος. τὸ μὲν οὖν δὴδεθὲν πᾶν λυτόν, τό γε μὴν καλῶς ἁρμοσθὲν καὶ ἔχον εὖ λύειν
ἐθέλειν κακοῦ· δι' ἃ καὶ ἐπείπερ γεγένησθε, ἀθάνατοι μὲν οὐκ ἐστὲ οὐδ' ἄλυτοι τὸ πάμπαν, οὔτι
μὲν δὴ λυθήσεσθέ γε οὐδὲ τεύξεσθε θανάτου μοίρας, τῆς ἐμῆς βουλήσεως μείζονος ἔτι δεσμοῦ καὶ
κυριωτέρου λαχόντες ἐκείνων οἷς ὅτ' ἐγίγνεσθε συνεδεῖσθε'. Zeyl emends Burnet's text at 41a7: see
Zeyl 2000: 28 n.36. For a slightly different emendation and a full discussion of the philological
issue, see Cornford 1937: 367–70.

[69] See e.g. *Phd.* 78b-c, and also *R.* 546a1–4 where the same principle is used concerning the
dissolution of the ideal city.

[70] For more details on the difference between essential and conferred immortality, see the insightful
study by Sedley 2009 who writes (155): 'Conferred immortality can exist only in a world in which
there is also essential immortality, since it requires an essentially immortal being to confer it'.

not be doing what he does *for the best*. The Demiurge's will is then obeying another principle, brought in so as to counterbalance the principle of diss-olubility: the principle of goodness which determines his every decision and action, as we have seen in detail concerning the body of the World Animal.

So, following Proclus' hint, we can isolate a single thread involved in some cosmogonical and zoogonical processes in the *Timaeus*. Imitating the teleological activity of the divine craftsman (*Tim.* 42e–43a), the lesser gods use dissoluble bonds to attach the human soul to the body through the marrow (73b3–4, c3, d6), and parts of the soul to specific parts of the body (69e4, 70e3), to implant organs within parts of the body (45a7, b4), and to attach parts of the body to one another (77e3, 84a3). The Demiurge, in turn, makes the lesser gods by using bonds that are dissoluble as such, but which will not be dissolved, because of the binding force of his will. When he makes the body of the World Animal, the Demiurge uses the most beautiful of bonds. Because this bond of proportion is a pure mathematical ratio, different from the things bound, but not superim-posed on them, as would a purely physical bond, it confers the greatest unity that can be conferred on physical elements. Still, this bond can in principle be dissolved. But it will not, because of the bond of the Demiurge's will. The Demiurge's will is thus supremely powerful: it overpowers the bonds that constitute the lesser gods and that are liable to dissolution. Yet, as Socrates puts it in the *Phaedo*, it is *to agathon*, that is, truly, what binds, which explains *in fine* why some beings such as the World Animal, the lesser gods and the rational soul are indissoluble.

The teleological programme advocated in the *Phaedo* thus develops into a *scala vinculorum*, as it were. Interestingly, this scale of bonds coheres with the different paradigms Plato has used to describe divine craftsmanship throughout the *Timaeus*: mathematical ratios confer the greatest unity on the things bound, whereas technical crafts[71] such as physical binding or weaving,[72] are invoked to describe mortal compounds, subject to dissolution. The obvious result of this scale of bonds is to lend a great continuity to the making of the World Animal and to the human animals that live and die within it. Most importantly, this continuity reveals the overwhelming presence of the good in the world, binding to one another the indissoluble world and the mortal beings within it.

[71] On the technical paradigms that govern divine craftsmanship in the *Timaeus*, see Brisson 1998: 35–50.
[72] For the weaving processes involved in the *Timaeus*, see *Tim.* 72c7, 76d4, 77e1, 78b3–7, d5, 79d3–4.

CHAPTER 4

The World Soul Takes Command
The Doctrine of the World Soul in the Epinomis of Philip of Opus and in the Academy of Polemon

John Dillon*

My purpose on this occasion is to explore somewhat further a thesis that I have proposed on a number of previous occasions, but primarily in my study of the Old Academy, *The Heirs of Plato*,[1] to the effect that, toward the end of his life, Plato, after having advanced a number of conjectures during his philosophical career as to the nature of a First Principle, was inclined to settle on the concept of a rational World Soul, with demiurgic functions, and that this was a doctrine that his faithful *amanuensis* in his last years, Philip of Opus, advanced on his own account, in the belief that in this he was developing the latest theories of his Master.

Plato, after all, seems to leave a rather confusing legacy to his successors, when it comes to First Principles. We have, on the one hand, the Good of the *Republic,* a first principle which is presented as being in some way "beyond" (*epekeina*) the rest of existence, of which it is the generative ground, as well as an object of desire or striving for all things; but then there is the Demiurge of the *Timaeus,* who is described as an Intellect, but who is represented as contemplating a Model in some way above and beyond himself, in his creation of Soul and of the world (unless the Demiurge and his creation are in fact mythical, and to be deconstructed – as was stoutly maintained, against the criticisms of Aristotle, by both of Plato's closest associates and immediate successors, Speusippus and Xenocrates); then there is the One of the hypotheses of the second part of the *Parmenides,* which may or may not have been intended by Plato as a first principle, but which was certainly taken as such in later times; further, there are the first principles set out in the *Philebus* (26Cff.), Limit, the Unlimited, and the Cause of the Mixture, which in turn seem to have a fairly close relationship to the One and Indefinite Dyad of the Unwritten

---

* This chapter first appeared, with slight differences, in C. Helmig (ed.), *World Soul – Anima Mundi. A Collection of Essays on the Origins and Fortunes of a Fundamental Idea.* Berlin: De Gruyter, 2019.
[1] 2003: 183–93 and 168–74.

Doctrines. All these, whatever else is to be made of them, would constitute first principles superior to anything that could be identified as a World Soul.

But then, last but not least, we seem to have the doctrine, firmly enunciated first in the *Phaedrus* (245Cff.), but particularly dominant in Book X of the *Laws,* of a rational World Soul as the first principle of all motion, and therefore of all creation. What are we to do with this apparent change of heart?

It might be said, admittedly, of the famous definition of soul in the *Phaedrus,* that all it, strictly speaking, does is to assert the immortality of soul, and to identify it as the source of all motion, but this does not preclude there being principles higher than soul that are unmoved; and indeed in the Myth we are presented with a whole array of Forms which the souls of both gods and mortals contemplate, which are certainly not presented as being dependent for their existence on any soul.[2] In Book X of the *Laws,* on the other hand, the situation is significantly different, and it is to that that I will now turn, before addressing the question of the position of Philip himself.

Let us first remind ourselves of the context, and then consider a series of key passages. The Visitor from Athens is concerned, at this stage of the conversation, to present his companions Cleinias and Megillus – neither of them, to say the least of it, accomplished philosophers – with a refutation of atheism, which he regards as a great evil, and profoundly subversive of good government. To do that, he has to bring to their minds the true nature of God. We must not forget this: his topic is not here the World Soul as such, or the originator of motion, or any type of intermediate being; we are concerned with God as first principle of all creation.

The Visitor starts in as follows (891Eff.):

> So it looks as if I must produce a rather unfamiliar argument. Well then, the doctrine that produces an impious soul also "produces" in a sense the soul itself, in that it denies the priority of what was in fact the first cause of the birth and destruction of all things (*prôton geneseôs kai phthoras aition hapantôn*), and regards it as a later creation. Conversely, it asserts that what actually came later, came first. That's the source of the mistake these people have made about the real nature of the gods.

> CLEINIAS: "So far the point escapes me."

---

[2] Indeed, at 249C, it is intimated that Forms confer divinity (though not explicitly *existence*) upon the soul of the philosopher.

VISITOR: "It's the *soul*, my good friend, that nearly everybody
            seems to have misunderstood, not realising its nature and
            power. Quite apart from other points about it, people are
            particularly ignorant about its origin (*genesis*). It is primal in
            rank,[3] born long before all physical things (*sômatôn emprosthen
            pantôn genomenê*), and is more than anything else the cause of
            all their alterations and transformations. Now if that's true,
            anything closely related to soul will necessarily have been
            created before material things, won't it, since soul itself is older
            than matter."[4]

    This certainly sounds promising, but by itself it cannot be said to get
us very far. Soul is asserted to be superior to body, and to the material
world in general, and to be the cause of its existence, but it itself is spoken
of as being "generated" (*genesis, genomenê*), which, if taken literally,
would imply some higher power again, such as would be responsible for
its generation.

    As the Visitor proceeds, however, it becomes much less clear that there
is any force in the universe superior to Soul. Let us turn now to the core of
the argument, at 896Aff.:

    So what's the definition of the thing we call the soul? Surely we can do
    nothing but use our formula of a moment ago: "motion capable of moving
    itself"?

CLEINIAS: "Do you mean that the entity which we call 'soul' is
            precisely that which is defined by the expression 'self-
            generating motion'?"
VISITOR: "I do. And if that is true, are we still dissatisfied? Haven't
            we got a satisfactory proof that soul is identical with the
            original source of the generation and motion of all past present
            and future things and their contraries, since it has been shown
            to be the cause of all change and motion in everything."
CLEINIAS: "Dissatisfied? No! On the contrary, it has been proved
            most adequately that soul is the most ancient of all things,
            since it has been shown to be the source of motion."

    We have now advanced to the position where Soul, being endowed with
self-motion (and thus, in effect, ungenerated and eternal), is presented as

---

[3] I take this to be the force of the slightly vague expression *en tois prôtois*, since the whole tenor of the
Visitor's argument is that Soul is *primary*, not just "one of the first creations," as Saunders translates
(Saunders 2004) – justifiable though that rendering might be in other circumstances.

[4] I borrow here the excellent, if perhaps rather excessively chatty, Penguin translation of Trevor
Saunders 2004, with minor alterations.

prior to all other things, and as the *cause* of all other things. One could still, perhaps, argue for a supreme deity which would be a sort of "unmoved Mover" (like the Good of the *Republic*), but we must reflect at this point, once again, that this whole argument is directed toward establishing the nature of *God,* so that, if the soul is *not* God, we are wasting our time establishing the existence and superiority of soul – unless we are then going to proceed to an investigation of whatever the *real* supreme principle might be. But in fact we never move beyond this demonstration of the nature and power of soul; on the contrary, the role of soul becomes ever more central and more exalted.

If we move on, for instance, to 896E, we learn that "Soul, by virtue of its own motions, stirs into movement everything in the heavens and on earth and in the sea." A long list of psychic states and functions then follows, which govern a long list of physical conditions, at the conclusion of which (897b1–3) we are told that the soul "governs all things rightly and happily, *when it takes a divine intellect to itself (noun men proslabousa theion)."*[5]

Here again, it could be objected, perhaps, that the *theios nous* here mentioned should logically be an entity superior to soul, but in fact such a supposition would be unjustified, as, with an interesting touch of dualism which we need not go into further in the present context, the Visitor envisages Soul alternatively taking "mindlessness" (*anoia*) to itself (897b3–4), in which case all things would be administered in an entirely opposite way, and it would be absurd, I think, to suppose that *anoia* here is being hypostatized. So all the Visitor really means to say is that Soul will act rationally rather than irrationally.[6]

This in turn, in my view, can be seen as assimilating Soul here to what must after all be taken as the supreme principle of the *Timaeus,* if we are prepared to demythologize the account of the demiurgic creation, as was certainly the position of Speusippus and Xenocrates – though it did not induce them to postulate a rational World Soul as their supreme principle – but must also have been the view of their successor Polemon, as I shall

---

[5] The text is sadly disturbed here, the chief mss. (A and O) reading ἀεῖ θεὸν ὀρθῶς θεοῖς, which really makes no sense. I must say that I favor, first, adopting the reading of L and Eusebius, θεῖον for θεὸν, and then Winckelmann's proposal ὀρθῶς θέουσα, "running on correctly," cleverly drawing on Socrates' etymology of *theos* in the *Cratylus* (397d), to which Plato may well be alluding here.

[6] I am conscious here of going against the thesis of Stephen Menn, in his most useful monograph, *Plato on God as Nous* (Menn 1995), in which he argues for the supremacy of *Nous* as a principle in Plato's later works, especially in the *Timaeus* (as the Demiurge), but he does not in fact devote much attention to *Laws* X. I would not wish to deny that Plato, at some stage in his development, may have favoured the concept of *Nous* as a supreme principle, but I think that he settled ultimately for a rational World Soul.

argue presently – who in turn passed it on to Zeno and the Stoic tradition, by which time a rational World Soul had become the accepted first principle.

But from these rather bold speculations let us return one last time to the text of *Laws* X, this time to 898Bff., where it is finally made clear both that the driving force of the universe is a World Soul, and that each of the heavenly bodies, which are in fact the "gods" that we have been in search of, is a (fiery) body guided by a soul of its own (898DE). At 899CD, the whole course of the argument is summed up, in a most significant manner:

VISITOR: Now then, Megillus and Cleinias, let's lay down limiting conditions for anyone who has so far refused to believe in gods, and so dispose of them.
CLEINIAS: What conditions do you mean?
VISITOR: Either he must demonstrate that we're wrong to posit Soul as the first cause to which everything owes its birth (*genesin hapantôn einai prôtên*), and that our subsequent deductions were equally mistaken, or, if he can't put up a better case than ours, he should let himself be persuaded by us, and live for the rest of his life a believer in gods.

We may note here how much the status of Soul has been enhanced from its first introduction at 892A. There, it was spoken of itself having a *genesis*, albeit one antecedent to all other things; here, however, it itself is the *prôtê genesis* of all things, and so, inevitably, the supreme deity. As for the other gods, whose existence and providential care for mankind the Visitor from Athens wants to establish, they are revealed as celestial deities subordinate to Soul, though each ruled by their own soul.

Having set out, then, in what I hope is a reasonably convincing fashion, the theological position taken up by Plato in his last work, a work in the editing of which Philip of Opus was intimately involved over many years, we may turn to an examination of the *Epinomis* itself.

The *raison d'être* of the *Epinomis,* as set out at the beginning of the work, is to give a more specific account of "what it is that mortal man should learn in order to be wise," on the grounds that that was not dealt with in the previous conversation. In fact, Plato himself seems deliberately to refrain from giving any details about this in the *Laws,* probably out of a conviction that it was better transmitted orally. This, however, gives Philip the opportunity to provide his own view of what the members of the Nocturnal Council of *Laws* XII – and indeed any man who desires to be wise – should be studying, and to lead up to that by providing a theological underpinning to justify it. It is this theological underpinning that I wish to dwell on in particular here, as it reveals most clearly Philip's distinctive philosophical position.

Now it is clear, I think, from the *Epinomis* that the supreme active principle in the universe favored by the author is in fact a rational World Soul, not transcending the physical world, but presiding in the celestial realm. This position may seem somewhat surprising, in view of what we think we know of the first principles favored by Philip's more distinguished contemporaries in the Academy, Speusippus and Xenocrates, and, if the evidence of Aristotle may be trusted (particularly in *Metaphysics* A 6), by Plato himself – basically, variations on the Pythagorean pair of Monad and Indefinite Dyad – but the evidence seems to bear this out.[7]

Let us look at some significant passages. There are four in particular that I should like to examine: 976D–977B, 982A–983C, 984BC, and 988A–E, all from the preamble, as it were, to the exposition of that science which Philip declares to be the supreme and most divine one – not dialectic, as one might expect from a Platonist, but rather astronomy, understood in its *Platonic* sense (that is, as expounded in *Republic* VII, 529–30).[8]

First, then, let us consider 976Dff. Here the Visitor from Athens begins his search for the single most basic science, without the possession of which, he says, "mankind would be the most mindless and senseless of creatures." This science he declares to be that of number – a gift to us from God himself. He then proceeds to explain what he means by God – a move interesting in itself, since Plato, in using the indefinite term *ho theos,* would never bother to provide any gloss for it:

> And I must explain who it is that I believe to be God, though he be a strange one (*atopos*) – and somehow not strange either, for why should we not believe the cause of all good things that are ours to have been the cause also of what is far the greatest, understanding (*phronêsis*)? And who is it that I magnify with the name of God, Megillus and Cleinias? It must be Heaven (*ouranos*) that has full claim to our honour and especially our prayers, as is the case for all the other daemons and gods also. That it has been the cause

---

[7] We must bear in mind, however, that this apparent unanimity may conceal considerable differences. Xenocrates' first principle, after all, is explicitly an Intellect, and *may* be regarded as immanent in the cosmos (cf. Fr. 15 Heinze/216 Isnardi Parente in Isnardi Parente 1982), while Speusippus' One is pretty clearly neither of the above. As for the Good of the *Republic,* it was certainly regarded in later times as being "above Intellect and Being," but it has also been claimed not to transcend Being (cf. Baltes 1997), and it is in fact nowhere specified in the text whether it is an intellect or not. In any case, both Speusippus and Xenocrates accorded a key role to Soul as efficient (and formal) cause of the universe in their respective systems, while Philip (and Polemon) may well, for all we know, have recognised the existence of Monad and Dyad as some sort of "Urprinzipien," being conditions for the existence of anything at all, while focusing on Soul as the primary *fully realised* principle.

[8] Dialectic does indeed appear briefly, in 991C – Philip, as a good Platonist, could hardly dispense with it altogether – but simply as a tool for pursuing astronomy.

of all the other good things we have, we shall all admit; that it really gave us number also we assert, and that it will give us more gifts yet, if we will but follow its lead. For if one enters on the right theory about it, whether one be pleased to call it World-Order (*kosmos*) or Olympos or Ouranos – let one call it this or that[9] – but follow where, in bespangling itself and turning the stars that it contains in all their courses, it produces the seasons and food for all. And thence, accordingly, we have understanding (*phronêsis*) in general, we may say, together with all number, and all other good things: but the greatest of these is when, after receiving its gift of number, one explores the whole circuit. (976e3–977b8)

This is surely a remarkable passage, even though the style be turgid. The old god Ouranos is pressed into service in a quite new role, as the *immanent* guiding principle of the universe, and assigned a demiurgic function (though proper also to the Good of the *Republic*), that of the ultimate provider of all good things to mortals, but in particular – by reason of the alternation of day and night, and the movements of the sun and moon and other planets – of number and reasoning in general.

There is not yet here, admittedly, any mention of a World Soul, but for that we do not have to wait very long. Let us turn next to 982Aff. Here Philip has just (981B-E) finished setting out his five-element universe (fire, water, air, earth – and aether[10]), each with its proper inhabitants, ending with a distinction between two basic types of creature in the universe, mortal and immortal. He now goes on to expand on this:

Let us therefore first observe that, as we state it, such creatures are of two sorts – for let us state it again – both visible, one of fire, as it would appear, entirely,[11] and the other of earth; and the earthy one moves in disorder, whereas that of fire has its motion in perfect order. Now that which has motion in disorder we should regard as unintelligent, acting like the animal creatures about us for the most part; but that which has an orderly and heavenly progress must be taken as providing strong evidence of its

---

[9] This seems to echo interestingly Plato's phraseology in *Tim.* 28b3–5 – though with the significant difference that here we are naming a supreme deity!

[10] Remarkably, Philip introduces *aithêr*, not as the highest of the elements, proper to the heavenly realm, as did Aristotle and Xenocrates, but the *second-highest*, below fire, in the area just below the Moon.

[11] This might seem to suggest that the heavenly bodies (for it is those to which he is referring) are composed not only of fire, but also of immaterial souls, but as Tarán points out (1975: 267), what Philip seems rather to have in mind (cf. 981D-E) is that they have slight portions of all the other elements also – a thoroughly materialist scenario, therefore.

intelligent life. . . . *The necessity of a soul which has acquired intellect (nous) will prove itself by far the greatest of all necessities; for it makes laws as ruler, not as ruled; and this unalterable state, when the soul has taken the best counsel in accord with the best intellect, comes out as the perfect thing in truth and in accord with intellect, and not even adamant could ever prove stronger than it or more inalterable, but in fact the three Fates (Moirai) have taken hold, and keep watch that what has been decided by each of the gods with the best counsel shall be perfect.*

This contains its fair share of obscurantist guff and contorted syntax, as is characteristic of Philip's prose, at least when he is trying to imitate the worst excesses of his Master's late style, but nevertheless it can be seen, I would suggest, that Philip is touching on some significant Platonic bases here. Specifically, he seems to be alluding to certain aspects of the myth of *Republic* X. The mention of the *anangké* of soul here would seem to be a reference, above all, to the passage 616C–617C, which presents us with the image of the great cosmic spindle, consisting of the outer circle, or "whorl," of the fixed stars, and seven inner circles, representing the planetary circuits, which rests on the knees of a personified Necessity, who turns it – that would presumably be the point of the otherwise rather vacuous remark that it acts "as ruler, not ruled" (by contrast to the *anangké* of *Timaeus* 48A, for instance, which is controlled by the Demiurge, *qua* Intellect). The probability that Philip has the *Republic* in mind here is strengthened by references to "adamant" (cf. 616c8: the staff and the hook of the spindle are made of adamant), and to the Fates (cf. 617b9–c10: the *Moirai,* daughters of Necessity, who sit around the spindle at equal intervals, and help their mother to turn it).

It should be clear that in the above passage Philip is presenting Soul as the supreme active principle in the universe. The various mentions of *nous* as something which it "acquires," or "takes counsel with" should not, I think, be taken to refer to some shadowy superior entity in which Soul participates, but rather as characterizations of its own proper mode of being, that is to say, rational or intellectual, on the model of the reference to Soul's taking on a divine *nous* in *Laws.* X 897b2, quoted above. The supremacy of Soul is confirmed a little further on, at 983Cff., where it is presented as creating all the various classes of being, from the heavenly gods on down, through the aetherial and aerial daemons, to the denizens of water, and finally men. And yet, in the middle of this, we suddenly find a reference to "God," being differentiated from the various levels of daemon, as not being subject to passions (985a5–8):

> For we know that God, who possesses the final end of divine fate,[12]
> transcends these affections of pleasure and pain, but has a share of intelli-
> gence and knowledge in every sphere.

There is really nothing else for "God" to denote here, however, than the
World Soul. This is confirmed a little later on, at the end of what is Philip's
elaborate preamble to his proposing of astronomy (which he manages to
identify with the dialectic of *Republic* VII, 531D–535A) as the highest
science. He is criticizing the primitive conceptions of divinity held by men
of former times, in contrast with the best thinking of the present day
(988b7–e3):

> And indeed there is much good reason to suppose that formerly, when men
> had their first conceptions of how the gods came to exist and with what
> qualities, and whence, and to what kind of actions they proceeded, they
> were spoken of in a manner not approved or welcomed by the prudent, nor
> were even the views of those who came later, among whom the greatest
> dignity was given to fire and water and other bodies, while the wonderful
> soul was accounted inferior, and higher and more honoured with them was
> a motion assigned to the body for moving itself by heat and coolings and
> everything of that kind, instead of that which the soul had for moving both
> the body and itself.
>
>   But now that we account it no marvel that the soul, once it is in the
> body, should stir and revolve this and itself, neither does soul, on our
> reckoning, doubt her power of revolving any weight. And therefore, since
> we now claim that, *as the soul is the cause of the whole*, and all good things are
> causes of like things, while on the other hand evil things are the causes of
> other things like them, the soul should be the cause of all activity and
> motion, and that activity and motion towards the good is the work of the
> best soul, while that tending towards the opposite is of the opposite,[13] it
> must be the good things have conquered and continue to conquer those
> that are not such.

Once again, Soul emerges as the cause of all things, here in contrast to
earlier theories[14] which wished to derive the world, including the gods,
from material principles, indicating that, for Philip, questions as to the true
identity and composition of the gods or of "God" can be answered by an
enquiry into the true source of motion, which is Soul. Despite the various

---

[12] What on earth does this really mean, one might ask? It comes across as a typical piece of Philippian
guff. One may take it, however, I presume, as according this entity ultimate control over the
workings of fate, such as is appropriate to a supreme being.
[13] This suggestion of dualism is doubtless inserted here by Philip as an echo of similar suggestions in
Laws X 896E, and is not, I think, to be taken too seriously.
[14] Doubtless those of the Presocratics, from Thales on down to the Atomists.

references to Soul "taking to itself *nous*," or the like, it seems clear enough that for Philip, and, in his mind, for his master Plato as well, certainly in the *Laws,* but perhaps going back as far as the *Republic* and the *Timaeus,* the supreme principle in the universe is a rational World Soul, immanent in the cosmos, and residing most particularly in the sphere of the fixed stars. The study of astronomy is therefore the contemplation of the structure and workings of God's mind. It is this that teaches us the wonders of number, and it is that, in turn, which endows us with wisdom, *phronêsis.*

I have already suggested that this scenario did not appeal to Speusippus or Xenocrates – though, as I have suggested, the Nous-Monad of the latter may well have been envisaged as residing in the heavens – it is described, at any rate, by the doxographer Aetius (Xenocr. Fr. 15 Heinze) as *en ouranói basileuousan.*[15] The question now remains as to whether any echo of Philip's take on Plato's First Principle may be discerned in the thought of Polemon, last head of the Old Academy.

There is unfortunately not much to go on here, as is the case with almost every other aspect of Polemon's doctrine, but there is one clue which, properly interpreted, may yield something. This comes in the shape of a bald doxographic report of Polemon's position on the nature of God, relayed by the same Aetius, as preserved by Stobaeus in his *Anthologia,* just below the report on Xenocrates mentioned above. The report runs as follows: "Polemon declared that the cosmos was God" (*Polemon ton kosmon theon apephênato*).

It might be thought that this sentence need only mean that Polemon regarded the cosmos as *a* god, and thus was not of any great interest. But the context in which it occurs excludes that interpretation. The whole section in Stobaeus is concerned with the nature and functions of the supreme God, so this must give Polemon's view on that subject. We are faced, therefore, with the assertion that Polemon's supreme principle can be described as *kosmos* – which, we may recall, is one of the alternative appellations which Philip suggested, at *Epin.* 977b2 (quoted above), for his supreme principle *Ouranos,* also an immanent divinity, which, as we have seen, turns out to be a rational World Soul.

---

[15] This may well be, as I have suggested in 2003: 102 n. 44, an intentional reminiscence of *Phdr.* 246E, where Zeus is presented as "the great leader in the heavens," but this, though employing figurative language, need not preclude Xenocrates' being serious about the immanent nature of the Nous-Monad.

There is, as I say, very little other evidence as to what Polemon thought about anything, but I believe that one can flesh out somewhat our understanding of his views by adducing a piece of evidence that had also been previously disregarded, the summary of Academic doctrine presented by Cicero, through the mouth of Varro, in his *Academica* I, 24–9, a passage which must derive substantially from Antiochus of Ascalon. However, while the Antiochian provenance of this is generally agreed, its validity as an account of any sort of Old Academic doctrine has been vigorously disputed, it being felt that it is a Stoic-influenced farrago concocted by Antiochus himself.[16]

This consensus, however, was forcefully contested, some little time ago now, by David Sedley, in an important article,[17] and I think that he is right to do so. When one looks carefully at this passage, one can discern that there is nothing there that could not have been propounded by Polemon, and that the similarity to Stoic doctrine results from the fact that Zeno learned a lot from his period of study with Polemon. Let us look at the relevant section:

> The topic of Nature, which they treated next (sc. after Ethics), they approached by dividing it into two principles, the one the creative (*efficiens = poiétiké*), the other at this one's disposal, as it were, out of which something might be created. In the creative one they deemed that there inhered power (*vis = dynamis*), in the one acted upon, a sort of "matter" (*materia = hylê*), yet they held that each of the two inhered in the other, for neither would matter have been able to cohere if it were not held together by any power, nor yet would power without some matter – for nothing exists without it being necessarily somewhere.[18] But that which was the product of both they called "body" (*corpus = sôma*), and, so to speak, a sort of "quality" (*qualitas = poiotês*).

What do we have here? It is a system of two principles, very like that of the Stoics, certainly – except that there is no suggestion that either of these principles is *corporeal* – but also quite compatible with that which would

[16] One recent expression of skepticism in this regard is provided by Gretchen Reydams-Schils 2013, but, though she scores some good points against my previous presentation of Polemon's position in Dillon 2003, she seems to disregard my position that, although Polemon, and even Xenocrates, would seem to have postulated the supreme deity as being immanent in the cosmos, they did not go so far as to assert that it was in any sense *material*. It was Zeno's innovation to declare that it was composed of at least a very special sort of matter, intelligent fire (*pyr noeron*), and this constitutes a significant "tidying-up" of the Old Academic position.

[17] Sedley 2002

[18] This is certainly reminiscent of a passage of the *Timaeus*, 52B: "everything that exists must necessarily be in some place (*en tini topôi*), which would assimilate matter here, interestingly, to the Receptacle of the *Timaeus*."

emerge from a nonliteral interpretation of the *Timaeus.* The active, demiurgic principle, which, as I have suggested above, must really be conceived
as a rational World Soul, whose contents are the Forms, acts on a passive,
infinitely malleable, "material" principle, to create a world of physical
bodies. The concept of *poiotês*, "quality," to describe, presumably, what
the active principle impresses upon the passive principle, seems to embody
a reference to *Theaet.* 182A, from which a scholastic mind could, I think,
derive the theory that an active (*poiêtikê*) principle possesses a *dynamis* to
impose *poiotêtes* on a passive principle, where it is also plain that Plato is
postulating an etymological connection between *poiein* and *poiotês*.

It seems a reasonable postulation that this summary of Academic
doctrine reflects the position of the Academy under Polemon, if not also
under Xenocrates. If it were a total concoction of Antiochus', it is reasonable to argue that Cicero would have made that accusation against him
(or allowed one of his spokesmen to do so), since he is not backward in
accusing Antiochus elsewhere of excessive enthusiasm for Stoicism. But
nowhere does he do that, so I think that we must assume that he felt there
was some plausibility to this account of Academic doctrine.[19]

If that is so, then where, one might one ask, does this leave such entities
as the Monad and the Indefinite Dyad of the "unwritten doctrines" (and
of Xenocrates), the Limit and Unlimitedness of the *Philebus,* or for that
matter the Good of the *Republic*? And how can those principles, and
indeed the active and passive principles of the present summary, be
reconciled with the concept of a rational World Soul? I must say that
I do not see that there need be any serious degree of discrepancy here. If we
turn back to Xenocrates, for a start, his Monad is also characterized as an
Intellect, but this Intellect is presented as interacting with a dyadic principle, and is the ultimate cause of motion in the universe, and that, on
Platonic principles, is properly the province of Soul. So if, as we must
suspect, Xenocrates' Monad has the same function in the universe as the
de-mythologized demiurgic principle of the *Timaeus,* then we are back to a
rational World Soul. It is merely a matter of terminology. The active
principle of the later Old Academy (I leave Speusippus out of the reckon-
ing, as his radical concept of the One excludes him from this consensus)
possesses the characteristics of rationality and of motivity, as it acts on a

---

[19] We do not, of course, know whether Cicero had any first-hand acquaintance with the doctrines of
the Old Academy other than though Antiochus, but it is reasonable to suppose that much more was
available to him that is available to us. Certainly, he was acquainted with such a work as Crantor's
treatise *On Grief,* which he made use of in composing his (self-) *Consolatio* on the death of his
daughter Tullia (*Tusc. Disp.* I 66).

passive principle to produce a physical world of the best type possible, and thus, it seems to me, is best described as a rational World Soul.

So it may after all be the case that Philip of Opus was right in his interpretation of Plato's final position on the nature of the first principle, and that at least the majority of his colleagues, from Xenocrates on, came to share his view.

CHAPTER 5

Begotten and Made
Creation as Cosmogony in Middle Platonism

George Boys-Stones

5.1 Introduction

In his account of how things came to be, Timaeus describes the first cause of the cosmos as its 'maker and father': ποιητὴν καὶ πατέρα τοῦδε τοῦ παντός (*Timaeus* 28c).[1] He apparently means god to be *both* an agent who plans and builds the cosmos out of the available material as a 'craftsman' might (he is δημιουργός already at 28a), *and also* a self-replicating being who finds the right conditions for procreation in the 'receptacle' ('mother' to his 'father' at 50d and 51a). Yet very little attention is in fact given, at least by modern commentators, to the second of these claims, that god is the father of the world. The 'craftsman' metaphor has been endlessly and minutely studied; but one has to go a long way through the literature to find any more than a passing acknowledgement of the claim that god is father.[2] But it was not always like this. Middle Platonists took both images quite seriously – and if we are interested in the difference it could make to our reading of the *Timaeus* to take the image of divine paternity as seriously as we take the image of divine craftsmanship, we could do worse than to look to them.

---

[1] At 28b we are told that the 'cosmos' is just another name for this 'whole', i.e. 'the whole heaven' (ὁ ... πᾶς οὐρανός).

[2] For example, neither Cornford 1937, nor more recently Broadie 2012, have any commentary on the 'father' metaphor. Johansen 2004: 81–2 is motivated to engage with it only to help explain the *absence* of the 'craftsman' in 50c-d. See also Sattler and El Murr in this volume. Vorwerk 2010 is an exception – although his conclusion, that god is 'father' to the world soul but 'maker' of its body, does not pretend to add to our comprehension of Plato's metaphysics (and may also be taken to stumble on 32c, where the cosmic body is 'begotten'). The ancients were much more concerned to give full weight to both metaphors (and it is no coincidence that Vorwerk's article is formally a study of the ancient commentary tradition): see for example Proclus, *On the Timaeus* i. 299.10–310.2 Diehl (*ad* 28c). Plutarch, *Platonic Questions* 2 thematises the question of why god must be maker *and* father, ostensibly supplying the conclusion that Vorwerk adopts – although, as I shall argue below, when Plutarch's views here are read in conjunction with his comments elsewhere it can be seen that this is only a first approximation of his full view.

That claim might come as a surprise. Conventional wisdom has it that Middle Platonists were just as focussed on the craftsman image as modern scholarship. Indeed, a contrast is regularly assumed between the Middle Platonist conception of the world as an artefact, and the 'biological' cosmic systems of both their predecessors in the Hellenistic Stoa, and their successors in the Platonist tradition, starting with Plotinus.[3] But I want to show that this is a mistake. I do not of course want to deny that Middle Platonists thought of the world as an artefact and something crafted: but I do want to affirm that they thought of it equally as a child and something engendered as well. On their view, these ways of thinking about the world are not alternatives – and, after all, Timaeus himself says that *both* obtain at once: god is maker *and* father. If it is a challenge of sorts to understand how both can obtain at once, I hope to show that it was a challenge Middle Platonists rose to and that, in doing so, they produced some of their most significant contributions to cosmology and metaphysics. Indeed, I shall argue that their answer to one of the most central questions of cosmology and metaphysics – how matter 'participates' in forms to take on cosmic order in light of their activity – depends on the way in which they deployed the metaphor of divine paternity in tandem with the model of craftsmanship. So it turns out to be every bit as important for Middle Platonists as it had been for the Stoics and would be for Neoplatonists to see the cosmos in biological terms – in their case, as an animal engendered by its father.

5.2   Begetting as a Distinct Mode of Making

Timaeus' claim that god is 'father' of the cosmos at 28e is not a one-off remark: the language of paternity and of 'engendering' (the verb he regularly uses is γεννᾶν) pervades the cosmogony of the *Timaeus*.[4] Nor does Timaeus make any effort to confine it to particular questions or topics. One might think, for example, that the 'craftsman' metaphor has a special claim to describe the role of paradigms in creation, and so to illuminate the crucial relationship between particulars and forms.[5] But the 'paradigm' to which god as craftsman looks in 28a is itself revealed at

---

[3] See especially O'Brien 2012; Michalewski 2014. Vorwerk 2010: 93 notes that Plotinus reserves the term 'father' strictly for the first hypostasis, and scrupulously avoids the phrase 'maker and father'.

[4] See e.g. 32c, 34a, b, 37c, 37a, d, 41a, 50d, 68e. To the explicit talk of generation (ἐγεννήθη), 48a adds language suggestive of intercourse (μεμειγμένη) and seduction (πείθειν) to describe the work of the demiurgic intellect.

[5] See for example the excellent discussion in O'Meara 2017, chapter 3.

30c-d to be a living creature – the most complete of all animals. What is more, the suggestion might be that it is identical with the maker himself, since we also told that the maker wishes his creation to be as much like *himself* as possible (29e3).[6] So even in sketching the role of the forms, what starts as a process of manufacture quickly becomes one of reproduction. To claim that the 'craftsman' image is somehow dominant in Timaeus' account, or is live in a way that the 'father' image is not, is simply false, at least as a report of how Timaeus structures his discourse.

But what, someone might ask, could the image of fathering possibly *add* to the image of crafting? One reason for thinking that the craftsmanship model has cognitive precedence in the explanatory economy of the *Timaeus* might be that it provides more detail and clarity than the image of fatherhood. And indeed, if one were to ask an ancient philosopher what it is that a father does to produce a child, they are as likely as anything else to say that he does something akin to what a craftsman does. Aristotle for example compares the male seed to a carpenter (τέκτων), who works with the material (ὕλη) it finds in the mother's womb (*GA* 1.22). But if the craftsmanship model helps us to think even about how fathering works, it seems right to give it precedence in guiding our philosophical understanding of Timaeus' cosmology. And indeed, it looks as if we find a Middle Platonist acknowledging just this. Plutarch, who devotes one of his *Platonic Questions* to the meaning of *Timaeus* 28c (Timaeus' claim that god is maker and father), says that begetting is not only analogous to 'making', it is in fact a species of 'making': 'For what is begotten has been made as well – but not vice versa' (*QPlat* 2, 1001A: ὡς γὰρ τὸ γεγεννημένον καὶ πεποίηται, οὐ μὴν ἀνάπαλιν, οὕτως ὁ γεννήσας καὶ πεποίηκεν). But on this account, if we have investigated thoroughly god's craft as 'maker', we have covered what he does as father *a fortiori*, at least as far as aetiology is concerned. There is, you might think, nothing more of any substance that we can learn.

But this goes by a little bit too quickly. For it might be true that fathering does not involve *types of cause* which are not more easily thought in the terms of the workshop, but that does not mean that the procedures of fathering are quite the same as the procedures of (ordinary) crafts. Imagine that carpentry, *were* in fact the means to make a child. Still, one would not expect the carpenter to approach that task as he might approach the task of making, say, a chair – or even some more complex, self-moving artefact such a theatrical automaton. One obvious and relevant difference

---

[6] I owe this point to Jonathan Griffiths.

is that the carpenter maintains unique creative responsibility for the chair
and the automaton, which he brings to completion himself. But it is
distinctive of a father that he does not 'complete' his child in the same
way. Rather, it is in the nature of fatherhood to give the child the capacities
to bring *itself* to completion – that is, to grow, develop and sustain itself.
If someone were to make a human being completely, in the way that a
carpenter makes a chair or an automaton completely, that person would be
a Frankenstein not a father. A child is a product of the father, and would
not exist without him; but in 'taking over' the making of itself from its
father, *this* product achieves ownership of itself, and agential and moral
independence from its parents.[7]

   This distinction is worth reflecting on, because one striking feature of
Timaeus' account is precisely his claim that god, at a very early stage, hands
over creative responsibility for the cosmos – and hands it over to agencies
which are part of the cosmos itself. This happens at *Timaeus* 41a-d; and
there is nothing discreet or subtle about the way it happens. It is trumpeted
to the reader in the form of an impressive speech by god himself (tr. after
Zeyl):

> 'O gods, works divine whose craftsman and father I am,[8] whatever has
> come to be by my hands cannot be undone but by my consent. . . . There
> remain still three kinds of mortal beings that have not yet been begotten;
> and as long as they have not come to be, the universe will be incomplete, for
> it will still lack within it all the kinds of living things it must have if it is to
> be sufficiently complete. But if these creatures came to be and came to share
> in life by my hand, they would rival the gods. It is you, then, who must turn
> yourselves to the task of fashioning these living things, as your nature
> allows. This will assure their mortality, and this whole universe will really
> be a whole. Imitate the power I used in causing you to be. And to the extent
> that it is fitting for them to possess something that shares our name of
> "immortal". . . . I shall begin by sowing that seed, and then hand it over to
> you. The rest of the task is yours.'

---

[7] Or, to think of this another way: it achieves agential equality with its father by becoming exactly the
sort of craftsman that he is – the sort that makes an animal (in this case, itself). I do not mean to
suggest, by the way, that there might not be other ways in which a 'completed' artefact could acquire
relevant forms of autonomy – precisely a question raised by *Frankenstein*, indeed. My point is only
that fathering, as a distinct form of production, guarantees it.

[8] That god is (craftsman and) father (δημιουργὸς πατήρ τε) of the created gods as well as of the
cosmos in which they are realised is of course no contradiction, especially if we think of the world
soul and created gods as features *of* the cosmos as a whole (and the only characterising features it has
at this stage), rather than alien infusions into it. See further below.

Someone looking to understand why the making of the cosmos is also a 'fathering' might easily start to find the explanation here. For just as in the case of fathering (but not, for example, the making of chairs) the producer hands over creative responsibility to his product at the earliest possible opportunity; and it is quite explicitly the created gods, not the maker, who bring the cosmos to 'completion' (from 'incompletion') – or, what it might not be too much of a stretch to translate as 'maturity' (from 'immaturity') (the words are τέλεος / ἀτελής). The model fits all the better if one is inclined to believe (as Middle Platonists unhesitatingly believed) that these created gods were as a collective identical with the world's soul, whose complex structure was described back in 34b–36d. This is not unreasonable: we know that at least some of the created gods are associated with heavenly bodies (40a–b), and the heavenly bodies are set in orbits which coincide with the circles which are constitutive of the world soul (see 38bff., esp. 38c and 40a). So it is a short step to supposing that the heavenly bodies and the movements associated with them are intended to realise in matter the complex formulae for the world's soul worked out in 34bff.[9] If you can be convinced of this, then the maker's commission in 41a–d is not simply to agencies which form part of the cosmos, it is to the living agency of the cosmos itself. The parallel with paternity is exact in this case: the father imbues previously unformed matter with a soul, which takes over the subsequent development of the animal as soon as it can. It is also important and obviously pertinent to the biological model that this soul (taking 'soul' now to be interchangeable with the created gods as a collective) is charged to act with exactly the same craft and creativity as that displayed by the maker in the first place: 'Imitate the power I use' he says (μιμούμενοι τὴν ἐμὴν δύναμιν, 41d). That the soul does so is something Timaeus makes a point of affirming subsequently (42e; 69c). Indeed, throughout the narrative describing the work of the created gods, the identical verbs of agency and craftsmanship that Timaeus had originally used for the work of the maker are now used of their work. We are very familiar with the fact that the divine maker is referred to as a 'demiurge' (28a): but they are 'demiurges' too (δημιουργοί: 75b; cf. 46e).

---

[9] This identification also makes sense from a mechanical perspective: if you think that the climatic conditions in the sublunary realm, the realm of 'nature' narrowly speaking, are affected and even determined by the approach and recession of the different stars and planets as they are carried around on their respective spheres, then you have immediately to hand the means to say (as for example Atticus so clearly does) that and how world soul governs nature. See Boys-Stones 2018: 217–18.

5.3   Transmission of Creative Agency in Middle Platonism

So far, I have only wanted to show that there is an opportunity in the *Timaeus* to find an explanation for Timaeus' language of divine fatherhood in the transmission of creative agency he posits from maker to product, and in the fact that this product is one capable (thanks to what the maker has already done) of 'completing' its own creation. What makes it seem clear to me that it was an opportunity embraced by Middle Platonists is their readiness – in stark contrast to anything one finds in the modern literature – to embrace the idea that there are in fact two distinct causal 'stages' operating in Timaeus' account: one identifying features of the cosmos for which the explanation is the direct and primary operation of the demiurge; another identifying features of the cosmos for which the explanation has to do with their causal operation in turn.[10] Take Plutarch, for example. His most important surviving work of cosmology deals, as its title indicates, not with the cosmos as such but with *The Procreation of the Soul in the Timaeus* – precisely on the premise that the defining act of creation was the production of an ordered world soul, which would subsequently go on to structure the rest of the cosmos. Plutarch's concern in this work is, in fact, to make the case that, unless one supposes that creation happened at a determinate time (something denied by many contemporary Platonists, who supposed the cosmos to be eternally pro-duced by its causes), it would be impossible to sustain the causal priority of soul with respect to the rest of cosmic order (*Procreation* 1013E-F):

> If the cosmos is ungenerated, there goes Plato's claim that the soul is prior to the body and starts off all change and movement from its position as leader and initiator, as he has said [cf. *Laws* 896e–897a].

We do not have the work entitled *How Does Matter Participate in the Forms?* (*Lamprias* 68); but the answer given in the completion of the title – *That it Produces the Primary Bodies* – is another clear signal that Plutarch understood there to be two relevant 'stages' to the process of creation. And since we know (not least from the *Procreation*) that soul, in its radical form, is an essential feature of matter for Plutarch, the first act of organising matter into the 'primary bodies' here, cannot but be the act by which order is brought to the soul as well. So the two stages implied by this title

---

[10]   I use the language of 'stages' to indicate the causal or metaphysical priority of one to the other (the effects due directly to the demiurge, in Plato's text, compared to those due to the work of the created gods). This allows, but is not meant to imply, a temporal sequence – although as we shall shortly see, Plutarch makes the case that the stages collapse if they are not temporally separated.

conform to (a) the creation of the world soul by god as described in the *Timaeus* (and explored in the *Procreation*) and (b) the subsequent work of that soul in developing the world to maturity. So if Plutarch says that fathering is a species of crafting (*Platonic Questions* 2, as quoted above), he does not after all mean that the former adds nothing to what can learn from the latter: on the contrary, his point will be that it is important to understanding *what kind of crafting* Timaeus has in mind: not just any sort of crafting (in particular, not the sort in which a craftsman completes the work himself); but *fathering*.

All this provides an explanation for the fact that Plutarch elsewhere can talk in what would otherwise seem paradoxical terms about the world soul doing the bidding of god but at the same time exercising creative agency of its own. For example, in the *Symposium of the Seven Sages* 163D-F (= 8C BS), soul is god's 'instrument' and acts by divine intention, even as it (the soul) 'accomplishes the most beautiful things' (τὰ κάλλιστα περαίνεται θεοῦ γνώμη). Apuleius says something very similar when he describes the soul as a generative agency (*virtute esse genetricem*), but at the same time avers that it 'serves the creator god and is on hand for all his plans' (*subservire etiam fabricatori deo et praesto esse ad omnia inventa eius*: *On Plato* 1.9 [199] = 8F BS).[11] Or again, consider Atticus, who is very clear that the whole realm of nature is within the immediate control of the soul, as well as the product of a creator god – to the extent that it comes to much the same thing for him if Aristotle fails to acknowledge a providential creator, and if he fails to acknowledge that 'nature' is really a 'soul', namely the world soul (fr. 8 des Places):

> Plato says that the *soul* puts everything in order, 'pervading everything'; that it is that which everyone else too can agree puts each thing in order; that nature is nothing other than soul. ... What ought to be work of rational, thinking soul, namely to 'make nothing in vain', this Aristotle attributes to nature. But he does not let nature a share in the word 'soul' [i.e. as Plato does].

On some accounts of the Middle Platonists, we ought to see it as a *tension* or even contradiction in them that the language of demiurgy is distributed

[11] Atticus fr. 8 quoted below shows how extensive he thinks is the creative work of the soul – as extensive as Aristotle's 'nature'; yet part of the wider context for this claim is to assert, against Aristotle, that the entire world, including everything made by soul, is also due to the providence of the primary deity (fr. 6; cf. frr. 12–13 for the identity of this demiurge with the form of the good).

between the demiurge and the world soul.[12] But to see it as a *tension* that
both the demiurge and the world soul are creators is to betray a prejudicial
commitment to the uninflected ideal of the workshop. I would, conversely, like to offer the very fact that Middle Platonists distribute the
language of demiurgy between the maker and the world soul as our
evidence that they had something else in mind. It is not a puzzle to be
solved that both maker and world soul create: it is an organic feature of
the 'biological' model which Middle Platonists were able to find in the
cosmogony of the *Timaeus*.

Clearly, an interpretation like this of what Timaeus tells us involves
exegetical choices which will not appeal to everyone. But it is worth
reflecting, finally, that it offers a close and philosophically construc-
tive reading of a significant passage (41a-d) which Plato's modern
readers effectively ignore altogether. For example, many recent commentators talk without embarrassment as if it is the maker himself
who performs the creative operations which the clear letter of the text
attributes to the subsequent planning and activity of the secondary
gods.[13] Those who do not go this far almost always describe the created
gods as if they are something like workshop assistants, there to serve the
master's designs and ends without personal investment in, or ownership
of, the outcome themselves.[14] (As if, then, the cosmos is (only) *for*

---

[12] Such accounts typically 'solve' the tension by moves whose very extremity might have cast doubt on
the reality of the problem – for example, when they deny that some Middle Platonists (including
Plutarch) believe in a pre-cosmic god who properly counts as a creator at all (Opsomer 2005;
Michalewski 2014).

[13] Of these, some elevate 'reason' to the status of a kind of superordinate agency for which maker and
created gods alike are merely the vehicles: see e.g. Strange 1985; Brisson 1995, 22. (So Brisson, since
the difference no longer matters to him, is happy, in fact happier, to make the *demiurge* the agent
responsible for the creative acts which Timaeus ascribes to the created gods: see e.g. 1995, 53; 2006:
12.) Others think that there is no handover because there is no maker distinct from the world soul in
the first place: see variously Archer-Hind 1888: 39–40; Grube 1935: 169–71; Cornford 1937: 34–9;
Cherniss 1944: 425–6 with 603–10 (Appendix II); also, more recently, Carone 2005.

[14] El Murr in this volume, for example, talks about the demiurge 'supervising' work which he
'delegates' to the lesser gods – but Timaeus does not talk at all about 'supervising', or of the sort
of delegation which would require it. (On the contrary, as we have already seen, he leaves the
created gods to their own work once he has made the handover: 'τὸ δὲ λοιπὸν ὑμεῖς', 41d.) Others
too talk about the created gods as 'assistants': e.g. Steel 2001: 113–14; Broadie 2012 (e.g. 18: 'The
ancillary demiurges are, as it were, extensions of him'); O'Meara 2017: 57. But this is also language
that Timaeus himself scrupulously avoids. (O'Meara 2017: 57 n. 56 appeals to ἀπεργάζεσθαι, 43a,
and ἐξεργάζεσθαι, 46e; but it is mindless causes, not the created gods, that are the subject of
ἐξεργάζεσθαι; and ἀπεργάζεσθαι is used frequently of the maker himself as well: e.g. 32b, 34a, 37c,
39e, 40a. Anyway, both words mean only that the agents see through the work at hand, not that
they do it *for* someone else.) I stress this point without of course wishing to deny that the created
gods *are also* doing things that the maker ordained (see 42e, 69c, 71b; Sedley 2007: 124 traces the
gods' invention of the eye to the maker's intention that there be sight). But the soul of any animal

the maker.)[15] But whatever the merits of this as exegetical gloss, it cannot be too strongly emphasised that this is exactly what it is – an exegetical gloss. Timaeus himself never describes the gods as 'assisting' the maker; they are given full creative autonomy in his description of them and are, as I noted above, consistently described as doing exactly what the maker himself was doing. (The language of assistance and service *is* to be found in Timaeus' account: but by contrast it is always and only used of the input of Necessity.)[16] The Middle Platonists might not be right; but they are truer to the text than most moderns are. And in the next sections I hope to show that they profit by it philosophically as well.

5.4   World Soul versus 'Aristotelian Form'

A reading of Plato's cosmogony which takes seriously the suggestion that the world is an animal, so seriously that it affects how we understand god's approach to making it, has its first great advantage in finding aetiological complementarity between the roles played by god and the world soul in creation. It shows that there is no tension to be resolved in the fact that god creates and the world soul creates as well: that is just how it is when we are dealing with animals. But there is more to be said than this: it finds a complementarity that is *well motivated*. By this I mean that Middle Platonists find in this model of cosmogony an elegant way to think about one of the central and most pressing issues in Platonic metaphysics: how it is that the paradigm forms come to be realised in a well-organised republic of potentially infinite particulars. The pitfalls here are legion, and well known. Not the least of them involves the question of how the divine maker is capable of operating at the level of unformed and chaotic matter so as to effect the realisation of the forms there at all. This is hard to square with the axiomatic principle of his unchanging eternity (required if he is to be a *grounding cause* for the world of becoming; Middle Platonists generally take him to be of the same ontological class as the forms, for example).

---

works to make the animal into the kind of mature specimen its father ordained it to be – although it would be eccentric in the extreme to say that it was merely 'assisting' the father in doing so.

[15] It is worth recalling that creation is described as a generous act on the part of the maker from the very beginning: 'He was good, and no jealousy about anything ever arises in the good' (29e). This would be at odds with the thought that the cosmos was created entirely for his own benefit, as an artefact typically is for the artisan. (Artisans may work for patrons, of course; but that is an extrinsic complication not envisaged by Timaeus' craftsman metaphor.) On the other hand, fathering might be considered a 'generous' act even if the father also benefits from having a child, just insofar as the child can be considered a beneficiary too.

[16] See e.g. 46de–e, 68e–69a with Strange 1985: 29.

We have seen that the narrowly 'artisanal' view of Middle Platonist cosmogony strives to see creation as a single process driven by a single creative agency. As a result, its answer, when faced with the question of how the gap between particulars and forms might be bridged, is to posit a whole class of intermediate entities – something like, perhaps very precisely like, Aristotelian forms: real but incorporeal essences, which *correspond* to the paradigm forms on the one hand, but are capable of being individuated by matter on the other. (There is for example just one species-form human, corresponding to the paradigm Human; in this matter here, it produces a particular human being, namely me; but it at the same time produces other human beings when it comes to be present in different matter.) The reason the move seems attractive is that it gives us something which the demiurge can make, something finite and immortal, yet something which at the same time can give determination to an unlimited number of individuals, beyond the horizon of what the demiurge can know. In fact, given that this is a solution to a problem which the same commentators see in Plato himself, it is often claimed as the defining and foundational move for Middle Platonism.[17]

There are, however, very serious problems with the attribution of this theory to Middle Platonists. The least of them is that it involves ascribing to Middle Platonists a very strained reading of Plato's text. For Plato seems clear that the demiurge recuses himself altogether from discussions about *how the species will turn out*. If our question is what it takes to be a 'human', for example, it is relevant that the whole morphology of the human body is due to the work of the created gods, whose deliberations on this score Timaeus describes at some length – from 69c (where we are reminded that they are 'imitating' god's creative agency) to 91d (which begins the briefer description of their work on the lower animals).

Worse still, there is no unambiguous appeal to 'Aristotelian forms' anywhere in our evidence for Middle Platonism. Occasionally, we see language that we might be inclined to read as language associated with forms of this kind, but nowhere at all do we see explanations or arguments that rely on our reading it this way.[18] Indeed, there are standard, unambiguous and repeated claims in our evidence for Middle Platonists which actually exclude the possibility of 'Aristotelian forms' playing a role in their metaphysics. For example, Middle Platonists insist that, while there is

---

[17] See Boys-Stones 2018: 234–5.
[18] A full discussion of relevant texts at Boys-Stones 2018: 234–5.

a one-to-one correspondence between the species and ('Platonic') forms, the forms are (multiply) instantiated *in individuals* – that is, in individual bodies and *not* in single species-forms. It is I myself, not the putative species-form inhabiting me (nor my soul, if that is different), which imitates the form Human.[19]

Finally, and most seriously of all from a purely philosophical point of view, it is very unclear that Platonist metaphysics gives us anything for 'Aristotelian forms' *to be*. On the face of it, Platonists have nothing to work with at the outset except matter and (paradigm) forms: but 'Aristotelian' forms cannot be either of these, not least because their job is to mediate between the two of them. Nor, for the same reason, can they be some combination of both. The product of paradigm forms acting on matter is body; but 'Aristotelian form' would need to be prior to body, because (always on the hypothesis) it is what gives the body determination.

'Aristotelian forms' in fact turn out to be nothing more than modern speculation about what Middle Platonists needed as a 'fix' for their ontology. But remember that the need for such a fix is premised on the view that Middle Platonists subscribed to the unmodulated, one-stage 'craftsmanship' model of cosmogony – a model which the denies the creative agency of the world soul as something distinct from that of its father. As soon as creative agency (and individuality) is allowed to the world soul, the world soul *itself* is available to mediate between the eternal realm of god with the forms, and the realm of nature over which it presides. It is the world soul which is engendered in matter by the eternal (and paternal) activity of god and paradigm forms, and the world soul which thereby has a real immanent presence in matter which allows it to take over its father's work as it causes the cosmos to grow to maturity / completion. The world soul is already there to do exactly the work that motivated the hypothesis of 'Aristotelian forms'. Plutarch for one is explicit in describing the world soul acting in this role, translating its understanding of the forms into the determining characteristics of the mortal species at *Procreation* 1024C:[20]

---

[19] See for example Alcinous, *Did.* 12.1, p. 167.5–7 (= 5F BS), where a ('paradigm') form is 'cause and principle of each individual thing being the sort of thing that the form itself is': τῆς ἰδέας οὔσης αἰτίας <καὶ> ἀρχῆς τοῦ εἶναι ἕκαστον τοιοῦτον οἷον αὐτὴ ὑπάρχει.

[20] Alcinous, *Didaskalikos* 14.3 (= 8A[3] BS) is probably best read in this light: the soul is first 'roused' within matter by god then, by being intent on the paradigms, 'receives' (i.e. conceives?) the 'forms and shapes' by which, presumably, it will go on to articulate the material world.

> [What Plato calls] the 'becoming' of the cosmos, when it had not yet
> become, is nothing other than the substance which is in [its] transformations
> and changes, [a substance] positioned between the impressor [sc. form]
> and the impressed [sc. matter], which transmits to the latter images derived
> from the former (γένεσιν δὲ τοῦ κόσμου μήπω γεγονότος οὐδεμίαν
> ἄλλην ἢ τὴν ἐν μεταβολαῖς καὶ κινήσεσιν οὐσίαν, τοῦ τυποῦντος καὶ
> τοῦ τυπουμένου μεταξὺ τεταγμένην, διαδιδοῦσαν ἐνταῦθα τὰς ἐκεῖθεν
> εἰκόνας).

The 'substance' Plutarch mentions here is the soul: and it is the soul whose
position – at once ontologically and epistemologically intermediate between
forms and matter (able to contemplate forms while effecting particulars, as
Plutarch says at *Procreation* 1025E) gives it the unique perspective needed
to complete the 'portrait' of the forms in matter which was the motivation
behind the father's originating act of creation.

I have enlarged elsewhere on how, exactly, the world soul is taken to go
about this task (Boys-Stones 2018: 231–4). In brief, what I have supposed
is that it aims to create a patterning of empirical qualities through the
sublunary realm which is isomorphic with its understanding of the forms
as a system. Something of this sort needs to be said because, although our
texts assert a correspondence between forms and natural species – as in the
passage from Alcinous that I quoted above – there is no real scope for a
form on its own (if such a thing can in fact be conceived) to set the pattern
for any natural species (again, considered independently of the ecosystem
as a whole). The reason for this is that the members of natural species (a)
are realised in empirical qualities which have no paradigmatic correlates in
the realm of forms in Middle Platonist thought (colours, textures and so
on), and (b) have the properties and features that they have with a view in
almost every single case to the environment in which they have to live. So
the world soul cannot create species *seriatim*, but only as parts of its design
for an entire ecosystem. If this is right, then we can see once again why the
natural order depends on an immanent intelligence – one that can conceive nature holistically and in relation to the forms; why 'Aristotelian'
forms' would be inadequate to perform such a role instead; and why no
explanatory room is left for the postulation of ('Aristotelian') forms once
one recognises the presence and activity of the world soul. What matters,
in short, is that the shaping and sustenance of the internal order of the
cosmos is due very directly to its soul – not because the soul is the ultimate
creator (it in turn is engendered through craft-like techniques by the
maker), but because what is created is an animal, and that is how animals
grow and sustain themselves.

5.5 Intelligence to Make the World Better

A further exegetical advantage to this emphasis on the world's growth (self-creation) as an animal begotten by god is worth noting. The reason, in the *Timaeus*, that we started to think about world soul at all is that Timaeus thinks that any whole thing in the visible realm will be 'more beautiful' (κάλλιον, 30b2) if it is intelligent; since the world is to be as beautiful as possible, the world must be intelligent – and soul is a condition for intelligence. This is normally taken as a straightforward, if stipulative, claim that intelligent things are more beautiful, or are better, than other things, *merely in virtue of their being intelligent.*[21] But one way of taking the claim might be to consider that intelligent beings[22] are more beautiful *because they can use their intelligence to make themselves more beautiful.* It is not implausible to suggest, for example, that intelligent beings will see to it that they maintain themselves in better order than non-intelligent beings are capable of doing. In this case, the beauty that Timaeus thinks they will excel in is beauty in a perfectly ordinary sense of the word, and there is nothing strange or stipulative about the claim. There is some support for this suggestion in what follows very shortly after 30b. For we are told that completeness is, at the very least, a necessary condition of beauty (ἀτελεῖ γὰρ ἐοικὸς οὐδέν ποτ' ἂν γένοιτο καλόν, 30c); but we have already seen that the world will be 'complete' only if it makes *for itself* and *by a creative intelligence like that of the maker*, the natural species within it (41a-d as quoted above). So here we are clearly told that the cosmos is more beautiful for being intelligent, but only for the mundane reason that it uses that intelligence to exercise creative care over itself and improve (complete) its physical structure.

Anyway, we know that, for Middle Platonists, at least, the world soul is not involved in purely 'contemplative' activity: in fact it is a model for us of how one can, and must combine the contemplative and practical lives (Plutarch, *Procreation* 1025E–1026A):

> The soul is at once contemplative and practical: it contemplates universals, and effects particular things, apparently having intellection of the former and perception of the latter.

---

[21] Cf. Sattler in this volume, p. 32 with n. 10. Salles, also in this volume, offers a slightly different answer to the same question for the Stoics.

[22] At least, intelligent beings within the empirical sphere, which is the domain Plato specifies here: ἐκ τῶν κατὰ φύσιν ὁρατῶν, 30b1. This is relevant to my claim, because it is more obviously open to embodied intelligent beings to make themselves more or less beautiful in a conventional sense – namely by acting in ways which affect their physical appearance.

This only makes sense as a claim if it is doing more than administering a system worked out already by the maker. It is, as his child, creating that system as well.

5.6   Conclusion

One could probably construct something functionally very similar to a Platonist system by appealing *only* to a model of divine craftsmanship, a model which avoided any talk of the cosmos as a living being, or of god as its father. But Atticus' attacks on Aristotle (as I touched on them above) suggest that such a model would lack the channels for providence to reach 'all the way down' to individual creatures within the cosmos – and ultimately would erode the grounding for value in the sublunary realm.[23] Plato's introduction of a world soul – *in addition to the maker* – was the way in which god's providence could be preserved and transmitted into every corner of creation. But it brings with it a reconceptualisation of the cosmos and of the means by which it was created. Contrary to most modern scholarship, I have argued that the Middle Platonists did not try to flatten out Plato's story into a purely 'artisanal' account of creation – a view of Middle Platonism which ought to have seemed suspect as soon as it required us to posit, in the face of all the evidence we have, that they also believed in 'Aristotelian' forms to mediate between paradigm forms and their particulars. On the contrary, Middle Platonists took the biological account of the cosmos very seriously, and understood the two-stage account of creation in its light, as exactly the sort of account one would have to give of the (pro)creation of an animal. This is significant for their physics and metaphysics as well, because once the role of the world soul is established on this model, it becomes available to mediate paradigm forms into the patterns of nature.

---

[23] See Boys-Stones 2016 and 2018: 325–6.

APPENDIX

The World Soul: Nutritive and Rational

It is an entailment of the general view that I have set out in this chapter that the soul is properly immanent in the material of the cosmos: it is not a separate substance infused, Frankenstein-like, into a cosmic body fully prepared by the maker, but is, to put it at its simplest, something realised in the movements of the heavenly bodies. (As with 'Aristotelian forms', the question of what else there is for the world soul to be would force itself upon us if we were to think otherwise.)[24] This would be why, as Proclus tells us, many earlier Platonist accounts of soul were explicitly mathematical: for the soul amounts to the description (or, better perhaps, the prescription) for what these movements must be.[25] In the course of the chapter, I have noted some advantages of a view such as this; but one might also worry that it compromises rather than supports the general position that the cosmos is an animal in the way that Platonists normally think about animals. For in discussing animals, Platonists are in general committed to the transmigration of the soul. But in this case, souls are separable from the body. It is true of course that the cosmic soul lacks both the need and the opportunity for transmigration; but if its soul is not even in principle separable from its body, is the cosmos to that extent less like the animals of the sublunary sphere?[26]

[24] Explaining the substance of the soul is a problem for many commentators: Archer-Hind identifies soul as the forms, construed as immanent realities (which is of a piece with his denying the reality of the separate demiurge: cf. n. 13): see 1888: 44. Commentators more typically suppose that there exists the ontological space between being and becoming for some 'intermediate' substance (e.g. Cornford 1937: 63): but I for one have a hard time conceptualising this space. Johansen stipulates without further justification a 'soul stuff' which is extended but not corporeal (2004: 140–42).

[25] When Middle Platonist accounts of the soul were not 'mathematical', they were what Proclus calls 'physical', that is to say, they described soul as some intrinsic property of matter (Plutarch was of this view) – and so, once again, immanent in the physical cosmos. See Proclus, *On the Timaeus* ii. 153.17–154.1 = 8L BS with Boys-Stones 2018, chapter 8.

[26] Another way of putting this worry might be to consider Sattler's claim in Chapter 2 of this volume that 'the World Soul is in fact more of a World *Nous*'. But Plato argues precisely that, in order to have *nous*, the cosmos must also have *soul* (30b)'.

In fact, quite the contrary is the case: this worry only arises at all if one precisely fails to appreciate quite how seriously Platonists take the thought that the world is an animal. For the worry arises only if one imagines that the world soul is to the world what the 'higher', rational soul of sublunary animals is to the animal. This is a natural thought because of course the world soul is in fact intelligent, and the model for the intelligence of individual rational souls. But one of the lessons we should have learned from seeing that the 'two-stage' creation is based on a biological model of making by begetting is that its *function* in respect of the world's body is more properly compared to the function that the 'nutritive' soul of an animal has for the animal. It is the soul responsible for sustaining the basic organic structures of the creature. For what the world soul does is what the animal soul first implanted in matter by the father does: to see to the animal's growth and development. But the nutritive soul is not a soul that anyone will think can transmigrate, or which is in any sense, other than the purely analytical, separable from its body.

Is it a relevant difference, then, between the cosmos and others animals that its nutritive soul is rational, while theirs is not? Yes and no. The cosmos is certainly a unique sort of animal, just because, unlike the animals of the sublunary realm, its soul is capable of maintaining the integrity of its body forever. There is then no *need* to distinguish a second soul which can be the vehicle for intellect in the way that becomes necessary for a situation where bodies decay (despite the best efforts of the nutritive souls), but minds are still required to live on.

But note too that it is not strictly accurate to say without further qualification that our nutritive souls are non-rational, and in some way different from the world soul. In fact they *are* the world soul, and a manifestation of its rationality – even if they are not capable of giving rationality to the individual animal whose nutritive souls they are. This is something Galen learned – rather to his disgust (*On the Formation of Foetuses* 700.17–701.6 = 8H BS):[27]

> One of my Platonist teachers said that the soul which is stretched through the whole cosmos forms embryos. I thought that the skill and power was worthy of it, but I could not bear to think that scorpions and spiders, flies and mosquitoes, vipers and parasitic worms were all formed by it; I thought an opinion like that came close to blasphemy.

Galen might not have liked the idea; but there is no suggestion that this was an unorthodox view for a Platonist of the period.

---

[27] For Galen's views on creation – and his distance from mainstream Platonism on this score – see Frede 2003, esp. 75–6. As in matters of soul more widely, this is probably a question on which later Platonists would disagree with their predecessors: see e.g. Wilberding 2017: 68–71.

CHAPTER 6

The De Motu Animalium *on the Movement of the Heavens*

John M. Cooper

The organizing topic of *On the Movement of Animals* is the nature and explanation of the self-locomotion of animals – an animal's movement of itself from place to place, for example, by walking or swimming or flying.[1] The treatise's ambition is to consider, and to provide a single unitary explanatory account for, all these movements taken together, as done by animals of *whatever* species – an account that covers and explains them all in a single, unified theory. In retrospect, at the beginning of the last chapter of the treatise, Aristotle refers to the movements in questio\n as the animals' "voluntary" movements, though he does not used the term *voluntary* or its derivatives even once previously in the treatise.[2] In general, the *De Motu Animalium* (*DMA*) aims to avoid going into differential details of the theory's application to the different animal species – those going from place to place in water, on land, or in the air. However, from the beginning, as his examples show, Aristotle is clearly focusing on the specific case of human animals, and, as for example in his discussion of

---

[1] We see this from the opening lines of chapter 1. However, Aristotle quite naturally includes within the scope of his enterprise in the treatise not only to explain the causes of the movement of, for example, the legs involved in walking (i.e., in moving the whole animal to a new place) but also the movement of other limbs, such as arms or head, in executing other tasks, ones undertaken while the animal as a whole stays put. Exactly the same causal principles are involved in both types of case, Aristotle thinks.

[2] See *tas hekousious kinēseis*, chapter 11, 703b3, contrasted explicitly with certain *akousious* or "countervoluntary" movements, and also with a large group of others that are at any rate *not* voluntary (*ouch hekousious*). These latter two groups are also in fact movements in place or locomotions taking place within the animal's body; some of them are movements of bodily parts other than those for locomotion, and in fact they are *self*-locomotions (ones that the animal itself causes), though Aristotle usually leaves that qualification implicit. One should note that the voluntary local movements that Aristotle is primarily concerned to explain are not to be identified simply as all and only the voluntary *actions* or doings of an animal: in fact, they include both the involuntary and the countervoluntary actions, as well as the voluntary ones. When an animal does something involuntarily or countervoluntarily out of ignorance or under force, its self-movements in doing it are caused by the same sort of combination of thought and desire that, on Aristotle's analysis in the treatise, are the ultimate and principal cause of its *voluntary* actions. (On this analysis, see my paper on the first part of *DMA* chapter 7 (down to 701b1): Cooper 2020.)

the "practical syllogism" in *DMA* 7 (701a28–b1), he does sometimes discuss separately the theory's application to nonhuman animals (of whatever type) and to human ones (on this see my paper "The Role of Thought in Animal Voluntary Self-locomotion," in Rapp and Primavesi, eds., *Aristotle's* De Motu Animalium). Still, the explanatory account that he develops aims to explain animal self-locomotion within the broadest possible animal context.

Moreover, Aristotle situates these *animal* movements alongside and in causal relationship to all the other types of movements taking place in the physical world as a whole. For him, the physical world's most characteristic and distinctive feature is that its contents are constantly in movement in many, many different ways, and in order to understand animal self-locomotions, he thinks, we must grasp them in relationship to the other ones belonging to the whole system of nature: how do they fit in, in relation to those? Though his principal focus is on the causes of movements that lie within the individual animal, he looks outside too, as we see already in chapters 1–4 of the treatise, both to the immediately environing conditions that are required for, and that help to explain, animal self-locomotion (e.g., the outside "springboard" an animal has to use to get itself going), and all the way out to the circular movements of the whole cosmos (this is my main interest in this short chapter) and to their ultimate totally unmoved cause. That is, first of all, because the ultimate causes of animal self-locomotion include the circular movements of the heavens and their eternal unmoved causes.[3] Animals would not have the capacities for self-locomotion – these being crucial parts of their natures – that they have if not for the regular and orderly movements of the stars, the sun and the moon in constantly bringing them into and sustaining them in existence.

We see already in chapters 3–5 that Aristotle thinks that in order properly to grasp even all the *internal* causes of animal self-locomotion, which is the main topic of his treatise, we must examine the self-

---

[3] Aristotle also has occasion, as we see already in chapters 4 (700a21ff.) and 5, and can see further in chapter 11, to discuss the other self-movements of some land-animals including humans: the automatic movements of breathing, of the beating of their hearts, the processes of metabolism of their food and growth, and even such involuntary movements as coughs (see chapter 5, 700a 21–25), as well as both the movements and non-movements of being awake and thus open to sensory inputs, and sleeping, and self-alteration in qualities (as when one blushes in embarrassment), as well as involuntary self-initiated movements in place of parts of the body (when getting angry or sexually aroused, say). He even alludes to the movements in place of inanimate things, insofar as those movements are due to voluntary (or involuntary) animal self-movement. But all these are side-issues for Aristotle in *DMA*; they are pursued for the sake of the full and rich grasp of what is *special* about animal self-locomotion that attending to them enables.

locomotion of the heavens, and the dependence of that movement upon an external unmoved mover's action upon them, in close comparison with that of animals living on and around the earth. Attending to the vastly more impressive self-locomotion of the heavens and its dependence on an eternal, external, absolutely and completely unmoved, mover leads us to recognize the need for an external unmoved mover in the human and other animal case, too. *This* external mover is in addition to the internal articulation through a limb and joint as what the animal moves itself with and to the external "springboard" off which an animal pushes itself, discussed in chapters 1 and 2 of *DMA*, animals need an *external* object as a cause of their self-locomotion: as we eventually see in chapter 6, this is an external object of *desire* that moves the animal to self-locomotion by being desired by it. Thus both an internal and an external source of self-movement, *connected together*, are required for animal self-locomotion, in addition to the joints and limbs (and the external relatively stationary springboard) recognized in the first five chapters of the work.[4]

In the first chapter of the treatise, in its third sentence, Aristotle tells us, explicitly appealing to what appears and is usually taken to be *Physics* VIII, that he has shown elsewhere "that the origin (*archê*) of [all] the other movements is what moves itself, of which the origin is what is unmoved, and that the *first* thing that brings about movement is necessarily unmoved."[5] He says that those conclusions have already been established "when [in *Physics* VIII] we were investigating whether or not there is eternal (*aidion*) change, and if there is such a change, *which* change that one is." He goes on immediately to claim that "we ought to grasp this" (i.e., these facts, including which change is the eternal one) "not only conceptually and in general (*tōi logōi katholou*), but also in connection with particular cases, i.e., with perceptible things. It is in fact on account of (*dia*) the latter that we search on the basis of general concepts [or arguments] (*kata tous katholou logous*), and we think we ought to make the concepts [or arguments] harmonize with perceptible things." He then proceeds, "For it is evident, in fact, in the case of these things

---

[4] Here I follow Ursula Coope's and Benjamin Morison's analysis in their contributions to the *DMA* Symposium Aristotelicum volume (Coope 2020 and Morison 2020 both in Rapp and Primavesi 2020).

[5] In citing *DMA* I follow the revised text of Oliver Primavesi in the Symposium Aristotelicum vol. edited by himself and Christof Rapp (see n. 2 above). Though I have consulted the German translation by Klaus Corcilius printed alongside Primavesi's text in the version available to participants at the Symposium in Munich in July 2011, the English translation, which attempts to follow the order of the Greek wording, is my own.

[i.e., perceptibles] that it is impossible to be moved if nothing is at rest; to begin with [this is evident] among animals. For if ever any of their parts is in motion, some [other part] is at rest. That is why animals have joints." (He continues immediately, in the last three sentences of the chapter, 698a18–b7, to explain how the joints in an animal's limbs function to make possible its self-movement from place to place.)

Thus we see already in the very first chapter of the treatise that Aristotle holds that in order to understand adequately the causes of the self-movement of animals from place to place, it is necessary to grasp these movements in close comparison with the eternal daily and monthly movements in the heavens and their eternal causes. In fact, perhaps surprisingly, he claims here that his theoretical investigations (in *Physics* VIII, and, I take it, elsewhere too) into the causes of the heavenly movements are *for the sake of* understanding the self-locomotions of animals. Moreover, he claims that if one considers the self-locomotion of animals directly and on its own one can see that, just as theory shows for movements in the heavens, this requires, besides the movement of certain of animals' limbs (the ones for locomotion), that other of their internal parts, viz. their joints, should be kept at rest. And in the remainder of the chapter he goes on to establish exactly *how* the joints in the relevant limbs function to make animal self-locomotion possible. Already here we see that Aristotle holds that in the animal case, as with the heavens, the ultimate origin of the movement is something that moves itself, which in turn has the origin of its movement in something unmoved, so that in both cases, necessarily, the first thing that brings about the movement is something unmoved.

Now, we know from *Metaphysics* Lambda that Aristotle holds that this unmoved thing in the case of the heavens is the eternal self-thinking origin of being for all substances, both supra- and sublunary ones. This mover imparts movement first and directly to the living heavenly bodies (the stars, sun, moon and planets), though it is something altogether *outside* them and therefore no *part* of what it sets in motion. In chapter 4 of *DMA* (699b32–4) Aristotle raises for discussion the question (which was already posed at the beginning of chapter 3, 699a12–14), whether there must be "something unmoved and at rest outside what is moved, that is no part of it, or not? And is it necessary for this to hold true in that way also for the universe (*epi tou pantos*)?" This turns out to be quite a complicated question, especially in relation to the animal self-movers (see chapters 3–5); it is only finally answered in chapter 6, at 700b30ff., where Aristotle compares the Prime Mover's mode of action upon the heavens with an animal self-mover's pursuit of an external end desired by it. In the animal case, he says (700b25–8, "the good that brings about movement is of such a sort [viz., as to be an end of things done for the sake of something else], not any or everything that is fine," and he clarifies by adding (b28–9) that "one must lay it down that [in this connection] the apparent good occupies the position of the good, as does the pleasant, since it is an apparent good." (Aristotle elaborates on this in the first part of chapter 7, where he explains how in both the human and the nonrational animal cases thinking, in the form of a practical syllogism, is the ultimate cause of self-locomotion, more than is the desire for the pleasure or good aimed at in the action. (On this, see my contribution to the Symposium Aristotelicum vol., ed Rapp and Primavesi; see the ref. in fn. 2 above.) The movement of the living heavenly bodies, on the other hand, is "in one way similar to that of each individual animal, but in another way different: that is why [the animate heavenly bodies are] moved always, but the movement of animals has a limit (*peras*). The eternally fine and that which is truly and primarily good, and not good at one time but not at another, is too divine and too deserving of honor to be [what it is] in relation to anything else" (700b29–35).[6]

It will help if at this point we pause to consider the progress of Aristotle's argument in the first five chapters of the *DMA* as a whole. Benjamin Morison offers the following brief account,[7] which I believe is correct, and illuminating especially for our present concern, the interpretation of Aristotle's answer (in chapter 6, 700b30ff.) to his question about whether there must be something unmoved and at rest outside what is moved, that is no part of it, and whether it is necessary for this to hold true in the same way for the universe as it holds for animals. "The upshot of the argument [of chapters 3, 4, and 5] is that Aristotle makes us aware that the analysis of self-motion he gives in chapters 1 and 2 . . . fails to give a good analysis of the self-motion of the universe; specifically, it cannot find a place for the mover of the universe. Since that mover turns out to be immobile, outside the self-mover [the living heavenly bodies], and no part of it, that should alert us to the fact that we shall need to introduce in the case of animals too a mover which is immobile, and external to, and not part of, the animal. In both cases (the universe, animals) this external mover is the *orekton* [the object of desire]. . . . [T]he underlying argument

---

[6] When an *animal* moves itself, the good or apparent good it pursues is good or apparently good *for itself* (and maybe *only* for itself). This is the limit (*peras*) referred to in this passage.

[7] See his article, a commentary on chapters 4 and 5 of the treatise, in the Symposium Aristotelicum volume ed. by Rapp and Primavesi (n. 2).

of chapters 3 through 5 has been preparing us for the necessity of introducing that mover in order to account for the facts of self-motion," even the self-locomotion of ordinary animals.

I mentioned just above that in fact for Aristotle, as I explain in my Symposium Aristotelicum paper "The Role of Thought in Animal Self-locomotion," the ultimate source of movement in animals is not any desire, but the animal's *thought about* the object it desires, that that is something good (or pleasant) for it to have or experience. So, given the parallels Aristotle argues for between the two cases of self-movement, that of the universe and that of animals, we should expect some parallel thought to feature in Aristotle's account of the movement of the living heavenly bodies. In fact, we learn about this in *Metaphysics* Lambda (*Metaphysis* XII 6–10), probably written before *DMA*. There Aristotle sets out and argues for his definitive theory about the eternally unmoved mover of the heavenly bodies, holding that it functions as a mover by being the constant object of the desire of the stars and planets, which sets and sustains them in their seasonally varying movements in their orbits. We learn there that Aristotle posits a soul for each of the moved heavenly bodies (sun, moon, and the five planets recognized in ancient astronomy – Mercury, Venus, Mars, Jupiter, and Saturn – as well as one for each of the "fixed" stars). These souls cause the respective movements of their respective bodies, as viewed from the earth, by their desire to approximate[8] to the eternal life of

---

[8] Aristotle is very explicit in saying (repeatedly) in *Metaph.* XII 7–8 that the movements of the stars (the fixed ones and the sun, moon and planets) are brought about by *final* causation (see esp. 1072b1–4), and that in fact they occur because of a desire that each of them has, out of love (erōs) for the Prime Mover (see b3, *kinei hōs erōmenon*, where the Prime Mover is the subject of the verb κινεῖ), to move in a circle ceaselessly and continuously for all time, because that is the nearest it can come to the life that that being lives, and indeed just *is*. Traditionally, Aristotle has been reported as holding here that the heavenly spheres that carry the stars round in circles do so in an effort to "imitate" the life of the Prime Mover so far as possible, but Aristotle never in fact speaks in terms of imitation (an idea more at home in Platonic and Platonist metaphysics). This misinterpretation goes back all the way to the great third-century AD commentator Alexander of Aphrodisias, who adopts this Platonizing interpretation in two places in his *Aporiae kai Luseis (De Quaestionibus)* (i 1, p. 4, line 3, and i 25, p. 40, lines 17ff., in *CAG, Supplementum Aristotelicum*, vol. 2 pt. 2, ed. I. Bruns (Berlin, 1892). In reading Alexander's exegeses one must always take care to remember that he always interprets Aristotle from the point of view of the philosophical questions current at his own time. That very often, as here, makes his exegeses very anachronistic (see Frede 2017). It is important to bear in mind also that, although it is clear that Aristotle counts the Prime Mover, in the way I have explained, as a final cause of the heavenly bodies' movements, this does not all preclude it also as operating at the same time as a moving cause (an aition ōs hothen hē kinēsis for their movements. The two modes of causation are by no means incompatible as explanations of the same fact or event, on Aristotle's theory: he explains in *Physics* III 3 that there are several causes of the same thing, but not in the same *way* (the art of the sculptor and some bronze are both causes of a statue *qua* statue, and not *qua* anything else it might be, 195a5–8, but in two different ways of being a cause); and nothing in his theory prevents a single item from being a cause of the *same* thing in two different ways

the unmoved Prime Mover as most effectively they can, namely, by the continuous, unceasing, but seasonally varying, circular movements of their bodies. Each of these innumerable souls *thinks* (indeed *knows*) the Prime Mover and the life that it in fact just *is*, as the best, most fine and beautiful (*kalon*), thing that can be conceived, and so each of these souls desires, with a form of rational desire (*boulêsis*) natural to the rational soul that it is, to lead that life as closely as it can, because it recognizes that life as such a surpassingly good and splendid thing. Thus on Aristotle's analysis the stars, the sun, the moon and the planets (i.e., everything constituting the heavens), as indeed we have seen he says explicitly in *DMA*, are self-movers in the same basic way as terrestrial animals, viz. by the agency of their individual souls, which are the unmoved movers of their bodies. (The only difference is that heavenly bodies have *only* rational desires, not the mix of rational and nonrational ones that motivate the self-movements of the terrestrials.)

This is in sharp contrast to the corresponding analysis that runs through the Platonist tradition from Plato's *Timaeus* through Plotinus and his Neo-Platonist successors. For them, there is a single World Soul that resides in what they postulate as the outermost sphere that constitutes the surface of the word-animal's body: this soul moves that animal it in a circular motion around its center for reasons of its own. Aristotle himself explains why his own theory, with many many souls, not a single one, doing the moving of the heavens, is better than those of his predecessors, in the last chapter (chapter 10) of *Metaphysics* Lambda (see 1075a25ff.): it avoids the many impossible or paradoxical results that, as he points out there, face them; he

simultaneously. Professedly following a 1993 article of Sarah Broadie, Enrico Berti, in his contribution to the Symposium Aristotelicum on *Metaphysics Lambda* (Berti 2000), which took place in Oxford in 1996, mistakenly argues at great length, and against the manifest and explicit textual evidence cited above (and accepted as a central part of her own account by Broadie), that for Aristotle the Prime Mover does *not* produce the movement of the animate heavenly bodies by being an end for the movements that it imposes, simply by arguing that it moves them as an *efficient* cause of their movements. In fact, as I have said (and Broadie agrees; see n. 2, p. 377: le Premier Moteur dans Lambda semble être [cause] efficiente aussi bien que finale, et selon moi il l'est), it moves them, unproblematically, with *both* sorts of causation at once. (Nonetheless, I agree with Berti, against Broadie, that the Prime Mover's activity is "contemplative" in its essential nature, not "kinetic," but *thereby* also "kinetic.") Berti has several times more recently defended his interpretation against the Prime Mover's final causality, most recently in Berti 2012. As for the living celestial animals, and their difference in kind from the terrestrial animals we know so well in our daily experience, see Laks 2020 nn. 12 and 13. Laks refers there to *De caelo* II 2, 258a29 and II 12, 293a20f., as confirming that Aristotle does, as I have said, think that apparent self-motions of the "outer heaven" (as viewed from the earth) is in actual fact due to the self-movement of the individual stars and planets by their individual souls. He refers also to Fazzo 2012 for her detailed account of the differences in kind between the bodies of terrestrial and celestial animals (for her discussion of this difference as indicated in the *De Motu*, see Fazzo 2012: 208) explicitly mentions in this connection only Empedocles, Anaxagoras and the Platonists among his contemporaries (he apparently has in mind here both Speusippus and Xenocrates), but his reasons for rejecting Timaeus' account, and by implication and in advance the Neo-Platonists' view, are clear enough. His proliferation of self-movers and their souls is not at all profligate; by emphasizing the close similarity between the ways in which heavenly self-movers and terrestrial ones move themselves, Aristotle can explain what is necessarily (because of our distance from them) more obscure (to us), in the right way, through what is naturally less obscure (to us), even if what is more obscure to us is, in the order of nature, perfectly clear, and indeed can be seen even by us to be *much* clearer, *once* it *is* grasped by precisely this means – but *only* then. We know in our own case and in our easily conducted study of other terrestrial animals, how souls move their bodies; we can readily use that knowledge so as to grasp the mode of self-movement of the heavenly bodies, by analogy and extension.

As so often, it is a great pity that Plotinus and after him the other New-Platonists did not appreciate these great merits of Aristotle's theory (as they also did not appreciate the merits of Chrysippus'). They ought not to have felt they needed to pledge allegiance to the *Timaeus* theory of a world-animal with a special soul of its own to animate its body, however fascinating in its own terms their theory certainly is. Either Aristotle's or Chrysippus' theory is adequate as they stand.

CHAPTER 7

Biology and Cosmology in Aristotle

James G. Lennox

7.1 Introduction

"Biology" and "cosmology" are not Aristotle's words, and asking why they aren't is a good place to begin.[1] After all, they have respectable Greek roots, and Aristotle wrote a number of works that look at first glance like contributions to these sciences.

But it is important to realize that these works – *On the Parts of Animals* (*PA*), *On the Generation of Animals* (*GA*), *The History of Animals* (*HA*), *On the Movement of Animals* (*MA*), *On Animal Locomotion* (*IA*), and *De caelo* (*Cael.*) – are all contributions to Natural Science (*physikê epistêmê*). Aristotle goes to considerable lengths both to stress the distinctive nature of the study of animals in comparison to the study of the heaven; but he is also open to the ways in which the results of each inquiry may contribute to the other, and the bulk of this essay will be focused on two such contributions.

We will begin, however, with Aristotle's views about how these two contributions to the science of nature differ from one another – in particular on their respective limitations. Next, we will turn to an argument in *Cael.* II which explicitly depends on premises borrowed from Aristotle's study of animal locomotion, *De incessu animalium*. We will then examine an influence that flows in the other direction, where Aristotle appeals to patterns in the movements of the heavenly spheres to account for certain patterns in animal generation discussed at the close of *GA* IV. We will conclude by considering two passages in which Aristotle argues that biological reproduction allows perishable organisms to "participate in the eternal and divine," a goal achieved without qualification only by those

---

[1] For an exhaustive survey of the use of the concept "cosmos" (*kosmos*) in Aristotle and pseudo-Aristotelian texts, and how his understanding of nature and the eternality of the natural world affects that usage, see Johnson (2018).

natural bodies that move eternally in circles and are the focus of the first two books of *De caelo*.[2]

Before moving on, let me state explicitly the conclusion of the somewhat complicated argument that follows. Though *De caelo* and the zoological treatises listed above are contributions to the scientific investigation of nature, the objects they investigate and our epistemic access to them are very different; and Aristotle is, as we will see, sensitive to those differences and their consequences. Those differences account for the limited contributions that these two domains of investigation can make to each other.

7.2   Two Kinds of Natural Substances

The elegant encomium to the study of animals that opens *PA* I.5 begins with a fundamental distinction among natural beings and its epistemological consequences.

> Among the substantial beings constituted by nature, some are ungenerated and imperishable throughout all eternity, while others partake of generation and perishing. Yet it has turned out that our studies of the former, though they are valuable and divine, are fewer (for as regards both those things on the basis of which one would examine them and those things about them which we long to know, the perceptual phenomena are altogether few). We are, however, much better provided in relation to knowledge about the perishable plants and animals, because we live among them. For anyone wishing to labour sufficiently can grasp many things about each kind. Each study has its attractions. (644b22–31)

Aristotle is drawing a distinction *among* different kinds of natural beings, *not* between natural beings and something else. The heavenly bodies do not come to be and pass away, whereas the living things all around us (and we) do. Unlike Plato, Aristotle denies that the ordered universe was created. The heavenly bodies are eternal; however, they are material and partake of circular motion in virtue of the nature of that material.[3] Yet Aristotle thinks all the evidence points to them not changing in any other way. Whether the heavenly bodies are ensouled or not (Aristotle clearly thinks they are), the differences between earthbound perishable animals and plants and eternal heavenly bodies are profound.

---

[2] For a third, equally interesting, interaction between the study of animals and of the heavens, see the preceding chapter by John Cooper in this volume.

[3] And as we will see, also in virtue of their form, although Aristotle is open about the paucity of evidence he has on this score.

That ontological distinction has an important *epistemological* consequence. Those eternal heavenly bodies are, in virtue of their eternality,
and perhaps their natural motion being circular, of surpassing value, not
only in themselves but as objects of knowledge. In a lovely simile, Aristotle
compares study of them to the pleasure accompanying a brief glimpse of
a loved one (644b34–5). Nevertheless, from an epistemological perspective the stress is on how limited our observational access to them is, in
comparison to the animals and plants around us – the latter, he insists,
"take the prize in respect of scientific knowledge (*epistêmê*)" (645a1–2).
Moreover, the rest of this encomium makes the case that if one studies
living things *in the proper way*, then "the nature that crafted them likewise
provides extraordinary pleasures to those who are able to know their causes
and are by nature philosophers." (645a9–10)

Cael. too makes it clear from the start that this study of the heavens is a
natural inquiry.

> The science of nature appears, roughly speaking, to be mostly concerned
> with bodies and magnitudes, the affections and motions of these, and
> moreover their principles, as many as there are of such substantial beings.
> For of things constituted by nature, some are bodies and magnitudes, some
> have body and magnitude, and some are principles of things that have body
> and magnitude. (268a1–6)

Aristotle appears to be introducing the science of nature quite generally, by
identifying its subject matter – but that subject matter is characterized very
differently from the way it is identified in *Physics* I-II. Here the stress is on
magnitude in three dimensions, and the principles (*archai*) eventually
identified are not matter, form and privation (as in the *Physics*), but
principles of magnitude.[4]

Dimensions of magnitude are defined in terms of continuous divisibility
in length, breadth and depth, and a natural body is said to be *complete*
insofar as it has all three (*pasas tas diastaseis*, 268b6–7).[5] That is, *diastasis*
refers to precisely the same thing as the English word "dimension." We
will return to this concept in Section 7.5, when we consider Aristotle's

---

[4] For an excellent discussion of the difficulties posed by the introduction to *Cael.*, see Falcon 2016,
423–436, esp. 428–432. It is interesting to compare these comments about the objects of natural
science with the list of things that exist by nature that opens *Ph.* II.1.

[5] Plato, in the *Timaeus*, argues that the Demiurge chose the form of the sphere for the cosmos on
grounds that it is most complete and like itself (*Tim.* 33b-c); and introduces the three pairs of
directional dimensions at 43b-c, but in a manner essentially unconnected to Aristotle's. See Falcon
2005, 31–36; Johansen 2009, esp. 18–24.

discussion, in *Cael.* II, of whether the cosmos has a "right" and a "left," where *diastasis* appears to have a quite different meaning.

What can we take away from this opening paragraph? First, while *Cael.* has many interesting connections to astronomy, Aristotle is clearly introducing a *natural* scientific inquiry here, whereas he views astronomy as a (subordinate) *mathematical* science.[6] *Cael.* occasionally relies on results established by mathematical astronomy, but always distinguishes its inquiry from the contributions borrowed from astronomy.[7] Second, the principles of natural inquiry that are in focus here are the three dimensions of bodily magnitude, not the principles and causes articulated in *Physics* I-II.

7.3 Defining the Object(s) of Inquiry: *De caelo* I–II

The first clear reference in *Cael.* to the account of the science of nature in the *Physics* is in chapter 2:

> Concerning the nature of the entire universe (*tês toû pantos physeôs*), whether it is infinite in magnitude or its whole bulk is limited, this needs to be investigated later. We must now discuss the parts of the entire cosmos according to form (*kat'eidos*), making the following our starting point: all natural bodies and magnitudes we say to be, in virtue of themselves, capable of moving in place; for we say nature is a principle of motion in [natural bodies] themselves. (268b11–16)

Here Aristotle assumes as an established principle the definition of nature defended in *Ph.* II.1: "nature" refers to a source of change in natural things themselves. He then argues, based on the additional assumption that all simple locomotion is either toward, away from, or around "the center," that there must be a "primary" body whose natural motion is circular, a natural body which is eternal and partakes of no other kind of change (270b1–8), a result confirmed by observation (270b11–16). Though posterity will call it the "fifth" element or "quintessence" and name it aether, Aristotle tends to call it the *first* element and only once suggests borrowing the name aether for it from Anaxagoras (270b20–25).[8]

---

[6] See *Physics (Ph.)* II.2, 194a7–12; *Posterior Analytics (APo.)* I.7, 75b14–20; I.9, 76a22–25; I.13, 78b32–79a16; *Metaphysics (Metaph.)* M.3 1078a9–18. For discussion see Lennox 1985; McKirihan 1978, 1992; Distelzweig 2013. The subordinate mathematical sciences are, as he says in the *Ph.* passage just cited, the "more natural of the mathematical sciences."

[7] Cf. *Cael.* II.10, 291a29–32, 291b9–10; II.11, 291b21–3; II.14, 297a2–6, 298a15–20.

[8] Falcon 2005; he also mentions the fanciful etymology for this term in Plato's *Cratylus*, 410b.

The outer heaven and its fixed stars move by nature in a circle. Though he mentions that there are two "light" bodies that by nature move away from the center and two "heavy" ones that move toward it, he postpones discussion of them until Books III–IV and spends the first two books on those spheres that move by nature *around* a common center, that of the earth. In this chapter I cannot, even in outline, discuss the argument in its entirety.[9] What I propose to do, in light of this volume's theme, is to focus on one extended argument in *Cael.* II that depends heavily on premises Aristotle explicitly borrows from his study of animal locomotion.

But before turning to that task, I shall draw attention to a methodological consequence of the epistemic limitations highlighted in *PA* I.5, limitations which lie behind his appeal to his study of animal locomotion in *Cael.* II, to be discussed in Section 7.5.

7.4   Epistemic Limits on Cosmological Inquiry

A number of the problems Aristotle faces in *Cael.* II derive from the apparent fact that the motions of the sun, moon and observable planets are much more complex than that of the fixed stars: in addition to partaking in the diurnal cycle of the outermost sphere, they also revolve in an easterly direction at various angles, different and variable speeds and distances from the center, within the band of the zodiac.[10] Since all these spheres are postulated to be made of the same natural substance, Aristotle needs to explain why the outermost sphere revolves in one direction while the others in addition move in the opposite direction and in all these variable ways. But he is acutely aware of the constraints he faces in thinking clearly about this question:

> Since circular movement is not opposed to circular movement, we must investigate on what account there are many motions, even though we are attempting to make the inquiry from a great distance – distant not so much

---

[9] An excellent presentation of the ontology of *Cael.* and its relationship to the arguments for the necessity of eternal, divine, unmoved movers in *Ph.* VIII and *Metaph.* XII can be found in Broadie 2009, 230–241, in Anagnostopoulos 2009.

[10] For the purposes of this essay, it is only the movements of the sun and moon that are important. For clear accounts of Aristotle's understanding of the astronomical theories of Eudoxus and Callippus (as reported in *Metaph.* XII.8 and commented on by Simplicius in his commentary on *De caelo*), see Heath 1913, Lloyd 1970, Ross Vol. II 1922, 382–95.

in respect of location, but much more in respect of having perceptual awareness of far too few of the attributes that belong to these things. (*Cael.* II.3, 286a3–7)[11]

Physical distance is only a problem because to really deal with this issue it would help to have perceptual experience of the objects being investigated, in particular to differentiate the spheres revolving in different directions, and at different angles and velocities. As interesting as this comment is, what follows it is equally interesting, in that it reveals the sort of move Aristotle makes when he lacks a solid observational basis from which to work.

> The cause of these things must be grasped from the following (*enthende*):[12] each of the things for which there is a function (*ergon*) exists for the sake of its function (*heneka ergou*). But the activity (*energeia*) of a divinity is immortal; and this is eternal life. So it is necessary that eternal motion belong to the divine. And since the heaven is such (for it is a sort of divine body), on this account it has its circular body which by nature moves forever in a circle. (286a7–12)

The starting point of this argument is a premise anchored firmly in the teleology of artifacts and living things here on earth – things with functions exist for the sake of their functions. The connection between that premise and the next is clearer in Greek than in translation, since *energeia* (as far as we know an Aristotelian neologism) is both etymologically and conceptually rooted in the idea that entities are most fully what they are when they are actively engaged in performing their characteristic functions – *energeia*. Since it was established in Book I that the heaven was one, eternal and complete (see the summary in the opening paragraph of Book II, 283b26–284a12), it qualifies as a sort of divine body. But that body has as its function eternal motion, and therefore (by the first premise) must exist *for the sake of* that eternal motion. In the passage we are about to look at, in which he considers whether the concepts of right and left are applicable to the motions of the heavenly spheres, Aristotle explicitly borrows functionally defined concepts of direction from his inquiry into animal motion to aid in solving a cosmological problem.

[11] For passages with a similar tone and message, see *Cael.* II.5, 287b29–288a2, II.12, 291b24–31 and 292a14–22. I've argued elsewhere (Lennox 2009, 211–213) that he is willing to do somewhat speculative thinking in this domain in order to establish an alternative method in cosmology to the *a priori* mathematical approach found in Plato's *Timaeus* and in the Pythagoreans.
[12] I am tempted to translate "from this world" (see *Phaedo* 107e), since Aristotle is about to state a starting point that is grounded in his biological investigations, but understanding *enthende* in that way is not necessary for the point I am making.

7.5   Cosmology Borrowing from Zoology

As we saw earlier, *Cael.* opens by declaring that the science of nature appears most of all to be concerned with bodies, magnitudes, their affections and their changes, and with their first principles. Recall that dimension of magnitude is defined in terms of continuous divisibility, and a natural body is *complete* insofar as it has all three *dimensions* (*pasas tais diastêseis*, 268b6–7).[13] What is initially surprising about this way of specifying the science of nature is its stress on *magnitude* and its *dimensions*.[14]

Nevertheless, in *Cael.* I.2 he reminds his readers that this is a natural inquiry: "all natural bodies and magnitudes are, in virtue of themselves, capable of motion in place" (268b14–16); Aristotle thus stresses that this is a *natural* inquiry while simultaneously delimiting its scope.

This stress on dimensions of magnitude is an interesting example of the *domain specificity* of scientific inquiry for Aristotle. Dimensions of magnitude play a number of central roles in the study of the cosmos – in differentiating the motions of the spheres from those of the four elements; in using results from astronomy for cosmological purposes, and for the discussion we are going to focus on here: whether directional concepts such as right and left have application to cosmological motion. In particular, it is Aristotle's distinctive view that there is an intimate relationship between the concepts referring to spatial dimensionality and those referring to directionality.

At the beginning of the second book of the *Cael.*, not long after reviewing weaknesses in the arguments of those who deny that the heaven is eternal,[15] Aristotle asks whether the right and the left are among the principles appropriate to the current inquiry.

---

[13] This passage also includes [i] an endorsement of the Pythagorean dictum that "the all and everything are defined by threes"; [ii] a claim that we take the number three from nature and make use of it in worship of the gods; and [iii] a claim that the completeness of three is shown by the fact that the first time we say "all" (rather than "both") is when we refer to three items. For further discussion of the epistemological questions raised by the method and style of the *Cael.*, see Bolton 2009, and Falcon and Leunissen 2015.

[14] Interestingly, *Cat.* 6 (on quantity (πόσον)) does not mention magnitude (μέγεθος) while *Metaph.* Δ.13 immediately divides quantity into plurality (πλῆθος) and magnitude (μέγεθος) based on whether the quantity is countable or measurable and whether it is divisible into discontinuous or continuous parts (1020a7–11). Then, consistent with *Cael.* I.1, it goes on: "Of magnitudes those continuous in one dimension are lengths, in two breadths, in three depths. Of these, limited plurality is a number, [limited] length a line, breadth a surface, depth a body" (1020a11–14).

[15] *Cael.* I.1–4 argues that there is a "primary body" which is ungenerable and indestructible and whose natural motion is circular, out of which the heavenly bodies are constituted. (For an illuminating discussion of how unorthodox this move was and Aristotle's reasons for taking it, see Falcon 2005.) In chapters 5–7 Aristotle mounts an extended argument against the idea that the cosmos is infinite;

Since there are some, such as those called Pythagoreans (for this is one of
their statements), who claim there to be a certain right and left to the
heaven, one should investigate whether this is so in the way they claim, or
in some other way – if indeed one ought to apply these principles (*tautas tas
archas*) to the body of the whole cosmos. (284b6–10)

Aristotle raises two concerns here. The more fundamental one is
whether these principles are applicable to the heavens *at all*, and in a
moment we will see that this is a well-motivated question. Assuming they
are, the next question is whether they are applicable in the way suggested
by the Pythagoreans, or in some other way. Aristotle responds immediately
to both questions.

For first off, if right and left are present in something, then one should posit
(*hypolepteon*), prior yet to these, the prior principles (*tas proteras archas*) to
be present in it. Now a determination was made regarding these matters in
our studies of the movements of animals, on account of these principles
being proper (*oikeîa*) to the nature of animals; for at least in animals it is
readily apparent that *all* such parts (I mean, for example, right and left) are
present in some animals, *some* of them are present in some animals, while
only above and below are present in plants. (284b10–18)

For the purposes of this discussion I want to highlight two claims here:

[i]   These principles are proper, or appropriate – *oikeia* – to the nature
      of animals.
[ii] A determination about them was made in the discussions of animal
      movements (*en tois peri tas tôn zoon kinêseis*).[16]

At this point, Aristotle is noncommittal on the question of whether "right"
and "left" apply to the heaven at all, but he insists that, regardless of how
one answers *that* question, the Pythagoreans have made a *methodological*
mistake. Among these "directional" principles some are prior to others,
and in particular some are prior to "right" and "left." Thus, if the
Pythagoreans are committed to attributing right and left to the heaven,
they ought to speak of those prior principles first. And so he goes on:

And if it is necessary to apply any of these to the heaven, it would be
reasonable (*eulogon*) that *the one present first in animals be present in the
heaven*. For there are three, and each is a sort of principle. The three I am
talking about are the above and below, the front and its opposite, and the

---

in chapters 8 and 9 against there being more than one cosmos; and in chapters 10–12 against the
cosmos being generable or destructible.
[16] The phrase used for the subject of investigation, περὶ τὰς τῶν ζῴων κινήσεις, is the same as that
used in the first sentence of *MA* in reference to *IA*.

right and the left. For it is reasonable (*eulogon*) that all these dimensions (*diastaseis*) are present in complete bodies. And "above" is a principle of length, "right" a principle of width and "front" of depth. (284b18–25)

There are two appeals to what is "reasonable" (*eulogon*) here. The first encourages us to suppose that if one of these dimensional pairs is prior to the others in the case of *animals*, so should it be in the case of *the heaven*. The second appeals directly to the opening chapter of *Cael;* if directional orientations are the *principles* of the three dimensions of magnitude, and the cosmos is complete (i.e., three-dimensional),[17] these pairs of directional concepts must be fundamental in cosmology as well.[18]

Oddly, the same term – *diastaseis* – used earlier to refer to the three dimensions of magnitude is now being use to refer to the three pairs of *directional orientation*. Nor is this mere homonymy: the three pairs of directional dimensions are first said to be sorts of principles, and then one-half of each pair is identified as the *principle* (*archê*) of one of the three *bodily* dimensions – "above" of length, "right" of width and "front" of depth. To get a better understanding of what is going on here, we need to take Aristotle at his word, and turn to his inquiry into the causes of differences in animal locomotion.

IA 2, 704b11–705a2 is a quite general discussion of first principles commonly used in natural inquiry. He identifies three principles in particular:

[i] Nature does nothing in vain, but always does the best for the being of each kind of animal given the possibilities, such that if things are better in a certain way, that is the natural state of affairs. (704b15–18)

[ii] The six paired directional orientations – above and below, front and back, and right and left. (704b18–22)

[iii] The origins (*archai*)[19] of movements in place – pushing and pulling.[20] (704b22–4)

These are said to be presuppositions of natural investigation in language reminiscent of the *APo* – but they are said to be presuppositions of natural

---

[17] Recall *Cael.* I.1, 268a22–24. "...of magnitudes body alone [vs. line or plane] would be complete; for body alone is defined by the three dimensions, and this is all [the dimensions there are]."

[18] On Aristotle's use of the concept εὔλογος see Falcon and Leunissen 2015, 217–240 in Ebrey 2015; they are responding to Bolton 2009, 51–82 in Bowen and Wildberg 2009; see too Karbowski 2014, 25–38. A classic and still valuable discussion is LeBlond, 1938. Both uses in this passage support the view that a claim is εὔλογος if it is consistent with more fundamental or general conclusions Aristotle accepts.

[19] A good example of the ambiguity in the use of this term discussed in note 31, below.

[20] Referred to as the functions (τὰ ἔργα) of motion at *MA* 10. 703a19–20.

inquiry, not of demonstration.[21] Elsewhere,[22] I've argued that the first of the principles discussed here plays the role of a *hypothesis*, as discussed in *APo* I.2, 72a15–24, and I think this is the right way to understand these directional dimensions as well. Their use in our *Cael.* passage, however, suggests that another sense of "presupposition" (*hypothesis*) is also in play. Establishing these directional dimensions as *archai* belongs to the investigation of animal locomotion rather than the study of heavenly motion. The results of the discussion in *IA* are being *assumed* in the *Cael.*, but are to be properly defined and established as principles elsewhere.[23] That is precisely in accord with his introductory remarks in *IA* 2, where he says we are to assume them in studying *all* of nature's works, not only animals. That the defining of these principles is appropriate (*oikeia*) to the inquiry into animal locomotion does not rule out their application elsewhere.[24]

Of the three presuppositions of natural inquiry mentioned in *IA* 2, the second is presented in terms that are already familiar to us:

> Next it is necessary to grasp how many and what sorts of dimensions of magnitude (διαστάσεις τοῦ μεγέθους) belong to what kinds of things. For while the dimensions (διαστάσεις) are six, there are three pairs: first, above and below; second, front and back; and third, right and left. (704b18–22; cf. 705a26–9)

Note that the three pairs of *directional* dimensions are identified immediately after saying that it is necessary to grasp the number and kinds of dimensions of *magnitude*; the discussion is thus likely to shed light on how these two uses of *diastasis*, noted above (p. 117) are related.

The inquiry into directional dimensions is taken up in *IA* 4–5. Before looking at the details, it is helpful to keep in mind that these are pairs of contraries and that Aristotle's pairs of contraries are seldom "equals." Cold is the absence of heat (*GA* II.6, 743a36, *Meteor.* IV.8, 384b26–7); the female is female due to an incapacity, the male due to a capacity (*GA* I.20, 728a18–21). In general, *Ph.* I.7 refers to one contrary as a "privation" and the other as "form" (189b34–190a13).

This inegalitarianism holds for directional pairs as well: above is more honorable than below, front than back, and right than left (*IA* 5, 706b12–13).

[21] For similar language in a very similar context, see Plato, *Meno* 86e4–5, 87b2–5.
[22] Lennox 1997, 199–214 [repr. Lennox 2001b, 205–224].
[23] For an exact parallel, see the discussion of the organs that function both for excretion and generation at *PA* IV.10, 689a4–b1, and the note to this passage in Lennox 2001a, 323–4.
[24] On this point see Leunissen 2010, chapter 5.

The three directional *pairs* are *in a way* principles, but one member of each pair is *more* honorable, and thus "more a principle," than its opposite.

Of the three pairs of directional concepts, *only* right and left are *restricted* to locomotive animals, and thus the discussion in *IA* 4 and 5 devotes most attention to them. But the discussion begins by tying all three pairs of concepts immediately to living things:

> Although[25] the dimensions (διαστάσεις) by which animals are naturally bounded are six in number – above and below, front and back, and again right and left – *all* living things have the above and below part. For above and below are present not only in animals, but also in plants. It [vis. above and below] is delineated by function and not by position in relation to the earth and the heaven alone. For from whence the distribution of nourishment and growth comes in each of these things is "above," and the extremity toward which this extends is "below." The first is a sort of source (*archê tis*), the second a limit; and above is a source. (705a26–b1)

Aristotle's account of these directional dimensions makes most sense if we understand him as saying that a full delineation of above and below requires both a reference to function *and* to cosmic orientation. Note that he goes on to say that the above and below are positioned alike in plants and animals, and then qualifies this by saying that "relative to the whole [cosmos] they are not positioned alike, but relative to function they are" (705b4–5). But this claim is restricted to above and below – front, back, left and right are defined *entirely* by reference to function with no direct reference to cosmic orientation.[26] That distinctive feature of above and below may account for these being the *primary* directional pair of opposites.

Sense perception is the distinguishing feature of animal life[27] and thus front and back are defined by reference to the orientation and position of the sense organs. Finally, Aristotle argues that "right" and "left" are restricted in application to animals that "act on their own so as to change in respect of place" (705b14–16). Not only are these delineated by "a certain function," but they are *not* delineated by position (705b17–18). Locomotive organs come in pairs, and in all of these pairs one side must be the source of motion. After providing evidence that this side is the same for all such animals and is what is designated as "the right,"[28] Aristotle concludes:

---

[25] For a discussion of the complex syntax of this sentence, see Lennox 2009, 194n12.
[26] See *IA* 4, 705b8–13: "For all animals have perception and front and back are defined according to this."
[27] *PA* II.1, 647a21–4; 8, 653b19–27: *De an.* II.3, 414b1–10.
[28] The evidence is given at 705b31–706a10.

> And due to the same cause the right sides of all animals are the same; for the source of motion is in every case the same and positioned in the same place according to nature; and the right is the source of motion. (706a10–12)

For any two animals, if they are oriented in the same direction, they will *by nature* originate locomotion from the same side, a conclusion laden with normative implications: "the right is both better than the left and separated from it. And that is why the right in human beings is most right" (706a18–21). He then generalizes the argument to all of the directional orientations, concluding that the other sources, the above and front, are *also* most in accordance with nature in mankind (706a24–6).[29]

Chapter 5 applies this understanding of "above" and "front" to animals differentiated by reference to how many feet they have.

> So, then, those animals in which above and front are distinct (διώρισται), as they are in human beings and birds, are bipeds (of the four points,[30] two of them are wings in the one case and hands and arms in the other). But those that have the front and above in the same [orientation] are either four-footed, many-footed or footless. (706a26–31)

In bipeds, and especially in man (birds have a pelvic articulation that tips them forward slightly), functional above and below are "in relation to the whole cosmos" (*pros to tou holou*, 706b4), while those with four or many feet, as well as those with no feet, are not upright, and thus their "above" is on the same axis of orientation as their "front," and thus front and above are not (directionally) distinct (cf. 706b2–9). This chapter concludes with a statement I have already had reason to discuss – that it is reasonable (*eulogôs*) that the origins (*archai*) are from these parts because origins are honorable, and the above, front, and right are more honorable than the below, back and left (706b11–13).[31] That thought, however, is immediately followed by another:

> But about these matters, the reverse statement also has merit (*kalôs d'echei kai to anapalin*), that it is because the sources are in these places that these parts are more honorable than the opposing parts. (706b14–16)

---

[29] On the idea that the better of two related principles should, if possible, be separated from the worse see *GA* II.1, 732a3–8.

[30] Aristotle is explaining that, though blooded and therefore in possession of four limbs, two of them do not qualify as "feet." The very next lines explain that by foot he means a part that has a "point of contact" (σημεῖον) with the ground for movement in place.

[31] A clear example where Aristotle is using *archê* to mean both the starting point or source of motion (the first use) and to mean the first principle of a science (the second use).

There are two ways of establishing that parts located upward, in front and on the right are more honorable. One can start with a prior assumption that the *locations* are more honorable and conclude that the parts located there will thus be honorable; or you can start by assuming that the *parts with certain soul functions* are more honorable, and conclude that their locations are for that reason more honorable.[32] Aristotle does not think it is *wrong* to attribute greater honor to one of each of these directional oppositions; but he aims to ground such attributions on a prior determination of the location of biological functions. As in our *Cael.* II.2 passage, Aristotle is presenting an inductively grounded alternative to the Pythagorean approach, and perhaps Platonists of a Pythagorean hue.

Finally, *IA* 6–7 (706b17–707a22) argue that there must be a common source of control over locomotion continuous with the locomotive parts, and that these parts will be distinguished by being on the right or the left and (when there are at least four parts) by being above or below. He rejects as irrelevant to locomotion the distinction between front and back on grounds that there is no natural backward motion (706b28–32).

It is now time to see how this inquiry into these concepts in its "appropriate" place, the study of animal locomotion, bears on the discussion of the motions of the heavenly spheres in *Cael.* II. That will be facilitated by a summary of the conclusions reached in *IA*.

1. First and foremost it is clear that the appropriate place to investigate these dimensions is indeed, as he said in *Cael.* II.2, in the study of animal locomotion. It is there that Aristotle defines them, *argues that they are origins or "starting points"* and makes the case for priority both *among* the pairs, and of one-half of each pair over the other.

2. Directionality is defined by reference to biological function, and two of the three pairs are defined by reference to animal locomotion.

3. "Above" and "below" can be applied both by reference to organic function *and* by reference to position relative to earth and heaven.

4. Only with respect to bipeds, and most completely with respect to humans, is there agreement between the results of applying cosmic or functional concepts of "above" and "below."

5. Right and left are concepts applicable *only* in the case of locomotive self-movers.

6. Right and left are delineated *only* by function.

---

[32] Lennox 1985, 143–64 [repr. in Lennox 2001b, 259–79] discusses this passage in relation to *PA* III.3, 665a9–21, Theophrastus *Metaphysics* 11a8–13, and Plato *Timaeus* 45a-b.

7.   All natural locomotion is forward, not backward.
8.   In all three pairs, one member of the pair is more of a "source" or "principle," and more honorable, than the other – in the case of right and left, it is the right.

The reference to *IA* in *Cael.* II.2 comes while it is still an open question whether "right" and "left" have any legitimate use is cosmology. Whether the answer be yes or no, an appropriate first step is to appeal to a worked out theory of these directional principles, to see what, if anything, is applicable to the inquiry into the movements of the heavenly spheres. This is the basis of the criticism of the Pythagorean methodology on the table – they have applied the concepts "right" and "left" to the cosmos independently from the other two pairs of directional principles. Aristotle appeals to *IA* specifically to defend a norm for their application: there are directional concepts *prior* to "right" and "left," so that unless it is appropriate to apply these prior principles to the heavens, it cannot be legitimate to apply "right" and "left."

> For this reason one might well wonder that the Pythagoreans spoke of only two of these principles, the right and left, leaving aside four that are no less important; for above and front are no less differentiated from below and back than right is from left in all animals. *I say "in all animals" because in some cases these directional principles differ by functional capacity only, while in other cases they also differ by their configuration, and while above and below are present alike in all the ensouled animals and plants, right and left are not present in plants.* And again, as length is prior to breadth, if above is the principle of length and right of breadth, and the principle of what is prior is prior, above would be prior to right – prior in generation, that is, since "prior" is said in many ways. (285a10–22; emphasis added)

Aristotle here follows the *IA* discussion in every detail. He begins by noting the difference between above and below and the other directional principles, that only they can be defined *both* functionally *and* spatially, and notes that they are the only pair that apply to all living things and not only animals, specifically noting that right and left have no application to plants. Not only is this passage tied directly to *IA*, however. He also refers back to the three dimensions of magnitude with which *Cael.* I.1 opens, first reminding us of the priority of *length to breadth*, and then invoking the idea, defended in *IA* 4, that "above" is *the principle of length* and "right" is *the principle of breadth*, in order to argue that above is the *prior* principle – thus underscoring the error of the Pythagoreans.

Why does Aristotle insist that these concepts are required for cosmological inquiry? The answer lies in the facts, established by astronomical investigation, that to account for the motions of the planets, sun and moon, one must suppose that while they partake in the diurnal movement of the outermost sphere of the fixed stars, they each have their own independent motions in the opposing direction. That he recognizes the problems in extending these concepts, appropriate to the study of animal motion, to the heavens is most obvious in the following attempt to justify this extension:

> But since we determined previously that such powers are present in things having a source of motion, and that the heaven is ensouled and has a source of motion, it is clear that it also has the above and below and the right and left. For it is not necessary to puzzle on account of the shape of the whole being spherical, how the one part will be right and the other left though its parts are all alike and always moving. It is necessary to suppose it is just as if it is one of those things in which the right differs from the left in shape, yet is enclosed in a sphere – it will still have the differing powers, but it will seem not to on account of the uniformity of its shape. (*Cael.* II.2, 285a27–b5)[33]

This is a very odd thought experiment Aristotle is inviting us to take part in, but what is clear from it is that it is the assumption that the outermost heaven is an ensouled mover moving in one direction only that sanctions the application of these concepts here. As Judson puts it, without the spherical body being ensouled "its [elemental] nature would make it move in a circle, but . . . there would be no explanation of the particular direction in which it happened to rotate" (Judson 1994, 161). Aristotle poses this very question in *Cael.* II.5 in the process of introducing an argument for the priority of the movement of the outermost sphere to the movements of those below it (287b22–288a12). From the standpoint of the impact of the arguments in *IA* 2–6 on this discussion, it is to be noted that this argument not only invokes the superiority of right to left and above to below, but argues for the outermost sphere rotating to the right by postulating that "Nature always produces the best among the possibilities" (288a3–5). The ordering of those principles of inquiry in *IA* 2 may well have been designed for extension to inquiries outside the narrow scope of animal locomotion.[34]

I conclude this discussion of the background in *IA* of the argument in *Cael.* II with three methodological points. First, we are not here discussing the dependence of cosmological demonstrations upon premises that are

[33] For further discussion of this passage see Judson 1994, 159.   [34] See Leunissen 2009, 245–71.

only appropriate to zoological demonstration. Aristotle's purpose here is *to establish the norms of inquiry* into *whether* and *how* these directional principles should be applied to the cosmos. And given that these directional pairs are *archai* of the three dimensions of magnitude, and given the centrality of complete (i.e., three-dimensional) magnitude to *Cael.*, there is a strong presumption *in favor of* their application.

Second, the fact that Aristotle appeals to the *IA* theory does not commit him to the claim that the *entire* theory of *IA* is relevant here, anymore than a person studying optics is committed to the claim that *all* of geometry is relevant to optical investigation.

Third, Aristotle's claim that the appropriate place to define these principles is in the works on animal locomotion should not blind us to the fact that there is an important dependence that runs in the other direction. The orientation of animals with respect to cosmic above and below is a central feature of the discussion in *IA* 2–6. Above and below are *prior* to right and left, and the most *natural* arrangement for *functionally* defined above and below is in alignment with *cosmically* defined above and below. So while *Cael.* II.2 appeals to, and depends heavily upon, the discussion of directional dimensionality in *IA* 2–6, the latter discussion also explicitly depends on a concept of cosmic above and below that derives from Aristotle's general understanding of the cosmos taken as a whole.

7.6   GA IV.10 and Solar Inclination

"A human being and the sun begets a human being."[35] So Aristotle claims in concluding *Ph.* II.2 (194b13). He often reminds us that "a human being reproduces a human being," typically in discussions of the role of form in explaining generation, and introduced by the connective "for."[36] But only here does he claim that the sun is also involved. Here is the phrase in context:

---

[35] A valuable paper by Devin Henry (Henry 2015, 100–118) forced me to rethink many of the issues I discuss in this section. Where I end up in disagreement with him I will note as I proceed. In addition, A. L. Peck's Loeb edition of *GA* has a lengthy appendix that discusses the context for this passage provided by texts in *Metaph.* Λ, *Ph.* IV and VIII, *Meteor.* I, *Cael.*, and *GC* II, and while I occasionally disagree with his interpretation of some of these passages and their significance, it is a valuable tool for the reader.

[36] A partial list: *Ph.* II.1, 193b12; II.7, 198a26–7; *PA* I.1, 640a25; *Metaph.* Z.7, 1032a25; Z.8, 1033b33.

Up to what point ought the natural scientist know the form and the what-it-is? Would it be just as a doctor [ought to know the form and what-it-is] with respect to sinew or a smith with respect to bronze, to the point of knowing "for the sake of what" in each case, and concerning those things which, while separable in form, are in matter? For a human being and the sun beget a human being. But how the separable exists and what it is, that is the work of the first philosopher to determine. (194b9–14)

W. D. Ross no doubt correctly sees the overall thrust of this passage as a rejection of separate forms as causes of coming-to-be – Aristotle repeats this phrase (minus reference to the sun!) in making that very point in *Metaphysics* Z.8 (1033b27–30), insisting that the ability of living things to make another one in form with themselves renders separate forms unnecessary. Regarding the reference to the sun, Ross also helpfully points to *GC* II.10. There, after reminding us of a series of propositions established in the *Physics*, including the eternality of locomotion and its primacy among kinds of change, Aristotle discusses the continuity of the recurring cycles of coming-to-be and passing away in nature, arguing that this must depend on some sort of contrariety in the eternal circular motions of the heavenly spheres as well. It is at that point in the argument that Aristotle makes a reference to the motion of the sun on the ecliptic:

> Wherefore the primary locomotion is not the cause of coming-to-be and passing-away, but the motion along the ecliptic,[37] for in this way the movement is both continuous and the motions are two. . . . The movement of the whole[38] is the cause of the continuity, and the inclination of the approach and withdrawal. . . . So by approaching and being near [the sun] generates, by withdrawing and being further away this same body destroys, and if it generates by approaching often, it also destroys by withdrawing often; for opposites are the cause of opposites (Selections from 336a31–b9)

This motion of the sun on the ecliptic circle, as the source of the patterns of the biological cycles of coming-to-be and passing away, is the backdrop for *Generation of Animals* IV.10.[39] Aristotle begins this discussion by claiming that for the most part the length of gestation is determined in accordance with an animal's life cycle (*bios*), and goes on to argue that

---

[37] *hê kata loxon kuklon*, literally "the motion along the inclined circle"; cf. *Metaph.* Λ.5, 1071a16–17.
[38] I.e., of the outermost sphere of the fixed stars.
[39] There are numerous difficulties associated with understanding Aristotle's views about the mechanism by which the sun transmits heat to the earth which I am putting aside: for a recent review of the problems, see Wilson 2013, esp. 48–50. Wilson concludes: "In the end Aristotle has no coherent theory as to how the sun can heat the earth" (50).

factors related to the sizes of animals account for their relative length of gestation. He then turns to the movements in the heavens and their relationship to life cycles.

> It is reasonable that the times of all the gestations, generations and life cycles tend[40] to be measured according to nature by periods. By "period" I mean day and night, month and year and the times that are measured in these units. And there are lunar periods – full moon and waning, and bisections of the times between these; for it is in accordance with these that it stands in relation to the sun, the month being common to both.[41] (777b16–24)

He goes on to argue that since the moon shares in the sun's light, it too contributes to all generation and termination of life, which are ultimately dependent on cycles of heating and cooling due to the sun's motions – ultimately, because while he acknowledges the role of weather patterns, he sees those as also dependent on "the period of the sun and moon" (777b34–5).

He concludes:

> So then, nature tends to count the generations and terminations by the numbers of these motions, but they are inexact on account the indeterminateness of the matter and the coming to be of many principles which, by impeding generations and destructions according to nature, are often causes of things happening contrary to nature. (778a4–9)

This discussion provides no evidence of "cosmic teleology,"[42] but it is clearly a case where the natural motions of the spheres of the sun, and to a lesser extent the moon, are directly responsible for the patterns of coming-to-be and passing-away that are taking place in the realm of animals and plants. As we can see from a related passage in *Metaphysics* Λ.5, 1071a13–17 where Aristotle lists the causes responsible for a human being coming-to-be, the sun's role is mentioned as an external moving cause. Because the natural rhythms of birth and gestation, life spans are set by patterns in the movements of sun, moon and stars, and because these patterns form the basis of measuring and counting those natural rhythms,

---

[40] *boulontai*, and again at 778a4. The abstract noun derived from this verb, *boulêsis*, has a technical meaning within Aristotle's moral psychology and in that context is typically translated "wish" or "will." However, in Aristotle's natural science, when "nature" is the subject of the verb, "tends" is a better translation. See LSJ: *boulomai* III.1, where in fact 778a4 is cited for this sense. Contrary to Henry 2015, I see no hint of teleology in this passage, unless one builds it in by giving nature a wishing or willing faculty.

[41] For a clear explanation of what Aristotle means by "the month being common to both" (i.e., sun and moon), see Peck 1942, 478–9, note c.

[42] As it is said to in Henry, 2015, 102–103.

nature can be said to count our "bio-rhythms" according to these patterns. That the rhythms of life don't perfectly align with the patterns in the heavens is hardly surprising, given the indefiniteness of our material natures, but the relationship between the lunar and solar cycles and lives (and deaths) of animals and plants is clear nevertheless.

7.7 Participating in the Everlasting and Divine

In the previous section, I argued that the relationship between Aristotle's understanding of the relationship between the pattern of movements in the heavens and those in the life cycles of animals and plants is an efficient causal one. There is, however, a teleological relationship of a complicated sort nearby, and that is the subject of my last example of methodologically interesting interactions between Aristotle's animal inquiries and his investigation of heavenly motions.

GA II opens by reminding the reader that the first book has argued that the male and female are principles of generation and has established the capacities associated with each and defined them. Looking forward to Book IV, he promises to later explain why some animals come to be male and others female – insofar as this is explained by necessary interactions of motive causes and matter. What he is about to do, however, is explain this fact by reference to "the better and the cause for the sake of something" (731b23–4) – and for this teleological explanation, he says, he must begin "from above."[43] What he means by this becomes immediately clear:

> For since some of the existing things are eternal and divine, while the others are able to be and not-be, and since the noble and divine is always, in accordance with its nature, a cause of the better in things that are capable, while the non-eternal is able to be and to participate in the worse and the better, and since soul is better than body, and the ensouled than the souless because of the soul, and being than non-being and living than non-living – for these reasons there is a generation of animals. For since the nature of such a kind cannot be eternal, that which comes into being is eternal in the way that is possible for it. Now it is not possible [for it to be eternal] in number (for the substance of existing things is in the particular, and if it were such it would be eternal) but it is possible in form – for which reason there is always a *genos* of human beings, animals and plants. (*GA* II.1, 731b24–732a2)

[43] Peck sees this as a reference to the heavenly bodies (1942, 129, note e) and translates "the upper cosmos," but there is nothing in the Greek to indicate this. For an epistemic reading see Balme 1992, 155. Cf. Henry 2015, 112 and note 24.

Aristotle does indeed begin "from above," appealing to a fundamental cleavage among beings (*onta*) – those that are eternal and divine and those that are able to be and not-be. Notice that, unlike the passage from *PA* I.5 with which we began, this is not a distinction among natural beings but among beings as such. The distinction here is a challenge to a superficially similar Platonic contrast between a realm of being and a realm of coming-to-be. In the *Timaeus*, Plato insists that things that are cannot come to be, and things that come to be never truly are (27d–28a), while for Aristotle, the fundamental contrast is *among beings*, between those that can pass away and those that always are. Aristotle does share with Plato what I call the Axiological Axiom: Being is better than nonbeing; which in the case of ensouled beings translates into living being better than not-living. And as he tells us in a related passage in *De anima* II.4:

> The soul is the cause and principle of the living body. . . . And that it is the cause in the sense of substantial being (*ousia*) is clear; for the substantial being (*ousia*) is in all cases the cause of being (*einai*), to live for living things is to be, and the soul is cause a principle of these. (415b10–11, 13–14)[44]

The soul, then, in the case of perishable living things, is the source and cause of their being. But how does this explain that there is a *generation* of living things? In virtue of being perishable, they cannot be eternally in an unqualified sense, i.e., as numerically one being – but they can be eternal in a way, in form. To understand what Aristotle has in mind, it is necessary to look to an earlier passage in the same chapter of *De anima*:

> For most natural of the functions in living things, as many as are complete and neither deformed nor generated spontaneously, is the production of another like itself, animal animal, plant plant, in order that it may partake, as far as possible, in the always and the divine; for all [perfect living things] strive for this and do whatever they do in accordance with nature for the sake of this. (But that for the sake of which is double, the *of* which and the *for* which.) Now since they are unable to partake of the always and the divine continuously, each one partakes in so far as possible, some more and some less, and it remains not itself but like itself, not one-in-number but one-in-form. (415a26–b7)

The ability of "complete" organisms to beget others alike in form (i.e., in soul) to them is a capacity of the *nutritive* soul – it is a form of *self-preservation*.

---

[44] This passage actually argues that the soul is the cause in *three* of the four senses of cause (the body being the material cause); I've excerpted the lines that parallel our *GA* II.1 passage.

It is worthwhile dwelling on what motivates this doctrine. One possibility is that it springs from philosophical reflection on what unifies the many and varied activities on display in the living world. Most of these activities appear to be aimed at self-preservation – activity devoted to reproduction, however, understood to include mating, nest or den preparation, nurturing and teaching newly hatched or born off-spring, etc. might seem to be an obvious exception. It is here where biologists turn for classic examples of "altruistic" behavior.

The idea of reproduction as a form of self-preservation can be seen as an attempt to deal with this problem: Every organism does what it does in the interests of self-preservation, but by the very nature of organic being, they inevitably die. Each organism can, however, continue to be in form, and thus *participate* in the everlasting and divine. It is a being alike in form that is the result of reproduction – and, "in the case of living things to be is to live, and the soul is the cause and principle of life" (415b12–14). The goal of reproduction in fact is *continued being* for the being that is reproducing. This is achieved not by "participation in the eternal species" (Shields 2015, 201), nor by maintaining "the sameness of the kind" (Johansen, 2012, 109); rather, reproduction achieves continuous being for one's soul, the *source* of one's being.[45]

What has this to do with cosmology? To answer that question we need to return to the latter chapters of *GC*. Aristotle concludes his study of coming-to-be and passing-away by facing a concern about whether reproduction really does secure participation in the eternal and divine. He has made the case that if coming-to-be in nature is to be eternal, it must be cyclical, like the motions of the heavenly bodies, rather than proceed in a straight line (337b34–338a17), and as we saw earlier, he had already indicated how general seasonal cycles were a consequence of the obliquity of the sun's motion along the ecliptic. But he then considers the coming-to-be of living things – reproduction seems to be, as our language of lineages suggests, linear, not cyclical.

> But human beings and animals don't return back to themselves so that the same being comes to be again (for it is not necessary, if your father came to be that you must, but if you have come to be, he must have – and this generative process would seem to be in a straight line). (338b8–11)

---

[45] This paragraph owes much to an ongoing collaboration with Cameron Coates; see Coates and Lennox 2020.

Aristotle sees, however, a way in which the generation of living beings is akin to the motions of the planets and stars, and he alludes to it in the very last lines of *GC* II.11:

> as many things as are not imperishable but in fact pass away, must return back again, not in number but in form. Wherefore water comes to be from air and air from water the same in form, not in number. But even if these <elements> are the same in number, this is not the case with those things the being (*ousia*) of which comes to be, being the sort of thing that is capable of *not* being. (338b14–19)

This passage is surely looking forward to a systematic study of biological generation. Plato, in the *Philebus*, has Socrates eloquently defend the assertion that generation is for the sake of being (54a8, c4), but it is hard to see how, in a Platonic universe, generation would ever *achieve* being. Aristotle twice echoes the words of the *Philebus*,[46] and sees, in the ability of living things to endlessly generate beings one in form with themselves, a way that generation not only achieves being but participates, in a way, in eternal being.

7.8   Conclusion

The most general message of this chapter is that the relationship between cosmology and biology in Aristotle is complex, multifaceted and bidirectional. Both are natural scientific inquiries and, while any knowledge of the eternal beings of cosmology we may achieve is to be prized, it is severely constrained by our limited epistemic access to them; by contrast, our access to knowledge of the biological world is essentially unlimited. In its attempt to apply directional principles to the heavens, *De caelo* II depends heavily on the functional account of directional dimensions in *De incessu animalium* – and these directional dimensions turn out to be conceptually more fundamental than the dimensions of magnitude with which *Cael.* I.1 opens. In *GA* IV.10, Aristotle outlines his views about how the rhythms of biological life cycles are partially governed by the movements of the Sun and Moon, a relationship which we exploit in measuring those life cycles. Here, biology relies on cosmology. And finally, in the natural drive to reproduce Aristotle sees a form of cyclical "returning to form" that allows those organisms able to replicate themselves to participate in the eternal and divine. In that sense, formal replication is a bridge between the biological and cosmological domains of the natural world.

---

[46] *PA* I.1, 640a17–18; *GA* V.1, 778b5–6.

CHAPTER 8

Recapitulation Theory and Transcendental Morphology in Antiquity

James Wilberding

The most pithy – and most famous – formulation of the thesis of recapitulation may be credited to Ernst Haeckel, a renowned scientist (1834–1919) and an ardent defender of evolutionary theory, who also published very successful popular works on biology and its social and philosophical implications: 'ontogeny is nothing other than a concise recapitulation of phylogeny'.[1] Haeckel presents the recapitulation thesis in its classic, evolutionary form: the development of the embryo recapitulates the historical, evolutionary development of the species. To illustrate this thesis with just one of Haeckel's examples: On his account, the human embryo in the third or fourth week is virtually indistinguishable from that of an ape, horse, dog or other mammals. None of these mammals at this stage bear any morphological resemblance to their adult forms; rather, all of them resemble a bean with a tail and two fins, and gill slits and gill arches. In other words, they all resemble a small fish, and this is because each of these species evolved historically from fish, and the embryogenesis of the individual follows the same developmental steps that the respective species went through during its evolution.[2]

The focus of scholarship on the history of recapitulation theories is largely confined to the eighteenth, nineteenth and early twentieth centuries, with ancient embryological theories being discussed at most in passing and very briefly.[3] This is certainly reasonable, both because of the high level of interest in recapitulation theory in early modern times and because of how little evidence there is of recapitulation theories in antiquity. Nevertheless, the surviving evidence deserves a closer examination than it has received thus far. In what follows I shall show that although there is some evidence of classic recapitulation theories among the Presocratics, Plato and Aristotle appear to have given up on these theories. This is not just because Plato and Aristotle rejected evolutionary theory. For as we

[1] Haeckel 1866: vol. 2, 7.   [2] Haeckel 1903: vol. 1, 17 and 276–7.
[3] See e.g. Gould 1977: 13–16.

shall see, it is possible to reconceptualise recapitulation theory in non-evolutionary terms. In fact, Aristotle and especially Plato and the Platonic tradition appear to share the two theoretical commitments that led certain natural philosophers in the eighteenth and nineteenth centuries to formulate the recapitulation thesis: (i) a commitment to the hierarchy of species and (ii) a commitment to a universal law of development. I argue that these authors develop these commitments, especially the former commitment, in specific ways that are not conducive to a theory of recapitulation.

This enquiry into ancient recapitulation theories has a two-fold significance to the study of ancient cosmology. First, recapitulation theory is fundamentally concerned with phylogeny, and in antiquity phylogeny was a central part of cosmogony. No account of the generation of the cosmos could be complete without providing some account of the origin of the various forms of life on earth, and especially of its most conspicuous inhabitants, human beings. Even Homer and Hesiod, our mythological starting point of Greek cosmology, were concerned to say something about the origin of human life, with later Greek cosmologists – most prominently Anaximander, Empedocles and Plato – following their lead. Secondly, and more importantly, given the precise connections that recapitulation theories seek to establish between phylogeny and ontogeny, uncovering evidence for recapitulation theories in antiquity can reveal important truths about ancient views on the nature of the cosmos. Not only can it shed light on certain conceptions of hierarchical ordering in nature, but it can show that some ancient thinkers were envisioning general laws of development governing the cosmos that applied both to species and to individuals.

8.1   Presocratic Evolutionary Theories of Recapitulation

There is fairly little to be said about evolutionary recapitulation theories in antiquity, largely because there were hardly any ancient advocates of evolution, but it is striking that the two most notable exceptions to this rule, Anaximander and Empedocles, appear to have emphasised certain parallels between phylogeny and ontogeny. The evidence on Anaximander suggests that he thought that human beings evolved in some sense from fish or fish-like creatures,[4] and it has been argued that he supported this evolutionary thesis by pointing to the fact that embryogenesis, too, consists in a development from an initial state of submergence in (amniotic) fluid.[5]

---

[4] See 12A10–11 and 30 Diels-Kranz, with discussion in Loenen 1954 and Barnes 1982: 15–17.
[5] See Osborn 1929, reported by Gould 1977: 14–15.

Empedocles presents a still more striking case. Although some of the details of his account of phylogeny must remain a topic of scholarly speculation, the main lines of his theory may be set out as follows.[6] His principles of Love and Strife, along with the four elements, form the cosmological background of this account. The account begins as the reign of Strife, during which all elements exist in separation, comes to an end, and Empedoclean phylogeny proceeds through a series of stages, each of which involves a chance coming together (due to the influence of Love) of simpler substances to form a single, more complex substance. Initially, the four elements come together to form homoiomerous substances such as flesh and bone, which are then in turn brought together in chance formations that result in isolated limbs and organs. These limbs and organs are alive and sentient. They are proto-organisms that are effectively our ancestors, and they are actively looking to combine with other proto-organisms.[7] When these combinations occur, what results are more complex organisms consisting of a collection of parts. Some of these, we are told, are fantastical such as the 'man-faced ox-progeny' and creatures with 'doubled-faces' and 'doubled-chests'.[8] These apparently perish quickly, or at least do not reproduce. Others, however, end up – again by chance – being so well put together as to be viable and ultimately even capable of reproduction, and these correspond to our present-day species.

This extremely brief account of Empedocles' theory of phylogeny certainly leaves much out, but it provides sufficient detail for us to appreciate some important parallels to his embryology. Chance, for example, is accorded the same prominent role to play in his embryology as in his phylogeny. Moreover, the morphological development in embryogenesis appears to run parallel to phylogeny, even if the surviving evidence does not record Empedocles himself drawing attention to this.[9] The development of the human embryo, for example, also proceeds from a

---

[6] There are two points of scholarly controversy that cannot be discussed here. One concerns how the various zoogonical stages are to be coordinated with the two cosmic periods of (increasing) Strife and Love, and the other concerns the prominence of chance (as opposed to teleology and design) in Empedocles' account. On both of these points I follow – and have otherwise benefitted from – Henry's discussion of ancient evolution (Henry 2016). See also Rudberg 1951. For a well-argued interpretation that diverges from the above on these two points, see Sedley 2007.

[7] 31B57–9 Diels-Kranz.   [8] 31B61 Diels-Kranz, cf. B60 and B62 with A72.

[9] Aristotle does call attention to the parallels, so perhaps Empedocles himself had done so, too. In *GA* 722b6–20 Aristotle criticizes Empedocles' embryological thesis (citing 31B63 Diels-Kranz) that such isolated parts could be alive and connects it to the historical phylogenic thesis (citing part of 31B57 Diels-Kranz) that comparable parts once lived on their own. The parallels might go well beyond what is suggested here, depending on how one interprets certain details of the cosmic cycles and the zoological and embryological passages. Cf. Gould 1977: 14.

state of isolated parts, which he understood to be proto-organisms that are already alive. Some of these are supplied by the father and others by the mother, and they all come together to form the entire embryo.[10] When these isolated parts come together to form more complex organisms, sometimes what results can be deformed – teratological cases of offspring born, e.g. 'double-headed' or 'double-backed'[11] – but barring extreme deformity the result is a human child. Thus, we have some evidence of Presocratic philosophers being committed to a hierarchy of species and to a universal law of development, such that the development of the individual (embryo) is governed by a universal law of development that applies to evolutionary development of the universal (species) as well.

8.2   Two Non-Evolutionary Variations on Classical Recapitulation Theory

Although evolutionary theory was almost universally rejected in antiquity, there are non-evolutionary versions of recapitulation. One approach to embryology in antiquity that bears some interesting parallels to recapitulation theory deserves some mention here, though it will not be the focus of the main discussion. This is what we might call cosmogonical recapitulation. This begins with the widely held belief that the individual human being is a microcosm that corresponds in certain salient points to the macrocosm of the universe. When applied to generation, this can result in a general law of development that covers both the universal case (cosmogony) and the individual case (embryology). Plato famously advanced a view along these lines in his *Timaeus* (see below), but it is possible to find it already in the Presocratics.

---

[10] 31B63 Diels-Kranz (= Aristotle *GA* 722b12). An anonymous referee has questioned whether Aristotle's report that Empedocles considered these simple parts to be living proto-organisms deserves credence. The parallel with the zoology would seem to speak for the veracity of Aristotle's report, though this possibly risks begging the question of Empedocles' commitment to recapitulation. Suffice it to say that, even if Aristotle is misrepresenting Empedocles on this point, the fact that an ancient thinker such as Aristotle interprets Empedocles along these recapitulationist lines is significant in its own right.

[11] 31B61 Diels-Kranz. The context of this fragment is phylogenic rather than embryological, but it is reasonable to assume that the descriptions were inspired by familiar teratological cases in embryology. The same goes even for the more mythological-sounding creatures, as some of Aristotle's remarks in *GA* show. In *GA* 4.3, for example, he might well have Empedocles' ox-faced humans and 'man-faced ox-progeny' (31B61 Diels-Kranz) in mind when he criticizes those who 'say that which is formed has the head of a ram or an ox' (*GA* 769b13–14, Peck translation in Peck 1942). Cf. Bien 1997: 70.

The pseudo-Hippocratic *De Victu 1* offers a particularly explicit illustration of this type of thinking. After having described the development of the embryo in chapter 9, in chapter 10 the author turns to the cosmos, offering this announcement as an explanation for what could otherwise be seen as a sudden change in topic: 'In a word, all things were arranged in the body [of the individual human embryo] appropriately, by fire itself, in order to make an imitation of the Universe, matching the small [organs] to the great and the great to the small'.[12] As Robert Joly has already noted,[13] the description of the embryo's formation in chapter 9 is rather vague, and the details of the microcosmic-macrocosmic correlations remain obscure. We learn that in both cases fire is the formative agent, and that certain organs in the human body correspond to parts of the cosmos: the cavity of the stomach to the sea, and flesh to earth, with three passages in the body (for air and incoming and exiting nourishment) corresponding in some way to three passages in the cosmos (of the sun, the moon, and the (presumably fixed) stars). This may not be much to go on, but it is enough to see that the author is envisioning human embryogenesis as a recapitulation of cosmogony.

The parallels envisioned here to hold between the universal and individual cases are certainly striking, but such cosmogonical theories lack what is the most conspicuous feature of classic recapitulation theories, since there is no talk here of the morphological development of higher animals running through the adult forms of lower animals. Let us therefore focus rather on a non-evolutionary version of recapitulation theory that preserves this important feature. Various such theories had in fact been advanced in the eighteenth and nineteenth centuries by German *Naturphilosophen*, prominently including Carl Friedrich Kielmeyer (1765–1844), Lorenz Oken (1779–1851) and Johann Friedrich Meckel (1781–1833), and by French transcendental morphologists such as Etienne Geoffroy Saint-Hilaire (1772–1844) and Etienne Serres (1786–1868). Although these biologists were not advocates of evolution, they were committed to two basic principles from which some version of recapitulation would seem to follow. First, there was the belief that the animal kingdom comprises a single sequence of living beings that progresses from the lowest and simplest to the highest and most complex. Second, nature was held to be unified in the sense that there is a single set of laws governing all processes of development. From these two principles it was thought to

---

[12] *De Victu 1* 10 (134, 5–6 Joly and Byl), after Joly and Byl's translation in Joly and Byl 2003.
[13] See Joly 1967: 12 n. 1 and 1960: 40–52.

follow that the development of the individual human embryo must in some sense climb up through the sequence of lower living things.[14] Whereas evolutionary recapitulation holds that the stages of the human embryo's development reflect the sequence of extinct ancestor-species out of which the human species evolved, according to non-evolutionary (or transcendental) recapitulation the human embryo's development reflects the hierarchy of the permanent and stable animal kingdom, with individual stages of the embryo corresponding to inferior adult animals that continue to exist today.

Thus, recapitulation theories are theoretically available to non-evolutionary natural philosophers. Nevertheless, although some subsequent ancient philosophers appear to be equally committed to these two principles – the hierarchical ordering of the animal kingdom and a universal law of development – they do not commit to recapitulation. In the following sections I shall argue, using Aristotle and the Platonic tradition as my main examples, that this is at least partly because the particular ways in which they conceive of the hierarchical arrangement of living things do not really lend themselves to recapitulation. Aristotle, who has been singled out as a thinker who could be seen as anticipating the recapitulationist movement, does propose a conception of the hierarchy of living things and their sequential development, but it is not sufficiently morphological. By contrast, Plato and the subsequent Platonic tradition develop a robust hierarchy of living things that is rich in morphological content but nevertheless refuse to see the morphology of higher animals as a further development of the morphology of lower animals.

8.3   Aristotle

Aristotle has been called 'the great-great-grandfather to the theory of recapitulation'.[15] He is certainly no evolutionary recapitulationist, as he defends the view that the entire universe and its contents – including the species of living things – are eternal. Rather, any claim of Aristotle being a recapitulationist must be understood in the spirit of the *Naturphilosophen* and the transcendental morphologists, which is to say that Aristotle has been supposed to envision that the development of the human offspring can be mapped onto an ascending scale of (permanent) species of living things. The scale follows from the ontological priority of soul-powers discussed in *De anima* 2.2–3. In the most general of terms, plants and

---

[14] See Gould 1977: esp. 37.   [15] See Gould 1977: 16, who attributes it to Needham 1959.

trees are the lowest form of life, having only the vegetative powers of soul (nutrition, growth and reproduction), followed by animals, which additionally also have powers of sensation, locomotion and (in some cases) representation, with humans occupying the top of the scale due to their possession of intellect.[16] It is against this background that some of Aristotle's remarks on the order of the embryo's development in *On the Generation of Animals* have been understood along recapitulationist lines. For he repeatedly likens the embryo in its earliest stages to a plant, particularly with respect to its soul-powers.[17] Initially, all of the seed's soul-powers are present only potentially, and the first activities to take place are those of the vegetative soul: nourishment, formation and growth.[18] The higher powers belonging to the sensitive and rational souls come in later. The former, being the actualities of their respective organs, may be said to be present once their respective organs have been formed. The power of sight is present once the eyes have been fashioned.[19] The latter, which by contrast is not the actuality of any bodily organ, is enigmatically said to be supplied 'from outside'.[20] Aristotle does not commit himself to an explicit timeline for these two developmental events, but the emergence of the sensitive soul certainly takes place after that of the vegetative soul, with the intellect presumably coming in still later.

Thus, Aristotle may say of embryos, 'at first all such things seem to live a plant's life'.[21] As we have just seen, there is good reason to think that this view is founded upon the *De anima*'s ontological priority thesis, but the parallels between early-stage embryos and plants go well beyond the fact that only vegetative powers are operative at this stage of ontogeny. They extend also to the *manner* in which these shared vegetative activities are executed. Aristotle emphasises not just that embryos nourish themselves but that they do so in the same way that plants do, because both are 'imperfect'.[22] One of the peculiarities of plants is that they have no need to transform the nourishment that they consume into 'ultimate nourishment', unlike blooded animals, for example, which have to transform their

---

[16] A more sophisticated characterisation of Aristotle's scale of life could introduce additional tiers, placing e.g. the zoophytes between plants and animals, and animals with representation between the other animals and humans, but the above is sufficient for our present purposes. In *GA* 2.1 Aristotle describes a different hierarchy of animals based on their methods of reproduction (viviparous, ovoviviparous, oviparous with perfect eggs, oviparous with imperfect eggs, larviparous), but this hierarchy plays no role in the recapitulation claims.
[17] See e.g. 731b5–8 and 741a24–7.   [18] *GA* 736b8–13.
[19] See *DA* 2 *passim*, e.g. 412a18–25 and 424a24–6.
[20] See *DA* 3.4–5 *passim* with 408b18–29 and 413b24–7; *GA* 736b27–9.   [21] *GA* 736b12–13.
[22] *GA* 740a24–5.

food into blood before it can be serviceable.[23] Plants find their nourishment ready-made, as it were, in an external source (the soil) and send out
roots to extract it. Likewise, embryos have no need to transform their
nourishment, because in the blood supplied by the mother they also find
their ultimate nourishment ready-made. Like plants, they send out their
'root' – Aristotle says the umbilical cord is in this respect functionally
equivalent to the roots of plants[24] – and take the nourishment they need.
Similarly, the manner of the early development of the embryo parallels that
of plants:

> Once the fetation has set, it behaves like seeds sown in the ground. The first
> principle <of growth> is present in the seeds themselves too, and as
> soon as this, which at first was present potentially, has become distinct
> (*apokrithê*), a shoot and a root are thrown out from it, the root being the
> channel by which nourishment is obtained, for of course the plant needs
> material for growth. So too in the fetation, in a way all the parts are present
> potentially, but the first principle has made the most headway, and on that
> account the first to become distinct in actuality is the heart.[25]

In both cases Aristotle describes a three-step process: (i) initially, there is a
principle of the living thing existing potentially in the seed, which (ii) then
comes to exist actually. In blooded animals this principle is the heart,
whereas in plants it has no name. (iii) Finally, roots (or the umbilical cord)
are sent out from the principle to the source of nourishment.[26]

   All of this goes a long way to explain why many scholars have thought
that Aristotle deserves to be included in the history of recapitulation
theory. This characterisation would also seem to gain still more support
from Aristotle's functionalism. He often defines forms, and especially
the forms of living things and their parts, in terms of the activities that
they perform. This would seem to allow for the multiple realisation of a
given form in different kinds of matter, so long as that matter supports that
form's essential functions.[27] Thus, if for Aristotle the plant and the embryo
are functionally equivalent, then they are equivalent *tout court*. And it is
perhaps also encouraged by the similarities to some of the remarks made
by *Naturphilosophen* that have been singled out as early statements of

---

[23] See *PA* 650a20–23 and 655b32–6.   [24] *GA* 740b8–10, cp. 725b22–6.
[25] *GA* 739b33–740a3, Peck translation in Peck 1942.
[26] See *GA* 739b34ff. and *PN* 468b16–9a9. Additionally, it might be noted that both principles are in
the 'middle'. In plants, the roots grow down from the principle, whereas the shoot grows upwards.
In blooded animals, Aristotle also speaks of the heart being a principle that lies between the upper
and lower portions of the body, e.g. *GA* 742b10–17 and 743b18–31.
[27] E.g. *DA* 412b10–a3; 413b11–13; *PA* 642a9–11, and Caston 2006: 320–22.

recapitulation theory. Carl Friedrich Kielmeyer (1765–1844), for example, has been counted among the earliest recapitulation theorists because of statements such as the following:

> These very laws, according to which the powers are distributed to various forms of organization, are the very same ones that governed the distribution of the powers to the various individuals of the same genus and – what is more – to one and the same individual in the various phases of its development. Even human beings and birds are, in their initial state, vegetative (*pflanzenartig*).[28]

The similarity to the Aristotelian account set out above is unmistakable.

Nevertheless, it is abundantly clear that Aristotle cannot be a recapitulationist in any strict sense of the term. This is because the parallels that Aristotle underlines between plants and embryos cannot amount to the claim that the embryo is *morphologically equivalent* to an adult plant. For embryos and plants do not even have the same homoiomerous parts. Plants have leaves and stems, whereas embryos consist of flesh and bone, and although plants and imperfect animals are bloodless, even at its earliest stage of development the embryo is a blooded creature.[29] Nor are Aristotle's commitments to functionalism sufficient to overcome this impasse. Although there is some functional overlap between certain parts, Aristotle cannot seriously maintain that embryos and adult plants are functionally equivalent. For adult plants possess many powers that embryos do not possess. They can, for example, reproduce, survive division and replace lost parts.[30]

8.4 Plato and the Platonic Tradition

We have now seen that although scholars had some good reasons to point to Aristotle as a proto-recapitulationist, his claims regarding the sequence of individual embryological development following the order laid out in the three-tiered hierarchy of living things fail to capture the crucial

---

[28] '[E]ben diese Gesetze, nach welchen die Kräfte an die verschiedene Organisationen vertheilt sind, gerade auch die sind, nach denen die Verteilung der Kräfte an die verschiedene Individuen der nehmlichen Gattung, ja auch an ein und dasselbe Individuum in seinen verschiedenen Entwicklungsperioden geschah: auch der Mensch und Vogel sind in ihrem ersten Zustande pflanzenartig' (Kielmeyer 1793/1993: 36). Kohlbrugge 1911: 447–8, for example, points to Kielmeyer as the first to formulate the recapitulation thesis. See also Gould 1977: 37 and Richards 1992: 19.

[29] See *GA* 740b3–4, and cp. *Meteor.* 388a15–19. Aristotle also emphasises that bones are formed in embryos in the first phase of formation (*GA* 744b28–32 and 745b4–5).

[30] See e.g. *DA* 413a16–19 and *PN* 467a6–30. And see Bos 2007.

morphological component of recapitulation theory. In this section I shall determine how close ancient Platonists came to developing – if not a theory of recapitulation – then at least a rough theory of transcendental morphology that could serve as a foundation for recapitulation. After all, the Platonic affinities characteristic of some of the early proponents of transcendental recapitulation theses, e.g. Fichte, Goethe and Schelling,[31] do raise some questions about how much of this can already be found in the ancient Platonic tradition. I shall argue that Plato's remarks pertaining to phylogeny in the *Timaeus* remain ambiguous on certain key points that make it difficult to determine Plato's exact commitments to transcendental morphology.[32] Then, I shall show that the subsequent Platonic tradition – I shall be focusing here on Plotinus – cleared away these ambiguities but did so in such a way that a transcendental morphology resulted that was unsuited to serve as a foundation to recapitulation theory.

There can be no question of Plato being labelled a recapitulationist for the simple reason that he provides no account of ontogeny. Virtually all that one finds about ontogeny in the Platonic corpus is this short and somewhat paradoxical passage in the *Timaeus*:

> 'the [female] desire and the [male] *erôs* bring [the male and female] reproductive parts together and, like plucking a fruit from the trees, sow into the womb as if into a tilled field living things too small to see and unformed, and then after having separated them again, they nourish them until they grow large inside [the womb] and after this they bring them to the light of day, completing the generation of living things'.[33]

The paradox lies in Plato's description of the embryo being, on the one hand, a miniscule living thing that only needs to grow larger, which suggests that Plato might be advocating some version of preformationism, and on the other hand something that still lacks form, which would speak against such a suggestion. In fact, there are good reasons to reject a preformatio-nistic interpretation of Plato's remarks on embryology, but it is still the case that Plato simply does not engage with the traditional questions regarding the order of the embryo's morphological development.[34]

In the domain of phylogeny, however, Plato sketches a rather innovative doctrine of evolution. Some qualifications are needed here, and they are

---

[31] See e.g. Richards 1992: 21–39.
[32] See Chapters 2 and 3 of the present volume for a discussion of Plato's *Timaeus*.
[33] Plato, *Tim.* 91c7–d5.
[34] For a more detailed discussion of this paradox, the above translation, and Plato's embryology more generally, see Wilberding 2015.

forthcoming, but let us first look at the context and content of this doctrine, which is outlined very briefly at the end of the *Timaeus*.[35] After having explained the generation of the universe and of human beings, the focus switches to the generation of birds, (non-human) land animals and aquatic creatures, which Plato seeks to explain by means of a process of devolution: all non-human creatures are inferior mutations of human beings. There appear to be at least two distinct mechanisms behind this process. One amounts to a quasi-Lamarckian appeal to use and disuse: those men who fail to exercise their rational souls, which in the *Timaeus* consist of circular motions in the head, are left with heads that are elongated and deformed, and their posture also changes on account of their heavy reliance on the powers of soul seated in their torsos, which push their chests out in front of their hips. Other morphological mutations are due to an act of divine, creative intervention. Thus, while in four-legged animals the transformation of human arms into forelegs might be explicable within this quasi-Lamarckian framework, the additional legs of certain land creatures – presumably insects and arachnids[36] – are not, and so an appeal to a renewed act of divine creation is required to account for them. Indeed, in the case of birds and aquatic creatures, no indications of anything Lamarckian are given. In fact, no morphological changes are explained at all in these cases,[37] as the focus is placed rather on their relocation into new habitats. In all of these cases, the intervention of the gods is intended as a just punishment designed to reinforce some funda-mental lifestyle choice: it is the humans who have foolishly sullied their souls who are banished from the pure air into the murky seas.[38]

Now for the qualifications. First, some scholars are inclined to take Plato's remarks here merely as an attempt at humour and insist that we should not count it among his genuine engagements with natural science.[39] This is partly because, secondly, the contextual occasion for this discussion of evolution is the transmigration of souls, and it is extremely difficult to disentangle the former thesis from the latter. In addition and more importantly, this is also because, thirdly, an evolutionary theory

---

[35] *Tim.* 91d6–92c3, and cf. 42c1–d2.   [36] Following Taylor 1928: 644.

[37] In the case of birds, we are told that feathers take the place of hair (91d7), but no cause of mutation is given.

[38] See *Tim.* 92a7–c1. Somewhat anomalous is the justification for the complete removal of legs and feet from snakes: rather than appealing to justice, the reason given is that they no longer have any need of feet (*hôs ouden eti podôn khreias ousês*, 92a6).

[39] E.g. Taylor 1928: 644 and Johansen 2004: 143. Perhaps this is also why Henry 2016: 319 entirely omits this passage from his short discussion of evolution in Plato, concluding simply that there 'is little in Plato that even remotely resembles evolutionary thinking'. Cf. Campbell 2000.

would seem to be incompatible with the theory of Forms. For the one-over-many principle demands that there should be a unique eternal, intelligible Form corresponding to each of these 'new' species. Indeed, the *Timaeus* places great emphasis on the fact that our sensible universe is itself a living thing has been modelled after an eternal, intelligible Form, the Form of Living Thing Itself, and that it follows from this fact that the sensible universe must contain 'the same kinds and numbers of living things as those which, according to the discernment of the Intellect, are contained within the real Living Thing'.[40] Furthermore, the birds, land animals and aquatic creatures are explicitly named (along with the stars) as the four kinds of living things that pre-exist in the intelligible model,[41] with the result that the 'evolution' of these species is in danger of collapsing back into creationism.

In light of this tension with the theory of Forms, it seems prudent not to insist too strongly on the truth of the evolutionary thesis in its most literal sense, though neither must it be entirely discounted. We are confronted here with a problem that is in fact an instantiation of a much broader and more familiar problem in the *Timaeus*. The *Timaeus'* entire account of creation is presented as an historical sequence of events that begins with the sensible world in a pre-cosmic state of chaos and sees the Demiurge, at first alone and subsequently with the assistance of the generated gods, bring this chaos step-by-step into the present state of cosmic order. There is a well-known disagreement, dating back to Plato's earliest exegetes and persisting today, regarding whether this account is to be understood metaphorically or literally. Taken literally, Plato is envisioning an historical timeline of creation, beginning at some datable starting point, with certain events in this creation taking place earlier than others, e.g. the stars were created before human beings.[42] The alternative is to take this talk of sequence and time metaphorically. On this interpretation, the cosmos never came to exist in any historical sense, rather it always existed in the state that it is now (and will always remain such) and the reason why Plato employed temporal and sequential language in this description of the cosmos was to highlight certain causal relations that bear upon the

---

[40] *Tim.* 39e7–9, Zeyl translation in Zeyl 2000.

[41] See *Tim.* 39e3–40a2, and cp. 30c2–31a1, 31a4–5, 41b7–c2.

[42] Ancient defenders of the literal interpretation include Atticus, Plutarch, Harpocration, Hippolytus, and Philo of Alexandria (for sources and discussion, see Baltes 1976: 38ff.), as well as Philoponus, who will be discussed below. Baltes 1999: 304 provides a list of modern literal interpretations, to which Sedley 2007: 99–106 may now be added.

everlasting cosmos.[43] Although there is no scholarly consensus on this issue, I believe there are good reasons to support the metaphorical interpretation over the literal one,[44] and I propose that Plato's evolutionary thesis should also be taken seriously but in a non-literal, i.e. non-historical, sense. In other words, we should understand Plato's point to be not that there was ever a time at which there were human beings but not yet any birds or turtles. Rather, Plato is committed to the eternity and immutability of all species of living things. When the temporal and sequential language of the evolutionary thesis is unpacked atemporally, we appear to be left with a thesis that is meant to suggest something about the relations among the eternal Forms of these living things.

There are obvious limits to how much can be said about the precise content of these relations, as Plato gives us precious little to go on. At a minimum it would seem to involve some claim about the ontological priority among the Forms corresponding to the various living things, though attempting to say anything definitive about the exact sense of priority involved proves very difficult. Some of these difficulties can be illustrated by reflecting on how some of Plato's characterisations of the relations that hold between these living things do not sit well with our general intuitions about the theory of Forms. For example, as Plato's theory of Forms is typically understood, there should be many distinct Forms of living things in the intelligible world – one corresponding to every species of animal in the sensible world. For convenience I shall be referring back to this conception of the intelligible world as the wheel model: every species of living thing in the sensible world is directly connected to a Form in the intelligible world, just as the points on the periphery of a wheel are connected directly by spokes to points on the hub. The problem is that in the *Timaeus* we find Plato saying things that are difficult to reconcile with the wheel model. We are told, as we briefly saw above, that there are only four kinds of living things in the intelligible world.[45] Moreover, some of Plato's remarks would even seem to call the distinctions between these four kinds into question. For the way that Plato characterises the lower animals as mere deformed human beings suggests

---

[43] Ancient defenders of the metaphorical interpretation may be said to include the majority of subsequent Platonists, including Xenocrates, Speusippus, Crantor (on all of whom, see Dillon 2003), and nearly all Neoplatonists. Plotinus' metaphorical interpretation will be considered below. Baltes 1999: 304 provides a list of modern metaphorical interpretations, to which I believe Johansen 2004 may now be added (see p. 91). Aristotle might well also belong to this group (*DC* 280a1, but cf. Dillon 2003: 25n49).

[44] See Wilberding 2006: 6–7.   [45] *Tim.* 39e–40a.

that they are all homologous, which is to say that the winged, land and aquatic animals are simply increasingly inferior instantiations of humanity. Similarly, humanity itself is portrayed as an inferior imitation of the universe. All of this creates the impression that Plato is not thinking of the intelligible principles of living things in terms of the wheel model. Rather, he is envisioning the totality of animals as forming either a single, linear, homologous ladder that begins with the universe and ends with the lowest of the aquatic creatures,[46] with each subsequent rung in the ladder being a more and more imperfect imitation of the one perfect living thing. Or else he might perhaps be envisioning the totality of animals after the model of a tree-chart, which would allow two or more kinds of animals to be directly subordinate to another species, e.g. various lower animals could be directly subordinate to the human species, as is perhaps suggested by *Tim.* 91e–92c. What the ladder-model (also known as the Great Chain of Being) and the tree-model have in common is that, unlike in the wheel model, not all animal species are directly represented by Forms in the intelligible world. Rather, at least some animal species and perhaps most of them are only indirectly represented there, insofar as they are imperfect instantiations of some other Form.

Unlike the wheel model, the ladder and tree models would seem to provide a promising foundation for the development of a theory of recapitulation, since they envision intelligible Forms of certain living things as sequentially emerging in some sense from other living things. But since recapitulation is a *morphological* thesis, in order for the Platonic theory of Forms to take on this foundational role, Platonic Forms must contain morphological content, and it is far from clear that this is the case. Although it might seem obvious that the Form of Human Being, for example, contains essential information about human morphology, e.g. that a human being has two legs, in the *Timaeus* there are no explicit indications that the Forms contain morphological content. Rather, the morphology of living things is consistently said to result from the creative decisions of the gods. This is particularly clear in the case of the generation of the 'first' human being. For in contrast to the Demiurge, who is said explicitly to look at the intelligible model as He creates the universe, the generated gods are *never* said to look at the Form of Human Being when they create the first human body. They do use a model, but their model is the universe itself in order that the human microcosm may be the best

---

[46] Unlike the other living beings (*zôa*), plants are created not as part of the imitation of the sensible world but simply to provide sustenance for other living things. See *Tim.* 76e–77c.

possible imitation of the macrocosm. Nowhere does Plato suggest that the uniquely human morphological features are derived from an intelligible Form, rather he says these features result from the amendments the gods themselves must introduce in order to accommodate human life to the material circumstances of the sublunary world.[47] The same is true of the lower, non-human animals,[48] whose morphological transformations, as we saw, are due either to the effects of quasi-Lamarckian use and disuse or to the intervention of the generated gods. Here again there is no claim about these morphologies deriving from the intelligible Forms. Indeed, it would seem to hold even of the universe itself. For while it is true that the Demiurge is said to look to the intelligible model, there is no indication that the spherical form of the universe is part of the intelligible model. Rather, He simply infers that this shape is best suited to the universe, given what he knows about the model (*Tim.* 33b–34b).

The situation with Plato, then, may be summed up as follows. Although he paid little attention to the order of formation of the embryo, Plato might have provided some important groundwork in the area of transcendental morphology. This, however, ultimately depends on whether he conceived of the organisation of the intelligible Forms of living things in terms of the ladder (or tree) model as well as whether he envisioned these Forms as having morphological content. The text of the *Timaeus* remains ambiguous on both points.

If we turn now to Plotinus as a representative of the subsequent Neoplatonic tradition,[49] we can see how he certainly did succeed in establishing a theory of transcendental morphology that cleared away the ambiguity on both points, but he did so in such a way that the resulting transcendental morphology is actually ill-suited to theories of recapitulation. In *Ennead* 6.7 he works out his own account of how the various living things are present in the intelligible world, and he shows a certain sympathy for the ladder and tree models. What interpretations like this have going for them is that they preserve the dignity of the intelligible world by refusing to admit the existence of Forms of ignoble creatures.[50] By recasting ignoble creatures as unnatural deformities of noble creatures,

---

[47] Thus, the human head is modelled explicitly to have the shape of the universe, but the body and limbs are added simply to keep it from rolling around (44d8–e2 and 69c6–7). The eyes and the ears are added to help make the revolutions in the head more like those of the universe by enabling us to study and reflect on them (47b5–e2 and 90c7–d7).

[48] *Tim.* 91d–92c.   [49] See also Chapter 14 of the present volume for a discussion of Plotinus.

[50] See Wilberding 2011.

the existence of these creatures in the sensible world may be adequately accounted for without debasing the intelligible world by positing Forms of them there.

Ultimately, however, he rejects these models in favour of something like the wheel model. His main objection to the ladder and tree models is that these models ultimately denigrate the sensible world. For to whatever extent the species found in the sensible world are not directly represented by Forms in the intelligible world, and that is to say, to whatever extent their forms are merely unnatural distortions of other, nobler species, to this extent the sensible world, qua imitation of the intelligible world, must be seen as a failure. For Plotinus, who wants to see the sensible world as a success story – it is the best possible imitation of the intelligible world – this conclusion is simply unacceptable.[51] Thus, Plotinus demands that there be Forms directly corresponding to *all* species of sensible living things:

> Since we maintain that this universe exists in accordance with the paradigm, as it were, of that one, the universal living thing must exist there too first, and, if its existence is to be complete, must be all living things. [...] All animals are in it, all that walk on and belong to the land here below, and, obviously, plants rooted in life; [...] and all the living beings in water [...] and the aerial living things are there.[52]

Plotinus' commitment to total inclusiveness is underlined by his willingness to explicitly accept even a Form (or perhaps Forms) of plants in the intelligible world, which goes well beyond what is set out in the *Timaeus*.

At the same time Plotinus is committed to maintaining the *Timaeus'* thesis that some animals are nevertheless inferior to others, but squaring this hierarchical ordering with the wheel model's inclusivity thesis requires some finesse. Plotinus begins by making a crucial distinction between a species being inferior and its being corrupt:

> But if it is by being spoilt (*kakuntheisa*) and made worse (*kheirôn*) that a principle forms a beast-nature, then originally it was *not* the principle that made ox or horse, and the form-principle of horse as well as horse will be corrupt (*para phusin*)! Rather, they are inferior (*elatton*) but not corrupt (*para phusin*). On the contrary, that [original principle] was in a way (*pôs*) even at the outset horse or dog.[53]

---

[51] E.g. Plotinus, *Enn.* 2.3.18.16–22; 2.9.4; 3.2.3; 3.8.11.29–33; 5.8.7–8. And see Wilberding 2011.
[52] Plotinus, *Enn.* 6.7.12.1–13, after Armstrong translation.
[53] Plotinus, *Enn.* 6.7.7.1–5, after Armstrong translation.

Non-human animals are not corruptions of nobler forms that cannot exist in their own right in the intelligible world. For there is a unique principle in the intelligible world corresponding to each species. The fact that all of these Forms exist side-by-side in the intelligible world does not prevent some of them from being inferior to others, a point that Plotinus drives home with an analogy. Just as humans are complex living things consisting of some parts (e.g. eyes and fingers) that are superior to others, so too is the Living Thing Itself, which for Plotinus comprises the intelligible world in its entirety, complex, consisting of many Forms, some of which are superior to others.[54]

In the following passage he also clarifies his contention that the principle responsible for forming a lower animal such as a dog or a horse was 'in a way (*pôs*)' already a dog or a horse in the intelligible world. Here he describes how each of these transcendent Forms – which he refers to here in typical Plotinian fashion as 'intellects' or 'intellect-principles' (*noes*) – is related to the immanent form-principles responsible for constructing the bodies of the various species of living things in the sensible world:

> For each [principle in the intelligible world] is actually one thing but has the power to be all; but [in the sensible world] we apprehend in each what it actually is; and what it actually is, is the last and lowest, so that the last and lowest of this particular intellect-principle is horse, and being horse is where it stopped in its continual outgoing to a lesser life, but another stops lower down. For as the powers unfold they always leave something behind on the higher level; and as they go out they lose something, and in losing different things different ones find and add on something else because of the need of the living being which appeared as a result of the deficiency; for instance, since there is not yet enough for life's purpose, nails appeared, and having claws and fangs, and the nature of horn; so that where the intellect-principle came down to, at that very point it comes up again by the self-sufficiency of its nature and finds stored in itself the cure for the deficiency.[55]

Let us start unpacking this passage by observing that, in contrast to Plato, Plotinus clearly ascribes morphological content to the Forms. Plotinus is effectively presenting an interpretation of the *Timaeus* that refuses to distinguish between the Forms and the generated gods. As we saw above, in the *Timaeus* it appeared to be the generated gods that were responsible for our respective morphologies, but Plotinus interprets these gods metaphorically: they are simply the immanent instantiations of the

---

[54] See Plotinus, *Enn.* 6.7.10.9–14.   [55] Plotinus, *Enn.* 6.7.9.34–46, after Armstrong translation.

transcendent Forms. This metaphorical interpretation helps him to reha-
bilitate the distinctly beastly morphological aspects of non-human animals.
Thus, whereas Plato described the generated gods as devising certain
morphological changes as *punishments*, for Plotinus even the baser morphological elements – claws, fangs, horns – are meant to be *beneficial*.
They help these creatures survive. And because this rehabilitation allows us
to value them as good features, they may be included in the intelligible
world – 'in a way'. What Plotinus means by this qualification is that while
there is a Form in the intelligible world corresponding to each species of
living thing, and this form does contain the species' distinctive features, in
the intelligible Form itself these distinctive features are present only in a
potential manner. This allows Plotinus to maintain that even the Form of
an ignoble creature, such as a dog, is 'perfect' or 'complete' (*teleion*) insofar
as the Form is not corrupt and contains all the information required to
create a dog,[56] while at the same time securing not only the nobility of the
intelligible world but also the greatest possible degree of unity for it. For
suppressing the species' distinctive features as potentialities helps assimilate
the Forms into a unity.[57]

This brief examination suffices to show that Plotinus may indeed be
credited with the development of a theory of transcendental morphology,
yet it also shows why Plotinian transcendental morphology is ill-suited to
serve as a foundation for recapitulation theory. The reason lies in Plotinus'
commitment to what I have been calling the wheel model. Transcendental
recapitulation theories require a particular variety of transcendental morphology. A suitable transcendental morphology must include at a minimum some claims about morphological continuity such as are found in the
ladder and tree models. That is to say, the morphologies of higher living
things such as human beings should represent further developments of
the morphological structures of lower living things, or, if viewed from the
inverse perspective of Plotinian emanation, the morphologies of lower
living things should be corruptions or degenerations of the morphological
structures of higher living things. A theory of recapitulation can then result
from applying such a continuous morphological scheme to ontogeny:
as the embryo develops morphologically into a higher living thing, it

---

[56] See e.g. Plotinus, *Enn.* 6.7.10.7. Plotinus is very careful never to call any species 'imperfect' or
'incomplete' (*ateles*). This commitment is what lies behind the emendation in modern editions of
ateleis to *euteleis* ('cheap') at 6.7.15.4.

[57] See e.g. Plotinus, *Enn.* 6.7.12.23–30.

passes through the morphologies of (certain) lower living things. As close as Plotinus appears to come to such an account of transcendental morphology at times, he ultimately rejects it. The morphologies of lower living things are no more degenerations of those of higher living things than is the eyebrow or the eyelid of the eye. Rather, despite their inferiority, their morphologies are wholly accounted for in their own right in the intelligible world.

It was noted above that Plato had little to say regarding the details of ontogeny. Our interest in Plato and the Platonic tradition lay rather in their possible contributions to transcendental morphology, an area which is fundamental to non-evolutionary recapitulation theories. As we have now seen, although Platonists, especially the Neoplatonists, did indeed work out sophisticated views on transcendental morphology, these views turn out not to be of the right kind.

A comparison of approaches to certain cases of teratology may serve as a helpful illustration of this point. Because recapitulationists envision the human embryo as developing through a sequence of morphological stages that correspond to the adult morphologies of lower animals, they are prepared not only to explain some cases of teratology as the result of an obstruction of development but then also to classify the resulting offspring as effectively possessing the same morphological structure as some other animal situated earlier in this sequence. If the offspring ends up bearing a greater resemblance to some lower animal than to its human parents, this resemblance can be accounted for because the lower animal's morphological structure is embedded in the sequence of human morphological development.[58] By contrast, although Neoplatonists certainly agree that cases of teratology are generally due to an obstruction of the embryo's development, they do not think that this is sufficient to explain whatever resemblance a human offspring might bear to an animal of some other kind K. Rather, they feel the need to posit an additional cause for such cases of resemblance, namely the World Soul, which is conjectured to supply the form-principles of kind K to supplement the human embryo's

---

[58] Consider, for example, this 1829 statement by G. Andral: 'Die Mißbildungen durch Hemmung der Entwicklung wiederholen meistens mehr oder weniger deutlich die normale Bildung bei den niederen Tierklassen. Dieser Satz geht unmittelbar aus dem Gesetz hervor, kraft dessen der Mensch während seines Fötuslebens die verschiedenen Organisationsstufen durchläuft, welche bei den niederen Tieren den bleibenden Zustand bilden' (cited in Kohlbrugge 1911: 449). For another example, see Haeckel 1866: 206.

development. These externally supplied form-principles were thought capable in extreme cases of even usurping the entire development, resulting effectively in an offspring of kind K, but the fact that these principles had to be supplied from outside shows that they are not envisioning the human embryo's development as running through a morphological sequence of lower animals.[59]

In fact, although in general the Platonists of late antiquity – like Plato himself – show little interest in determining the order of formation of the embryo,[60] some of their offhand remarks on the sequence of formation actually show a greater affinity to one of the greatest critics of recapitulation theory than to classic recapitulation theory itself. Karl Ernst von Baer (1792–1876) fiercely criticised the recapitulation theories of his time, proposing an alternative theory that envisioned certain other parallels between ontogeny and (transcendental) phylogeny. According to von Baer, there is once again a universal principle of development governing phylogeny and ontogeny, but rather than proceeding from the imperfect to the perfect and ascending through a morphological hierarchy of lower animals, all development is described as a process of *individualisation* that begins with the universal and progressively adds levels of differentiation. Thus, for von Baer, in its early stages of development, the human embryo is not to be identified with any specific lower animal; rather, it is simply a *generalised* animal that has the potential to acquire the characteristics of any number of different species.[61] Let us close, then, with this final passage, which deserves more commentary than is possible here and in which Ammonius Hermeiou, a Neoplatonist active in the fifth and sixth centuries, anticipates in a way von Baer's view that ontogeny proceeds from the universal to the particular, even if not quite in the sense that von Baer was later to envision:

> You should know that nature proceeds from the more universal to the more particular and that the particulars pre-exist in potentiality in the more universals, for example: out of the seed that has been sown [nature] creates first the flesh-bit, as the doctors say, in the womb, which is a body. The body is universal. But this *qua* body is in actuality, but *qua* ensouled is in potentiality. For it is not yet actually ensouled. But when it has been nourished and grown, it is ensouled, and is said to be actually ensouled, but potentially an animal

<hr>

[59] See e.g. Philoponus *In Phys.* 201,10–202,21 and Proclus *In Crat.* §82. Both passages are discussed in greater detail in Wilberding 2014.
[60] See Wilberding 2016: 129–33.   [61] See Gould 1977: 52–63 and Richards 1992: 55–61.

(*zôon*), [since] it does not yet have part in sensation and motion. When it already partakes of these, it becomes an animal actually. And when it is born (*ekkrithê*) and partakes of reason, it becomes rational actually.[62]

---

[62] Ammonius *In Isag.* 104,32–105,8. To be sure, Ammonius is not advancing a morphological thesis like von Baer's here. He is simply recasting Aristotle's psychological thesis about the embryo proceeding from the least perfect state (vegetative living thing) to the most perfect (rational living thing) into a thesis about moving from the universal to the particular. But both agree (for very different reasons) on the direction of the universal law of development. By contrast, Philoponus stays closer to Aristotle's original formulation (*In DA* 214, 11–25).

CHAPTER 9

The Stoics' Empiricist Model of Divine Thought

George Boys-Stones *

9.1 Introduction

The Stoics believed that order is brought to the cosmos by divine agency. Their principal reason for believing this is the 'argument from design'.[1] So much is well understood. What is less well understood is the Stoics' commitment to the further belief that this divine agency must have rationality which, in kind at least, is identical with the rationality that we humans have. Indeed, this is so little understood that, as we shall presently see, most modern commentators end up effectively, or even quite deliberately, denying the fact altogether. For this reason, it is worth pausing at the outset to register just how clear and explicit the Stoics are on the point (Cicero, *Nature of the Gods* 2.78–9 = *SVF* 2.1127):

> And necessarily, since there are gods, they are alive; and not only alive, but possessed of rationality, and united in a sort of political union and society, governing the one world as a commonwealth, and a [common] city. It follows that they have *the same rationality* (*ratio*) as the human race, that there is the same truth in both cases, the same law.

The reason that it is a simple entailment of the gods' having rationality that they have the same rationality as human beings (so that this claim applies equally to the one Stoic creator god as to created divinities within the cosmic system) is that there is only one thing that rationality is, that truth is, and that thinking is (*SVF* 2.1128). If something, anything, is rational, it cannot but be the case that it is rational exactly as we humans are.

Note that the argument from design does not secure this conclusion on its own. It is quite possible to argue from the premise that the cosmos

---

* This chapter owes a lot to discussion with audiences in York, Paris, Seoul, Mexico City – and Athens, where I gave a version of it as the 2019 Michael Frede Memorial Lecture. I am especially grateful for feedback and suggestions from Francesca Alesse, Gretchen Reydams-Schils and Ricardo Salles.
[1] See esp. Cicero, *Nature of the Gods* 2.87–97; Epictetus, *Diss.* 1.6.7.

seems well designed to the conclusion that it is the product, not of thoughtful craft, but of a craftsman-*like* teleology. One might use the language of skill, planning, thought and craftsmanship to describe the teleological causes involved, but without being committed to the view that they relate to human processes of planning, thought and so on except homonymously. As it happens, one of our fullest accounts of the argument from design in Stoicism is also evidence that Aristotle had appealed to the argument before them; indeed the Stoic argument is presented as an elaboration of Aristotle's argument.[2] But, on most accounts, Aristotle is committed to a teleological explanation of cosmic order that is 'impersonal' – and insofar as it relies on a god who 'thinks', his thinking is nothing like that undertaken as such by human craftsmen.[3] In Aristotle's hands, at least, the creator god to which the argument from design invites us to infer would be an expositional device to help us think about what (teleological) benefits accrue to the cosmos in virtue of its being an effect of the 'first unmoved mover'.[4] On one reading, this is exactly how we should approach the 'Demiurge' in Plato's *Timaeus* as well: not as a mind that plans the cosmos just as a human might in his place, but as a cause which is compared with human craftsmanship only for reasons of exposition.[5] So it is very important that the Stoics insist that god's creative activity relies on his thinking, and that his thinking is just the sort of thinking undertaken by human craftsmen. If the argument from design goes through, it follows for the Stoics, in a way that (true or false) it does not *follow* for their predecessors, that there is a creator god who thinks in exactly and unequivocally the way that humans think.

The reason that it might be tempting to resist this conclusion is that it is difficult to see how it is *physically* possible that god thinks as we think. The Stoics have a lot to say about the development and operation of human thinking, so we know that, in their view, human thinking relies

---

[2] Cicero, *Nature of the Gods* 2.94–5. Note that there is no evidence of an argument from cosmic design any earlier than this: Plato, *Timaeus* 28b-c is properly a 'cosmological' argument; Xenophon, *Memorabilia* 1.4.2–19 (discussed by Sedley 2007: 75–86), concerns the design of human beings, not the cosmos.

[3] That is human craftsmen *qua* craftsmen; but I say this without prejudice to the question of whether humans are capable of the sort of theoretical contemplation characteristic of divine intellection, and also whether this sort of noetic activity is a precondition for discursive thought in humans. See Norman 1969; Gerson 2005, chapter 5.

[4] The assumption, then, is that the argument from design comes from an 'exoteric' work, probably *On Philosophy* (it is fr. 12 Rose³) where more technical language would be inappropriate.

[5] E.g. Menn 1995; Gerson 2005: 128–30. (Against this, see e.g. Johansen 2004 and 2014; Broadie 2012.)

on complex prior conditions. In particular, it depends on the ability of humans to have perceptual experience – which in turn presupposes both sense-organs and the existence of an ordered cosmos with which they can interact in relevant ways. But the Stoic god does not have sense-organs (*SVF* 2.1058); and even if we could find some feature of his constitution capable of sensation, the very fact that he is the creator of cosmic order immediately entails that he cannot have acquired his thoughts from *experience* of cosmic order, as human being do. (It is no answer to the question being posed here to refer back to a cosmos he might have made and experienced in the past.)[6] This was a problem that was noticed in antiquity: 'If there has to be a maker of this universe, he is not going to make it by setting his mind on the things that are in it when it does not yet exist' (Plotinus, *Enn.* 5.9.5.20–21).

In what follows, I want to offer some possible answers to these worries, and to show that the Stoics did have available the means to explain how god came to acquire thought which is, in the relevant ways, exactly like the thought of human beings. I offer it as a contribution to the present volume because, among its other conclusions, one thing that this will make clear is that the Stoics are quite serious in inviting us to consider god as an animal, indeed the animal par excellence. Most accounts of the Stoic god entail the view that god's operations, starting with his mental operations, are only homonymously like those of creatures within the cosmos,[7] so that in truth he is only homonymously an animal at all. Some accounts even welcome the entailment as a way of 'naturalising' the Stoic god. But on my view, the Stoics are committed to the position that god's thinking is qualitatively identical to our own. This saves the irreducible reality of the object of Stoic theology – but it does it precisely by insisting that we can learn about him through Stoic zoology as well.

---

[6] For one thing, not all Stoics believe in cosmic recurrence (Philo, *Eternity* 76–8; Cicero, *Nature of the Gods* 2.118). Assuming eternal recurrence, and assuming that god is able to keep thinking through the conflagration (see e.g. Plutarch, *Common Conceptions* 1077D-E, Epictetus, *Diss.* 3.13.7, with Reydams-Schils 2006: 83 and Alesse 2011–12: 374 n. 41), it might well be the case that there was never a time when god acquired his rationality. But that does not relieve us of the need to *explain* it (any more than, for example, the eternity of Aristotle's world relieves him of the need to explain its structure).

[7] Gretchen Reydams-Schils finds middle ground here, arguing that god has a rationality which is qualitatively similar to that of humans, but a distinctive way of using it – in particular, because god does not have or require *ennoēmata* (see esp. 2006: 90–91; although note that this position has to face down texts which explicitly say that god does have *ennoēmata*: e.g. *SVF* 2.83, p. 28.26–8).

9.2   Craftsman-like Thoughts of the Stoic God

I do not, of course, wish to deny that there are *some* ways in which god's thinking must be different from ours. God's thought takes in the cosmos as a whole, determines what happens in the cosmos as a whole, and, as a consequence, does not allow of error, as ours does. But that is a difference of, as it were, quantity, not quality: nothing is hidden from god (or beyond his control), while a great deal is hidden from us and outside our influence to determine it. But the *quality* of god's thought must be just the same as ours. Indeed, there is a case to be made that the Stoics are the first philosophers who not only believe but have good reasons to believe that god thinks in just the way that we do.

Consider again the argument from design, and allow that this gives the Stoics good reason to stand alongside Plato and Aristotle in believing that cosmic order requires a teleological explanation – in other words, that its evident orderliness and beauty must be explained by the specification of some end, some common goal by reference to which all of its parts are unified into a single, well-functioning organism. The Stoics, however, differ from Plato and Aristotle in the options they have for identifying this 'end' as something with traction on the process of creation. Both Plato and Aristotle are in a position to say that there exists some entity *prior* to the emergence of cosmic order which specifies in advance what form that order will take: the form of the good in Plato, or the first unmoved mover in Aristotle.[8] It is open to them to say (whether in fact this is precisely what they did say) that the very nature of these entities is such that matter conforms to them, and so acquires cosmic order under their influence.

The Stoics, however, do not allow that it is even a possibility that models like this could exist independently, or have any effect of their own on matter. It is an axiom of Stoicism that only a body can have an effect, and it can only have its effect on another body (e.g. *SVF* 1.90; 2.341, 363). So the material from which the cosmos is made is the only 'precosmic' entity that can exist. But that material cannot carry the pattern for cosmic order without itself *already being ordered*. In other words, Stoic

---

[8] Some qualifications: (1) 'prior' to the cosmos means 'logically prior', without prejudice to the question of whether the cosmos had a temporal beginning; (2) the specification of what the cosmos will look like is in both cases 'ideal': the cosmos does not end up looking exactly like the form of the good, for example; but its order is explained by its approximating it as far as possible – which is enough for the argument; (3) it only matters for immediate purposes that Plato had the metaphysical resources to give an account such as this, not whether he did in fact dispense with a thinking creator god.

teleology cannot operate through the bare activity of a paradigm for the order that there is to be, because that paradigm would already be the order it was supposed to explain.

The Stoics need something that stands in a slightly more complex relationship with future cosmic order. Given the basic material for the future cosmos in state S_1, they need to find some fact about this material that (1) is itself part of this material in state S_1; (2) is capable of specifying some *alternative* state, S_2, for this very material (namely the state in which it is the cosmos); and also (3) is a state that has direct or indirect causal influence over the material, so that it is able to bring it about that the material assumes state S_2. To put this in other words, they need something which is realised in matter, which specifies a structure not yet realised in matter, and which can act to realise that structure. Or, in other words again: a mechanism for the *representation* of certain ends and an *intention* to realise them. But this sounds precisely like the specification of a mechanism for thinking.[9] In short, the possibility that there is thinking before cosmic order comes to be, and thinking in very much the sense that we recognise it and engage in it ourselves, is the obvious way, if not the only way, in which the Stoics can incorporate teleological causality within a metaphysical framework of strict corporealism.

9.3   'Rationalist' Models for Divine Rationality

9.3.1   'Cartesian' Rationalism?

That the Stoic god might *need* to think perhaps does not take too much arguing for. But one might be tempted to suppose, nevertheless, that god's possession of thoughts, and of rationality, is to be explained in a way very different from that in which we explain how humans come by rationality and thinking. This has to do with the problems I raised at the outset of the chapter. Human rationality is formed by empirical processes which do not seem to be available to god. For example: our thought relies on there being an ordered cosmos, and our having sense-organs to experience it. (From our experience come concepts; from concepts, rationality: cf. esp. *SVF* 2.83.) God does not have sense-organs; nor does he have an ordered

---

[9] The basic template of the argument I suggest here can be found in Plato, *Philebus* 35a-c, where Socrates argues that desire (for future satisfaction) entails the existence of soul (or, let us say, relevant psychological functions) as well as mere body, because body on its own cannot be 'in contact with' the object desired but not yet present.

cosmos to reflect on. We invoke god to *explain* the order that the cosmos has, as its cause. There is no order (or strictly: no *particular* order) for him to experience until he has determined it.[10] These considerations make it natural to conjecture that the Stoics adopted a very different explanation for god's rationality.

One possibility, for example, is to suppose that rationality is 'given' in the nature of god's substance – to that extent (but with the important qualification that he is *also* corporeal and extended) a sort of Cartesian *res cogitans*. But this would be a disappointing answer. For one thing, it rather asserts than explains god's thinking. For another, one might wonder why the complicated mechanisms of empiricism as the Stoics describe them are needed for creatures *within* the cosmos if there exists some substance of which the capacity to think is already a property. (In this context it is worth observing that Stoics account for human souls, in fact all souls, as *parts* of god as he pervades the universe as cosmic soul, e.g. *SVF* 1.495, 2.633, 634, 774. If that is the case, then the reason that different explanations are needed for human and divine thinking could not be that the human mind lacks the appropriate participation in divine substance in its thinking form.)

But there is an even more serious reason to hope that the Stoics did not conceive of god in these terms. For if this model entails that there are thoughts innate to cosmic substance which genuinely and meaningfully specified the end for the cosmos – thoughts that are prior to but also causes of cosmic activity – then the Stoics would not be far from admitting the existence of something uncomfortably like Platonic 'forms'. It is worth recalling at this point that the Stoics defined reason as something constituted by concepts (*ennoiai*); what is more, they probably thought that it is not just any set of concepts from which reason is constituted, but that some at least are essential to the collection of concepts forming reason. Indeed Chrysippus is quoted as saying that reason is a 'bundle' of '*certain concepts and preconceptions*' (*ennoiōn te tinōn kai prolēpseōn athroisma*, *SVF* 2.841). So to say that reasoning is part of god's substance would be to say, not just that god has an analytical capacity of a certain sort, but that there are concepts, indeed there are theoretically identifiable concepts, that god innately possesses. (The alternative, which involves denying that

[10] E.g. *SVF* 2.318, 1107. However, there is a 'most basic' state of determination, namely the finest, or most rarefied, form matter is capable of taking – into which every other state can be 'resolved' but which itself cannot be 'resolved' into any other state. See Salles 2005: 70–72. This is important for the suggestion that I develop below, because it gives a determinate 'default' state of substance from which god's self-perception can begin.

concepts form an essential part of god's rationality, also amounts to a denial that god's rationality is the same in kind as human rationality.) Now, we know that Stoics could talk about the 'thoughts of gods', and even use the language of Plato's forms to do so;[11] but in the usual picture of Stoic metaphysics, this language is a deflationary move against Plato (forms are *nothing but* the thoughts that god has). This move works well so long as the view is that these thoughts are posterior to god – produced by god's mental activity. But if some of god's concepts are innate, then they do not depend on god's mental activity – exactly the opposite: they are its necessary condition. There is in fact no further explanation for the innate concepts that god has. But in this case, not only are they 'thoughts of god', they are also *principles* – they are among the irreducible first causes for everything that subsequently happens. That is why I said that they do not just look like Platonic forms, but look *uncomfortably* like Platonic forms.[12]

It is not surprising then that there is no Stoic evidence that articulates the possibility that concepts, or any of god's thoughts, are 'principles', or uncaused causes. On the other hand, we do have explicit testimony which rules it out that they are uncaused first principles. Varro, in his review of philosophical history at Cicero, *Academica* 1.39 (part = *SVF* 1.134), tells us that Zeno explained mind, not as something given in primary substance, but as something posterior to it:

> Zeno's views about nature were, first, that this 'quintessence', out of which his predecessors thought sensation and mind were made [cf. 1.26], had no place among the four elements: he determined that fire is that substance which gave rise to everything, including mind and sensation.

9.3.2 'Spinozan' Rationalism?

If Descartes cannot help us with a non-empiricist approach to the Stoic god, perhaps Spinoza can? It is one of Spinoza's more eye-catching claims that God's thoughts exist in a one-to-one correlation with extended bodies – and, more than this, that the very same reality can be adequately described either in the language of divine thought or in the language of

[11] See Reydams-Schils 1999: 145–7; 2005; 2006; 2010: 197–9; Alesse 2011–12, esp. 380.
[12] A 'Platonising' position like this is proposed by Alesse 2011–12, esp. 374–5. Her principal ground is the alleged 'implausibility' of attributing to god mental operations such as (her example) abstraction to universals. She does not say what makes this implausible.

physical extension.[13] That the Stoics might have thought something similar is a view most fully elaborated in recent literature by Gretchen Reydams-Schils.[14]

Reydams-Schils focuses her account on the so-called seminal principles (*spermatikoi logoi*), which we know are supposed to function somehow as the 'seeds' of particular entities in the cosmos. She supposes that these things (whatever exactly they are) can be viewed from two perspectives. From one perspective, they express a *thought* (namely the thought of a particular thing), which is why they are called *logoi*; but from another perspective they are structural facts about particular pieces of substance, facts which account for the way a given piece of substance develops. (This is why they have the quality of 'seeds', *spermata*.) And all divine thinking, she suggests, is like this. God is to be thought of as a dynamic substance who moves and changes and restructures by the 'logic' of his own physical constitution – a logic that can, if you like, be expressed as the laws of physics. But all of these moves and changes and new structures also have a mental aspect to them. In other words (and just as in Spinoza) god's thoughts are numerically identical with parts of his physical structure.[15]

As with the 'Cartesian' reconstruction, our explicit evidence offers some opposition and no support to this 'Spinozan' view. *Academica* 1.39 (quoted above) stands against it once again: god's thinking is not, in this case, specified independently of his substance, but it is still not *posterior* to this substance, which is the position ascribed there to Zeno. And (although there might be other ways of construing this passage) Seneca at least suggests that there is a gap between the thoughts that god has and their material instantiation (Seneca, *On Benefits* 6.23.5):

> Nature thought us *before* she made us (*cogitavit nos ante natura quam fecit*); nor are we such a trivial work that we could have escaped her notice.

But just as important as the recalcitrance of our explicit evidence are the severe theoretical problems that a 'Spinozan' view would have for the Stoics.

---

[13] See *Ethics* 2 prop. 7: 'The order and connection of ideas is the same as the order and connection of things' (*ordo et connexio idearum idem est ac ordo et connexio rerum*; cf. scholium: 'the mode of extension and the idea of that mode is one and the same thing, but expressed in two modes').

[14] See esp. Reydams-Schils 2005 and 2006; but also e.g. Long 2003: 11–13.

[15] There are of course other ways of construing the idea that *spermatikoi logoi* are god's thoughts: Alesse 2011–12: 379, for example, puts more emphasis on the idea that these things express the principles of what is to be, rather than the thing itself.

In Reydams-Schils' reconstruction it is crucial that god is denied *repre-sentational* thought. If god thinks 'lion', it is not by entertaining a concept, namely the concept 'lion', which stands in a certain relationship to some fact about the universe. God's thought 'lion' just is a lion, or at least some structure in nature (i.e. the *spermatikos logos*) that will develop into a lion. But if god's thoughts are identical with cosmological features, then god cannot be said to *plan* for the world at all – certainly not in the sense of entertaining different possible courses of action and choosing one rather than another, since it is impossible for god to entertain counter-factual possibilities on this account. But this compromises the 'craftsman' model whose more literal acceptation, I suggested above, was an entailment of the Stoics' bringing teleology into a materialist cosmological outlook. If god cannot plan, then he cannot operate teleologically.

A response to this might be to suggest that what really happens is that god's thoughts (and so the cosmos) roll out in an orderly sequence – perhaps each simply determines the next, so that there is only one possible direction for the cosmos. A view like this would, on the face of it, be compatible with the Stoics' views about fate, and eternal recurrence. (God only ever does follow the one course of action.)[16] But, again, it comes up against both textual evidence and theoretical concerns. Textual evidence, because the Stoics seem to imply that god has a choice when they say that he makes for himself *whatever he wishes*.[17] Theoretical, because a view like this is hard to square with the insistence, built into the argument from design which brought us to consider a creator god in the first place, that utility and beauty are both maximised in the cosmos (Cicero, *Nature of the God* 2.87). The Stoic theory of fate is careful to specify that, whatever one thinks about fate, it should not dislodge or supplant the view the cosmos is explained by concern for these things as well: it does this by making an identification between fate and providence (*SVF* 1.176). The point is not only that things happens inevitably, but that they happen the way they do because god thinks it best. On the current view, however, there is no mechanism to guarantee that the inevitable order is the one that maximises either beauty or utility.

Another problem with the 'Spinozan' model is that it obscures the important distinction that the Stoics make very early on in the process

[16] Cf. Alesse 2011–12: 377–9.
[17] *SVF* 1.1009 (ad init.: μεταβάλλον δ'εἰς ὃ βούλεται); Seneca, *Letters* 65.2 (*causa autem id est ratio materiam format et quocumque vult versat*). Of course, it is possible that god is constrained to 'wish' just one thing; but that makes an appeal to his will redundant.

of cosmogony between the 'ruling faculty' of the cosmos on the one hand (the *hēgemonikon*), and the divine as it is present in the rest of the cosmos on the other. (The distinction is to be found in human beings: our souls pervade our whole bodies; but part of the soul, the part designated the 'ruling faculty', is to be found specifically in the chest, around the heart, and it is there, and only there, that we think.) The Stoics argued over where the 'ruling faculty' of the cosmos was to be found: some identified it with the pure fire of the aether, around the periphery of the heavens; others identified it with the sun; at least one Stoic located it with the earth.[18] All, however, were clear that it existed in a very well-defined area within the cosmic system. But what this means is that, when god thinks, for example, 'lion', the material substrate of the thought is just there, in the aether or the sun, or wherever the ruling faculty is taken to be. But of course no actual lions are to be found in the sun or the aether; not even the *spermatikoi logoi* of lions are to be found there.[19] As long as lions are in existence, they do not exist at the location of god's thoughts about them. This consideration is a strong reason to believe that god's concepts are, after all, representational.

Finally, it is relevant to note that Reydams-Schils' account falls foul of the problem of universals. For Reydams-Schils needs to be able to claim (and does claim) that god makes certain things 'like' each other.[20] At the very least he has to be *conscious* that certain things are 'like' each other if the universals which we human beings form in our minds are to correspond with thoughts in god's mind. Now this is already a problem of sorts for the Stoics because, in consequence of their rigorous corporealism, the Stoics are nominalists and committed to the position that, as a matter of fact, no two things *are* alike (e.g. Seneca, *Ep.* 113.16). But things are even worse if god's thoughts were identical with entities in the world. For if this were the case, not only can no two things be alike, but god would be incapable of entertaining the thought that they were alike. For god's thought would have to be instantiated in some reality, in this case some actual likeness. But no such likeness exists; therefore god could not think it. But if that is the case, then the isomorphism between god's mind and our own – the claim that we have the same rationality in any sense – is put under impossible strain.

18 *SVF* 2.644 (DL 7.139); for earth, *SVF* 2.643, and 3, Archedemus fr. 15.
19 Texts such as *SVF* 2.1074 make it clear that the *spermatikos logos* is what is as it were implanted where god's mind has withdrawn. And see further Section 9.5.
20 Cf. esp. Reydams-Schils 2006: 91.

9.4   An Empiricist Model for Divine Rationality

The 'rationalist' accounts of divine rationality considered above force the Stoics further in the direction of either Platonism or mechanical necessity than they seem to want to go. They are impossible to square fully with a sincere desire to bring teleology into a materialist cosmology, and they contradict the qualitative convergence between human rationality and divine rationality which surviving texts of Stoicism seem keen to emphasise. So, despite the obvious challenges which an empiricist account of divine thinking will have to face, there is motivation enough to see whether we can find the resources within our evidence to suggest answers to them. In what follows, I want to show that we can make some progress on this front by taking the Stoics much more closely at their word, that is, in treating god as an animal, whose operations, including his mental operations, are relevantly like those of animals within the cosmos. It is true that his are unrestricted, while those of creatures within the cosmos are heavily circumscribed by their environment. But this makes a difference only to the *range* of questions it is appropriate to ask about god on the one hand and animals on the other. The question of god's birth or infant development does not arise, for example; nor of divine disease or hunger or passion.[21] But where the questions are the same – for example, what motivates activity, or how (in the case of rational animals) rationality is constituted – our initial assumption ought to be that the elements for an answer will be the same as well.

9.4.1   Divine Perception

There are, to recap, two main challenges that an empiricist account of divine rationality has to meet: (1) god cannot have empirical experience because he lacks sense-organs; (2) there is no appropriate object of empirical experience for him to have. (To have the sort of experience that can result in concept-formation, and thereby rationality, presupposes an ordered cosmos; yet that in turns presupposes god's thinking.)

In fact, it turns out to be very easy to deal with (1). It is true that god does not have sense-organs, but it is false that this entails that he lacks the ability to perceive. Our fragments are explicit that, on the normal Stoic view, god did have the power of perception. A number of fragments say as much, at least on the most straightforward reading of them: see e.g. DL

---

[21] In general, god is self-sufficient and does not experience need: see *SVF* 2.604.

7.143 = SVF 2.633;[22] DL 7.139 = *SVF* 2.634;[23] and perhaps Seneca, *Blessed Life* 8.4.[24] But there is unambiguous testimony that this was the normal Stoic view in a passage which tells us that *one* Stoic disagreed with it – Zeno's pupil Aristo of Chios (Cicero, *Nature of the Gods* 1.37 = SVF 1.378):

> [Aristo] thinks that the form of god cannot be grasped, denies that there is sensation among the gods – and doubts altogether whether god is animate.

It is very clear from the way Cicero reports this that Aristo was, in this matter as in others, the exception: in denying that god had the power of perception, Aristo was claiming something that no other Stoic claimed. And this fragment also hints at one reason why his view was the outlier: it might be hard to maintain that god was animate at all if one denied that he had perception.[25]

The reason that confusion has arisen over the question of divine perception has to do with the seductive, but ultimately mistaken, view that perception requires sense-*organs*. It does in some zoological systems – for example that of the Epicureans.[26] But it does not in the Stoic system. As far as the Stoics are concerned, sense-organs are instruments for perception specifically *of the external world*. But the Stoics think that any

[22] The cosmos is 'ensouled substance capable of perception'. Someone might argue that the cosmos is not to be taken as identical to god in this context; but even if that is right, it does not undermine the value of the fragment. DL infers that the cosmos is capable of perception from the fact that the cosmos is an animal; but god is an animal (DL 7.147 = SVF 2.1021); so either way, the fragment is evidence that god is capable of perception.

[23] Chrysippus seems to have given substance to the idea of god as *intellect* pervading the whole cosmos by explaining that the purest part of the aether pervades everything else 'perceptually', *aisthētikōs*. Bénatouïl (2009: 35) argues that this passage applies to the perceptual capacities of the inhabitants of the world rather than to god himself; but these inhabitants include plants, which we know do not have perception (cf. SVF 2.458, p. 150.11–12).

[24] Seneca talks about god discovering himself through extension to 'externals' (*in exteriora quidem tendit*) in a way relevantly like the way in which the stimulus of external sensory evidence gives animals the means to reflect on themselves. I take it that the mechanism of 'co-perception' lies behind the latter thought: just as in Hierocles, the fact that we see other things in relation to ourselves helps us to appreciate *that* we see ourselves too – and so, in this case, helps us actually to reflect on ourselves. (In the case of god, the *exteriora* cannot be outside him in quite the same way, but they can be those things which he creates or intends to be distinct from his mind itself, including his 'affordances'.)

[25] For perception (with impulse) as part of the definition of an animal, see again n. 22 above; also Hierocles, *Elements* I.31–3: 'An animal has two things which differentiate it from what is not an animal: perception and impulse'.

[26] In Epicureanism, perception just is the entrance of certain atomic structures (namely *eidōla*) into the body from outside, through the sense-organs: see *Letter to Herodotus* 46–53. Seneca argues for self-perception (*constitutionis suae sensus*), and against the idea that we learn about our bodies through experience, in *Letter* 121.7–10.

animal has a prior and more basic form of perception of its own immediate constitution (*SVF* 2.852; Seneca, *Letters* 121.6).[27] Indeed, since this is the primitive sense of 'perception', the Stoics make a point of applying a different, technical word to the perception of the external world – 'co-perception' (*sunaisthēsis*); the idea being that when an animal perceives something outside its body, it already has to be seeing its body *as well*, and in relation to what is external.[28] The fact that all perception of the external world must be co-perception comes to be part of the Stoics' argument (against, for example, Epicureans) that perception in the radical sense is of the self. There is a particularly compelling version of this argument in Hierocles, who points out that we need to perceive the very organs of sense-perception if we are to use them to perceive things outside the body as well (*Ethical Elements* I.55–II.3):

> We ourselves [perceive] our eyes and ears and the rest. And so, when we want to see something, we strain our eyes towards the visible thing, not our ears. And when we want to hear, we direct our ears, not our eyes. When we wish to walk, we don't use our hands for this, but our feet and the whole of our legs. In the same way, we don't use our feet but our hands when we want to take or give something. Hence the first proof that an animal perceives its whole self is co-perception (συν(αί)σθησις) of the limbs and the functions for which they are provided.

Self-perception, by contrast, does not need any organ: rather – and this is a large part of what Hierocles is attempting to persuade us of here – it is a primitive operation of the soul.[29] So sense-organs turn out not be any part of the Stoic understanding of perception *as such*, and the fact that god lacks sense-organs *only* tells us that he cannot perceive anything external to himself. But this leaves it open that he can perceive himself – and, if he can, then of course he can perceive everything there is.

I have argued that the Stoic god possesses the capacity to perceive. It is also clear that nothing in what we know of god prevents him from

---

[27] Reydams-Schils (2005: 82) is wrong, then, to attribute 'a kind of self-awareness' to god as an *alternative* to perception: there is nothing for such 'awareness' to be *except* perception.

[28] *Sunaisthēsis* has a different sense in Stoicism from its use in Aristotle, and its subsequent use in Neoplatonism, where it means something like 'self-awareness'. See discussion in Boys-Stones 2007: 84–5. Since I shall mention the theory of 'affordance' below, it might be interesting to note the degree to which the account of affordance in Gibson 1977 – as something perceived in the external environment by an animal – converges with Hierocles' of the 'co-perception' of the external world. The two authors even use the same illustration, that of an animal (co-)perceiving of a crevasse whether it is too wide for it to jump: Gibson 1977: 79; Hierocles, *Elements* II. 34–46.

[29] Note that, at *Elements* IV.24, Hierocles identifies the 'perceiving capacity', *aisthētikē dunamis*, not as something the soul *has*, but as what it *is*. This explains the emphasis on the immediacy of self-perception in Seneca, *Letters* 121.6–10.

employing this faculty. But does he do so? An argument from Hierocles shows us that he *must* – that self-perception is not just a theoretical capacity for god, but a permanent and inalienable feature of his being.

At *Elements* III.56–IV.53, Hierocles argues that animal self-perception can be inferred from: (1) the fact that an animal has a tangible soul as well as tangible body, (2) the fact that soul is blended with the body (in the technical Stoic sense of complete blending, so that there is no part of the animal where body and soul are not co-present), (3) the fact that the soul is a perceptive capacity (*aisthētikē dunamis*), and (4) the fact that the soul is a cohesive force (*dunamis sunektikē*). All these things being true, says Hierocles, it cannot but follow that an animal perceives itself. But we are in a position to apply exactly the same argument to god. God too has: (1′) a tangible active principle as well as tangible matter (passive principle) (*SVF* 2.1051), (2′) the active principle blended throughout with the passive principle (*SVF* 2.310), (3′) perceptive capacity (see references above), and (4′) an active principle which is cohesive (e.g. *SVF* 2.448; Plutarch, *Abandoned Oracles* 425E). It follows, then, that god is not just capable of perception, but must be always and actually perceiving, that is, perceiving himself.[30]

It is natural to ask, finally, how this can be so – in virtue of what features it is the case that god can (and does) self-perceive. As it happens, our evidence tell us very little about what the constitutive basis is of the perceptive capacity in general – what it is about some entity (any entity) such that it possesses this capacity.[31] But it seems reasonable to suppose that the perceptive capacity, in parallel with the cohesive capacity mentioned by Hierocles in the argument outlined above, is an emergent property of the basic constituents of the soul – or, in the case of god, of the blend of active and passive principles. On any account, in fact, the cohesive capacity can only be the potential created by the primitive relationships of blending and resistance between the active and passive principles. And it is easy enough to make sense of this: the active principle is active upon the passive principle everywhere, and encounters resistance

---

[30] This has the added benefit, on my account, of giving the Stoics something to replace the position of Aristotle (and Plato on the 'non-literal' reading: see n. 5 above) that god, as intellect and as pure actuality, must always be thinking. The Stoics can say that their god is necessarily and always engaged in perception (which in turn either is, or will lead to cognition). For those scholars at least who think both (a) that rationality is innate to god's substance and also (b) that god does not necessarily perceive, what guarantees that god will always – or ever – in fact think?

[31] The only definitions or explanations we have of perception relate to perception of the external environment, not in fact perception *per se*: e.g. *SVF* 2.850.

from it everywhere; this would be the basis for explaining its potential to sustain patterns in it. (A similar story could be told for the relationship of the soul to the body – albeit the effect is limited in this case by their own constitution, namely as soul and body, from elemental modes of the blend of principles.) Perhaps the perceptive capacity can be explained in parallel terms: for example, as the patterns of movements, or alterations to its own patterns of movement, that arise in the active principle just because of its contact with the passive principle.[32] (This would cohere with the fact that the Stoics called perception of self 'internal touch': *SVF* 2.852.) Again, in this case the perceptive capacity of the soul would arise in just the same way. In fact, if something like this is right, the soul's evident capacity for perception is an argument *a fortiori* that the active principle has this capacity – itself a happy conclusion, since we know anyway that the soul inherits its capacities from god (see again references in Section 3.1 above).

9.4.2   Divine Concept-Formation

There is good reason to think that it is an entailment of the way that the originative substance is constituted that it self-perceives. But is its self-perception enough for the formation of concepts?

As I observed at the outset, there is no patterned order for god to consider, no repeated experiences of different qualities, and this was already seen as a challenge for the Stoics in antiquity. But there is some evidence that the Stoics might have worked quite hard to find middle ground between giving divine perception too little to work on (for example because, in its originative state, substance is perfectly uniform: in this case, there is not enough diversity to engender concepts) and giving it too much (for example, if god started transforming himself at random, and all the infinite variety of changes through which he is capable of undergoing became available to his perception: in this case there is not enough order to engender concepts).

The evidence I have in mind comes in the form of the elaborate, hierarchical series of transmutations to which the Stoics appeal in their account of how god ends up transforming himself into the cosmos. This is neatly captured in *SVF* 2.581 (DL 7.142):

[32] See Helle 2018. (This would be in effect the '"metaphysical" principle' which Brittain 2002: 269 sees is needed behind the text of Hierocles.) God's perceptual and cohesive operations are also linked in *SVF* 2.633.

The cosmos comes about when, from [pre-cosmic] fire, substance turns through [pre-cosmic] air into moisture; then the denser constituent of that produces earth, while the rarefied constituent is thinned out further: this, when it has become even more rarefied, gives rise to fire. Thereupon out of these elements animals and plants and all other natural kinds are formed by their mixture.

Accounts of Stoic cosmogony are inclined to abbreviate the sequence, partly because the details are rarely relevant,[33] and partly because it is obscured by the use of the same terms for different states of substance (for example, 'fire' both of the originative state of substance and for the cosmic element which is the last produced in this account). But it is worth pausing to consider that god in his originative form evidently does not have the power to change *immediately* into just anything he wants. For example, he cannot change directly into the cosmos, or even the cosmic elements. First he has to change into a form of (pre-elemental) 'air'; then a form of (pre-elemental) moisture.[34]

The epistemological relevance of this starts to become clear if we consider something else about self-perception for which Hierocles gives us clear evidence. According to Hierocles, self-perception is not restricted to the qualitative accidents of the body in the present moment. Indeed, it might not even begin with these, properly speaking, but with what we might call the 'affordances' of the body.[35] The first thing an animal perceives is its constitution *and what it can do with it*. Hierocles gives many examples of this: 'winged creatures have a grasp of the provision and suitability of their wings for flying', for example (*Elements* I.52–3). In fact, once again, this is crucial for the animal's development towards

---

[33] The thought is probably that the proximate state of pre-cosmic matter will be 'spermatic' moisture (DL 7.135), from which elemental earth is 'precipitated', while elemental air (which in turn feeds the fires of the heavens: *SVF* 2.572, 690) is 'exhaled'. But moisture is not the most basic state of substance, which is identified with the most rarefied state of substance: see again n. 10 above.

[34] Cf. Salles 2015: 24–5.

[35] For the idea of 'affordance' see Gibson 1977. Gibson differs from the Stoics in assuming that perception is first of the environment, so that he *only* considers environmental affordances. (The Stoics consider these too, but as the object of an extended use of perception, what they call co-perception: see discussion above.) But that difference of scope aside, his notion of 'affordance' works well to describe what the Stoics have in mind – not least in his insistence that the perception of affordances *precedes* the discrimination of the qualities through which they are delivered to the senses (1977: 75). I am not convinced, then, that animal self-perception at the most basic level is 'complex' or 'quasi-conceptual' in the way assumed by Brittain 2002: 256–74. Indeed it *could* not be (because it could not be basic, as Hierocles insists) unless one supposes that 'quasi-concepts' are hard-wired – a position on which Brittain starts to converge (266), but ultimately (and rightly) steers away from (266 n. 39). That a new-born does not perceive itself in conceptual terms at all is, I take it, the ultimate point of Seneca, *Letters* 121.11–13.

co-perception, that is perception of the external world; because it is not enough that the animal perceives its own sense-organs, it needs to perceive their affordances, that is, the possibility of using them for one thing rather than another (see again coll. I.55–II.3 quoted above).

If we put these two facts together, then it turns out that god, even in his original, homogenous, state, has more to perceive than that very state: he may also perceive, immediately, what he is capable of doing in that state.[36] But while that enriches his perceptual data, it does not do so to the point of confusion, because he is not able, immediately, to do an infinite number of things (even though, ultimately, matter is infinitely determinable). For example, he is not able to transform himself immediately into a cosmos, or into the cosmic elements, or even into the pre-cosmic moisture from which they are produced. There is a finite number of things into which he can transform himself, or parts of himself; for all we are told, perhaps pre-cosmic air is the only thing.

So it turns out that, in his original state, god has access to just the limited complexity of empirical data – sensibilia that share some qualities but not others – needed to start the process of concept-formation. From here one can see how easy it would be, in principle, to develop the story as god discovers an increasing diversity of sensibilia through the further exploration of the affordances of successive modulations of his substance – until (1) he has a rich enough conceptual set appropriately articulated in such a way that he now has reason; and (2) his concepts include all the irreducible qualities of matter, from which 'synthetic' structures (such as the cosmos, as it is constructed from the four cosmic elements) can be designed and planned, much as a human creative artist makes designs on the basis of the materials available to her, and her understanding of the qualities it is capable of assuming.

In short: it is possible to account for the mind of god on the assumption that it is constituted and that it operates on the very same empiricist principles that the Stoics use to explain animal cognition in general, and human rationality in particular. To suppose that this is how the Stoics accounted for god's rationality avoids both bare stipulation on the one hand, and the real conceptual problems which face non-empiricist attempts to explain divine thinking on the other; and it allows us to take

[36] Cf. perhaps Epictetus, *Diss.* 3.13.7, which might be translated to say that, at the conflagration, Zeus, no longer thinking about the cosmos, 'forms a concept of the way he himself is organised' (ὁ Ζεὺς αὐτὸς ἑαυτῷ σύνεστιν καὶ ἡσυχάζει ἐφ' ἑαυτοῦ καὶ ἐννοεῖ τὴν διοίκησιν τὴν ἑαυτοῦ οἵα ἐστί), and comes to have just those conceptions that have to do with himself (καὶ ἐν ἐπινοίαις γίνεται πρεπούσαις ἑαυτῷ).

the 'craftsman' model of divine creative activity consistently and seriously as an attempt to include cosmic teleology in a radically corporealist view of reality.[37]

9.5   The Road to Creation

I end with a very brief sketch of how the creation of the cosmos proceeds – and especially how god's intentions are realised in the life of the cosmos.[38]

Surviving texts on Stoic cosmogony are not as helpful as one might have hoped. They tend to bifurcate into those on the one hand that describe (in rather 'Presocratic' terms) the turnings of substance (for example DL 7.142 as quoted above), and those on the other which hint at the role of the *spermatikoi logoi* in engendering animals and plants. There is little overlap between the two. Nevertheless, one thing does seem to emerge: that it is in the course of the transformations of god into the various elements that the division I alluded to earlier between the mind of god (the *hēgemonikon*) and the rest emerges. And it seems to me natural to suppose that this is the point where the *spermatikoi logoi* come into their own. Their role, I suggest, is far from being that of unifying god's mind with his creation, as Reydams-Schils suggests. On the contrary, it is precisely to allow some degree of *distance* between god's mind and the operation of the cosmos he plans. This is especially important given that he plans for the existence of further, autonomous intellects, since we need to be able to square a meaningful sense of their autonomy with the claim that everything happens as god plans. It is not clear that this would be possible if every individual cosmic event were a way of describing a concurrent divine thought.

A good starting point is DL 7.136. After the turnings of the whole, we are told that god creates a divide between himself in the moisture and the rest of substance bent to his purpose:

> God, intellect, fate and Zeus are one thing – which is called by many other
> names too. In the beginning, when he is by himself, he turns the entirely of

---

[37] It could be relevant to note here that matter is said to yield perfectly and immediately to god's wishes (*SVF* 2.1107). One might worry that, if effort and perseverance were involved, it would require more complexity than I am allowing the divine mind at this stage in the explanatory process: for example, some conceptualisation of the future, which is ruled out by the Stoics as an object of perception (*SVF* 2.879 at p. 236.2–3). (Note that perception of divine 'affordances' is, then, perception of present capacity, not future potential.)

[38] For detailed discussion of early Stoic cosmogony, see especially Salles 2015; also Hahm 1977, chapter 3; Cooper 2009: 101–15.

substance through air into water. As in [animal] generation, the seed is contained [i.e. in moisture], so this spermatic principle of the cosmos is retained in the water as such [a seed]. He makes the matter into something he can work with[39] towards the birth [*genesis*] of each thing in turn. Then he generates, first, the four elements: fire, water, air, earth.

God here is the seminal principle of the cosmos as a whole: in other words, I take it, has a plan for the development of the whole.[40] But as such he contains the seminal principles of each part of it which, as the plan develops, become dispersed (*SVF* 2.1027):

The Stoics declare that god is intelligent, a skilful fire following a route towards the birth [*genesis*] of a cosmos, encompassing all the spermatic principles by which each thing comes to be according to fate.

See also *SVF* 1.497 [part]:

As all the parts of a single [organism] grow from seeds at the appropriate times, so the parts of the universe, among which are animals and plants, grow at the appropriate times. And, as principles for these parts enter the same seed and are mixed together, and again are distinguished out when the parts are produced, so all things come from one, and from all things one is compounded, the cycle pursuing its route harmoniously.

So we can talk now about divine reason being everywhere in one sense; but not because the guiding intelligence, the divine mind, is everywhere (DL 7.138–9):

The cosmos is organised with intelligence and providence ... since intellect pervades every part of it, just like the soul in our case – but more through some parts, less through others. It has gone through some parts as *condition* [*hexis*], e.g. bones and sinew; some as intellect, e.g. the *hēgemonikon*. So the whole cosmos is an animal, ensouled and rational, with the aether as its *hēgemonikon*.

The fact that the seminal principles only really come into their own at this later stage, where a separation develops between the divine mind and the rest of the cosmos, seems to me fatal in itself to the notion that seminal principles are *thoughts*, in the sense of being acts of thinking. In fact the seminal principles represent just what we get in just those places of the cosmos where the divine mind has planned for something to happen *but is*

[39] *euergon*: cf. Aristotle, *Ph.* 2.2, 194a33–4.
[40] So he can also be thought of as the (singular) governing 'nature' of the cosmos: e.g. *SVF* 2.1024.

not itself present.[41] They are, so to speak, the 'encoding' of particular areas of the universe. This more 'impersonal' understanding of what (*spermatikoi*) *logoi* are is encouraged by the occasional use of the term *arithmoi*, numbers, or perhaps 'formulae', to describe them (*SVF* 2.744; 3.83; Cornutus, *Theology* 7, p. 8.7–9 Lang).[42] It is probably wrong to think of them as *thoughts* – a translation which in any case already stretches the possible meaning of the word *logos*. They are rather the 'expressions' of thoughts, that is, of god's intentions.

9.6 Conclusion

My argument has been (1) that the Stoics must have addressed the question of how god thinks; and (2) that they must have assumed that just the same sort of empiricist model underpinned his thinking as underpins the thinking of human minds. They must have assumed this because (3) it is actually required for their reconciliation of teleology with a radical corporealism.

Above all, what is important to stress is that the Stoics are committed to the position that god thinks, and acts skilfully in creation on the basis of his thought, in a way that relates very straightforwardly to the way in which humans think and plan. There is nothing metaphorical, alien or homonymous about the way that god thinks. Whether or not the Stoics were the first to argue this depends on one's interpretation of the earlier tradition;[43] but they were arguably the first who *had* to think it, that is, who had well-motivated philosophical reasons to think just this. That makes their theology more radical – and perhaps more important for later theories of god and creation, including Christian theories – than people often recognise.

---

[41] Note however that, if god's mind is located in a part of the cosmos from this point, god as a whole remains present throughout the cosmos, on the precise analogy of a soul in a human body: so god's awareness of the cosmos as a whole remains immediate, and a case of *self*-perception, requiring no organ.

[42] Alexander and Plotinus variously compare them to 'immanent form': *SVF* 2.306, 1047; Plotinus 5.7.3.

[43] Including, as well as Plato and Aristotle, certain of the Presocratics: cf. e.g. Sedley 2007: chapters 1 and 2 for Anaxagoras and Empedocles respectively.

CHAPTER 10

Why Is the Cosmos Intelligent?
(2) Stoic Cosmology and Plato, Timaeus 30a2–c1

Ricardo Salles*

The Stoics maintain that the cosmos as a whole (understood as the complex system composed of the Earth, its atmosphere, the planets and the fixed stars, as well as the laws that govern their motion) is *intelligent* in the sense that it is an agent capable of thinking. Their contention is not that the whole cosmos thinks, since some parts do not think, e.g. mountains and trees, but that it thinks as a whole, in just the same way as I have parts that do not think but I am, as a whole, something that thinks. In this chapter, the second in a series of two essays on the subject,[1] I explore a family of Stoic proofs for the intelligence of the cosmos – 'F_1' – and its Platonic background in *Tim.* 30a2–c1. The basic-argument structure of these proofs runs as follows: (a) the intelligent is better than the unintelligent, but (b) the cosmos is better than everything else; therefore, (c) the cosmos is intelligent. Given this argument-structure, there is a close connection between these proofs and the Timaean proof. The connection has been brought out, and carefully studied, by David Sedley in an important study on ancient cosmology.[2] Sedley concentrates on the strong similarities between them. However, there are also significant differences between the two, and these shed at least as much light on the nature of F_1 as the similarities do. These differences are the focus of the present chapter.

---

* Earlier versions of this chapter were presented at the '13 Taller de Filosofía Antigua del Instituto de Investigaciones Filosóficas' in Mexico City (UNAM) in February 2017, the V Congreso de la Asociación Latinoamericana de Filosofía Antigua (ALFA) in Rio de Janeiro in September 2017, and the University of Michigan in February 2018. I am indebted to these audiences for discussing with the issues that I raise here. I owe special thanks to David Sedley for his detailed and extremely helpful written comments on the penultimate version. The research for this project benefitted from financial the support from three research projects: PAPIIT-UNAM 400517 and PAPIIT-UNAM 403620.

[1] See Salles 2018a.

[2] See notably Sedley 2007: 225–30. The Timaean proof is also discussed by Sattler in Section 2.2 and by Boys-Stones in Section 5.5 (Chapters 2 and 5 of the present volume).

The argument-structure of F_1 is no doubt borrowed from the Timaean proof But as I intend to show, the philosophical ideas on which the premises of F_1 are based, and especially those behind the key notion of something 'better than' something else, are new. The specific reason why the cosmos is better than everything else according to F_1 is that everything exists for the sake of the cosmos, and the reason why the intelligent is better than the unintelligent is that the latter exists for the sake of the former where existing 'for the sake' of something means existing for its benefit: everything exists for the benefit of the cosmos and the unintelligent exists for the benefit of the intelligent. These ideas, I shall argue, have no parallel in the Timaean proof which is not teleological in any important sense. The notion that everything exists for the sake of the cosmos is surely present in Plato's cosmology, for instance, in *Laws* 10 903b4–c5 (cited below as **T4c**). But the *use* of this idea to prove the intelligence of the cosmos, as in F_1, is a Stoic innovation.[3]

One problem that I bypass in this chapter and that is not addressed either in F_1 or in any of the families of Stoic proofs for the intelligence of the cosmos is that of the object of cosmic intelligence. What does the Stoic cosmos think about? One way to approach this question is by asking what is the characteristic activity performed by that part of the cosmos which the Stoics regard as the seat of its intelligence, namely its 'ruling part', or *hēgemonikon*.[4] Some Stoics identify this part with the sun, others with the layer of ether that surrounds the sublunary cosmos, and still others with Earth, the spatial centre of the cosmos. Whatever is achieved by the activity of this part may be rightly identified as the product of cosmic intelligence and, therefore, as the object at which the cosmos is directed when it thinks. The intuition here is that thinking and intentional action are closely linked to one another: if A is an intelligent being that does B intentionally, B is an object of thought of A and, in general terms, for anything X that A does, doing X intentionally requires that A thinks about X. So going back to our question – what does the Stoic cosmos think about? – one general answer would that, since everything that occurs in the cosmos is the product of cosmic intelligence, everything that occurs in the cosmos is also an object of its thinking, which raises the question of

---

[3] Plato's teleology is also discussed by Hankinson in Chapter 13 of the present volume.
[4] See e.g. *SVF* 2.499 and 634. The Stoic conception of the ruling part of the cosmos is discussed by Vimercati in Sections 11.2–11.4 of Chapter 11 of the present volume. See also Boechat 2017.

how cosmic intelligence is related to divine intelligence and of how, if they are not identical, they complement each other.[5]

10.1   The Argument-Structure of F₁

The argument-structure of F_1 – (a) the intelligent is better than the unintelligent, but (b) the cosmos is better than everything else; therefore, (c) the cosmos is intelligent – is clearly reflected in three sources for this family.[6]

> **T1a:** Cicero, *ND* 2.21 (*SVF* 1.111b)
> That which makes use of reason is better than that which does not make use reason; nothing, however, is better than the cosmos; therefore, the cosmos makes use of reason.
> **T1b:** Sextus Empiricus *M* 9.104 (*SVF* 1.111a, < *LS* 54F, < *BS* 12.16)
> And again Zeno says: 'The rational is better than the non-rational; but nothing is better than the cosmos; therefore, the cosmos is rational. And likewise for what is intelligent and animate. For the intelligent is better than the unintelligent and the animate is better than the inanimate; but nothing is better than the cosmos; therefore, the cosmos is intelligent and animate'.
> **T1c:** DL 7.142–3 (< *SVF* 2.633, > *LS* 53X, < *BS* 12.13)
> Chrysippus in the first book of *On Providence*, Apollodorus in his *Physics*, and Posidonius say that the cosmos is an animal that is rational, animate and intelligent. It is an animal to the extent that it is an animate sensitive substance. For the animal is better than the non-animal, but nothing is better than the cosmos, and therefore the cosmos is an animal.

The proofs in **T1b** and **T1c** differ is some respects from that in **T1a**. The demonstrandum in **T1b** is not just the intelligence of the cosmos, but also, more generally, its rationality (which comprises intelligence, but also the powers of impression, assent, sensation, and impulse), and, still more generally, its possession of soul (which comprises rationality but also the five senses – sight, smell, hearing, taste and touch – as well as the powers of speech and reproduction).[7] The same applies to the demonstrandum of **T1c**. These, however, are minor differences considering that, from a

---

[5] For the form and content of Stoic divine intellection, see Boys-Stones, Chapter 9 of the present volume, as well as Cooper 2003: 219–28, Long 2003: 11–13, Reydams-Schills 2005: 584–92 and 2006, and Alesse 2011–12.

[6] In addition the texts cited below, see Philo, *Prov.* 1.24–6 (> *SVF* 2.1111) and Cicero, *ND* 29–30 (*LS* 47C, *BS* 12.11).

[7] For the division of reason into impression, assent, sensation, and impulse, and for the dsitinction between reason, perception, speech and reproduction as the four basic powers of the Stoic soul see *SVF* 773–911 (esp. 823–78).

Stoic perspective, the possession of a particular capacity entails the possession of any other capacity located at the same level or at the lower levels.[8] So
the proof of the intelligence of the cosmos attempted in **T1a** is also, *a
fortiori*, a proof of its possession of rationality and soul. Furthermore, **T1b**
and **T1c** are extremely important for determining the authorship of F_1. **T1c**
mentions that is was accepted by Chrysippus and later by Apollodorus
and Posidonius, and **T1b** points out that F_1 has its origin in Zeno, an issue
to which I return shortly.

We may notice that none of the three passages explains the proof.
They are silent about how each of the premises is established – why the
intelligent is better than the unintelligent and why the cosmos is better
than everything else – and about how the inference works from these
premises to the conclusion that the cosmos itself is intelligent. The sources,
however, do report a fourth member of the family, significantly different
from the three examined so far, in which an interesting account is provided
of how the proof works. This fourth member is reported again by Cicero, a
little later in the *De Natura Deorum*.

> **T1d:** Cicero, *ND* 2.37–8 (> *SVF* 2.1153, < *LS* 54H, *BS* 12.14)
> For nor is there anything other than the cosmos which has not some-
> thing missing, and which is totally fitted, perfect and complete in all its
> elements and parts. For Chrysippus skilfully says that just as the shield-
> cover exists for the sake of the shield and the sheath for the sake of the
> sword, so too with the exception of the cosmos all else is generated for the
> sake of other things. For instance, the crops and fruits which the earth
> produces [are generated] for the sake of animate beings, and the animate
> beings for the sake of human beings (the horse for transport, the ox for
> ploughing, the dog for hunting and guarding). Humankind itself – being
> in no way perfect, but a particle of what is perfect – has arisen in order to
> contemplate and imitate the cosmos. But the cosmos, since it embraces
> everything and there is not anything that does not exist in it, is totally
> perfect. How then could it lack what is optimal? But nothing is better than
> intelligence and reason. Therefore, the cosmos cannot lack this.

Given that this proof is attributed to Chrysippus and that, according to
T1c, Chrysippus also accepted the Zenonian proof, it is likely that
Chrysippus regarded the proof reported here, not as a new one, different
from Zeno's, but as a stronger version of the Zenonian proof intended to
bring out its validity and its soundness.

---

[8] See *SVF* 2.458 and 988–9 discussed in Inwood 1985: 18–27. On the Stoic *scala naturae*, see also
Akinpelu 1967 and Hahm 1994.

It is not easy, however, to grasp the Chrysippean version and some analysis is needed. The passage contains four different claims that are all supposed to play a role in the inference, either as premises or conclusions. One – *Structure* – concerns the teleological structure of the cosmos. The cosmos is a whole whose parts exist either for the sake of one another or for the sake of the whole. Thus, fruits and crops, and presumably plants in general, exist for the sake of 'animate beings' (*animantia*), i.e. animals. Animals, in turn, exist for the sake of human beings (*homines*). And human beings themselves exist for the sake of the cosmos. The cosmos, however, does not exist for the sake of anything else. It stands, therefore, at the apex of the teleological structure that governs the natural world: every natural being exists either directly or indirectly for the sake of the cosmos. The term that I translate as 'for the sake of' is '*causa*', which is clearly used in the sense of a final cause. In fact, it could hardly possess a different meaning. For instance, it could not refer to an *efficient cause* since it makes little sense in this context to say that the sword, for example, is the efficient cause of the sheath or, more significantly, that animals are the efficient cause of plants. The second claim – *Order* – establishes a general criterion for determining the order in which natural beings exist for the sake of one another. Unintelligent beings exist either directly or indirectly for the sake of intelligent ones, but no intelligent being does so for the sake of an unintelligent one. *Order* is implied by the examples given in the passage. The third claim – *Completeness* – asserts that there is no natural body that is not part of the cosmos since nothing exists outside it: 'it embraces everything and there is not anything that does not exist in it' (*omnia conplexus est neque est quicquam, quod non insit in eo*). The fourth claim, *Intelligence*, functions merely as the conclusion of the argument: the cosmos must be intelligent.

Given these four claims, the inference seems to proceed as follows. The cosmos must be intelligent, as *Intelligence* demands, because, if it were not, then, given *Order*, the cosmos would exist for the sake of some intelligent being, which is impossible. For this natural being would have to be either part of the cosmos or not, but neither option is acceptable: it could not be one of its parts because, given *Structure*, the cosmos does not exist for the sake of its parts, and it could not be either something that is *not* one of its parts because, given *Completeness*, there is no natural being that is not a part of the cosmos, since nothing exists outside the cosmos.[9]

---

[9] An alternative interpretation of the proof, suggested to me by James Wilberding and Vincenzo Carlotta, could be that, since the cosmos is perfect in the sense that it is the most 'final' being (i.e. it

If we compare the Zenonian versions in **T1a-c** to the Chrysippean version in **T1d**, we notice at once two significant differences: one is that the latter contains three premises whereas the former only two; the other is that the latter expresses the relation between the cosmos and its parts, and between the intelligent and the unintelligent, in terms of one existing for the sake of the other, whereas the former expresses these relations in terms of one being better than the other. Assuming that the latter version is indeed a revision of the former, we may venture some hypotheses to explain these differences.

As regards the second difference, one hypothesis is that *Structure* and *Order* are intended to explain the two premises of the proofs in **T1a-c**. The intelligent is better than the unintelligent – first premiss in these proofs – *because* the unintelligent beings exist for the sake of the intelligent ones; and the cosmos is better than everything else *because* every natural being exists for the sake of the cosmos but the cosmos does not exist for the sake of anything else. The general principle behind these two theses would be that the comparative value of something depends on its place within the teleological structure to which it belongs. The higher up it is located the better it is compared to the other items in the structure. In this vein, something is the best – as is the case with the cosmos according to *Structure* – if it occupies the highest place, i.e. if it is that for the sake of which everything else exists and that does not exist for the sake of anything else.

In connection with the first difference, the premiss that appears in **T1d** that is missing in **T1a-c** is *Completeness*. This premiss is important in the argument because, as a matter of fact, the proof is invalid without it. The mere conjunction of *Structure* and *Order* is insufficient for inferring that the cosmos is intelligent. This conjunction certainly implies that the intelligent being for the sake of which the cosmos would exist if it were unintelligent, is not one of its parts. But it does not rule out that such an intelligent being exists. For this being could be something that is not part of the cosmos. To rule out this possibility it must established – as *Completeness* does – that nothing exists that is not part of the cosmos. In other words, the role of *Completeness* is to cancel a possibility that the Zenonian version leaves open and that threatens the validity of the proof. Thus, in Chrysippus' distinctive contribution to F_1 would be to provide a

is the being for the sake of which the greatest number of other beings exist), and since intelligence is optimal, then the cosmos must be intelligent since something perfect in the sense above cannot lack something optimal. My main concern with this reconstruction is that it makes no clear use of the thesis, central in **T1d**, that I call 'Order', namely, that the unintelligent exists for the sake of the intelligent.

teleological basis to the Zenonian proof and to add a premiss that secures its validity. This is something important that we must bear in mind in Section 10.3 for the explanation of the difference between F_1 and the Timaean proof. For although the Zenonian proof bears some striking similarities to the Timaean one, when we look at it from the angle of the Chrysippean proof, it becomes evident that F_1 as a whole differs significantly from the Timaean proof. As will be seen, the central difference is that F_1 rests on a teleological theory that we may describe as 'cosmocentric', implied in *Structure* but absent from the Timaean proof, namely that the cosmos is a whole whose parts exist either for the *benefit* of one another or for the *benefit* of the whole in such a way that the cosmos is the ultimate *beneficiary* of everything that exists in the cosmos. As I argue in the next section, this is indeed how *Structure* should be understood.

10.2   The Teleology of the Chrysippean Proof

In order to bring forth the cosmocentric character of F_1, we may use one additional principle, based on the notion of benefit. According to *Benefit*, for any two natural beings A and B, A exists 'for the sake of' B if only if A exists for the benefit of B. This principle is strongly suggested in the examples given in **T1d**. For instance, in the artefacts example – the shield-cover and the sheath – they both exist for the sake of the shield and the sword *because* arguably they benefit them somehow. A shield out of its shield-cover or a sword out its sheath, for example, may be damaged and become useless. Likewise, in the plants example, plants exist for the sake of animals *because* they benefit them inasmuch as animals feed on them and need them for their survival. And similarly, in the animals example, the horse, the ox and the dog exist for the sake of human beings because they benefit them at least in the sense that they help us to perform tasks needed for our survival (transportation, ploughing, hunting and guarding). The human example is puzzling since it is not immediately clear why human contemplation would benefit the cosmos in any way, an issue that I tackle momentarily.

Further evidence for cosmocentrism may be gathered from a number of sources. One is Plutarch in a passage dealing with how, according to Chrysippus, animals exist for the sake of human beings.[10]

---

[10] For additional passages dealing with this particular issue see the testimonies of Porphyry and Lactantius in *SVF* 2.1152 and 2.1172 (with commentary and notes in Long-Sedley 1987: 1.331–3 and 2.330–31) as well Cicero, *ND* 2.154–62, which provides a long list of examples.

T2a: Plutarch, *SR* 1044D (*SVF* 2.1163b, LS 54O)

In book 5 of *On Nature*, he [sc. Chrysippus], having said that bugs usefully wake us up, that mice force us not to dispose of each thing carelessly, and that it is likely that nature, taking delight in variety, loves beauty, says literally that the evidence for this would come mainly from the tail of the peacock. For this evinces that the animal was generated for the sake of the tail and not vice versa, but in virtue of the male's being generated in this way, the female followed as a concomitant.

T2a reports a series of examples given by Chrysippus to explain how the lower, unintelligent, animals exist for the benefit of human beings. The notion of benefit is conspicuous. Consider the peacock example. Given that nature, i.e. presumably *our* nature, loves beauty, watching the tail of a peacock gives us pleasure and this is precisely the reason why peacocks exist at all and why peahens, needed for the reproduction of the species, also exist at all. Another source is Epictetus in a passage that refers to the teleological order the cosmos in terms very similar to those used in the Chrysippean proof.

T2b: Epictetus, *Diss.* 1.6.18–22 (< LS 63E, BS 29.7)

So then [god] constitutes each of the animals [in a certain way:] one in such a way as to be eaten, another in such a way as to serve in agriculture, another in such a way as to produce cheese and the other for another similar use. But for such activities what is the use of being capable to understand, and distinguish between, impressions? But god introduced the human being as a contemplator of himself and of his works; and not only as a contemplator, but as an expounder of them. For this reason, it is shameful for the human being to begin and to stop where irrational animals do, and he should rather begin there, but stop where nature stopped relative to us, and it did so in contemplation and understanding and a way of life in harmony with nature.

The focus of **T2b** is on two things: the difference between the place that we occupy in the teleological order of the cosmos and the place occupied by lower animals, and the normative consequences of this difference. As in **T1d**, the lower animals exist for the sake of us and we exist for the sake of the cosmos. The notion of benefit is conspicuous here too. But, as in **T1d**, no explanation is offered of how our contemplation of the cosmos – the end for which we exist – benefits the cosmos. However, there is no doubt that for Epictetus it may do so. Consider the following passage.

T2c: Epictetus, *Diss.* 2.5.24–5

What is the meaning of the statement that some external things are natural and others unnatural? It is as though we took ourselves to be detached beings. For while I admit that it is natural for the foot to be clean, yet if you take it as a foot and not as something detached, it will be appropriate for it to step into mud and trample on thorns, and sometimes be amputated for the sake of the whole. Otherwise it will no longer be a foot. That is the way we should also view ourselves. What are you? A human being. If you view yourself as something detached, it is natural for you to live to old age, to be wealthy, and healthy. But if you view yourself as a human being and a part of some whole, for the sake of that whole it is appropriate for you now to be sick, now to set sail and take risks, now to be in need, and maybe even die before your time.[11]

The passage explains how anything may be viewed from two different perspectives – as something detached and as part of a whole – and argues that what is natural from the latter perspective may not be natural from the former. In this context, Epictetus suggests that any part of a whole may be in a state that positively or negatively affects the whole and, in particular, that the harm of a part may benefit the whole. For example, a given situation may require that I trample on thorns, and so harm my foot, in order to avoid a greater damage to my body as a whole.[12] The intuition we are invited to share is that, by analogy, a given situation may require that I suffer some harm in order to prevent a greater harm to some whole (*holon ti*) to which I belong. And this would apply to cases where the whole in question is the cosmos itself, which in Stoic cosmology is often referred to as 'the whole'.[13] Our passage, however, does not disclose how the states of individual beings could affect the cosmos as a whole and, in particular, how contemplation, a state of human beings, could affect cosmic intelligence, a state of the cosmos as a whole. By a 'state' I mean what in modern metaphysics is often called an 'event', i.e. the exemplification of a property by a body.[14] Thus my contemplation of the cosmos is the exemplification by me of the property of contemplating, which the Stoics would classify as a 'disposition' or 'dispositional property' (*hexis*) as opposed to a quality or qualitative property (*poiotēs*). Likewise, the cosmos' thinking would constitute the exemplification by the cosmos of the property of thinking, which is also a disposition.

---

[11] Slightly modified trans. from Long 2002: 200–201.
[12] Other passages where this analogy is drawn include Epictetus, *Diss.* 2.6.8–10 (citing Chrysippus) and 2.10.5–6.
[13] See for instance the evidence collected under *SVF* 2.522–5 and Epictetus, *Diss.* 2.10.5–6.
[14] See **T2e** below. For a discussion of the Stoic theory of events see Bobzien 1998: 26–7 and more recently Salles 2018b: 142–50.

It is clear from **T2c** that for Epictetus our states in general may affect the cosmos as a whole. But how? Let me indicate, first, one way in which it is not clear how they could affect it and, second, two ways in which they surely can. The Stoics, like some Preplatonics and unlike some critics of them, notably Aristotle, think that meteorological phenomena in the sublunary cosmos may affect the supralunary cosmos, and also that the stability of the supralunary cosmos is needed for the preservation of the cosmos as a whole. One prominent example given by the Stoics are the exhalations (*anathumiaseis*) emitted by the sea and all the large bodies of water on Earth, which feed the celestial bodies and, in particular, the sun which is necessary for the endurance of the whole cosmos.[15] Thus, exhalations are needed for the very endurance of the celestial bodies and, given the role of these bodies in the preservation of the cosmos as a whole, for the endurance of the cosmos as a whole. In this respect, it may be rightly qualified as a beneficiary of the exhalations. But how could our states, according to the Stoics, affect this complex system? In general how could they affect meteorological phenomena and have, thereby, an impact in the operation celestial bodies and on the cosmos as whole? Plato, for example, seems to have thought that they can, and that they actually do, and it seems to be wrong simply to assume that ancient Greek philosophers did not have ecological concerns derived from a belief in our impact on our environment.[16] But there is not enough evidence to ascertain the position of the Stoics on these questions.

Now, there are at least two ways in which our states may affect the cosmos as a whole. One affects the completeness of the cosmos. Whether or not we contemplate affects the completeness of the cosmos, since the rationality of a cosmos in which I contemplate is more complete than that of a cosmos in which I do not, and in this respect my contemplation does benefit the cosmos a whole.[17] The other affects the effectiveness of cosmic intelligence. In Stoic cosmology, cosmic intelligence is supposed to determine the states of each and all of its individual parts. Consider, for

[15] See e.g. *SVF* 2.663, 677 and 690.
[16] See e.g. *Critias* 109c–112e with discussion in Carone 1998: 128–32. The opposite view is advocated in Attfield 1994: 77–90. On this question see also Westra-Robinson 1997.
[17] See e.g. Marcus Aurelius, *Meditations* 7.9. which suggests that the cosmos is constituted by the sum all things, that all things are divided into genera, and that each genus as its own characteristic perfection and, hence, that contemplation and the use of reason in general, as the characteristic perfection of human beings, is constitutive of the cosmos as a whole. This theme also appears in classic Stoic texts on our role in the cosmos and its connection with happiness and duty such as *DL* 7.88 (*SVF* 1.162d) and Cicero, *Fin.* 3.64 (*SVF* 3.333, *BS* 30.45).

instance, an important passage of Sextus Empiricus on the ruling part of the Stoic cosmos – the seat of cosmic intelligence – as the source of all the powers of its parts.

T2d: Sextus Empiricus, *M* 9.102 (< *BS* 12.16)
For the beginning of motion in every nature and soul seems to proceed from the ruling part, and all the powers that are dispatched to the parts of the whole are dispatched from the ruling part, as from some kind of spring, and hence every power that exists in the part also exists in the whole because of being passed on from the ruling part that lies in it.

At a physical level, cosmic intelligence acts on the parts of the cosmos by causing its individual parts to take on a certain amount of tension (*tónos*). For example, it may cause some of its parts to take on the amount of tension needed for their endurance as unified wholes. This would occur, for instance, in lifeless entities such as stones. But it may cause other parts of the cosmos to take on, in addition to the amount of tension needed for their endurance as unified wholes, the amount of tension required for performing an activity such as contemplation, as would be the case in human beings who are actually contemplating.[18] In this picture, the *effectiveness* of cosmic intelligence – its ability to bestow a given amount of tension to its parts – will depend on the success of its action, i.e. on whether the parts of the cosmos do take on the amount of tension intended by cosmic intelligence. For this reason, any state of any part of the cosmos, including human contemplation, does affect cosmic intelligence. If I failed to contemplate at a time when cosmic intelligence requires me to do so, my failure would limit its effectiveness. This does not mean that I could fail to contemplate when cosmic intelligence requires me to do so, as if my actual states could be at variance with cosmic intelligence. This would represent a breach in determinism, something that Stoic cosmology rules out. As is reported by Plutarch, for example, in a passage where he quotes Chrysippus' treatise *On Nature*:

T2f: Plutarch, *SR* 1050a (< SVF 2.937, < BS 19.9)
But given that the organization of the all things proceeds in this way, it is necessary that it be in accordance with this organization that we are in whatever state we happen to be, whether, at variance with our individual nature, we are ill or maimed or whether we have become grammarians or

---

[18] For how the ruling part of a natural being in general acts on its other parts, see Aetius, *Placita* 4.21.2–4 (< SVF 2.836, < LS 53 H, < BS 13.13) and Calcidius, *in Tim.* 220–21 (> SVF 2.879, > LS 53G, BS 13.14); for how the ruling part of the cosmos acts on its other parts, see DL 7.138–9 (> SVF 2.634, LS 47O, BS 12.13). I discuss this issue extensively in Salles 2018a.

musicians [. . .] for it is not possible for any particular thing, not even the smallest one, to occur otherwise than in accordance with common nature and its reason.

Chrysippus concurs with Epictetus in **T2c** on the notion that in a given situation cosmic intelligence may require that I suffer some harm for the sake of the whole. But Chrysippus stresses the deterministic aspect of the theory: any state in which I happen to be is necessarily in accordance with cosmic intelligence.[19] Thus, the states of the parts of the cosmos cannot be at variance with cosmic intelligence. In this sense cosmic intelligence is always fully effective. But even so there is an important connection between the effectiveness of cosmic intelligence and the actual states of the parts of the cosmos: cosmic intelligence is fully effective *because* all actual states of the parts are in accordance with it. At least in this respect, cosmic intelligence is affected by the states of the parts of the cosmos, and human contemplation in particular has an impact on it.

Now that we have seen that cosmocentrism, the view that everything exists for the benefit of the cosmos, is a key element in F_1 we may rightly appreciate the difference between F_1 and the Timaean proof. As I indicate at the end of the next section, cosmocentrism is a form of teleology already existent in Plato's *Laws*. But it not developed in the context of a proof of the intelligence of the cosmos and, in any case, it is absent from the Timaean proof.

10.3 Plato and F_1

I now turn to the relation between F_1 and the Timaean proof for the intelligence of the cosmos. How much of F_1 is already present in this proof? We must begin by looking at Plato's text.

T3a: Plato, *Tim.* 30a2–c1
   Wanting everything to be good and nothing to be bad as far as possible, and so gaining control of all that was visible though not at rest but in motion wrongly and disorderly, god brought it from a state of disorder to one of order, believing that order was absolutely better than disorder. However it is laid down that it was, and that it is, impossible for the best to do anything but the most beautiful. In consequence, he found out by reasoning that, among the things that are naturally visible, nothing unintelligent will ever be as a whole a better work than that which has

---

[19] For a general discussion of cosmic determinism, see Bobzien 1998: 28–58, Salles 2005: 3–29 and also Vogt, Chapter 12 of the present collection.

intelligence, but in addition that intelligence is incapable of accruing to something without a soul. By means of this reasoning he built the whole putting intelligence in soul and soul in body in order for the finest and the best naturally possible work to have been completed. Therefore, in line with our likely account, this is how it must be said that this cosmos was generated as a truly ensouled, intelligent animal by god's providence.

There is no question that in its Zenonian version F_1 has much in common with this proof. As in the Zenonian proof, the 'cosmos' whose intelligence is proved by Timaeus is surely the system composed of the Earth, the planets, the fixed stars and the laws that govern their motion. In fact, there are detailed references to each of these components at *Tim.* 38b5–40d5, and in general terms the whole of the *Timaeus* is a lengthy account of how each of the components of the cosmos in this sense of 'cosmos' exists for a purpose. Furthermore, the two premises of the Zenonian proof are paralleled in the Timaean proof through the claims that the cosmos is the 'best' (*to kalliston*) and that the intelligent is 'better as a whole' (*holon holou kallion*) than the unintelligent. The same applies to the conclusion that the cosmos is an 'animal, ensouled and intelligent' (*zōon empsuchon ennoun*), which is practically the same as the conclusion in F_1 except for the use in **T4a** of the term '*ennoun*' instead of '*noeron*' for 'intelligent' (ζῷον ὁ κόσμος καὶ λογικὸν καὶ ἔμψυχον καὶ νοερὸν in **T1c**). Thus, the basic-argument structure of the Timaean proof is apparently the same as that of F_1 in its Zenonian version, namely (a) the intelligent is better than the unintelligent, but (b) the cosmos is better than everything else; therefore, (c) the cosmos is intelligent. This evident closeness between the two proofs could hardly be fortuitous. On the contrary, it intimates that Zeno knew the Timaean proof well, and that he intentionally imitated its language and its structure.

There are, however, several differences that evince that Zeno and Chrysippus went well beyond Plato in central respects. In what follows, I discuss three main differences. The former two concern the Zenonian proof as stated in **T1a-c**. They are, as Sedley correctly observes, relatively minor. The third, however, is substantive and concerns the Chrysippean version in **T1d**.

The first difference resides in the use of the adjective 'as a whole' (ὅλον ὅλου) to qualify how the intelligent is better than the unintelligent, a qualification that we do not encounter in the Zenonian proof.[20] The qualification is stated by Timaeus as follows 'nothing unintelligent will

ever be *as a whole* a better work than that which has intelligence'. We may
surmise, in the absence of evidence to the contrary, that this is a purely
rhetorical device to stress that the intelligent is indeed better than the
unintelligent. It is also possible, however, that the adjective is intended to
have a logical function that is not purely rhetorical, namely to stress that
intelligence, unlike other many positive properties, is one whose possession
is, all by itself, sufficient for its possessor to be better than anything that
lacks this property. The issue of whether intelligence is the only positive
property that is sufficient all by itself for the superiority of its possessor was
addressed by the Megarian Alexinus of Elis through a series of parodies of
F_I and by later Stoics who confronted Alexinus.[21] So the use of the
expression '*holon holou*' in the *Timaean* proof could be an anticipation
of this discussion. The issue, however, was not discussed either by Zeno or
by Chrysippus who seem to be unaware of Alexinus' objection. At least,
the proofs belonging to F_I that are attested for them do not register their
position regarding this discussion. So if '*holon holou*' in the Timaean
proof did have the logical function of introducing the idea that intelligence is sufficient for superiority, we could conclude that the Timaean
proof is philosophically more sophisticated than the Zenonian or
Chrysippean proofs.

The second difference is that the Timaean proof, unlike the Zenonian
one, restricts the scope of the thesis that nothing unintelligent is better
than something intelligent to the realm of 'naturally visible things'.[22] This
difference rests on a general difference between Platonic and Stoic ontology. In Platonic ontology, visible things are opposed to Forms, which
occupy a higher realm of reality and, given this ontology, the restriction of
the scope of the thesis that nothing unintelligent is better than something
intelligent to the realm of 'naturally visible things' is needed because
something unintelligent in the realm of Forms could be better, in some
sense, than intelligent beings in the realm of bodies. In particular, the
Forms themselves are unintelligent, but they are nonetheless better, in
some sense, than the intelligent beings that live in the realm of bodies (e.g.
the Form of Human Being would be better, in some sense, than human
beings themselves). In Stoic ontology, by contrast, the restriction above is
not needed because the realm of bodies (and hence of visible things) is,
strictly speaking, the only one there is: everything that exists in a proper

[21] For which see Sextus Empiricus, *M* 9.109–10 and Cicero, *ND* 3.23, discussed in Schofield 1983:
34–5 and 37–8, Sedley 2007: 211, 219 and 229–30, and Meijer 2007: 129–32.
[22] Sedley 2007: 225, 228.

sense is corporeal.[23] This difference between Platonic and Stoic ontology is certainly important. But it has more to do with the general difference between Platonism and Stoicism than with how the Zenonian and the Timaean proofs are themselves designed.

We may now consider the third difference. Suppose that we look at the Zenonian proof from the angle proposed by Chrysippus in **T1d**. In particular, suppose that *Structure* – the principle that all natural beings other than the cosmos exist, either directly or indirectly, for the benefit of the cosmos – captures the reason why, according to the Zeno, nothing is better than the cosmos. If it does, then this explanation is a major difference between the Zenonian and the Timaean proofs. For in the Timaean proof, the reason for this, if any, cannot be teleological.

To begin, in the Timaean proof there is not really an explanation of why the cosmos is better than all other natural beings. Firstly, in the passage Plato uses the comparatives 'more beautiful' (*kallion*) and 'better' (*amei-non*) as materially equivalent: something is better if and only it is more beautiful. Therefore, none of these concepts helps to explain the other. Secondly, the fact that the cosmos was created by a demiurge does not explain either why the cosmos is the best or the most beautiful. For according to **T3a**, this cosmos is the most beautiful and the best that the demiurge could create: 'it was and it is impossible for the best to do anything but the most beautiful' (30a6–7). The idea here, presumably, is that, of all the cosmoi that the demiurge could create, the present one is the cosmos he chose to create because it is the most beautiful and the best and, given that the demiurge himself is fully rational, he could not create a cosmos that is not the most beautiful and the best. This, however, does not explain why the present cosmos is the best and the most beautiful *in the first place*.

So, why could this reason be? It cannot be that everything exists for the benefit of the cosmos To appreciate why it cannot, consider how the expressions 'more beautiful' and 'better' are employed in **T3a**. They appear twice: first, at 30a7, in connection with the thesis that the visible was brought to order from a state of disorder because order is absolutely *better* than disorder (*pantōs ameinon*); secondly, at 30b2, in connection with the

---

[23] Although Stoic ontology does include incorporeal entities, these are dependent on bodies in the sense that they inherit their properties from the bodies that they characterise (e.g. the size of the place occupied by my desk is the same as the size of my my desk) and, for this reason, no incorporeal entity could be, *in itself,* better than a body.

thesis that, in all that is visible, nothing unintelligent is *more beautiful* as a whole (*holon holou kallion*) than something intelligent. However we understand their meaning in each of these two places, their meaning is *not* that *A* is 'better' or 'more beautiful' than *B* when *B* exists for the benefit of *A*. This is especially clear in the first example: the claim there is surely *not* that the orderly is better than the disorderly *because* the latter exists for the benefit of the former in some sense, and especially so in the sense that the pre-cosmic disorderly motion is needed for the endurance of the cosmic order: this claim would make little sense in the context of the *Timaeus*. Therefore, if the notion of being 'better than' is to have a uniform meaning throughout **T3a**, the visible cosmos is not better or more beautiful than any other natural being in the teleological sense that all natural beings other than the cosmos exist for the benefit of the cosmos. What could be, then, the implicit explanation in the Timaean proof of why nothing is better than the cosmos? One possibility is that the present cosmos is, of all possible worlds, the most beneficial to human beings, which would be the reason why the demiurge chose to create it. This anthropocentrism is, in fact, strongly suggested further in the *Timaeus*. As has been pointed by Sedley (1989: 374–81), at least some of the most important parts of the Timaean cosmos exist for the benefit of human beings in the specific sense that they serve the purpose of bridging the gap between human and divine intellection and, in more general terms, of helping us to achieve the ideal of godlikeness (*homoiōsis theō*).[24]

To summarise, we have noted that the notion that the cosmos is optimal is common to F_1 and the Timaean proof. However, in F_1 the cosmos is optimal because all other natural beings exist for its benefit, as the Chrysippean version of F_1 emphasises. In the Timaean proof, however, no explanation is given of why it is optimal. I have argued, however, that there are elements for thinking that in the Timaean proof the cosmos is optimal because it is the most anthropocentric and, if so, the sense in which the Timaean cosmos is optimal is sharply different from the cosmocentric sense in which the Stoic cosmos in F_1 is optimal.

It is worth remarking that the idea that all natural beings beings exist for the sake of the cosmos, in the specific cosmocentric sense that they exist

---

[24] See Sedley 1989: 374–81 and 1997: 316–22. Sedley refers especially to *Tim.* 46e–47c on the cause of vision: we see in order to contemplate celestial motion, which is something that benefits us precisely because it helps us to imitate it. This anthropocentrism, Sedley explains, also found, in an even stronger form, the *Phaedo*.

for its *benefit*, is not alien to Plato's cosmology. It emerges, for example, in *Laws*, Book 10 as a central component of the cosmology developed there.[25]

> **T3d:** Plato, *Lg.* 10 903b4–c5
>
> Let us persuade the young by means of arguments that all things have been organized by the caretaker of the whole for the sake of its preservation and excellence, and that each part of this plurality does and suffers as far as possible what is appropriate. Rulers have been appointed as commanders over each one of them down to the smallest details of their actions and passions, bringing about the ultimate purpose [of each]. Even you, most wretched fool, are a part of this plurality, a tiny one, which strives and longs for the whole but that does not realize, concerning this very fact, that all generation comes about for the sake of the whole, in order for a happy existence to belong to the life of the cosmos, and that it does not come about for your sake but that you [come about] for its sake.

The passage explicitly states that all things in the (visible) cosmos exists for the benefit of the cosmos in the sense that its purpose is to secure its endurance, referred to here as its 'preservation' (sōtēria). Moreover, in *Laws* 10 Plato also claims that the cosmos is ensouled and that its soul is intelligent. The role of this claim in the overall argument of the book – which is to prove, against the atheist, the existence of god – is essential. Given that the cosmos must be governed by a soul rather than by the mechanical interaction of the four elements (893b–897a), and given also that this soul must be intelligent (897b–d), god must exist if god is identified with this soul (899a). In fact, the 'caretaker' referred to in **T3d** at 903b4–5 is no other than the intelligent soul of the cosmos. Therefore, the inferential connection between the claim that everything exists for the sake of the cosmos and the claim that the cosmos is intelligent is different in *Laws* 10 and in F_1. In F_1 the latter claim is inferred from the former, as we have seen. But in *Laws* 10 the order is reversed: the claim that everything exists for the sake of the cosmos is inferred from the claim that it is intelligent. The particular inferential connection put forward by F_1 has no precedent in Plato.

---

[25] For which see Carone 1998: 132 with reference to other passages in the *Timaeus* e.g. 30c–d, 39e–40a and 41a–c and Johnson 2008: 122–4.

10.4 Conclusion

I have argued that F_I is indebted to the Timaean proof at *Tim.* 30a2–c1 inasmuch as it uses exactly the same argument-structure and nearly the same terminology, but that the philosophical basis of the two proofs differ significantly. In both cases, the thesis that the cosmos is intelligent because it is optimal is central. The reasons given for its optimality, however, are largely different. In the Timaean proof, the issue is not addressed systematically. But there is reason for thinking that the cosmos is optimal because it is, of all possible cosmoi, the most beneficial to human beings, which reveals the presence of an anthropocentric cosmic teleology, consistent with other parts of the *Timaeus*. In F_I, by contrast, this is not so. As is brought out by Chrysippus in his version of F_I the cosmos is optimal because all other natural beings exist for *its* benefit. This reveals a cosmocentric teleology that sharply departs from the anthropocentric view probably presupposed in Timaean proof. Cosmocentrism is not alien to Platonic cosmology, and in fact there is evidence in the *Laws* that Plato was, at least in that dialogue, an advocate of cosmocentrism in the sense that he believed that all natural beings exist for the benefit of the cosmos. But there is no evidence that he used cosmocentrism to argue for the intelligence of the cosmos. F_I, therefore, introduces a major innovation in ancient cosmological thinking.

CHAPTER II

Cardiology and Cosmology in Post-Chrysippean Stoicism

Emmanuele Vimercati

II.I Introduction

This chapter focuses on some developments of Stoic cardiology in the post-Chrysippean tradition and on their application to the reading of the cosmos. In this regard, my aim is to investigate the role of the heart and the image of the world as a cardiovascular system enlivened by a network of blood vessels. Within this picture, I would then like to show that in later Stoicism not only the heart, but the blood first and foremost, was used in explaining the essence and features of the soul, and eventually employed as a model to explain the universe. I will thus highlight the existence of a 'hematic' variation within cardiocentrism, which allows some Stoics go better justify the spreading and the action of the soul within the body, and that of god throughout the cosmos. By doing so, the post-Chrysippean tradition recalls Empedocles' position, thus breathing new life into early Stoicism. These innovations demand greater attention than what has been given to them by modern scholarship.

Therefore, this topic will be first of all studied in Diogenes of Babylon, who stresses the importance of the heart in the human body in the wake of his master Chrysippus, yet apparently providing a different definition of the soul as (made of) blood. The chapter will then briefly consider Posidonius, whose cardiocentrism – though not strictly 'hematic' – differs from that of both Aristotle and Chrysippus and is crucial for his understanding of living beings and natural phenomena. Lastly, the chapter will focus on the cardiological image of the cosmos in Seneca and Manilius, who often represent the universe as a cardiovascular system with aspects of originality compared to the previous tradition. In particular, I will show how persistent – though not unanimous – the idea was according to which the soul is made up of blood, and the intellectual functions should be placed within the heart, as Diogenes had stated following in Empedocles' footsteps.

11.2 Diogenes of Babylon on Cardiology, Hematology and Cosmogony

After an introduction on cardiology in early Stoicism, this section mainly focuses on Diogenes' understanding of the human soul and its possible application to the origin of the cosmos. First of all, it should be noticed that, regarding the placement of intellect inside the human body, the ancient tradition used to mention three main locations, namely the head, the blood or the heart. The latter two organs were often associated, depending on whether priority was given to the blood, which has the most even blending of cosmic elements and the body fluids and forms the cardiac wall, or to the heart, which serves as receptacle and propeller for blood. Encephalocentrism was referred to Alcmaeon of Croton, and subsequently associated to Plato[1] and to some works from the *Corpus Hippocraticum*;[2] hematocentrism was originally ascribed to Empedocles,[3] while cardiocentrism was mainly attested in Aristotle,[4] Praxagoras,[5] and in the Hippocratic treatise *On the Heart*.[6] As for the Stoics, the very first members of the school shared the definition of the soul as *pneuma enthermon*,[7] but were seemingly hesitant about the actual placement of the ruling part. For even though the sources diverge, Cleanthes seems to have placed the ruling part within the head, while Zeno and Chrisyppus located it in the heart.[8] In particular, Chrysippus deemed that the psychic *pneuma* that makes up all of the soul's superior functions, dwells inside the heart's left ventricle.[9] Starting with Chrysippus, then, cardiocentrism became the Stoic leading theory, and was seemingly never abandoned.

But apparently not all of Chrysippus' followers shared his opinion regarding the heart's central role. A passage from Theodoret recounts

---

[1] *Tim.* 44d5–6; 69d–70b; the chest is rather considered as the location of human courage (*thymos*; *Tim.* 70b–73d; see also Manuli–Vegetti 1977: 29–53 (on the brain-centered tradition), 55–76 (on the blood-centered tradition), 77–99 (on the tripartite scheme of Plato and Philolaos).

[2] See especially *On Diseases* III 2–4; *Sacred Disease* 17.

[3] See Theophrastus, *On Sense Perception* 10; 23; 25–6 = fr. 24A5 and 31A86 DK; Aëtius, *Plac.* IV 17, 1 = fr. 26A7 DK)

[4] See below.

[5] On the Stoic dependence on Praxagoras see *SVF* II 897; Steckerl 1958: 4; Hahm 1977: 160–63; Tieleman 1991: 122–3. On the *pneuma* in Praxagoras see, recently, Lewis 2017: 256–9 (the heart as the source of *pneuma*), 275ff. (on the role of *pneuma*).

[6] See below.   [7] See *SVF* I 135, 522; II 773.

[8] See *SVF* I 499 and II 836 [1] (Aëtius reports that, for Cleanthes and other Stoics, the ruling part of the cosmos is the sun, which plays the same role as the head in our body); II 838; see also II 908–10; III [DB] 29, 33.

[9] See *SVF* II 897 [2].

different types of cardiocentrism, depending on the ruling part being placed either inside the heart or within the blood, in the pericardium or – more generally – inside the chest. The author states: 'Empedocles, Aristotle and the Stoic school placed the ruling part inside the heart. And, among them, in turn, some placed it inside the heart itself; others within the blood. And some in the pericardial membrane, others in the diaphragm'.[10] In this passage, Empedocles and the Stoics are precisely mentioned in regard to the possible variants of cardiocentrism. The fact that the centrality of the heart or chest did not coincide with that of the blood can also be presumed by a text from Eusebius, which states that according to Empedocles, 'the ruling power (*hêgemonikon*) is neither in the head (*kephalê*), nor in the chest (*thôrax*), but rather in the blood (*haima*); whence in whatever part of the body this ruling power is more largely diffused (*paresparmenon*), in that part men excel (*proterein*)'.[11] Therefore, cardiocentrism and hematocentrism seem to be two (partially) different theories, the latter being sometimes presented as one possible articulation of the former.[12] As I shall argue, these variations also help us in better understanding Diogenes of Babylon's position. For Galen states:[13]

> None of these arguments, then, is valid, nor is that in which Diogenes says, 'The governing part is the member which first draws in nutriment (*trophê*) and *pneuma*; and the member which first draws in nutriment and *pneuma* is the heart'. [. . .] In the same way he also used arguments against himself.[14] He says: 'That which causes a man to make voluntary movements (*tas kata prohairesin kinêseis*) is a certain psychic exhalation (*anathymiasis*); but every exhalation arises from nutriment; therefore, that which first causes voluntary movements and that which nourishes us is necessarily one and the same'. When Diogenes writes this, we shall say that for the moment we do not challenge his saying that the substance of the soul is an exhalation, whether from nutriment or from *pneuma*, lest we cause him complete distress. [. . .] And he himself forgot the doctrines of his own school when he says that the soul is blood, as Empedocles and Critias had supposed. But if he should follow Cleanthes, Chrysippus and Zeno, who say that the soul

---

[10] See Theodoret, *Cure for the Greek Affections* V, 22 (ed. Canivet) = fr. 31A97 DK; instead of 'Aristotle', other manuscripts report 'Aristocles'.

[11] Eusebius, *Preparation for the Gospel* I 8, 10 (= fr. 31A30 DK).

[12] See *SVF* II 879, where the Stoics are credited with cardiocentrism and the rejection of hematocentrism.

[13] *PHP* II 8, 40–48, 164–6 De Lacy (= *SVF* III [DB] 30; trans. De Lacy, modified). For a close discussion of Galen's own physiological theory in a teleological context, see Hankinson's contribution to the present volume (Chapter 13).

[14] De Lacy 1980–84: 1.166 accepts *kath'heautou* (arguments against himself), instead of *heautou* (his own arguments).

is nourished from blood, but its substance is *pneuma*, how will the source of nourishment and the cause of motion remain the same, since it is the blood that nourishes and the *pneuma* that causes motion?

Galen shows that Diogenes was a supporter of cardiocentrism, as was Chrysippus. This stance is also confirmed in a passage by Aëtius, in which both Diogenes and Chrysippus located the ruling part 'in the arterial ventricle of the heart, which is pneumatic'.[15] Despite the concurrence with his master, Galen recognises that Diogenes 'forgot the doctrines of his own school'; after all, there would be no point in mentioning him should his arguments comply with Chrysippus', who was Galen's polemical target. Diogenes did not share his predecessors' positions, according to which the soul *is the pneuma*; rather, he deemed that the essence of the soul is the blood. By associating these two assertions – the cardiocentric thesis and the blood-like nature of the soul – to his affinity to Empedocles, Diogenes seems to have been largely autonomous within the Stoic school, thus playing a much eclectic role compared to that of Chrysippus and the other early Stoics. This very eclecticism was at the basis of Galen's accusation of incoherence.

But let us proceed step-by-step. First and foremost, Galen testifies to Diogenes' affinity with Empedocles' and Critias' stance. The key passage in Empedocles reads as follows:[16]

> For Homer too thinks that for men thought about mortal things is in the blood. [. . .] And Empedocles seems to speak as though the blood were the organ of understanding (*noêma*):
> [the heart] nourished in seas of blood which leap back and forth, and there especially (*malista*) it is called understanding by men: for men's understanding is blood around the heart (*haima perikardion*).[17]

Aristotle also recounts that Critias embraced similar stances,[18] stating that 'perceptiveness is the most proper feature of the soul, and this is due to the nature of blood'. The two passages thus prove that (1) the organ of human intelligence is the pericardial blood; (2) blood nurtures the heart itself; (3) perceptiveness is the most specific feature of the blood and the soul. This information is also confirmed by other passages regarding Empedocles, namely one by Theodoret[19] stating that the ruling part

[15] Aëtius, *Plac.* IV 5, 7; that Diogenes refers here to Diogenes of Babylon is confirmed by Tieleman 1996: 81.
[16] Porphyry, *On Styx*, in Stobaeus, *Eclogae* I 49, 53, p. 424, 9–19 = fr. 31B105 DK.
[17] Trans. Inwood 2001: 136.   [18] See Aristotle, *On the Soul* I 2, 405b5ff. = fr. 88A23 DK.
[19] See Theodoret, *Cure for the Greek Affections* IV, 5, 8 = fr. 31A97 DK.

resides within the blood, and another one by Theophrastus[20] stating that understanding (*phronein*) is achieved through the blood. Lastly, in Empedocles, the blood is also seen as the cause for human breathing (fr. 31A74 DK), together with air or the *pneuma* (fr. 31B100 DK). These insights help us to better understand Diogenes' position and its difference with his predecessors. For, since humans excel among other beings where the blood is most widespread – the heart – then clearly the blood's excellence depends upon its capability of being diffused in the body. This very diffusion also makes sense-perceptions possible, and thus the intellective functions of the soul. The latter would be concentrated in the cardiac region, where the flow of blood is much greater. However, unlike the heart, which is placed in a precise position, the blood's nature better represents the blending of the body fluids and the functions of the soul, which are not concentrated in a single place, but rather spread out in different organs.

According to Diogenes, therefore, the soul – which is blood – is an exhalation produced by both nourishment and the *pneuma*, that is, it is produced from corporeal functions. The blood-like nature of the soul, however, does not imply rejecting cardiocentrism, since the blood has its largest concentration inside the cardiac region, from which it then spreads throughout the body. In this manner, Diogenes' stance is in line with Chrysippus', though in an eclectic variation. For blood is the means by which the psychic principle and its functions spread inside the human body. But Galen's stance also shows how important Empedocles' psychology still was in Hellenistic Stoicism, and – as will be shown below – possibly even in the Imperial era.

However, Diogenes' position is different from Empedocles', both because cardiocentrism had advanced in the meantime, and because such progress had been integrated by Diogenes within Chrysippean Stoicism. Galen's text, in particular, intertwines the presentation of Chrysippus and the Stoics with Hippocratic and Peripatetic themes. In fact, in the Hippocratic and cardiocentric work *On the Heart*[21] the nourishment of the ruling part of the soul is referred to as 'not visible blood', which differs

---

[20] See Theophrastus, *On Sense Perception* 10 and 23 = fr. 31A86 DK.
[21] Which is the only one in the *Corpus* to place human understanding (*gnōmē*) in the heart (see X 3); also, Manuli–Vegetti 1977: 101–9; Potter 2010: 54; Duminil 1983: 308–12. This has led scholars into thinking the text had to be from a later date (see Duminil 1998: 180–81; Leboucq 1944: 18; Oser-Grote 2004: 94–6, with previous references; Potter 2010: 55–6).

from nourishment coming from the stomach and the intestines.[22] Since in the same context the Stoic technical term *hêgemonikon* occurs, the reference to 'not visible blood' might anticipate Diogenes' claim that the soul is an 'exhalation' made of blood. In this regard, however, Diogenes' dependence upon Aristotle is more relevant. For Galen credits Diogenes with a thesis according to which the principle of nourishing and the principle of voluntary motions (*tas kata prohairesin kinêseis*) are the same. As has been noted,[23] the Aristotelian footprint of such terminology is mirrored in Galen's attention for the Peripatetic tradition and for some of its analogies with Stoic psychology. In particular, in the work *On the Parts of Animals*, Aristotle claims that 'in sanguineous animals the blood exists for the sake of nutrition of the body (*trophês heneken*)' and that it 'is contained, as in a vase, in the heart and vessels'.[24] In other passages, the Stagirite presents the heart as the location of *pneuma* and, therefore, as the principle of sense-perception and locomotion for sanguineous animals.[25] For Aristotle this depends on empirical and theoretical reasons,[26] among which natural heat should be mentioned, which is innate in the cardiac region and sometimes expressed in terms of psychic ignition.[27] Natural heat is what mainly distinguishes the heart from the brain, which for Aristotle is cold and without blood.[28] In this account, the Stoics might well have seen a motive of inspiration for their notion of the soul as *pneuma enthermon*; in any case, the association of heart, blood and *pneuma* as responsible for the nutritive and sensitive functions is clearly attested in Aristotle.[29] However, no less relevant in the Stagirite is the notion of exhalation (*anathymiasis*),[30] which is related to the process of nutrition of animals as a result of the flux of

---

[22] *On the Heart* XI 1–3; on this kind of blood see Duminil 1998: 257 n. 56 (the Hippocratic author has apparently some problems in determining the nature of reason, which has a material subject different from air and blood; for the Stoics this could be the *pneuma*, I think). The distinction between the two kinds of nourishment may have to do with the difference between the vital and the psychic *pneuma*. On the heart as the source of blood see *On Diseases* IV 33.

[23] See Tieleman 1996: 67–79.   [24] Aristotle, *PA* II 3, 650b2–13.

[25] Aristotle, *PA* II 10, 656a28; III 3, 665a10ff.; *Somn. et vig.* 2, 455b34–456a11; on the *pneuma* and the heart see also Praxagoras, frs. 31–2 Steckerl.

[26] Aristotle, *PA* III 4, 666a18–22; see also *GA* II 6, 742b33–7.

[27] Aristotle, *Iuv. et sen.* 4, 469b6–20; 22, 478a29–30; also, Manuli–Vegetti 1977: 117–27.

[28] Aristotle, *PA* II 7, 652a–b.

[29] See Aristotle, *Somn. et vig.* 2, 456a; *Iuv. et sen.* 22, 478a27ff.; Lanza–Vegetti 1971: 543–9, 788–96; Manuli–Vegetti 1977: 113–56; Frampton 1991: 293–6; Jori 2005: 24–5, 34–5; Oser-Grote 2004: 90–92 (also on Aristotle, *HA* I 17).

[30] Heraclitus' definition of the soul as 'exhalation' is reported by Aristotle himself, followed by Arius Didymus (Aristotle, *On the Soul* I 2, 405a25–6; Arius Didymus in Eusebius, *Preparation for the Gospel* XV 20, 2; see also Heraclitus, fr. 22 B 12 DK; *SVF* I 139; 141; 519–20; II 847); also, Solmsen 1961: 22–4; Finkelberg 2013.

nourishment through the vessels, its transformation into blood and its nutritive function for the body.[31] Thus, the three terms of Diogenes' definition – exhalation, nourishment and *pneuma* – occur in the same context also in Aristotle, with reference to nutrition, production of blood and the state of sleep which depends on the ascent of *pneuma* into the higher region of the body.[32] In general, despite the uncertain legacy of Aristotle's works in the Hellenistic age,[33] the analogies between the two authors are significant and perhaps not accidental, since Diogenes' conception of the soul is associated by Galen to that of the Peripatetics.

However, Diogenes also deviates from Aristotle's cardiocentrism, since the argument with which he places the ruling part inside the heart is a clearly Stoic one. For, while the Peripatetics apparently stressed the role of the heart starting from its nutritive function,[34] in Diogenes this rather depended on the strict relation of mind, discourse and speech.[35] Since discourse is 'meaningful articulate speech' (*sêmainousa enarthros phônê*) and 'speech does not come out from the head, but clearly from a place lower down', the mind (*dianoia*) should be located not in the brain, but in the heart.[36] It is also relevant to note here that the localisation of the mind depends on the emission of speech, which is a meaningful breath (*pneuma*) coming from the centre of the body, or, in Stoic terms, is the *logos prophorikos* expressing the *logos endiathetos*. This comparison is confirmed by Galen, who quotes Chrysippus in claiming that 'it is absolutely reasonable (*eulogon*) that the part in which all these things take place is the part in which the act of going through a discourse (*logos*) is performed, and that we speak (*legein*) and think (*dianoeisthai*) there'.[37] The relation of both speech and thought as expressive of human discourse is also worth noticing here. As will be shown below, in both Chrysippus and Diogenes placing the *logos* in the heart also affected some aspects of their cosmology, since

---

[31] Aristotle, *Sens. et sensib.* 5, 444a10–13; *Somn. et vig.* 3, 456b18–19; but see also *Probl.* XIII 6, 908a29–b11, where, according to the Heracliteans, exhalation in the human body is said to take place just as it does in the universe.

[32] Aristotle, *Somn. et vig.* 3, 457a.   [33] See Lennox 1994 and 2001b: 110–26.

[34] See Alexander of Aphrodisias, *On the Soul*, esp. pp. 39, 23–40, 3 Bruns; Tieleman 1996: 73–9.

[35] See *PHP* II 5, 8, 130 De Lacy (= *SVF* III [DB] 29); Diogenes wrote also a work *On voice* (*SVF* III [DB] 17; and Isnardi Parente 1991: 257–63).

[36] See again *PHP* II 5, 8, pp. 128–30 De Lacy; also *SVF* II 894 and 910 (for Chrysippus speech comes from the heart). On the heart as the source of voice see also Praxagoras, fr. 33 Steckerl.

[37] Galen, *PHP* III 7, 34–5, 219 De Lacy (trans. De Lacy, slightly modified); see also *ibi* II 5, 15–20, 131 De Lacy. The centrality of the heart in the human soul was sometimes compared to the body and paws of a spider, or to the tentacles of an octopus (*SVF* II 827; 879; Ramelli–Lucchetta 2004: 436–8).

for the Stoics the *logos* stands not only for human understanding and speech, but also for the universal physical principle.

In this regard, Diogenes' cardiocentrism is clearly attested also with reference to the generation of the world and the role played by god, which Diogenes explained in allegorical terms. For according to Philodemus, 'in his work *On Athena* Diogenes of Babylon writes that the cosmos is the same as Zeus or that it contains Zeus just as a man contains his soul'.[38] The analogy between the world and the human being is confirmed in the following lines, in which the presentation of the gods and the parts of the cosmos depends on the description of the human soul and on the question as to whether its ruling part should be posited in the brain, as 'some Stoics think', or rather in the chest, as according to Chrysippus and Diogenes.[39] This question is directly related to the nature of the world, since, as Cicero remarks in a parallel passage, Diogenes moved from mythology to physiology.[40] Accordingly, as common in ancient Stoicism, Diogenes gave physical relevance to his allegorical survey, since Athena represents human wisdom, but also ether, i.e. the noblest of the elements. This is why for Chrysippus the ruling part of the cosmos was located in the heavens, an assumption shared presumably by Diogenes too.[41] For this reason, moving from the location of the ruling part within the human body, Chrysippus' and Diogenes' cardiology was applied to the origin of ether. For, according to Diogenes, 'Chrysippus says that the ruling part of the soul (*hêgemonikon*) is in the chest, and that Athena, who is wisdom [and ether, as said above], was born there'. Therefore, we can suppose that Diogenes located the ruling part of the cosmos in the light of the role of the heart within the human body. But Diogenes' definition of soul as blood allowed for a more effective cosmological application. Since blood is a fluid substance that is widespread throughout the living body, one can easily understand Diogenes' definition of god as cosmic soul,[42] that is a substance that is widespread in the whole universe. In fact, since god, *pneuma* and ether were strictly related according to the Stoics,[43] the ether was no less diffused in the cosmos, for it was at the origin of the cosmic elements,[44] and only in the heavens was it found in its purest form.[45] This universal diffusion of god-*pneuma*-ether was crucial in ensuring the

---

[38] Philodemus, *On Piety* 15 (= *SVF* III [DB] 33).   [39] See also *SVF* II 908–11.
[40] See Cicero, *ND* I 41 (= *SVF* III [DB] 34).   [41] See DL VII 138–9; Boechat 2017: 84ff.
[42] *SVF* III [DB] 31.   [43] *SVF* II 447; 471; 664.   [44] *SVF* I 154; 530; 532; 534; II 327.
[45] *SVF* II 644.

physical cohesion of the world and its theological unity.[46] In so doing, some Stoics referred precisely to Empedocles.[47]

However, the supposed predominance of the heart apparently clashed with the mythological account, which attested the generation of Athena from the brain of Zeus. In order to solve this inconsistency, (Chrysippus and) Diogenes introduced a distinction between the place of conception and the place of birth. Thus, Athena was conceived in the heart, which is the centre of diffusion of *pneuma* and the spermatic activity,[48] but was born from the head, since speech comes from there.[49] The relevance attributed by Diogenes to speech in the attempt to locate the ruling part of the soul has been already noted above. Therefore, quoting Hesiod's *Theogony*,[50] Chrysippus and his supporter Diogenes explained the generation of Athena-ether as a process internal to Zeus (*endon tou Dios*), who had swallowed Metis, the goddess of wisdom.[51] Diogenes' interpretation was thus related to the centrality of the heart as the source of mental products. For, the role of Zeus, as father of the gods and ruler of the cosmos, refers to the relation of heart, mind and speech in human beings.[52] Thus, the conception of Zeus does not directly involve his partner Metis, so much so that he is referred to as the maker of the world only through *logos*. This is presumably why, in Philodemus' passage, Zeus is called 'male and female', playing both roles in the conception of Athena and being responsible for the generation of gods and goddesses, who are aspects of the single cosmic Zeus.[53]

In sum, Diogenes seems to have embraced a peculiar position within both the Stoic and cardiocentric traditions. By drawing on different sources, he seemingly reached an autonomous synthesis, which owed to Empedocles, Aristotle and Chrysippus, but that could not be attributed to any of them. As seen above, the eclectic nature of such synthesis was itself the basis of criticism by Galen, who accused Diogenes of having

[46] Unlike Aristotle who, as is well known, limited the ether to the heavens. The intelligent and organic nature of the cosmos, which is based upon the widespread nature of god, is well depicted by Ricardo Salles in his contribution to this volume (esp. Sections 10.1 and 10.2).
[47] See *SVF* II 447; for Empedocles, too, human nature has a structure equivalent to that of the universe, since they share the same blending of cosmic elements (see frr. 31B107; 109; 110 DK).
[48] See e.g. *SVF* II 828; 873; 911.
[49] One should note here that Praxogaras had already seen the heart as the source of semen, so as the place of conception (fr. 34 Steckerl).
[50] Vv. 886–91.
[51] See Galen, *PHP* III 8, pp. 222–32 De Lacy (= *SVF* II 908); Obbink 1996: 20–21.
[52] See Ramelli–Lucchetta 2004: 439–40; this is confirmed by Justin, *First Apology* 64 (= *SVF* II 1096).
[53] See e.g. *SVF* III 302, and Algra 2009: 239.

contradicted himself and having betrayed the foundations of his own School. However, the importance given to the heart and blood-system will leave an important trace in later Stoicism.

11.3 Posidonius on Cardiology and Cosmology

In this context, some traces of Posidonius' cardiology are preserved: they will hereby be explored in relation to his cosmology. This will be achieved through the doctrine of *pneuma*, which is distinctive for the heart, the soul and the cosmos itself. Posidonius' cardiocentrism is clearly attested by the sources,[54] as well as the importance he gave to the blood in order to explain human nature.[55] It is noteworthy that Posidonius stressed the role of the blood's warmth and coldness in the body, as well as its density and rarefaction, in order to show the differences between individual human natures. This proves that he was familiar with Aristotle's studies on the nature and distribution of blood,[56] and that he gave them a psychological application. The 'movements' of the soul were thus related to the flow of blood and to its heat and density, that is to the temperature and the general condition of the body. In particular, since blood is warmer and denser near the heart, Posidonius believed that in that very region the functions of the soul should dwell, especially the superior ones. Therefore, although he notoriously distinguished three 'powers' (*dynameis*) in the human soul,[57] he did not 'divide' the body in the same manner. In so doing, Posidonius distanced himself from two opposite but equally problematic positions: that of Plato, who had distinguished three different *ousiai* in the soul (appetitive, spirited and rational), locating each of them in a different part of the body;[58] and that of Chrysippus, who had referred the three aspects of the soul not only to a single substance, but also to a single faculty. On the other hand, in order to avoid these opposite risks – the disintegration of the soul and the monistic reduction of its functions – Posidonius spoke of three 'powers' in relation to a single substance located in the heart.

---

[54] See Galen, *PHP* VI, 515, p. 368, 20–26 De Lacy (= Posid., fr. 146 EK).

[55] See Galen, *PHP* V, 442–3, pp. 321–2 De Lacy (= Posid., fr. 169 EK), with reference to Aristotle.

[56] See Aristotle, *PA* II 647b–648a; 650b–651a; Tieleman 1996: XXII–XXVIII; Tieleman 2003: 30–39, 202–6, also on Posidonius' Aristotelising tendencies.

[57] See Galen, *PHP* VI, 515, 368, 20–26 De Lacy (= Posid., fr. 146 EK). As to whether Posidonius actually spoke of 'faculties' (*dynameis*), see Tieleman 2003: 202–6.

[58] See Tieleman 2003: 34.

The importance given to heat in living beings explains both the vital role of blood and Posidonius' standard definition of the soul as *pneuma enthermon*.[59] For, whereas the cardiac origin of *pneuma* had already been highlighted by Aristotle, only with the Stoics does *pneuma* become the very essence of the soul and the divine substance spread in the universe. This helps us understand how Posidonius' cardiology also influenced his cosmology. In his view, 'the universe is a living creature. And it is "animate" [ensouled] as is clear from our human souls being a fragment (*apospasma*) from that source'.[60] Thus, the analogy between the cosmos and the human beings is grounded in the nature of the soul, which – as said – was placed in the heart. In addition, we know that Posidonius located the ruling part of the cosmos in the ethereal heavens and that this claim was based on the analogy between mind/soul and world/body.[61] Now, since *pneuma* plays a crucial role in locating the soul in the heart and in its diffusion through the whole body, the relation between cosmos, human body and its soul becomes more understandable.[62] This relation is described in a passage of Eustathius' *Commentary to the Iliad*, in which the author affirms: 'The expression "his spirit left his bones" reveals that a soul spirit has been diffused (*psychikon ti pneuma paresparthai*) even in the bones of the living, as the philosopher Posidonius also says in *On Soul*.'[63] The vocabulary used by Eustathius is clearly Stoic, and one should assume that Posidonius conceived a similar relation between the universal *pneuma* and the body of the world, being penetrated in all its physical parts by the seeds of god's intelligence. For, the cohesive power of the intelligent *pneuma* in both the human beings and the universe was repeatedly stressed by Posidonius.[64]

Based upon these assumptions is also his approach to meteorology and geography as cosmological sciences. In fact, the location of the ruling part in the heavens depended on the heat of those regions, which presided over the density of the atmosphere, the circulation of the stars and, ultimately, the life of the universe.[65] This is why, since the stars were living beings, they were also enlivened by the heat of their substance, as was the case for

[59] See DL VII 157 (= Posid., fr. 139 EK).
[60] DL VII 143 (= Posid., fr. 99a EK, trans. Kidd 1999).
[61] DL VII 138–9 (= Posid., frr. 14, but also 21 and 23 EK); Boechat 2017: 81–97.
[62] See Posid., frr. 100–101, 28a–28b EK; such a relation is already attested in the previous Stoics: *SVF* I 106; II 368, 546, 836 [1], 838; also, Brouwer 2015: 27–8.
[63] See Eustathius, *Comm. ad Hom. Il.* XII 386 (= Posid., fr. 28b EK, trans. Kidd 1999).
[64] See again DL VII 143 (= Posid., fr. 99a EK); *Scholia in Lucani Bellum Civile, Pars I, Commenta Bernensia* IX 578 (= Posid., fr. 100 EK); also, Aëtius, *Plac.* I 7, 9 (= Posid., fr. 101 EK).
[65] See frr. 49 (p. 67, ll. 62ff.); 130 (p. 121, ll. 15ff.); 131b (pp. 123–4, ll. 12–19) EK.

blood inside the human body.[66] And then, 'since the temperature of the atmosphere is judged in relation to the sun, there are three distinctions which are most fundamental and contribute to the constitution of animals and plants, and to the semi-organisations of everything else under the air [i.e. on earth], or in the air itself, namely excess, defect and mean of heat'.[67] In this sense the temperature of the human body, too, was associated with that of the external environment, showing how their combination contributed to shaping human behaviour. The grounds for their differences 'are that the emotional movements (*tôn pathêtikon kinêseôn*) of the soul follow always the physical state, which is altered in no small degree from the temperature in the environment (*tês kata to periechon kraseôs*). For he (*sc.* Posidonius) makes the point too that even the blood in animals differs in warmth and coldness, thickness and thinness, and in a considerable number of other different ways'.[68] Lastly, the notion of *pneuma* also seems to be presupposed in the explanation of earthquakes, which were related to the penetration of air into the hollows of the earth,[69] as if they were ducts for the flow of cosmic breath.

In sum, the heat and density of blood and *pneuma* were at the origin of Posidonius' cardiological explanation of human beings and the life of the universe. Interestingly, on some of these aspects our main source is Seneca, who developed some of Posidonius' assumptions, as we shall see below.

11.4 Seneca and Manilius on the Cosmos as a Cardiovascular System

Seneca and Manilius deserve closer inspection, since they provide two more or less contemporary accounts of the physical world and the heavens inspired by the previous Stoic tradition, nonetheless rich in original aspects. For, in these terms, Seneca's debt to the medical Pneumatism and Manilius' reception of the Stoic milieu in his astronomical framework have been also recently re-emphasised.[70] Notably, both Seneca and Manilius reaffirmed a 'cardiovascular' reading of the universe as a circulatory system of

---

[66] See also Posid., frr. 13; 123; 132 EK. The Aristotelian background of these assumptions is helpfully highlighted by James Lennox in his contribution to the present volume (Chapter 7); see also Boechat 2016.

[67] Strabo II 3, 1 (= Posid., fr. 49 EK; trans. Kidd 1999).

[68] See again Posid., fr. 146 (p. 161, ll. 85ff.) EK (trans. Kidd 1999).

[69] See DL VII 154 (= Posid., fr. 12 EK); also frr. 230 and 232 EK, the source being Seneca (*NQ*).

[70] See Verbeke 1945: 143–57; Le Blay 2014: 63–76 (on Seneca); Salemme 1983: 27–56; Lapidge 1989: 1393–7; Colish 1990: 313–16; Ramelli 2008: 196, n. 1 (with further references); Ramelli 2014; Volk 2009: 226–34; Boechat 2017: 97ff. (on Manilius).

blood and *pneuma* in the vessels, applying then this model to their interpretation of natural phenomena. This is first attested in a passage of Seneca's
Natural Questions:

'I think that the earth is controlled by nature, and on the model of our
own bodies, in which there are both veins and arteries; the former are
receptacles for blood, the latter for breath. In the earth too, there are some
passages through which water runs, others through which breath does; and
nature has created such a resemblance to the human body that our
ancestors too spoke of "veins" of water'.[71]

The comparison between the world and the human beings is here
grounded in the fact that both the earth and the human bodies have veins
and arteries. These vessels are responsible for the flux of blood and *pneuma*
in the bodies, and of water and air on the earth. Then, this analogy is based
on the common nature of the world and the humans. This comparison
continues in the following paragraphs, where the case is made of the burst
of veins in the bodies and channels in the earth, from which blood and
water spring.[72] Both cases are made to depend on the law and the will of
nature (*legem naturae voluntatemque*). As to the vascular flux, blood is
considered 'a quasi-part of us [. . .], and yet it is also matter' (*quasi pars est
sanguis nostri, et tamen est materia*), and it is responsible for the vital
functions of the body.[73] Elsewhere, Seneca mentions the argument according to which the nature of the soul lies in the blood (*NQ* VII 25, 2), and
besides, blood flow is what brings the human body together with the air
and water channels in the cosmos (*NQ* II 3, 2). Yet, it is not surprising that
Seneca attributes the air a major role, since the air is also the vital breath
(*spiritus*) of living beings, or their *pneuma*. The association of air and
pneuma is recalled by Seneca himself, when he says that it is the 'vital
and active breath nourishing all the things', and that also the winds can be
called soul (*anima*), or living breath.[74] For 'the air is a part of the
world, and a necessary one',[75] first and foremost since it is provided with
internal unity and, in turn, it provides unity to the cosmos.[76] This is the
standard Stoic doctrine of the *continuum*,[77] which Seneca develops here
in vascular terms, since the air is spread over the whole world through
its proper vessels.[78] As the author says, 'unity' is to be intended as a
'continuity without gaps' (*unitas est sine commissura continuatio*), or as a

---

[71] Seneca, *NQ* III 15, 1 (trans. Hine 2014); see also III 2, 1 and VI 14, 1, where the same image
is used.
[72] *NQ* III 15, 3–8.   [73] *Ibi* II 3, 2.   [74] *Ibi* VI 14, 1.   [75] *Ibi* II 4, 1.
[76] *Ibi* II 2, 1; 6, 2 and 6; 8,   [77] Sambursky 1973: 1–20; Sambursky 1987: 132–47.
[78] *Ibi* VI 14, 1; 16, 1.

'non-interrupted connection' (*non intermissa coniunctio*).[79] The unity of air is thus an internal or substantial 'cohesion', which differs from a mere composition of parts and does not depend on external agents.[80] Secondly, air is responsible for the 'tension' of the world, its balance and cohesion.[81] For 'one can infer that unity is characteristic of air just from the fact that our bodies hold together. What else could make them cohere, apart from breath? [...] What motion could it have except tension? What tension, except from unity? What unity, unless it existed in air?'[82] Thirdly, air is responsible for the movement of the earth,[83] being located inside it as if it were its breathing faculty, and not coming from outside, since elsewhere Seneca claims that the earth is full of air, both the one that we experience upon the earth, and the vital one – i.e. *pneuma*. Incidentally, this assumption plays a major role in understanding the aetiology of earthquakes. Fourthly, air is powerful, having a generative and nutritive force,[84] since this 'spirit' inside the earth is the nourishment of trees, plants and everything which grows upon the earth. But, above all, the vital breath gives nourishment to the fiery ether, the stars and the celestial bodies which live on terrestrial exhalations.[85] In general, in Seneca, the analogy between microcosm and macrocosm, much more than upon the heart, seems to be based upon the nature of blood and on the vascular system, which guarantee the continuity and dissemination of the psychic substance in the universe.

In other terms, the same image of the world is preserved also by the contemporary Roman astronomer Manilius, whose reception of Stoic ideas should be assumed, at least in a few passages – though his sources are not easily identifiable in detail. In Manilius' *Astronomica*, traditional Stoic cosmology is well attested, including the living nature of the world[86] organically harmonised by universal 'sympathy',[87] the immanence of an intelligent and provident god that spreads over the world as breath or 'spirit' (*spiritus*, translating *pneuma*),[88] the role of nature in determining fate and the unchangeable physical laws,[89] and the influence of the stars on

[79] On this sort of *coniunctio* (or blending) see Wildberger 2006: 7–13.   [80] *Ibi* II 2, 1–4.
[81] See also Seneca, *Cons. ad Helviam* VIII 3; *De ira* II 31, 7; also, Lapidge 1989: 1399–1400; Wildberger 2006: 73–8 (on the tension and *pneuma*).
[82] Seneca, *NQ* II 6, 6 (trans. Hine 2014).
[83] *Ibi* II 11, 1–2; on the tonic movement of the cosmic *pneuma* see also Marcus Aurelius, *Medit.* VI, 38.
[84] Seneca, *NQ* V 6; 18, 1; VI 14, 1; 16, 3; 21, 1; further occurrences in Vottero 1989: 758–9.
[85] Seneca, *NQ* VI 15; 16 and 24; recently, Brouwer 2015: 24–8.
[86] See Manilius, *Astron.* I 247–54;   [87] *Ibi* II 60–135.   [88] *Ibi* IV 886–935.
[89] *Ibi* I 478–99; III 66–82; IV 14–15.

the structure and the parts of the human body.[90] In this general framework
inspired by Stoic orthodoxy, two aspects are interesting for the aim of this
study: the relation between macrocosm and microcosm, and the assertion
of the incorruptibility or eternity of the world. The relation between the
parts and the whole is expressed by Manilius through the comparison
between the world and the human beings. Physically speaking, both the
universe and the human beings have a body equipped with proper limbs,
related to one another and kept alive by the spirit or the soul. For Manilius
claims: 'This fabric which forms the body of the boundless (*immensus*)
universe, together with its members composed of nature's diverse elements, air and fire, earth and level sea, is ruled by the force of a divine
spirit (*vis animae divinae*); by sacred dispensation the deity brings harmony
and governs with hidden purpose, arranging mutual bonds between all
parts, so that each may furnish and receive another's strength and that the
whole may stand fast in kinship despite its variety of forms'.[91] And
elsewhere: 'Now learn how the parts of the human frame are distributed
among the constellations (*divisas hominis per sidera partes*), and how the
limbs are subject each to a particular authority; over these limbs, out of all
the parts of the body, the signs exercise special influence'.[92] These passages
reveal an assimilation between the nature of the cosmos – an *animal*
penetrated by the universal *pneuma* – and that of the living beings –
animals penetrated by their soul, which is a spark of the divine *pneuma*
disseminated in the universe.[93]

In this view of the cosmos, the centrality of the heart is reiterated by
Manilius on several occasions, beginning with the first lines of his work, in
which he intends to know the *praecordia mundi*. This knowledge indeed is
'a more fervent delight'.[94] Broadly speaking, *praecordia* here signifies the
intimate recesses of the universe, or the mysteries less visible to man.
Strictly speaking, however, the term refers to the heart and the regions
around or in front of it. In Manilius, this concept is especially important in
describing the universe, but it is already attested in Seneca as to human
nature. Beyond a strictly biological or metaphorical meaning,[95] in Seneca
praecordia also refers to the heart as the seat of the *animus*. The *praecordia*
are in effect the site of the emotions and their control by way of reason.
They are, for example, the seat of adulation, fear and desire, but also of

[90] *Ibi* II 452–6.   [91] *Ibi* I 247–54 (trans. Goold 1977, also here below).   [92] *Ibi* II 453–56.
[93] This doctrine is also attested in Seneca, *NQ, Praefatio*.
[94] Manilius, *Astron*. I 16–19 ('impensius ipsa / *scire iuvat magni penitus praecordia mundi* / quaque
regat generetque *suis animalia signis*, / cernere et in numerum Phoebe modulante referre', *my italics*).
[95] See e.g. Seneca, *Prov*. 6.53; *Cons. Marc*. 26.27; *Vita beata* 20.5; *Ep*. 66, 37; 95, 25; *NQ* IV*b* 13, 5–6.

steadfastness of spirit (*firmitas animi*),[96] making the heart the centre of human biological and psychological life. A similar stance was embraced by Manilius, proposing that the seat of the mind in beings should be the heart.[97]

One must also remember that *praecordia* is closely related to the term *perikardion*, with which Empedocles had qualified the blood that constitutes human understanding (*haima perikardion*). From Aristotle (*PA* II 10, 672b) we also gather the fact that *praecordia* had to correspond to the Greek term *phrenes*, the see of intellect. This is not surprising, since Theophrastus had recounted that according to Empedocles, understanding (*phronein*) is achieved through pericardial blood.[98] The word *praecordia* was thus extremely significant and referred to a cardiologic tradition that dated back to Empedocles and Aristotle, the traces of which we have also found in Diogenes. Seneca and Manilius were undoubtedly aware of such tradition, since their cardiocentrism recalls typical elements of its Stoic reception. In a passage, Manilius states: 'Can one doubt that a divinity dwells within our breasts (*habitare deum sub pectore nostro*) and that our souls return to the heaven whence they came? Can one doubt that, just as the world, composed of the elements of air and fire on high and earth and water, houses an intelligence which, spread throughout it, directs the whole (*hospitium menti totum quae infusa gubernet*), so too with us the bodies of our earthly condition and our life-blood (*sanguineas animas*) house a mind which directs every part and animates the man?'[99] This passage is significant for various reasons: firstly, it confirms the presence of the cardiocentric paradigm in Manilius, which is here applied to the psychological sphere and – by analogy – to the cosmological one. We thus find confirmation of how the study of the individual soul had been oriented towards understanding the universe, the heart being a shared principle at both levels. Moreover, the soul as vital principle is here explicitly associated with the blood, by which it is constituted. Just as the blood, the soul too guarantees life within the whole organism, since it spreads throughout all of its parts. This seems to prove the existence of a 'hematic' variant in the cardiocentric thesis; for, in this case, the soul's blood-like nature is considered in conjunction with the intellect that rules the human body. Lastly, just as the blood and soul within the human

[96] Seneca, *Ep.* 20, 1; 45, 7; 74, 3.   [97] Manilius, *Astron.* IV 929–30.
[98] See Theophrastus, *On Sense Perception* 10 and 23 = fr. 31A86 DK.
[99] Manilius, *Astron.* IV 886–93.

body, the divine intellect too rules the universe, throughout which it is spread. All of these elements agree with what we have found in Empedocles' and Diogenes' cardiocentrism.

Manilius applied thus the notion of *praecordia* to his interpretation of the cosmos, using cardiology as an image of universal nature. In particular, the astronomer associated the seat of the heart with *signa*, i.e. with the signs of the zodiac, which were considered capable of influencing the nature and activity of living beings.[100] This theory reappears throughout his work, when Manilius refers to nature as the 'first cause and guardian of all things hidden', which 'by fixed laws united separate limbs into a single body'. In this rational order, the constellations, 'deployed by the central region, occupy the heart of the universe' (*mundi praecordia*),[101] thus assuming the role of the cosmic soul as command centre.[102] In this framework, the references to Apollo[103] point to the sun as guardian of the zodiac and thus as *hêgemonikon* of the world.[104] This entire conception reflects a number of traditional astrological assumptions; yet, as associated with nature as a principle and with the pivotal role of the heart, it seems quite close to Stoic positions. After all, Cleanthes had already claimed the ruling function of the sun within the cosmos.[105]

In sum, Manilius' *Astronomica* thus offer a peculiar synthesis of the living nature of the world, expressed in cardiological terms. It should also be noted that Manilius rejected the cyclical recurrence of the world, and possibly its very generation:[106] besides, he also considered the universe to be boundless.[107] Such a complex of theories is attested nowhere else in the history of Stoicism. Interestingly, the coexistence of these claims does not seem to have affected Manilius' reception of the main body of traditional Stoic cosmology, and especially the doctrines of the universal *pneuma*, fate and divination – unlike for example in Boethus and Panaetius, in different ways. This eclectic integration of orthodox and heterodox theories distinguishes Manilius from the previous Stoic tradition, but does not seem to have influenced the rest of Imperial Stoicism.

11.5   Conclusions

Post-Chrysippean Stoicism thus aligns with the cardiocentric paradigm that had been consolidated by Chrysippus, even though later tradition

---

[100] See also Volk 2009: 16–17; Schwartz 1972: 601–14.   [101] Manilius, *Astron.* III 47–65.
[102] See Schwartz 1972: 614; Boechat 2017: 103–5.
[103] See e.g. Manilius, *Astron.* I 19; III 62; IV 144.   [104] See Boechat 2017: 108.
[105] See DL VII 138–9.   [106] Manilius, *Astron.* I 182–7, 518–23.
[107] *Ibi* I 13–15, 247–8, 294–5, 330, 488–90; II 23; also, Habinek 2011.

displays notable differences with this theory. In particular, starting with Posidonius, Chrysippus' psychological and cardiocentric monism is rejected, whereas in Diogenes blood becomes a psychic substance in a proper sense. Among the reasons for this choice was blood's widespread nature, which allowed for a better explanation of the soul's distribution within the living body and the articulation of psychological functions. A similar paradigm was subsequently applied to reading the cosmos, interpreted as a cardiovascular system with a heart and blood vessels. The heart contained the ruling part, while the psychic substance was funnelled into the fluxes of air and water which populate the universe. In this context, in the Imperial era traces can still be detected of Empedocles' stance and terminology, possibly through Diogenes' mediation. This model of the human being and of the cosmos was thus in compliance with Chrysippus' thought, yet it deviated from it in significant ways, in order to achieve a more suitable explanation of human and cosmic psychology.

CHAPTER 12

The Agency of the World

Katja Maria Vogt

12.1 Introduction

The Stoics put forward two premises that appear to be in tension. First, they claim that the active principle is the sole source of movement and cause of everything. Second, they offer a *scala naturae* according to which kinds of entities differ by the way in which they move and jointly co-cause all movement in the world.

> ONE CAUSE: There is one cause, namely god, which is the cause of everything.

> MANY CAUSES: Compounds, which are parts of the world, jointly co-cause the world's movement.

This One-Many Problem is the Stoic version of what is later called the problem of free will and determinism, or so I argue. As the Stoics conceive of the problem, the challenge consists in showing how both premises – One Cause and Many Causes – are true. The plan for this chapter is not to reconstruct Stoic solutions to their version of the free will/determinism problem. Instead, my goal is to defend my reconstruction of what, for the early Stoics, the problem is.[1] It is easy to go wrong here, in particular since the Stoic notion of causality differs in a number of deep ways from ours.[2]

Nevertheless, my aim is not merely to get clear about differences between Stoic and later ideas. I argue that the Stoics get crucial ideas right. The puzzle, as they see it, does not place human reasoners in a natural world, as if human agency was the exception in a domain otherwise

---

[1] Throughout the chapter, I focus on early Stoic philosophy. I set aside, for example, Epictetus.

[2] My argument is indebted to the work of others, in particular Bobzien 1998; Coope 2007; Sauvé-Meyer's contrasting of the Stoic notion of causality with modern notions (2009); Frede 2011; one sentence by Cooper in which he signals that, if there is to be a solution to the Stoic analogue of the problem of freedom and determinism, it must rely on the fact that the reason of each human being is a portion of God's reason (2003: 240); and finally, Schaffer 2010 and 2013.

regulated by the laws of physics. Many Causes makes this explicit: human beings are only some of the many parts of the world that jointly co-cause its movements. Human reason, animal and plant souls, and the so-called tension that individuates sticks and stones are literally portions of the world's reason. The movement by which all these compounds move does not compete with – or in any other way add to – the movements of the active principle. Hence the impression that One Cause and Many Causes are in tension dissolves. The Stoic proposal, though phrased in historically distant terms, strikes me as attractive, both because it looks at humans together with animals and other parts of the world and because of its upshot for human agency. Our reasoning, including our decision making by which we set ourselves in motion when we act, constitutes some of the causes that co-cause the world's overall movements.

What remains puzzling, however, is that our reasoning is subject to norms. When we think about what to do, presumably we should aim to figure out what is, on consideration, right. We should think carefully, not assent rashly, and so on. If our reasoning, however, is some of the movement that is under way in the corporeal world, then it is not clear how these norms fit into the picture. Ultimately, the puzzle is how norms for practical reasoning fit into the physical world.

This reconstruction, I submit, has the virtue that it does justice to a wide range of evidence. It recognizes that the Stoics address human movement in the context of a *scala naturae*, that is, in a theory about the movements of all macroscopic compounds in the world: stones (and what is like them), plants, animals, people. And it predicts what indeed we find: a wide range of texts about the status of human assent, indicative of the awareness that this is not an easy topic.

After some remarks on how we should not describe the Stoic puzzle (Section 12.2), I turn to One Cause (Section 12.3) and Many Causes (Section 12.4). The rest of the chapter is spent with a reconstruction of how One Cause and Many Causes fit together (Section 12.5), and a concluding discussion of which problems, if any, remain (Section 12.6).

12.2 How Not to Describe the Stoic Puzzle

One thing is fairly clear: there is no such thing as a "will" in Stoic philosophy, and *a fortiori* there is no free will.[3] This means, first of all, that the Stoics do not conceive of a faculty that they call the will or that we

---

[3] Cf. Frede 2011, Bobzien 1998 and 1999, Cooper 2003, Vogt 2008: 185–189, Vogt 2012.

could plausibly identify as the kind of faculty other philosophers call the will. It also means that the Stoics do not take themselves to address the kind of scenario that is later described in terms of alternate (or alternative) possibilities.[4] In the alternate possibilities scenario, an agent stands, as it were, at a crossroads. She considers several courses of action as options and assents to one of them, thereby deciding to perform this action rather than another. The agent is free, the thought goes, insofar as she can do either. Contrary to this type of picture, the Stoics think that an agent's assent reflects her current state of mind. Given who an agent is, such-and-such is what she is going to do. When we praise an agent, it is not because she chose the better course of action over the worse; it is because she was such as to perform a good action.[5]

Suppose, then, that the Stoics do not conceive of a free will. Do the Stoics conceive of determinism? Let me stipulate a conception of determinism: determinism says that the state of the world at a given time t_1 plus the laws of nature, understood as the laws of physics, "fix" the way things go thereafter. Understood this way, determinism is alien to Stoic physics in at least two ways: with respect to the relevant notion of physics, and by extension with respect to the relevant notion of laws.[6] Both differences run deep. Put simply, Stoic *phusikê* – Stoic study of nature – is a kind of biology, or at any rate, it is in important respects a kind of biology, perhaps even a kind of theology.[7]

With a view to scholarly conventions, I continue to refer to Stoic *phusikê* as Stoic physics. But I construe this notion broadly, to accommodate that Stoic physics is a distinctive kind of enterprise. Let us stipulate that, whatever else biology is, it is the science of living beings. The Stoics take it that the world is a large-scale, complex living being.[8] This living being has a biography, a life cycle. Moreover, this living being has a commanding-faculty, a *hegemonikon*, which guides its movements.[9] This makes it seem rather like other living beings, whose movements are governed by the kinds of souls they have. The world, according to the

---

[4] Cf. Frankfurt 1969.   [5] Frede 2011: 81–82.

[6] Cf. Maudlin 2007 on the relevant conception of laws: laws make things happen in a certain way and their existence enables us to explain why things happen in these ways.

[7] Cf. for example Diogenes Laertius 7.147 (LS 54A) and Cicero, *On the nature of the gods* 1.39 (LS 54B). Cf. Sattler, chapter 2 in this volume, on cosmology as biology and theology in Plato's *Timaeus*.

[8] On Stoic conceptions of god and the cosmos, cf. Salles 2009.

[9] Cf. Salles 2018. The questions of how the *hegemonikon* relates to the world's reason and divinity as described in other contexts need not be resolved for present purposes. Cf. for example Diogenes Laertius 7.147 (54A) on various Stoic ways to describe god.

Stoics, is the best living being, indeed, a divine living being.[10] Stoic physics, then, is a distinctive approach to nature, where physics, biology, and theology blend.[11] It is rather unlike the physics that modern philosophers have in mind when referring, in discussions of determinism, to the laws of physics.

What, then, about the notion of the law? The Stoics speak of the law of the world. Should we assume that they conceive of deterministic laws of biology, laws that govern the behavior of a living being? Arguably, the answer is "no." The Stoics refer to the active principle as god, reason, law, and more. Each of these designations picks out a dimension that interests the Stoics in a given philosophical context. The claim that the world is governed by law takes pride of place in political philosophy. The law, as the Stoics conceive of it, governs how we should relate to other parts of the world, and in particular to fellow human beings. The Stoics are literal cosmopolitans: the world is our only real home.[12] The law that we are most fundamentally subject to is the law of the world.[13] This law (singular) is about the ways in which we should relate to all other parts of the world, including all other human beings. It is thus rather unlike the laws (plural) of nature as they come to be understood in the context of the natural sciences.

To take stock, the basic notions of the problem of free will and determinism are alien to the Stoic framework. The Stoics do not conceive of a free will, of physics in the sense in which physical determinism understands it, and of the laws of physics (or even, the laws of biology). It should be plain, then, that the Stoics do not conceive of the problem of free will and determinism. It is also plain, however, that they conceive of something in the proximity. Otherwise it is hard to make sense of the fact that the Stoics discuss – seemingly in great detail – how assent is "up to" agents, to the effect that they are the authors of their own actions.[14]

---

[10] Cf. Sedley 2007, chapter VII "The Stoics" on the world as a divine living being.

[11] On ancestors in Plato and resonances with Plato's arguments, cf. Sattler, Chapter 2 in this volume, and Salles 2018 as well as Chapter 10 in this volume.

[12] Details of Stoic cosmopolitanism are contested, in particular with respect to whether the cosmic city is thought to be populated merely by a smallish group of sages; cf. Schofield 1999. In Vogt 2008, I argue that according to the Stoics all human beings share the world as their home. This means that we are subject to demanding norms. We ought to live up to the ideals of relating to everyone as a fellow-citizen. Cf. Clem. Strom. 4.26 (= SVF 3.327) on the universe as the only real city governed by law.

[13] Cf. Vogt 2008 on the Stoic conception of the law.

[14] Cf. Vogt 2014. I say "seemingly" because, given the state of the evidence on Stoic philosophy it is difficult to judge the extent to which the Stoics were interested in some questions as compared to other questions. The fact that much material on assent survives may also be reflective of the interests of source authors.

The stage is set, then, for asking what the Stoic version of the problem looks like.

A final preparatory disclaimer: Stoic proposals can seem alien, perhaps even obscure, not least insofar as the Stoics propose that the world's biography recurs identically in eternal cycles.[15] Doesn't the theory of eternal recurrence dissolve any grip one may have on the notions of time, past, present, and future? Aren't these notions basic to any understanding of agency, assuming that agents don't predict their actions but deliberate about what to do?[16] Along these lines, one might hold that Stoic views are not just different from other philosophical outlooks. Worse than that, one might think, they are so outlandish that my method, which aims to make sense of Stoic philosophy, is misguided.

Against this line of thought, one may argue that contemporary physics can also seem to dissolve our ordinary, agential grip on time. Today it remains a difficult task even to describe the problem of how agency fits into the natural world in compelling terms. The presumed obscurity of Stoic premises should not keep us from taking their views seriously.

12.3   One Cause: The Active Principle

It is often said that there are several Greek terms that can be translated as cause. These terms – *archê*, *aitia*, *aition*, and more – have a range of uses or meanings, one of them being cause. The flip side of this observation is less often noted: there is no one word in ancient Greek philosophy that maps onto our term cause. These considerations bear on the foundational premise of Stoic physics, according to which there are two so-called principles. So far, this may seem to accord to a familiar pattern in ancient philosophy: one or two or more "principles" are appealed to as fundamental to all of reality. The way in which the Stoics think of the two principles, however, is anything but familiar.[17] Here are two relevant texts:[18]

> **T1** The Stoics think that there are two principles of the whole, that which acts and that which is acted upon. That which is acted upon is unqualified substance, i.e., matter; that which acts is the reason in it, i.e., god. For this,

---

[15] Salles 2003.
[16] This is a slogan formulated and discussed by Levi 1997: "prediction crowds out deliberation."
[17] Cf. Vogt 2018 on Stoics theory of causality.
[18] I render all fragments that are included in Long and Sedley 1987 in their translation, at times with changes by KMV.

since it is everlasting, constructs every single thing throughout all of it. (DL 7.134 = LS44B)

   T2 They [the Stoics] say that god is mixed with matter, pervading all of it and so configuring it, shaping it, and making it into the world. (Alexander, *On mixture* 225, 1–2 = LS45H)

According to these texts, there are two principles: god, also called active principle or reason; and matter, also called passive principle. Together, they constitute the universe, conceived of by the Stoics as a "whole" (*holon*). Both principles are everlasting, ungenerated and indestructible.[19] Both are corporeals and qua corporeals, they are existents. Existence here contrasts with mere subsistence, which is the ontological status the Stoics ascribe to noncorporeals. Both principles are three-dimensional and offer resistance.[20] Matter, the passive principle, is entirely unqualified, but at every given point in time it is inseparably connected to some quality or other. It is through the active principle, which pervades matter, that bodies are individuated and qualified.[21] Matter is divisible but does not by itself divide up into parts.[22] It is because matter is subject to various ways of being qualified by the active principle that there are compounds. Compounds, on this picture, are the elements (fire, air, water, earth) and eventually ordinary bodies as we encounter them on a macroscopic level (stones, plants, animals, people, etc.). Here is a complete list of compounds, as the Stoics conceive of them: the elements (already qualified), soul in the sense of fiery breath, ordinary objects, and the world as a whole.

   This summary contains, in condensed form, much of Stoic physics, and I elaborate on some of it below. For now, I want to turn to the notion of a principle. What is translated here as principle is in Greek *archê*, and though *archê* can mean cause it does not mean cause in Stoic philosophy. The fact that there are two principles does not mean that there are two causal powers. It means that there are two sources – or beginnings or starting points – of the universe. The upshot of this line of thought is significant: if the active principle is a cause, it is not a cause qua being a

---

[19] DL 7.134; SE M 9.75–6 (= SVF 2.311 = LS 44C); Calcidius 292 (= SVF 1.88, part = LS 44D); Calcidius 293 (= LS 44E).

[20] On corporeals being three-dimensional, see DL 7.135 (= SVF 3 Apollodorus 6, part = LS 45E). On resistance, cf. Galen, *On Incorporeal Qualities* (SVF 2.381 = LS 45F). It is difficult to know whether the Stoics agreed on corporeals offering resistance. Cf. Brunschwig 1999, 210–11; Cooper 2009, esp. notes 10 and 11; and Marmodoro 2017a, chapter 6 "Stoic Gunk" and Marmodoro 2017b.

[21] 7.134; Calcidius 292; Calcidius 293.

[22] This is a distinctive Stoic proposal: there are no basic material constituents – particles, atoms, or anything of this sort. Cf. Marmodoro 2017a, chapter 6 "Stoic Gunk"; Marmodoro 2017b.

principle; for otherwise the passive principle would also be a cause, and it is not. To be a principle, thus, is something other than, and more fundamental than, being a cause.

Both principles are corporeal. Corporeality is necessary for being a cause, or in other words, for acting. But it is not sufficient. Matter is corporeal insofar as it is acted upon. God is corporeal insofar as he acts. Compounds are corporeal insofar as they act and are acted upon. The active and passive principles are blended through and through, without thereby one of the principles losing its nature as active or passive.[23]

What is standardly translated as "the active [principle]" is *to poioun*, literally "the making principle." Instead of saying that there are two principles, that which acts and that which is acted upon, one could say that there are two principles, that which makes and that which is affected, *to paschon*. In these terms, god is the making principle.

I take it that scholars have refrained from this translation because it might be misleading: it might suggest, falsely, that *to poioun* makes *to paschon* – that it makes matter. This is not the Stoic proposal. Instead, the proposal is that *to poioun* makes everything in the sense of making all compounds, everything that is a blend of active and passive principles, namely the elements and macroscopic entities of all sorts. The active principle constructs and thereby individuates each part of the world. In this kind of making, the material is available to the maker. The making consists in configuration and shaping, thereby making each part of the world what it is.

The term *to poioun* arguably exploits several dimensions of the verb *poiein*: it can mean "to bring about, to cause" and it can mean "to make something so-and-so." This latter meaning is suggestive for current purposes. The Stoics claim that matter, on which *to poioun* acts, is entirely unqualified. It is never actually in existence in this unqualified way: it is always acted upon and qualified – made so-and-so, in Greek, *poion* – by *to poioun*. Literally, the "how-maker" makes things "so-and-so." Another way in which one might refer to *to poioun*, then, is "the qualifying principle." Arguably, this captures rather well what *to poioun* does. Its disadvantage is that it may sound too weak, as if the active principle was merely a modifying cause.

---

[23] The Stoics conceive of three kinds of mix: juxtapositions (*parenthesis*), like beans and rice, every bit touches other bits, but none loses its integrity; fusion (*sunchusis*) when two things intermix to the extent that they go out of existence and make up some new body; blending (*krasis*), complete reciprocal pervasion and co-extension, but both bodies retain their natures. The argument works by elimination. God and matter aren't fused; they are either juxtaposed or blended; they are not juxtaposed; they are blended. Alexander, *On mixture* 216,14–218,6 (LS 48C).

The active principle, further, is a self-moving power (*dunamis*) and moves everything else:

> **T3** ... So there exists a power which in itself is self-moving, and this must be divine and everlasting. For either it will be in motion from eternity or from a given time. But it will not be in motion from a given time; for there will be no cause of its motion from a given time. So, then, the power which moves matter and guides it in due order into generations and changes is everlasting. So this power would be god. (SE M 9.76 = LS44C)

Let me summarize the ideas we covered so far in two premises, Making and Moving.

> Making: The active principle qualifies matter and thereby individuates entities in the world.
> Moving: The active principle imparts movement on matter and on the entities in the world that it makes.

Making and Moving are diachronic *and* synchronic. This combination is captured in sources that describe the Stoic god both as "proceeding" a certain way in "creating" the world, and at the same time as "pervading" the world in ways that individuate the compounds which are the parts of the world:

> **T4** The Stoics made god out to be intelligent, a designing fire which methodically proceeds toward creation of the world, and encompasses all the seminal principles according to which everything comes about according to fate, and a breath (*pneuma*) pervading the whole world, which takes on different names owing to the alterations of the matter through which it passes. (Aetius 1.7.33 = LS 46A)[24]

Making and Moving are diachronic insofar as the active principle causes the biography of the cosmos. The world is a living being with a recurring life-span, beginning and end.[25] This is especially salient in texts that describe the beginnings of a world cycle, where the active principle qua designing fire makes the elements, and in texts that describe conflagration as the world's periodic end.[26] But the diachronic dimension of Making

---

[24] Similar claims are made about the commanding-faculty (*hêgemonikon*). According to SE M9.102, the beginning of motion in every living being proceeds from its commanding-faculty. This beginning, however, is not simply temporal priority. When a living being moves and the movement originates in its soul, then the living being's motion is contemporaneous with the commanding-faculty's "initiation" of the movement. On this and related passages, cf. Salles 2018.

[25] On fate cf. Sauvé Meyer 2014.

[26] Many of the key texts are in chapter 46 of LS. Cf. especially Aristocles (Eusebius, *Evangelical preparation* 15.14.2) = LS 46G and Cicero, *On divination* 1.125–6 = LS 55L.

and Moving is not limited to the beginnings and ends of world-cycles. Throughout each cycle, the world is a living being with a life that proceeds temporally. Diachronic causality, hence, is a stable dimension of the active principle's Making and Moving.

And yet it is not the case that the active principle *first* makes the parts of the world and imparts movement on them, and then these parts are by themselves the sources of movement in the world. Instead, the active principle continuously makes, moves, and imparts the power of movement on the parts of the world that it makes. Making and Moving are synchronic insofar as all parts of the world and their activities co-cause the total activity of the world. Synchronic causality is contemporaneous with diachronic causality at all times other than beginning and end of each world cycle, for at these times compounds do not exist.

12.4   Many Causes: Compounds

All entities in the world are connected with each other in what we might call a physically, or biologically, "real" way.[27] Each entity in the world is individuated *as well as* connected to all other entities in the world by the active principle, which in this context is described as designing fire and breath. It is on account of the way in which the active principle pervades everything that the world is one and whole, its parts being inseparable and mutually coherent.[28] The world is a whole with parts: all compounds in the world, including human beings, have the status of parts of a whole. Let me, accordingly, formulate Making and Moving with a view to this part-whole relationship.

Making(part): The active principle qualifies matter and thereby individuates parts of the whole.

Moving(part): The active principle imparts movement on matter and on the parts of the whole that it makes.

The active principle, then, is the Maker (individuator) and Mover (that which imparts movement) both on the level of elements and on the level of compounds such as stones, plants, animals, and people. For present purposes, I set aside how individuation and movement work on the level of the elements.[29] My focus is, instead, on compounds that we may call

---

[27] Sauvé Meyer 2009; Marmodoro 2017a chapter 6 "Stoic Gunk" and Marmodoro 2017b.
[28] Aetius 1.7.33 = LS 46A; Calcidius 293 = LS44E.
[29] Qua designing fire, the active principle first creates the four elements. Cf. LS 46, Cooper 2009, Salles 2009.

ordinary bodies, or macroscopic compounds: sticks and stones and the like, artifacts, plants, animals, and human beings. By pervading parts of the whole – the world – in distinctive ways, the active principle makes compounds the kinds of compounds they are. This is how the Stoic *scala naturae* is organized. It proceeds via the dimensions of Making and Moving, now considered with respect to the kinds of entities there are in the world:

> **T4** Of that which moves, some have the cause (*aitia*) of movement in themselves, while others are moved only from outside. That which is moved only from the outside is transportable, like logs and stones and every material thing which is sustained by tenor alone . . .
>
> Animals and plants have the cause of movement in (*en*) themselves, and so, quite simply, does everything sustained by physique or soul, which they say also includes metals. . .
>
> Some things of this kind, they say, are moved out of (*ex*) themselves, and others by (*aph'*) themselves: the former are the soulless things, the latter are the ensouled.
>
> Ensouled things are moved by themselves when an impression occurs within them which calls forth an impulse . . .
>
> A rational animal, however, in addition to its impressionistic nature, has reason which passes judgment on impressions, rejecting some of these and accepting others, in order that the animal may be guided accordingly.
>
> (Origen, *On principles* 3.1.2–3 = SVF 2.988 = LS 53A)

Stones and similar compounds are individuated by a given tenor; they can only be moved from outside. Plants are individuated by natures; they have the cause of movement in themselves, where this means they move out of themselves, with the movement of growth. Animals are individuated by souls; they have the cause of movement in themselves, where this means they move by themselves, namely via impressions and impulse. Rational beings are individuated by reason; they have *logos* in addition to impressions and impulse, and their conduct is guided by assent to and rejection of impressions. This provides us with another dimension of Making and Moving, one that attends to kinds of compounds.

> Making(kinds): Compounds are qualified such as to be compounds of a certain kind via the kind of presence the active principle has in them.
>
> Moving(kinds): Depending on the kind of presence of the active principle in them, compounds play a certain role in the overall movement of the world.

The Stoic *scala naturae*, it turns out, is at the center of their theory of causality. It ascribes to each kind of compound a kind of movement that is reflective of its nature. In effect, the Stoics offer a version of a distinctively ancient take on causality. Rather than locate causality in cause-effect chains or in laws that govern chains of causes, causality is located in the natures of entities.[30] On the Stoic account, then, *all* compounds contribute to the world's overall movement. Why? Or, to be more precise, why not only those that are in one way or another moving "out of" or "by" themselves? While stones, logs, and so on do not have a source of movement in themselves, they are nevertheless pervaded by the active principle. Thereby they are part of an interconnected whole, and they are such that they can be moved. To be moveable is not the same as to be able to move or to act, but it is sufficient for participation in causal relations.

Though artifacts are no natural entities, and hence not included in a scale of nature, we may note that they too participate in the causal nexus among all compounds. In this respect a knife is like a stone: moveable from the outside. A person may use the knife to cut paper, just as she may take a stone and put it on paper, using the stone as a paperweight. Via these routes, artifacts participate in the causal connections between all compounds in the world.

12.5   The Stoic Puzzle

At this point we have sketches of both sides of the One-Many Problem with which I began. According to my proposal, the Stoic version of the problem that is later discussed in terms of free will and determinism is a One-Many Problem. It can be formulated in terms of causes:

ONE CAUSE: There is one cause, namely god, to the effect that this cause is the cause of everything.

MANY CAUSES: Compounds, which are parts of the world, jointly co-cause the world's movement.

---

[30] On cause-effect chains cf. Sauvé-Meyer 2009. Frede puts things as follows: "Perhaps the most crucial difference is that nobody in antiquity had the notion of laws of nature, meaning a body of laws which govern and explain the behavior of all objects, irrespective of their kind. For the most part, at least, philosophers believed [. . .] that the most important factor for one's understanding of the way things behave is the nature of an object" (2011: 15). Cf. Sedley 1998 on on Platonic causes and Coope 2007 on Aristotle's conception of agents as causes.

and in terms of agency:

ONE AGENT: There is one agent, namely, god.

MANY AGENTS: Components of the world, notably stones/etc., plants, animals, and human beings, move by being moved, by themselves, through themselves, or via their reasoning; they are thereby agents to lesser or higher degrees.

Both formulations highlight a feature of Stoic theory that is so far under-appreciated in the literature.[31] The Stoics are not, from the get-go, focusing on how human agency fits into the world. Their question is not how the movements of one privileged kind of entity – human beings – relate to the physical world. Instead they ask how the movements of *all compound entities* relate to the *one* cause of everything: the active principle.

Consider Mara who has a dog named Fred. A Stoic philosopher may ask "how does Fred's running to the door when Fred hears Mara come home fit into the physical world?" just as she may ask "how does Mara's concern for Fred, which makes her come home early, fit into the physical world?" Along similar lines, she may ask how it fits into the natural world that the trees in the nearby park grow, or that when Mara throws a stick Fred runs and brings the stick back to her. The best that a modern reply to the problem of free will and determinism can do, it might seem, is to explain how Mara sets herself in motion. The Stoics find this insufficient. They seek an account of causality that makes sense not only of Mara's, but also of Fred's, the tree's, and the stick's movements. That is, the Stoic One-Many problem genuinely addresses how it is that, while there is one cause for everything, there are many causes.

On this picture, human action is not as special a case as later philosophy makes it seem. Like other philosophers, the Stoics are interested in human action. But human action, for them, is not the sole exception in a world of physical determinism. Instead, human action is, as the Stoic *scala naturae* has it, at one end of a scale. The scale is organized according to the extent to which parts of the world are themselves sources of their movements. Sticks have a source of movement in themselves only to the extent that the tension which makes something a stick also makes this stick an object that can be moved from the outside: carried by a dog, for example. Plants have the source of their movement in themselves insofar as they grow and decay. Animals have the source of their movement in themselves insofar as their

---

[31] For example, even though Frede (2011) discusses how ancient philosophers locate causality in the natures of entities, he adopts the perspective of later authors who are interested specifically in human agency.

movements are guided by perception, as when Fred hears Mara approach the door and runs to the door. Finally, human beings have the source of movement in themselves to the extent that they rationally respond – assent or reject – to impressions, thereby setting off the impulses for their actions. For example, Mara's assent to "I should get home to feed Fred" sets off her action of going home to feed Fred.

According to the Stoics, compounds move with movement that is imparted on them from the active principle. Their movements co-cause the movements of the world. Their ability to move resides in the way in which the active principle pervades and individuates them: as tenor (sticks and stones, papers and knives), soul (animals, plants), or reason (humans). One way to put this, in the case of humans, is that every human being's reason is a portion of the world's reason. This formulation hones in on why the Stoics do not face the question of how human beings can be the authors of their own actions: human reason is literally a portion of the world's reason. Whatever problems the Stoics run into, it is not the case, on their picture, that the active principle (god/reason/etc.) is something over and above or separate from the reasoning of human agents. The Stoics, as is plain also in this respect, do not run into the problem that is later discussed in terms of free will and determinism.

Relatedly, the Stoics do not encounter the question of how a "mental" cause – a human being's deliberation, decision, and the like – fits into the otherwise physical world. Stoic corporealism cuts across distinctions that are fundamental to later philosophy of mind, distinctions between the material and immaterial, the physical and the mental. According to the Stoics, all movement in the world is due to the world's reason. Portions of the world's reason make parts of the world causes of movement (and in the case of objects like stones, such that they can be moved from the outside).[32] A later philosopher might infer that, for the Stoics, all causes are mental. But this would be a mistake, for the mental, in later traditions, is thought to be *not* physical. For the Stoics, reason – god, the active principle – is corporeal, and so are the minds of humans, the souls of animals and plants, and so on.[33]

---

[32] On Stoic proofs for the intelligence of the world and Platonic ancestors of these proofs, cf. Salles, Chapter 10 in this volume.
[33] This does not mean that Stoic accounts of thinking do without any incorporeal items. Thoughts have incorporeal linguistic counterparts, *lekta* ("sayables"). But the role of *lekta* is not such that the Stoics face the kind of problem that is later discussed in terms of mental causation. *Lekta* are effects, not causes. As effects, they are incorporeal, and outside of causal relations. The world's parts are interrelated causes that co-cause everything that can be truly thought or said about the world.

12.6 Conclusion

Human beings are some of the many compound causes that co-cause the movements of the world. There is, however, one respect in which human beings are the exception. They are the only entities in the universe, as the Stoics conceive of it, whose movements are subjects to norms of reasoning. Perhaps the faculties and psychology of some animals include aiming to do better at some task. Conceivably Fred the dog aims to do well – run fast, etc. – in carrying the stick back to Mara. However, whatever norms apply to animals or other nonhuman compounds are not norms of their own reasoning. Only humans, the Stoics hold, assent to and reject impressions concerning what to do, so only humans are subject to norms of assent.

According to the Stoics, this is how human beings are genuinely and fully agents: they are self-moving via their reasoning. They are not, thereby, self-moving in the best kind of way, for they can fail to live up to norms. The perfect reason of the sage and of god prescribe what is to be done. In this sense, even god is subject to norms (Marcian 1 = SVF 3.314 = LS 67R).[34] In god's and the sage's case, however, this does not mean that there can be failure to live up to norms. For them, perfect action reflects the state of mind the agent is already in. This is what the Stoics call self-action, *autopragia*, and freedom (DL 7.121 = LS 67M).

Among the "many" causes that jointly cause the movements of the world, human beings play a special role after all. To repeat, they do not play a special role because, qua imperfect reasoners, they may go for the worse alternative between two possible courses of action. To the Stoics, this would appear to be an odd and unattractive notion, comparable to arriving at a conclusion that has nothing to do with the considerations one was thinking through. As the Stoics see it, the totality of one's state of mind at a given time does not permit that one does anything other than what one does.[35] Human beings are imperfect reasoners, then, because their state of mind typically falls short of that of the wise person. One's current state of mind reflects one's past thinking. In the past, an agent may have adhered only imperfectly to epistemic norms, which makes it even harder to become better and to assent only as one should.

It was not my aim in this chapter to present the Stoic solution for their analogue to the problem of free will and determinism. It is not my aim,

---

[34] Analogously, virtuous people are simultaneously ruling and complying with rule (Stobaeus 2.102,13–16).
[35] Cf. Bobzien 1998: 276–301; Frede 2011; Vogt 2012.

therefore, to explore in any detail how the Stoics conceive of norms of assent and their role in agency. Instead, it has been my aim throughout to get clear about the contours of the problem the Stoics face. To this end, a question that is genuinely hard must be identified; an analysis of the Stoic view which makes the problem disappear is not satisfactory. Why? Because as much as the Stoics do not face the problem of free will and determinism, and as much as human beings are qua parts of the world genuine agents, there *must* be a problem which the Stoics recognize – otherwise they would not go to such lengths discussing related matters, and otherwise it is unlikely that later authors would engage with the Stoics as contributors to this debate to the extent that they do.

Rather than make the problem disappear, my reconstruction locates the problem. A version of the problem of free will and determinism shows up in Stoic philosophy because, though a human being's reason is a portion of the world's reasoning, human reasoning is not straightforwardly an instance of the world's (and that is, god's) reasoning. It is not as if, according to the Stoics, god reasons through us, as it were via the reasoning in our minds. Instead, the way in which reason (god, the active principle) individuates a human being and constitutes her reasoning faculties reflects that compared to god we are lesser entities. We are not as far removed from god as other compounds, for after all we are reasoners. But human reasoning is subject to norms and thereby it differs from god's reasoning. In Stoic philosophy, the notion of freedom comes up here: only a wise person is free, and the wise person's state of mind is not inferior to god's. A wise person's reason is perfect.[36]

Perfect reasoning translates into perfect action. Human beings can do better and worse in the ways in which they assent to impressions, thereby generating what the Stoics call impulses (*hormai*) for their actions. Impulses are movements of the corporeal mind. They are, as it were, the conclusions of thought about what to do. If there is no external impediment, impulse sets off action.[37] A wise person is the best part of the world one can possibly be, both with respect to her thinking and with respect to the actions her thinking sets off.

The hardest task for the Stoics, I propose, lies here: in accounting for norms of assent – and for the way in which imperfect reasoning, reasoning that needs to adhere to norms, is a portion of perfect reasoning. Though the testimony is in many ways inconclusive, one thing is plain. The Stoics

---

[36] Cf. Vogt, 2008, chapter 3 "Wisdom: Sages and Gods"; Frede 2011.
[37] Cf. Inwood 1985; Vogt 2008, pp. 168–78.

put much effort into discussing assent to impressions and how this assent is in an agent's power – or, as they put it, how assent is up to us.[38] The sources, I conclude, confirm my proposal: the "hard" puzzle, for the Stoics, is how norms fit into a corporeal world.

Despite this remaining puzzle, the Stoic outlook as I described it seems inherently attractive. A plausible theory of human agency, we may agree with the Stoics, approaches human movement alongside the movements of other living beings. The Stoic outlook may also seem attractive *because* of the problem that remains. A philosophical theory can be compelling not only via the answers it offers to questions; it can also be compelling in where it locates and how it conceives of the hardest questions. It seems true, or at any rate it seems to many philosophers today, that it is one of the hardest tasks to find out how norms fit into the physical world.

---

[38] This notion – up to us – is at the heart of Stoic and later discussions. Cf. Destrée, Salles, and Zingano 2014; Vogt 2014.

CHAPTER 13

God and the Material World
Biology and Cosmology in Galen's Physiology

R. J. Hankinson

For Galen there can be no serious biology without cosmology:

> When anyone looks at the facts with an open mind, and sees that in such a slime of fleshes and juices there is none the less an internal intelligence, and looks at the structure of any animal whatsoever (for they all give evidence of a wise Creator), he will understand the excellence of the intelligence in the heavens. A work on the functionality of the parts, which at first seemed to be of little importance, will then be rightly thought to be the source of a precise theology,[1] something far greater and finer than all of medicine. It is useful not just for the doctor, but even more for the philosopher who is eager to gain an understanding of the whole of Nature. I think that everyone who honours the gods should be initiated into this work, which is quite different from the mysteries of Eleusis or Samothrace, which give only feeble proofs of what they set out to teach; the proofs of Nature are plainly to be seen in all animals. (1: The Functionality of the Parts [UP] IV 360–61 Kühn = 17.1, ii 447,16–448,9 Helmreich, 1907-9; trans. here and elsewhere after May 1968)[2]

That passage comes towards the end of Galen's resonant summary (the 'Epode', as he calls it) of his lengthy treatise on the marvellous functional adaptiveness of animal structures. The reference to theology is not merely adventitious. The whole thrust of the work is to demonstrate that the only reasonable result of such an investigation will be an acknowledgement of,

---

[1] *akribês theologia*: Frede (2003: 85) notes that this is the only place where Galen uses the term *theologia*.

[2] Texts of Galen are generally cited, where possible, first by way of the edition of Kühn (1821–33), which is still the best, indeed the only, available text for large chunks of Galen (although that situation is slowly being remedied); where better editions exist, I usually cite them as well. Margaret May's 1968 annotated translation of *UP* (which she renders 'On the Usefulness of the Parts of the Body') is still extremely valuable, particularly for identifying the structures which Galen is describing (or trying to describe), although superseded in some respects by subsequent scholarship. I have opted for 'functionality' to the alternatives for rendering the notoriously problematic '*chreia*': others have preferred 'use', 'utility', 'function'. As her translation is keyed only to Helmreich, from here onwards I refer only to that text.

indeed an unqualified admiration for, the consummate skill exhibited by the Creator of the animal kingdom, whom Galen calls, in a nod to Plato, the *dêmiourgos*.[3] Only someone blinded by a sterile, mechanistic ideology could fail to draw the obvious inference to His existence and supreme wisdom (Galen has at the forefront of his mind here Epicurus and other anti-teleological Atomists; but − typically − his scorn ranges much wider than just that). Galen's moriology, his account of animals' parts, in contrast with Aristotle's, from which he derives inspiration but which he seeks to correct in its fine detail, is a work of natural theology.[4]

UP was composed relatively early in Galen's long and productive career. At the end of his life, he revisited the same themes in his *apologia pro doctrina sua, My Own Opinions*:

> I do not know whether the world was created, or whether there is anything outside it or not. Moreover, ... I have no knowledge as to whether the creator of everything in the universe is corporeal or incorporeal, or where the divine power is located.[5] This is the same as those powers that are manifested in this world by activities that can only be the result of a Creator; thus they themselves point to God. ... I have no knowledge of their substance; but I know from their activities that they exist, since the organization of all living things comes from them, and they are revealed in divination and dreams.[6] The activities of God ... have become even clearer in their power: he cured me once of an illness I had,[7] and they can be seen in the salvation of those at sea who are about to suffer shipwreck, when they firmly believe that they will be saved by the signs that they see. Clearly this signifies some wonderful power; indeed I have experienced it myself.
> (**2**: *My Own Opinions [Prop.Plac.]* 2.1–3 = 56,12–58,16 Nutton 1999)[8]

---

[3] Usually simply transliterated as 'Demiurge', but sometimes rendered 'Craftsman' or 'Artificer'; I have generally followed May in preferring the translation 'Creator'.

[4] I deal with the 'Epode', and with Galen's religious language and orientation in general, in my forthcoming.

[5] On the sense of this, see Frede 2003: 94–7.

[6] Galen professes to believe in divinely inspired dreams: he was, he tells us, told by a god in a dream not to accompany Marcus Aurelius on his German expedition in 169: *My Own Books (Lib.Prop.)* XIX 18–19, = 142,15–20 Boudon-Millot 2007. His father was similarly inspired to have him expensively educated as a doctor: *The Order of My Own Books (Ord.Lib.Prop.)* XIX 59 K = 99, 24–100, 4 Boudon-Millot 2007; *Prognosis* XIV 608, = *CMG* V 8, 1, 76,2 8–78, 2 (Nutton 1978). *Lib.Prop.* and *Ord.Lib.Prop.* are also edited in Müller 1891. See also n 40 below.

[7] This is probably the cure he elsewhere attributes specifically to Asclepius; he managed to avoid going with Marcus Aurelius to Germany by telling the emperor that the god had told him not to; Marcus accepted his excuse (*Lib. Prop.* XIX 19, = 142,11–20 Boudon-Millot 2000; cf. *Treatment by Venesection* XI 314–15). See Frede 2003: 90–91.

[8] Nutton constructed his text from a variety of sources (partial Greek, Arabic, Latin and Hebrew exemplars); the recently rediscovered complete Greek text of *Prop.Plac* is edited in Boudon-Millot and Pietrobelli 2005. The difficulties of this chapter are dealt with in Frede 2003: 89–98.

So Galen writes, with disarming personal frankness, in the first substantial part of what Vivian Nutton (1987) has aptly described as his philosophical testament. His theology[9] is of a piece with his rather better-known views regarding souls: their existence is evident from their effects, the activities for which they, and only they, can be responsible. How they do what they do, and what, in substance, they are, is, by contrast, highly obscure; but fortunately, at least from the standpoint of medical practice, these obscurities are of little import *Prop.Plac.* 3.1, 58,22–60,6; 15.1–2, 116,5–118,10 Nutton 1999).

The relation between God, the divine creator and organiser of the world, and practical science is less direct (see *The Doctrines of Hippocrates and Plato* [*PHP*] V 777–82 = 586,7–590,11 De Lacy 1978–94). But Galen is convinced that one can only form a fully-rounded and accurate picture of the complexity of its structures by properly understanding its genuinely teleological nature: 'Let us then make you skilful in Nature's art, so that we may call you … a natural philosopher (*phusikos*)' (*UP* 3.10, i 175,18–20 H).[10] *UP*, his magnum opus on the subject, is a reworking of Aristotle's *de Partibus Animalium* (*PA*), with the avowed purpose of fleshing out what he takes to be the deficiencies which derive from Aristotle's refusal to countenance the actual creative activity of an actual Creator (cf. *UP* 1.8, i 14,13–15,12 H).

13.1   The Hand of God

Even so, his treatment is still greatly, and acknowledgedly, indebted to Aristotle's. Book 1 is devoted to a detailed examination of the structure of the hand, and how perfectly designed it is when considered in the light of the functions which it has to perform. It follows, while greatly expanding upon, Aristotle's account in *PA* 4.10. Galen begins by praising Aristotle's contention that man has hands because he is the most intelligent of animals, rather than *vice versa* as Anaxagoras had mistakenly held (*PA* 4.10, 687a7–18; cf, *UP* 1.3, i 3,25–4,5 H). Hands are the basic human tool (the 'tool of tools', as Aristotle puts it: *PA* 4.10, 687a20–21; cf. *UP* 1.4, i 6,6–8 H): 'Every soul has through its very essence certain faculties, but without the aid of tools it is helpless to accomplish what it is

---

[9] Frede 2003 is the best exploration of this issue; see also Kudlien 1981.

[10] This emphasis on becoming a 'natural philosopher' recurs elsewhere (e.g. 11.18, ii 170,8–9 H and 12.14, ii 222,17 H). At the very end of treatise (17.2, ii 449,15–19 H), Galen claims that the 'greatest benefit' of a proper teleological understanding accrues to the natural philosopher, by inculcating respect for this immense providential power.

by nature disposed to accomplish' (*UP* 1.3, i 4,11–13 H). Galen points to the way in which newborn animals try to make use of parts which have not yet fully developed:

> Every animal has, untaught, a perception of the powers of its own soul, and the supremacy of its parts[11] ... how can one say that animals learn the functionality of their parts from the parts themselves, when obviously they know their functionality even before they have them? ... The other animals acquire their skills by instinct rather than reason. (**3**: *UP* 1.3, i 4,23–5,19 H)

The discussion of the hand functions as the template for every other inquiry into structure and morphology:

> Let us investigate this supremely important part of the human body ... not simply to determine whether it is useful, or suitable for an intelligent animal, but to see whether it is in every respect so constituted that it would not have been better had it been made any differently. (**4**: *UP* 1.5, i 6,18–22 H)

Galen is motivated partly by his desire to expound the advanced discoveries of contemporary anatomical physiology, some of them his own.[12] But more importantly, he aspires to exhibit in detail the extraordinary adaptiveness and complexity of animal structure in general, something underappreciated even by the great men of the past:

> Why did Plato ... speak so slightingly of the functionality of the fingernails? And why did Aristotle, who was adept at explaining the workmanship of nature, overlook so much of their functionality? Plato[13] says that, like certain bad workmen, the gods who fashioned men made nails grow on his fingertips as if they were practising in advance the formation of the claws that would be necessary in other animals. Aristotle,[14] on the other

---

[11] Galen mentions calves butting before their horns grow, baby boars trying to slash with non-existent tusks, and puppies biting with soft teeth, as the well as the facts that birds and snakes, raised from eggs without their parents, will instinctively follow their natural modes of behaviour, i.e. flying, swimming, crawling. Compare 15.7, ii 365,2–366,4 H, on animals' instinctive knowledge of how to acquire nutrition, and of what sort of nutrition is appropriate; see also *The Formation of the Foetus* (*Foet.Form.*) IV 687–702, = 90,27–106,13 Nickel 2001 (*CMG* V 3,3, 2001), and §5 below. Similar examples are adduced, although with very different argumentative ends in mind, by Lucretius: 5.1028–40.

[12] A case in point: detailed dissective anatomy has shown that the sexual parts are not initially differentiated in the foetus: *UP* 14.7, ii 304,17–305,6 H; see §4 below. Galen is also an important source for competing physiological theories and especially Stoic theories, for which see Vimercati's contribution to the present collection (Chapter 11). For a discussion of Plato's physiological theory in connection with the structure of the cosmos, see El Murr's contribution (Chapter 3).

[13] *Tim.* 76d-e.   [14] *PA* 4.10, 687b22–5.

hand, says that the nails were formed for protection, though he does not say from what. (**5**: *UP* 1.8, i 11,21–12,13 H)

Plato supposes that fingernails are vestigial, in themselves useless, dry-runs for later, better things. Aristotle at least tries to give a functional account of them; but it is insufficiently precise and detailed – indeed, it is just wrong. The nails' real function is to allow us to pick up different sorts of object by providing a firm and resistant backing for the soft and sensitive flesh of the fingertips (1.5–7, 10, i 6,18–11,20, 20,15–24 H; even so, they need to be kept at the right length: 1.5, i 10,5–11,20 H). Moreover, they are of exactly the right degree of hardness: they are firm, but more yielding than bone, hooves or claws (1.11, i 20–22). This makes them prone to being worn down and broken off, so to compensate Nature has made them capable of growing when the animal as a whole has stopped doing so (i 22,16–23,5): 'Thus everything about the nails shows the utmost providence on the part of Nature' (i 23,5–6). As such, they are prime exemplars of what Galen is fundamentally trying to prove. Only those who are insufficiently familiar with it, or blinded by dogma, incompetence or idleness, can fail to appreciate the marvellously fine construction of things:

> I mentioned Aristotle and Plato not to refute what they have wrongly asserted, but rather to show why I was impelled to begin a discussion of these matters. There was a great disagreement (*diaphônia*) among doctors and philosophers of old concerning the functionality of the parts. Some of them believed that our bodies are formed neither for the sake of anything nor with any skill, others that they are formed for some purpose and skilfully, but with one claiming one use for each of the parts, and another another.[15] I sought first to discover a criterion for resolving this disagreement, and then to put together one universal method which will enable us to discover the functionality of each part, and its attributes. (**6**: *UP* 1.8, i 12,13–23 H)

The key, in Galen's view, is to understand the co-operative nature of the functioning of the structures and the systems they embody. Galen quotes from the Hippocratic *Nutriment* 23: 'Taken together, all the parts are in sympathy; taken severally, the parts in each part co-operate for their

---

[15] May's translation has Galen here distinguish sharply between the old doctors and philosophers, making the former only the holders of the view that everything is formed by chance, the latter the advocates of design. But this, while a possible rendering of Galen's Greek, is not a possible rendering of his thought: foremost among his targets in *UP* (and indeed elsewhere) are the materialist and anti-teleological Epicureans; while for Galen, Hippocrates is a paragon of the proper teleological approach.

effect'.[16] Every part (of the body) co-operates in a general shared enterprise; and so do the parts of the parts as well. All are perfectly organised components of an extraordinarily complex and finely tuned piece of machinery; and any complex piece of machinery must be the work of a craftsman. This is, of course, a staple of design-arguments down to Paley and beyond, before some of us at any rate became comfortable with the possibility of blind watchmakers. Galen is only one of many such theorists in antiquity;[17] but his is the most thorough-going, empirically informed and carefully worked-out development of the position; nobody else does it with the same degree of anatomical detail and explanatory ingenuity. Plato (unlike Aristotle) rightly invoked divine creation, but as **5** emphasises, he did not get its specifics right. If one looks closely enough, the workmanship is more perfect than even Plato could have comprehended.

Which takes us back to Galen's creationist theology.[18] Bad divine workmanship is not, for Galen, an option, at least not one that can be generalised across structures which hold for entire species, as it would have to be if there were something fundamentally wrong, or inadequate even, with human fingernails. Nature occasionally gets things wrong on an individual basis, but only very rarely: five is – as Galen demonstrates at some length in Book 1 of *UP* (1.23, i 60,6–61,21 H) – the ideal number of human fingers. While there are cases of individuals born, like Anne Boleyn, with an extra finger, this happens 'only once in ten thousand times ten thousand cases'[19] (*UP* 17.1, ii 444,3–7 H). If a human craftsman (or artist: *technitês*), such as the pre-eminent sculptor Polyclitus,[20] 'made an error of this sort just once in a thousand statues, you would not condemn him, but would rather say that his detractors had no judgement' (*UP* 17.1, ii 444,7–9 H). Galen's constant refrain is the extraordinary, providential skill evidenced in the work of Nature (which should here be capitalised as well), or, equivalently for him, the Craftsman. Galen adopts Aristotle's slogan 'Nature does nothing in vain', repeating it regularly, and in

---

[16] See Craik 2017: 205, for Galen's appropriation of this text; and see in general 204–7.

[17] The Stoics also employ design-arguments, and in support of a similar view of the craftsman-like rationality of the Universe: see Boys-Stones in Chapter 9 of the present collection.

[18] Creationist theology is also discussed in connection with Plato and the Stoics by Sattler and Boys-Stones in Chapters 2 and 9 of the present collection.

[19] Not – of course – the claim that this occurs literally once in every 100,000,000 times; 10,000 – a myriad – is merely a conventionally large number, which, when multiplied by itself, yields an unconventionally large number.

[20] Galen likes to invoke the great sculptors: even Phidias (see **9** below) and Polyclitus are not good enough so as only to go wrong once in every few thousand sculptures, which is Nature's error-rate (*UP* 15.7, ii 364,15–365,2 H; the subject is breech-births).

numerous variant forms,[21] but re-interprets it to make it an invocation of divinely directed, intentional teleology.

13.2   The Hymn to Nature and the Nature of Beauty: Matter, Form and Function

This is most conspicuous in a passage where Galen describes this work as a 'sacred discourse' and a 'Hymn to Nature', the Creator (*UP* 3.10, i 174,7–8 H). The 'hymn' takes the form of expounding the brilliance and attentiveness to detail of the divine creation, a far better tribute than burning incense and making sacrifices (*UP* 3.10, i 174,4–19 H).[22] This act of reverence involves a comparison between the universe as a whole and its microcosmic, animal counterparts:

> The ancients[23] ... say that an animal is, so to speak, a little universe, and that you will find the same wisdom displayed by the Creator in both his works. 'Then show me', you say, 'a sun in the body of animal'. What a thing to demand! Are you willing to have the sun formed from the substance of blood, so prone to putrefy and so filthy? ... This, and not the failure to make offerings and burn incense, is true sacrilege. I will not show you the sun in the body of an animal; but I will show you the eye,[24] a very brilliant instrument, resembling the sun as closely as could be achieved in an animal's body. (7: *UP* 3.10, i 177,10–20 H)

The filthiness and corruptibility of the matter of the human body was emphasised a couple of pages earlier, in a vivid passage on the nature of true beauty (*UP* 3.10, i 174,19–175,20 H; cf. 175,23–176,3 H). Beauty is purely a matter of form, and form is related to function; genuine artists admire perfection of structure no matter what material it is realised in. Indeed, proper beauty just *is* functional excellence:[25]

---

[21] See e.g. *UP* 1.18, 1.23, 2.15, 3.10, 4.15, 5.5, 6.1, 6.17, 7.8, 9.16, 10,3, 10.14, 11.5, 12.14, 13.2, 13.8, 15.4, 15.5; i 46,9–11, 61,14–15, 110,4–5, 165,25–166,5, 231,19–24, 267,11–14, 299,13–15, 358,25–359,6, 391,25–392,8, ii 47,19–22, 69,6–8, 108,26–109,5, 123,18–19, 222,14–18, 237,18–238,6, 263,1–3, 349,23–350,7, 359,5–9 H, etc.

[22] See my forthcoming, §6.

[23] Galen does not here specify whom he has in mind; but Plato in the *Timaeus* is an obvious candidate (esp. 42e–47e, on the creation of humanity by the lesser gods). He never mentions the Hippocratic *Regimen* 1, the clearest example of such views in the entire corpus; but he had his own reasons for thinking this text spurious, and he rarely refers to it. There is a probable (so May thinks, 1968: 636 n 36), if nameless, reference to *Regimen* 1.6–7 at *UP* 14.7, ii 306, 26–307, 3 H.

[24] The discussion of the eye occupies the whole of Book 10 (ii 54,20–113,5 H); see §4 below.

[25] See also *Thrasybulus* 10, IV 821–2, = 44,18–45,6 Helmreich 1983; and Sedley 2017: 235–42.

If you are seeking to discover the proper form for the eye or the nose, you will find it by correlating structure and activity *(energeia)*. This is the standard, measure and criterion of proper form and genuine beauty, which is nothing but excellence of construction. (**8**: *UP* 1.9, i 17,20–18,1 H; cf. 11.13, ii 152,14–153,26 H)

Nature will add purely cosmetic adornment when it can do so without loss of functionality; ears are pretty, as well as being perfectly suited for gathering sound.²⁶ Pubic hair grows necessarily as a residue in the loins, since they are warm and wet; 'but it also makes a covering and an ornament for the parts there, as the buttocks do for the anus,²⁷ and the foreskin for the penis'.²⁸ Aesthetic adornment is sometimes a matter of decorum or decency; Galen is easily shocked by what he sees as immodesty and indecorousness. But even if purely aesthetic considerations are secondary in comparison with those of the functional, the fact that they can be discerned at all is further evidence for the existence of a providential and intelligent Creator. Galen sums up:

> Disregard the differences in matter, and consider only the bare art itself, bearing in mind when you inspect the structure of the eye and of the foot that one is the instrument of vision and the other of locomotion. If you think it proper for the eyes to be made of matter like the sun's, or the feet to be pure gold instead of bone and skin,²⁹ you are forgetting the matter *(ousia)* of which you have been formed. Bear it in mind, and reflect whether your matter is celestial light or slime of the earth. ... You would never demand an ivory statue of Phidias if you had only given him clay; equally, when blood is the operative material, you will never obtain the bright and

---

²⁶ On the other hand, he claims that the beauty of the eye is 'often disregarded, since its functionality is so greatly admired' (ii 153,8–10 H); I don't know what to make of this.
²⁷ 'Apes have absurd bodies to go with their ridiculous souls' (1.22, 3.16, 11.2, 15.8, i 58,13–59,16, 193,23–194,22, ii 117,12–15, 367,15–22 H); one reason for their ridiculousness is their shameful lack of buttocks (11.13, ii 153,6–8 H; cf. 15.8, ii 367,15–21 H). Aristotle concurs regarding the buttocklessness, but draws a functional rather than an evaluative conclusion; quadrupeds have no buttocks, since they don't need to sit down, but generally they do have tails; apes 'equivocate' between quadruped and biped, and thus have no buttocks, like quadrupeds, but no tail, like bipeds: *PA* 4.10, 389b1–690a4. Tails also serve to 'cover and protect that part which serves for voiding excrement'; but Aristotle does not suggest that this also serves the cause of propriety. Galen agrees that humans are the only animals that properly sit: 3.1, 3.3, i 126,22–127,4, 131,15–133,8 H; n 30, below.
²⁸ 11.13–14, ii 152,14–162,12 H, esp. 153,3–8, 162,4–8; cf, 15.3, ii 346,1–4 H, with reference also to the labia majora and minora.
²⁹ Given the functional role which it is supposed to fulfil, it is good that the foot is made of bone and skin, indeed skin which is particularly tightly connected to the underlying flesh; *UP* 3.10, i 172,5–173,11 H.

beautiful body of the sun or the moon. They are divine and celestial, and
we are mere figures of clay; but in both cases, the art of the Creator is
equally great. (**9**: *UP* 3.10, i 175,20–176,9 H)

This section of *UP* deals with the construction of the foot, in a very real
sense a pretty mundane structure: 'Who will deny that the foot is a small,
ignoble part of an animal?' (*UP* 3.10, i 176,9–10 H). But it is ideally
constructed for what it has to do; moreover, like the sun, it is in the best
place it could possibly be, given its functional role (176,10–177,8 H).[30]
Humans, being rational, need working hands (above §1), and since
properly functional hands need to be kept free, they need to be bipeds.[31]
This is turn demands a particular architecture for the legs and feet (and the
spine: §3 below), which entails that human feet cannot be small and hard,
like those of the horse, and hence cannot be built for speed. However,
'man, who was to tame the horse with his intelligence and his hands, had
no need of speed for himself' (3.1, 123,18–19 H). Galen deals with these,
and other, related functional requirements for the feet, at length at the
beginning of *UP* 3 (3.1–6, 123-9-142,2 H).[32]

13.3   Teleology, Design and Material Constraints: The Eyelashes and the Spine

Things are indeed organised for the best, provided at least that the best is
properly understood. However, the power of Galen's Demiurge, great
though it is, is limited by the material he has to work with, unlike
'the God of Moses', 'who could make a horse or an ox out of ashes' if he
so desired (11.14, ii 158,25–6):

> Has our Creator then commanded only these hairs [sc. the eyelashes] to
> always maintain the same length, and do the hairs preserve it as ordered
> because they fear the injunction of their Lord, or reverence the God who
> commands it, or themselves believe it better to do so? This is how Moses

---

[30] I deal with this passage on the supreme functionality of the structure of the universe in Hankinson
      1989.
[31] Humans sit in order to keep their hands free for use (which is why they uniquely have buttocks: see
      n. 27). Being a genuine biped, with fully prehensile hands, is a feature of being a perfect (in the
      sense of properly equipped) rational animal. At 14.6, ii 298,7–299,2 H, Galen writes that animals
      with all of the senses are 'close to perfect', even if they have no limbs, like fish. If they do have limbs,
      then they are better if, like lions and dogs, they have hands 'in a way'. Better still are the more
      dextrous and erect bears and apes; 'but only man has an actually perfected hand and the intellectual
      power to use it as well, a power than which there is nothing more divine in animals'.
[32] See my forthcoming, §7.

reasons about Nature (and it is better than Epicurus's way). However, we should adopt neither, and continue to derive the principle of generation (*archê geneseôs*) from the Creator in everything generated, as Moses does, but then add the material principle (*hê ek tês hulês*) to it. (**10**: *UP* 11.14, ii 158,2–11 H)

Even so, Galen does allow that the eyelashes may, in a sense, do what their Creator tells them to:

He has made these hairs feel the necessity of preserving always an even length since it was better thus.[33] ... But it was not enough just to will that they be so; for even if had wanted to make a man out of a rock all of a sudden, it would be impossible. This is where my teaching, and that of Plato and the other Greeks, differs from that of Moses. (**11**: *UP* 11.14, ii 158,11–23 H)

God's power is circumscribed by material constraints. This is, as Galen says, Platonic in origin: the creator-gods could have made man longer-lasting but less intelligent by making him largely bony, but thought it better not to do so (*Timaeus* 75a–c). Design involves choices and compromises. If there were no restrictions at all on the divine ability to create at will, we might indeed criticise the Creator's failures to make things better. But as there are, such criticisms are misguided and ignorant. Time and again, Galen remarks that particular structures represent the best and most elegant design-solution to a complex set of problems, most generally created, as in the *Timaeus* case of the trade-off between intelligence and longevity, by the conflicting requirements of functional excellence and survival.

At the end of Book 12, Galen deals with a particularly complex case, the spine. It has four basic functions as (i) a foundation for the body, (ii) a path for spinal cord, (iii) 'a safeguard', sc. for the spinal cord, and (iv) an 'instrument of motion' for the back as a whole. It also has the subsidiary function of protecting the viscera, which is 'a necessary consequence' of the others.[34] Each of the requisite functions entails certain structural facts:

---

[33] Eyebrows and eyelashes naturally preserve the optimum lengths required to fulfil their functions of preventing things flowing down into the eyes from above, or penetrating into them from in front, without hindering ability of the eye to see: 11.14, ii 157,13–158,1, 159,3–160,3 H; see also 10.7, ii 79,20–80,19 H.

[34] This too is a common theme: the amniotic fluid's primary role is to provide a stable and protective environment for the growing foetus; but it also lubricates the birth canal: 'Nature's works are altogether ingenious; as I have shown many times, she makes additional use for the better of all things that will otherwise exist of necessity' (*UP* 15.5, ii 355,1–4 H). On such secondary functions, see Hankinson 1988.

(i) Because it is like a keel[35] or a foundation for the animal, it has been made of bones, indeed hard ones. (ii) Because it is a pathway for the spinal cord, it is hollow inside. (iii) Because it is like a city-wall for the spinal cord, it is fortified with many ramparts all around it; ... And (iv) because it is an instrument of motion ... it has been made of several bones, united by joints. (**12**: *UP* 12.11, ii 217,2–11 H)

Condition (iv) entails that it be flexible, and so jointed. But if (iii) is to be satisfied, it must be firm and strong as well. Had this been the only desideratum, or if it had simply had to function as piece of rigid scaffolding to make walking erect a possibility, as (i) demands, it could have consisted of a single (albeit hollow, given (ii)), bone (12.10, ii 211, 17–212, 21 H). But since it is better for the spine to be jointed (212,22–213,21), the number of the vertebrae is also excellently chosen:

Nature considers the aims not piecemeal, but always conjointly.[36] In terms of its intrinsic value, the activity is primary, and safety comes after it; but for lasting health, safety comes first and the activity is secondary.[37] ... I intend to show now for the spine, as I did before for the arms and the legs,[38] that no better or more accurate combination of activity and resistance to injury could possibly be imagined. (**13**: *UP* 12.10, ii 213,21–214,4 H; cf. **4**)

Galen promises, rather extravagantly, to explain why there should be exactly the number of vertebrae there are, and why they should be organised into the major groups (cervical, thoracic, lumbar) which we still recognise today, there being seven cervical, twelve thoracic, and five lumbar vertebrae, in addition to the os sacrum[39] (*UP* 12.12, ii 217,12–218,3 H). The actual explanation is long, convoluted, and digressive; indeed it lasts until well into the following book, where he examines the distribution of the nerves from

[35] The keel image is common in Galen: cf. *UP* 3.2, i 131,6 H; 12.10, ii 211,18; 12.11, 217,3; 13.3, 247,10 H; at *Foet.Form.* IV 682, = 86,20–21 Nickel 2001, the image of 'a foundation or keel' is used for the blood vessels, which Galen thinks are the first parts of the embryo to be formed, by outgrowth from the womb-lining.

[36] This is a central part pf the method adumbrated at **6** above.

[37] This point is made elsewhere: see e.g. 1.11, i 20,25–22,5 H; 2.17, i 117,1–118,7 H. On the ideal number of vertebrae, see 12.12, ii 217,12–221,4 H,; and 12.13–16, ii 221,5–233,8 H, on the protective function of the vertebral processes; on the prevention of neural injury, cf. 13.3, ii 240,25–247,23 H. Compare the case of the eye, §4 below.

[38] See *UP* 2.1–19, ii 64,10–123,8 H; 3.1–16, ii 123,9–194,26 H (arms); cf. 17.1, ii 442,9–448,7 H (legs).

[39] Galen's account contains a number of errors and inconsistences. Here, he writes that the sacrum consists in the human of four bones, as it in fact does in sheep, goats, and pigs, rather than the five of the actual human spine. He fails to mention the coccyx altogether (although at 13.7, ii 260,26–262,3, he describes it as being a cartilaginous outgrowth from the sacrum), while in his early *Bones for Beginners* II 731–2 K, he says that the coccyx is a bone additional to the sacral three: see May 1968: 574 n. 46.

spinal cord, and the role of the various muscles, ligaments and vertebral processes.[40] He begins by dealing in general terms with the need for a multiplicity of flexible vertebrae ('not two, or three, or four'), to protect the spinal cord, as well as allowing the back to flex while preserving the integrity of the cord (218,3–219,13 H). Then, after a rambling discussion of how, among other things, the vertebral processes protect the spine and its precious cord by acting as a sort of impact-absorbing crumple-zone (12.15, ii 225,14–229,3 H), Galen returns to his initial theme:

> It is now clear why ... there are four main divisions of the whole spine. Since the thorax lies in the middle, and is contained on each side by the neck above, and the lumbar region below, and since the sacrum forms a common support for all of them, the principal divisions of the whole spine were necessarily four. After I have finished the present account, you will hear why one of them is composed of seven vertebrae, another of twelve, a third of five, and the last of four. (**14**: *UP* 12.16, ii 229,10–20 H)

There are four spinal regions, apparently, because there are four separate general areas of the body. Or at least three, with a single underlying foundation, the sacrum. The promised final accounting for the precise distribution of the vertebrae does not in fact materialise until the middle of the following book (13.7, ii 260,1–262,3 H). Because the human stands erect, the vertebrae need to decrease in size as they go up; in addition they have to fulfil the functions of distributing appropriate pairs of nerves to different organs, as well as generally supporting the entire structure. The account is complicated, multi-faceted, and, in truth, not very satisfactory:

> The lower vertebrae have to be as much bigger than the ones lying on top of them so as to support them without pain. .... Since they were to be like this, the whole thorax needed twelve of them, since it happened that this number agreed with the gradual increase, and with the generation of the thorax as a whole. (**15**: *UP* 12.16, 260,9–13 H)

And the rest of the passage is no more lucid. Nevertheless, Galen hopefully sums up:

> It has now become perfectly evident why the neck is constructed from seven vertebrae, and correspondingly the thorax from twelve, the lumbar region from five, and why the sacrum and all the other parts of the spine are exactly the size that they are. (**16**: *UP* 12.16261,19–23 H)

---

[40] Galen rightly points out, however, that these issues are inter-related and cannot be readily divided up: *UP* 12.16, ii 232, 27–233, 8 H.

Whatever the shortcomings in its actual execution, however, a fairly clear picture of Galen's overall project begins to emerge. Close examination reveals that the internal structures of animals are too complex to be the results of mere chance, or indeed (although Galen does not emphasise this, presumably out of respect for Aristotle), of undirected, immanent teleology. The degree of co-ordination required to optimise the results in light of material constraints, and in particular the need to secure the maximum degree of functional effectiveness consistent with the demands of resistance to injury and the preservation of life, tells conclusively against any possible alternative. Indeed, supreme artistic skill is manifested precisely by making the best of a not terribly good job, of contriving the optimal use of constrained resources (as well as by adding ornamentation, where possible); Galen's God is better, and more intelligent, than Moses'. Any competent, conscientious investigator not in the grip of mechanist dogma will have to acknowledge the hidden hand of intelligent design. But even so (consistently with **2** above), *how* the designer manages to bring about the results that he does may be utterly, indeed irremediably, obscure.

13.4   The Creator's Skill Made Manifest: Vision and the Reproductive System

This final, sceptical feature of Galen's cosmological teleology will better emerge from a consideration of two other structures in which Nature's pre-eminent skill and providence are most clearly exemplified: the eyes and the genitalia. Artistic excellence is primarily manifested in terms of form rather than matter (**8, 9** above, §2). At the end of the 'Epode', Galen remarks that the Creator's creative brilliance is evidenced, if anything, even more in lesser animals: 'the smaller the animal, the greater the wonder it will excite, just as when craftsmen carve something on small objects' (*UP* 17.1, ii 448,13–15 H). He describes an intricate miniature of 'Phaëthon drawn by four horses, each with a bit in its mouth, and teeth so small that I did not see them at first, until I turned it around under a bright light, . . . yet none of this displays more perfect workmanship than the leg of a flea' (17.1, ii 448,16–449,11 H). This is particularly clear when one remembers that the flea is no mere static representation, but a living, functioning animal. Still,

> If the Creator's skill is so great when manifested incidentally, as one might say, in insignificant animals, how much greater must we estimate his wisdom and power when manifested in animals of some importance. (**17**: *UP* 17.1, ii 449,11–14 H)

Let us return to the eye, the functional description of which occupies the whole of Book 10 of *UP*, and in which Galen manifests more openly than usual his genuine religious sensibility.[41] Again, he focuses on the structural complexity and the brilliance of the design-solutions that Nature has contrived to deal with a series of pressing problems deriving from the conflicting requirements of functional excellence on the one hand, and safety and longevity on the other. Thus the cornea needs to be both extremely hard, to fulfil its protective function, yet also wafer thin to allow light through without hindrance (10.3, ii 62,6–65,8 H). Galen addresses an imaginary 'Reviler of Nature':[42]

> The cornea, since it is made thin, hard, and dense, must immediately become clear as well, in order to be best suited for the transmission of light, just like horn which has been carefully pared down and polished. We cannot plan such things in advance as Nature can. But can we still judge it after the fact, and criticize any of the things she has made on the grounds that it would have been better to construct them in some other way? . . . For myself, I think that most of us cannot do even this. . . . If they cannot suggest some construction better than the one which actually exists, they should admire the one that does. So, Reviler of Nature: show us which of the other seven circles at the *iris*[43] would be better suited to producing the cornea. Or, if you can't do that, and if you think it wasn't good for it to grow out of the hardest circle, then show us what you would have done better in the case of the outgrowth of this tunic, had you been in Prometheus' position. (**18**: *UP* 10.3, ii 64,7–65,2 H)

But even though the cornea is admirably contrived, 'there are three difficulties which necessarily attend such a construction and which you, most clever accuser, if you had been put in Prometheus' position, might well have failed to take into consideration. Not so Prometheus himself, however' (ii 65,13–17 H). These 'difficulties' are (i) the problem of nourishing the cornea, since it cannot be endowed with veins and arteries; (ii) the fact that it should cause pain in the lens, by abrading it; and (iii) the fact that it should scatter the light, thus rendering clear vision impossible.

---

[41] When he turns (reluctantly: most people have no time for that sort of thing) to giving his geometrical account of the optics of vision, he does so, he says, because he was told to do so by a god in a dream: *UP* 10.12, ii 92,23–93,10 H (cf. n 6 above). This account occupies the rest of the book: 10.11–15, ii 93,23–113,5 H. For a critical analysis of Galen's arguments here, and his pretensions to geometrical exactitude, see Lloyd 2005.

[42] Cf. 17.1, ii 440,8, 443,1, 446,3–5 H ('enemies of Nature').

[43] In fact, the entire ciliary area; the 'seven circles' include the choroid membrane, the retina, the vitreous body, the lens, the sclera, and the cornea; see May 1968: 467–8 n. 10, on the problems with, and inadequacy of, Galen's anatomy of the eye.

Next (ii 62,6–69,6 H) Galen describes the complex structure of the eye and its various 'humours' and 'tunics', all of which combine to produce the optimum mixture of functional excellence with protection from damage, and so to resolve the difficulties. The vitreous humour directly nourishes the cornea, which protects the lens (so it does not require its own veins and arteries). It also stops it from abrading the lens, and prevents the dispersal of the light, while also being perfectly transparent, since although dense it is very thin:

> The Creator of animals . . . saw first how to bring it about that the cornea should be nourished; second that it should not touch the crystalline humour at any point; and third that it should not scatter its light: and he solved all of these problems with a single clever device. (**19**: *UP* 10.3, ii 66,6–11 H)

The 'single clever device' is the 'choroid tunic', the structure of which Galen proceeds to marvel at in characteristically gushing terms. For all their sophistical cavilling, if the 'Revilers of Nature' only understood the proper account of the mechanism of vision and the complexity of its carefully and providentially contrived structures, they would have to admit that nothing could have been constructed more durably and efficiently. Rhetoric aside, however, Galen's actual description of the anatomy of the eye, although detailed, is both seriously deficient, and hard to interpret (see n 43).

Book 14 of *UP*, which deals with the reproductive system, opens with the following claim:

> Nature had three principal objectives in constructing the parts of the animal: she made them either for the sake of life itself (the brain, the heart and the liver), or for the sake of a better life (the eyes, the ears, the nostrils), or for the continuance of the species (the genitals, the gonads, and the uterus). (**20**: *UP* 14.1, ii 284,20–285,1)

The following chapter expands upon Nature's 'wonderful artistry': 'Nature has given all animals organs for conception, allied to the power to produce great pleasure, and . . . an extraordinary desire', which drives even the most foolish of animals towards sex (14.2, ii 285,27–286,7 H).[44] The location

---

[44] This powerful and irrational drive to pleasure has its drawbacks: foetal developmental problems are often caused by human stupidity ('untimely intercourse' and faulty regimen of the mother: 14.7, ii 308, 23–309, 1: cf. 11.10, ii 143, 24–144, 6 on the damage wrought by drunken and gluttonous parents). Sexual pleasure and desire are imparted by the 'testicles' in both male and female: 14.9, ii 313–16 H; cf. *Semen* IV 569–70, = 120, 24–122, 12; cf. 572–3, 585, = 124,7–19, 136, 9–18 De Lacy 1992. Sexual excess can be seriously debilitating: 'some have even died because of too much sexual pleasure': IV 588–9 = 138, 28–140, 10 De Lacy 1992.

of the vagina 'below the stomach' is 'appropriate', in that it is 'far away from the facial organs';[45] moreover, it is easily distensible, and ideally constructed to receive the ejaculated semen (14.3, ii 286–8 H). But as soon as it does so, the uterus contracts around the semen to retain it (cf. *Semen* IV 513–16, = 64,13–68,2 De Lacy 1992), compressing it, and not allowing its parts to separate (14.3, ii 288,11–290,20 H). The vagina needs to be firm, to facilitate the introjection of semen, but also elastic, to allow for birth:

> So, to make room for two functions which are opposed to one another, Nature has given it contrary qualities in just proportion, making it hard enough so that it can maintain a reasonable breadth and straightness when receiving the semen, while mixing in enough softness to make it capable of expanding and contracting easily. (**21**: *UP* ii 289,20–290,2 H)

Galen goes on to contend (14.4, ii 290–91) that the number of cavities in the womb of different animals corresponds to the (normal? The maximum?) number of offspring; this and the equivalence of nipples to cavities, and the timely arrival of lactation should be enough to convince people that none of this can be a matter of chance (at least if they aren't shameless blockheads).[46] But what is the role of necessity here, and what of the Creator?

> Do all these things in the breasts and the uterus occur because the organs (*organa*) themselves know what they're doing, by reasoning? If so, they would no longer be instruments (*organa*), but rational animals, understanding both the proper time and duration of the activities. But if you add to their structure a certain natural necessity which leads them to these things, they will be instruments and parts of the animal, and still exemplify the remarkable technical skill of the Creator. Those who wish to represent the orbits of the planets construct their models by instilling in them a source of their motions by means of certain mechanisms (*organa*), which continue to operate as though their creator was present and controlling them in every

---

[45] Another example of Galen's prudishness; compare his treatment of the penis (15.1, ii 338,9–342,20 H), and his railing against those who 'wantonly abuse every orifice of their bodies' (3.10, i 173,21–174,4 H); see Hankinson, forthcoming, §6.

[46] Galen endorses the widespread ancient belief (which goes back at least to Parmenides: 22 B 17 DK, a fragment preserved by Galen) that male fetuses are located in the right 'cavity' of the womb, females in the left (14.4, ii 292,22–293,4 H), although sex differentiation in the foetus takes time (14.7, ii 304,17–305,6 H). He also subscribes to the Aristotelian view (*GA* 1.20, 278a17–20) that females are generally colder and inferior to males (14.6, ii 296,8–301,25 H); and to the idea that even so things are better that way (ii 299,3–23 H).

respect.[47] In the same way, I think, each of the parts of the body, following a certain dependence and sequence of motion, operates always because of the original cause, without requiring a controller. If we cannot give a clear account of all the works of nature, since they are pretty hard to explain, we must at least try to know what all of them are.[48] (**22**: *UP* 14.5, ii 294,26–295,18 Helmreich 1907-9; cf. 14.8, ii 310,8–313,7 H: the breast/uterus link also evinces 'amazing skill')

Galen leans towards the view that the internal process of generation, after the mixing of the two sorts of semen in the womb, and the subsequent nourishment of the conceptus by maternal blood, continues as the result of a pre-set programme, as Aristotle suggests in *GA* 2.1, 733b32–734b19 (cf. 2.5, 741b8–15). Aristotle analogised the way in which the semen's 'movements (*kinêseis*)' construct the embryo to the operation of *thaumata* (734b9–18), mechanical devices designed to follow out certain determinate patterns as soon as they are set in motion by an initial impetus.[49] Galen uses, while not fully endorsing, the same image in his late treatise on embryology, *The Formation of the Foetus*:[50]

> When people construct *thaumata*, they supply the original motion, but then depart, while their constructions continue to function in a skilful fashion, at least for a little while. In the same way, the gods construct the seeds of plants and animals in such a way that they are able to transmit these motions even though they are no longer acting on them. (**23**: *Foet. Form.* IV 688, = 92,16–21 Nickel 2001)

In *UP*, Galen admits that 'it is difficult to give a clear account' of foetal development, in particular of how the blood vessels are contrived to convey nutrition from the mother to the developing foetus. But even so, 'when these things are accurately observed in dissections, they immediately compel the observer's admiration' (*UP* 15.4, ii 346,16–21 H). The affinity for vein with vein and artery with artery as they grow out of the uterus like the roots of trees, and then unite, like a tree-trunk, and then finally divide and are inserted into their appropriate foetal viscera, are clear signs of providence and design (15.4, ii 347,21–351,25 H).

---

[47] Galen does not say that that this is in fact how the heavenly bodies operate too; but it is a reasonable inference that he thinks so. This would add another level to his version of the microcosm-macrocosm analogy.

[48] Cf. *PHP* V 558, = 404, 5–6 De Lacy 1978–84: the foetus has within itself the source of its governing powers. On Galen's embryology, see Hankinson 2017: 255–66.

[49] Types of mechanical toy: see Berryman 2002 and 2003; in this context, see Hankinson, 2017, 259–63.

[50] *Foet.Form.* IV 652–702, = *CMG* V 3.3, Nickel 2001.

In the construction and management of the baby *in utero*, Nature evinces another characteristic feature that argues irresistibly for creative intelligence: economy of the parts and their functional design.[51] In a lengthy argument (*UP* 15.5, ii 351,20–359,9 H), Galen discusses the reasons for the existence in the foetus of the urachus for voiding urine into the amniotic fluid, and its lack of a sphincter muscle, unlike in the developed systems of bladder and urethra. This is perfectly rational, 'since a muscle has, with good reason, been put into them to let nothing pass except at the bidding of reason, but in embryos this would be superfluous and in vain; and Nature does nothing in vain' (ii 359,5–9). The foetus differs from 'animals already born ... since it is governed for a very long time like a plant, and it derives more functionality from the veins; so Nature made them strong from the outset' (15.6, = ii 359,9–360,6 H). In a similar vein, he notes the pre-natal existence, and post-partum closure, of the foramen ovale (15.6, ii 360,13–363,1 H), and the functional adaptiveness of the closure of the cervix during pregnancy (15.7, ii 363,11–364,3 H). But in all of these cases, our ability to give a complete explanation is doomed to frustration. If we are honest and clear-eyed, we can certainly know *that* things are so contrived; but *how* they are is beyond our comprehension:

> Their individual functionality, then, is an indication of the fact that Nature contrives all of these things skilfully. But the power by which she achieves them is beyond our understanding – we would not even believe initially that there was such a power, if we had not clearly witnessed it on many occasions. (**24**: *UP* 15.6, 363,1–6 H; cf. **2** above)

The same also holds of the penis (15.1, ii 338,3–442,20 H). Its location, its functioning, its peculiar substance, its only intermittently erectile condition,[52] all argue for supreme divine design. The penis must be perfectly hard during coitus, not only to enable penetration, but also to unbend the urethra to facilitate maximal ejaculation, as well as straightening the vagina, ensuring penetration of the cervix by the semen (15.3, ii 344,5–345,12 H). Even so,

> These are the things that our Creator wanted to be made; but ... do not try ... to find out how they came be to like this. ... You wouldn't even have known that they were, had you not learned it from dissection. It is enough that you have discovered ... that every part has been formed in

---

[51] See again Hankinson 1988.

[52] An issue also considered by Aristotle (*PA* 4.10, 689a19–30), although of course he does not attribute it to divine workmanship. See Frede 2003: 78–9.

such a way as its functionality demands; if you try to inquire how it came
to be this way, you will be convicted of insensitivity not only to your own
feebleness, but also to the Creator's power. (**25**: *UP* 15.1, ii 342,4–13 H)

Michael Frede (2003, 78–9) has suggested that Galen thinks that any such
inquiry would be impious, a hubristic attempt to try to go beyond what
humans are capable of comprehending. Perhaps; but Galen may simply be
making a fairly banal point about the limits of human understanding. Even
if we can't say how it was done, in the sense of expounding the mechanisms
with which it was created and by which it continues to function, we have to
admit that it *was* done purposively. Denying that would be impious indeed.

13.5   Conclusions: The Evidence of the Providential Universe

This sort of agnosticism is entirely characteristic of Galen's whole approach
to science, and indeed of his theology. If you are open minded and
conscientiousness enough to reject materialist dogma, and simply see
things for what they are – to be, that is, a genuine *phusikos* (3.10, i
175,8 H) – the reality of the divine presence in the world will be manifest:

> Who would not immediately conclude that some intelligence of remarkable
> power was walking the earth and penetrating every part of it? For you
> see animals generated with remarkable structures everywhere. (**26**: *UP* 17.1,
> ii 446,7–11)

Moreover, it is reasonable to think that it is actually active, and descends
from the celestial regions:

> Is any part of the universe more insignificant than that around the earth?
> Yet even here some intelligence manifestly descends from the bodies above,
> and anyone who sees this is immediately forced to admire the beauty of
> their substance. . . . It is reasonable to assume that the intelligence dwelling
> in them is as much better and more perfect than that in the earthly bodies as
> their bodily substance is purer. For when animals are engendered in mud
> and slime, in marshes and in rotting plants and fruits, which yet display a
> wonderful indication of the intelligence which constructs them, what must
> we think of the bodies above? (**27**: *UP* 17.1, ii 446,11–23 H)

This is a striking claim, unparalleled anywhere else in his voluminous
oeuvre – but there is no reason to doubt its sincerity. Galen continues in
this comparative vein:

> You can appreciate the nature of human intelligence when you consider
> Plato, Aristotle, Hipparchus, and many others like them. When a surpass-
> ing intelligence comes to be in such slime – for what else could you call a

thing composed of fleshes, blood, phlegm, and yellow and black bile? – how great must we think the pre-eminence of the intelligence in the sun, moon and stars. (**28**: *UP* 17.1, ii 446,23–447,8 H)

The heavenly bodies must then be transcendently intelligent. Moreover, it is probable that their intelligence permeates down to the earth along with their light:

> It seems to me that a certain … intelligence pervades even the very air surrounding us; certainly the air could not partake of the sun's light without receiving its [sc. intellectual] power too. I am sure you will regard all these things in the same way when you examine carefully and justly the skill manifest in animals, unless, as I have said, you are prevented from so doing by some rashly propounded doctrine concerning the elements of the universe. (**29**: *UP* 17.1, ii 447,8–16 H; this is immediately followed by text **1** above)

In the middle of the long final chapter of *Foet.Form.*, in which he avows his uncertainty about the nature and detailed functioning of divinity in the world, Galen remarks on the ability of children to produce any sound we ask them to, without having any idea about the mechanisms by which they are produced. This suggests that either the functional parts still retain within themselves the animating soul which produced them, or that the various muscles are themselves animals, or at least that they are capable of understanding and obeying the rational soul. But all of these views seem extravagant, and no convincing argument can be found in support of any of them. (IV 696–7 = 100,14–29 Nickel; cf. **3** above)

Less acceptable still is 'the view of one my Platonist teachers', that all of the parts of animals are constantly under the tutelage of the World Soul (700–701 = 104,25–106,2 Nickel; cf. *Prop.Plac.* 13.5, 106,14–23 Nutton 1999), which seems to him to be impious.[53] Again, Galen can come to no even plausible conclusion as to how the Creator effects his creations, or how they subsequently operate; but that He does do so is, for all that, perfectly clear to any but the most purblind mechanist. Even the Aristotelian view that development of the foetus is merely the following out of some pre-set vegetable programme in the seed seems unacceptable,

---

[53] Because then the World Soul would be responsible for bad things like spiders, scorpions and snakes: there is an evident tension here with Galen's eulogy of the Creator's magnificence in *UP*; the tension can be at least diminished by emphasizing the idea that such banausic details would be beneath the World Soul's dignity.

although some things tell in its favour; while the idea that the foetus is generated by the rational soul seems just as unacceptable (700 = 104,15–25 Nickel).[54]

Still, the basic facts remain. And in *UP* Galen comes closest, albeit tentatively, to suggesting, at least in outline, some mechanism for the general divine influence and control of the terrestrial world, as passage **29** hints, on the back of the transmission and propagation of light. This is no more than a sketch, the details of which he admits he is unable to fill out. But the facts of causal influence are there, even if their mechanisms are barely if at all understood. In a quite different context, discussing how apparently insignificant initial causes can have widespread and ramified effects in bodies, he instances the action of the torpedo-fish, in conveying a shock through a solid bronze spear into the arm of a fisherman (*Affected Parts* VIII 421–2). There too, he says, we have no idea how the effect is contrived or of the modality of its transmission. But it would be the height of foolishness and empirical irresponsibility simply on those grounds to refuse to admit that it has been so transmitted; and just the same is true, he thinks, at bottom, in regard to the relation between God, the universe and its animal denizens. Cosmology, then, is not just a model for biology: it is an integral and indissoluble part of it.[55]

---

[54] I deal with this passage in greater detail in Hankinson, 2017, 263–6.

[55] This is a greatly revised and written-up version of the talk I gave to the Mexico conference in 2016. I should like to thank the participants for their questions and comments, both at the session and informally, in particular Barbara Sattler and George Boys-Stones; to Ricardo Salles, for organising the whole thing so beautifully, as well as for his comments and encouragement, I owe a special debt of gratitude.

CHAPTER 14

At the Intersection of Cosmology and Biology
Plotinus on Nature

Lloyd P. Gerson

14.1 Nature and Embodied Souls

Plotinus uses the word 'nature' (φύσις) in two ways, one of which is rooted in the tradition, and one of which is not. He uses 'nature' to refer to the essence or type of thing that something is. For example, the nature of body or form or the Good.[1] For our purposes, the far more important use of the term is for the lowest part of the soul of the cosmos.[2] This requires a bit of explaining. The soul of the cosmos (sometimes 'the soul of the universe', although the distinction need not delay us here) is Plotinus' version of the soul created by the Demiurge in Plato's *Timaeus*, set by him within and around the body of the cosmos.[3] This soul is said by Plato to be the ruler of the cosmos, that is, the principle that guarantees that the cosmos is orderly and, more to the point, that it conforms to the Demiurge's goal of making an image of eternal being that is as good as possible.

All soul – including the soul of the cosmos, the souls of human beings, and the souls of all animals and plants – both has life and also provides life to whatever is ensouled. This claim is derived from the Platonic argument for the immortality of soul in *Phaedo* to the effect that soul (ψυχή) is not only what gives life to living things but that it does so by being life, that is, by being essentially alive. So, though soul can be separated from body, it cannot be separated from the life that it is.[4] 'Nature' is the name for life that is other than or distinct from *intellectual* life. I will return in a moment to the explanation why the principle of intellectual life is distinct from the principle of non-intellectual life. So, all kinds of lives for the vast array of animals and plants have as their principle nature. The *scala naturae* is determined by the hierarchy of psychical faculties possessed by all living

---

[1] See for body, III 6 [26], 6.33–4; for form, III 6 [26], 4.41–43; for the Good, VI 8 [39], 13.28–40.
[2] See III 8 [30], 4.15–16; IV 4 [28], 13.3–5, 27.11–17; V 2 [11], 1.17–18.
[3] See Plato, *Tim.* 34A–C.   [4] See Plato, *Phd.* 102A10–107B10. See IV 7 [2], 2.5–6, 9.6–29.

beings.[5] That is, nature at the lowest level contains minimal psychical function, specifically, growth and reproduction; animals have higher psychical functioning including sensation, and human beings alone have the highest psychical functioning which includes the above along with an intellectual faculty. Thus, human beings are a sort of 'hybrid' with the psychical functioning that belongs to nature and an 'other soul' which is rational or intellectual.[6]

Nature is the lowest part of the soul of the cosmos whereas the higher or highest part is that which is engaged in governing cosmic order and conformity to the eternal intelligible paradigm of the Living Being eternally contemplated by the Demiurge.[7]

Given all the above, one might suppose that nature informs the bodies of living things, that it is, as Aristotle says, the inseparable *entelecheia* of the animated body.[8] Plotinus, however, argues that this cannot be so.[9] If the soul is an inseparable entelechy of the body, then it is analogous to the shape of the statue in relation to the statue itself. But for a number of reasons, this cannot be how the soul operates in relation to the body. The argument why a rational soul cannot so operate is the familiar one drawn from the possibility of conflict between soul and body and the possibility of incontinence or *akrasia*.[10] But I leave this argument aside for now since the overall position is intended to cut much deeper, that is, to show that no type of soul, no variety of nature, can be an inseparable entelechy. The general argumentative strategy is to show that psychical functioning in a living being is localised or specifically distinct from the extended body in a way that the shape of the bronze is not separate or divided from the statue. Even in plants, assuming as Plotinus does, that its psychical principle of growth is in its root, soul is not extended throughout the plant in the way that the shape is.[11]

That the lowest part of the soul of the cosmos or nature cannot be the form of a body obviously leaves us with the question of what determines the body to be the kind of body that it is. What, after all, is the form of the body? In order to appreciate Plotinus' answer to this question, we need to have recourse to one of his fundamental metaphysical principles.

---

[5] See I 4 [46], 3.15–24; II 2 [47], 9.20; II 3 [52], 16.7. The issue is extensively discussed by Wilberding in his contribuition to the present volume (Chapter 8).
[6] The 'other soul' is the real person or self. It is the soul 'in the principal sense'. See I 1 [53], 7, 9.20–21, 10.1–7; II 1 [40], 5.20–21; IV 7 [2], 1.22–5.
[7] See Plato, *Tim.* 30C-D.   [8] See Aristotle, *De an.* B 1, 412b5–6.   [9] See IV 7 [2], 8[5].
[10] See Plato, *Phd.* 88C1–95A3; *Rep.* 436A8–440A2.   [11] See Caluori 2015.

For Plotinus, every principle has an 'internal' and an 'external' activity' (ἐνέργεια).[12] The basis for this metaphysical claim is simply that the first principle of all, the Good or the One, is essentially diffusive (*bonum est diffusivum sui*).[13] The premises for the argument that concludes with the diffusiveness of the Good are that the Good is the source of the being of everything that is and that it itself is nothing but unlimited or infinite activity.[14] So, there is nothing that could be that is not. We determine what could be from what is (*ab esse ad posse*). So, for the topic I am considering, if there is such a thing as this cosmos, then we know that, ultimately, the cause for the being of this is the Good or One and that there could not not be a cosmos. For if, *per impossibile*, there were no cosmos, then the Good would be grudging or withholding or defective in some way. But that is impossible.

From this metaphysical basis, we infer the following. The soul of the cosmos (including its lowest part, nature), itself an intelligible principle, will necessarily produce whatever it is possible for it to produce. The bodies of living things, specifically, their anatomy both external and internal, are necessary products of the internal activity of soul or nature.[15] So, animals and plants have the structure they have because they have the kinds of soul that they have. This is not an unaristotelian point in itself. Nevertheless, Plotinus wishes to avoid the problem Aristotle faces because he holds both that soul does not come to an already existing body (else ensoulment would be an accidental change) and that soul is the first actuality or entelechy of a body. This seeming contradiction is avoided

---

[12] For the important distinction between 'internal' and 'external' activities, see II 9 [33], 8.22–5; IV 5 [29], 7.15–17, 51–5; V 1 [10], 6.34; V 3 [49], 7.23–4; V 4 [7], 2.27–33; V 9 [5], 8.13–15; VI 2 [43], 22.24–9; VI 7 [38], 18.5–6, 21.4–6, 40.21–4. For the specific employment of this principle to the relation between soul and embodied living being, see I 1 [53], 4.13–16; IV 3 [27], 10.31–35; IV 4 [28], 14.1–10, 18.4–9, 29.1–15; IV 5 [29], 6.28–32, 7.17–18. For the embodied expression of soul as a 'shadow' and 'image' of the soul itself, see IV 4 [28], 14.1–10, 18.4–9, 29.1–5. Also, I 1 [53], 12.24; IV 3 [27], 27.7–8.

[13] The Platonic provenance of this is *Republic* 508B6–7, where Plato says that the power of the Good 'flows out' (ἐπίρρυτον) as from a treasure trove.

[14] On Plotinus' use of the term ἐνέργεια for the One see V 4 [7], 2.28–39, especially 35, 'internal activity'(συνούσης ἐνεργείας); V 1 [10], 6.38; VI 7 [38], 18.6: f rom the activity [of the Good]' (παρ' ἐκείνου ἐνεργείας); VI 8 [39], 20.9–15, especially 14–15: 'If, then, activity is more perfect than is substantiality, and the first thing of all is most perfect, activity would be primary' (εἰ οὖν τελειότερον ἡ ἐνέργεια τῆς οὐσίας, τελειότατον δὲ τὸ πρῶτον, πρῶτον ἂν ἐνέργεια εἴη); VI 8 [39], 12.22–37, especially 25, 'because the activity is not different from it [the God]' (ὅτι μὴ ἕτερον ἐνέργεια καὶ αὐτός) and 36, 'for the Good is activity alone, or it is not activity at all' (ἢ γὰρ ἐνέργεια μόνον ἢ οὐδ' ὅλως ἐνέργεια); VI 8 [38], 13.5–9.

[15] See III 8 [30], 4.5–10, 7.13–14; IV 4 [28], 20.22–5.

by maintaining that, although soul is a form (εἶδος), it is not a form inseparable from the body and *a fortiori* it is not the first actuality of that body.[16]

The shape that the body has is given by nature. It is a sort of 'shadow' (σκία) or 'trace' (ἴχνος) of soul cast down by nature.[17] That shape or form is the last level of intelligibility in the universe. Beneath or beyond that is matter, which is utterly unintelligible – in effect equivalent to Aristotle's prime matter – and hence pure privation and non-being.[18] The animated body is, accordingly, not the ensouled body in the Aristotelian sense, but an image of the soul or nature that determines the kind of thing that that animated body is.[19]

In maintaining that the animate body is distinct from soul, even in the case of non-rational souls, Plotinus wants to maintain that what are inexactly called 'soul-body conflicts' can be explained as the experiences of animated bodies over against the souls that govern them. Souls are 'impassible' in relation to the bodies that experience all the travails of embodiment.[20] Thus, the bodies of living things have their own desires and their own passive states.[21] The souls, particularly of rational living beings, can either accede to or reject these desires. Analogously, the sensations which are the passive states of animate bodies are distinct from the cognition of these states by souls which is true sense-perception.

Nature thus operates at the bottom of the scale of intelligible being. Its product, visible or sensible form, is the limit of intelligibility. Beyond that which is intelligible is matter, that which is unqualifiedly unintelligible, although without matter there could not be a sensible cosmos. As we have

[16] See I 1 [53], 4.19–20; III 8 [30], 2.22; IV 4 [28], 15.8–10.
[17] See III 8 [30], 2.28–30, 4.5–10, 7.13–14; IV 3 [27], 11.8–12; IV 4 [28], 18.1–9; VI 4 [28], 15.15–18 .
[18] Plotinus rejects Aristotle's distinction between matter as potency and privation, as applied to prime matter. Matter can be potency only as a function of actuality, for which, *ex hypothesi*, there is none in pure matter. Hence, matter is pure privation. See II 4 [12], 16.3–8 arguing against Aristotle, *Phys.* A 1.9, 192a19–22.
[19] See III 4 [15], 1.8–15 for the clear formula: matter informed by nature = body. In this passage (see ll.15–16), Plotinus does attribute δύναμις to matter. But this is not the potentiality that something *with* matter has owing to the kind of thing it is; rather, it is the potentiality whose prior 'actuality' is the actuality that is the One. That is, since the One is the source of the quasi-being of matter, matter is potentially all the (material) things that the One is really and virtually.
[20] See III 6 [26], 2.34–7; IV 4 [28], 19.1ff, 26–7. It is to be noted that Aristotle, because he believes the intellect is a 'kind of substance' (οὐσία τις), thinks that intellect is impassible. See *De an.* A 4, 408b19–20. Plotinus agrees with Aristotle that intellect is separable and impassible, but he goes further in claiming this for soul as well. In part, this is because Plotinus follows Plato in not making a sharp distinction between intellect and soul and in part for the philosophical reasons sketched above.
[21] See esp. IV 4 [28], 20.

already seen, since there actually *is* a sensible cosmos, there must be one and so matter is a necessary condition for the necessary production that leads back ultimately to the One or Good itself. In the next section, I want to turn to the thesis of the famous treatise III 8 [30], 'On Nature and Contemplation and the One'. This will prepare us for the last section in which I will consider the newly reinvigorated thesis of panpsychism and how Plotinus' account of nature compares with this.

14.2 Nature and Contemplation

Plotinus begins III 8 with the hypothesis – first offered playfully and then seriously – that all of nature engages in contemplation (θεωρία). Although everything informed by nature contemplates, each does so according to its ability. Even the earth contemplates, and even though it does so minimally, we might say, it is not so clear what this claim amounts to or what successful contemplation is supposed to be for anything other than human contemplators of intelligible reality. We begin to get a sense of what Plotinus has in mind when he says that all action (πρᾶξις) and all production (ποίησις) are done for the sake of contemplation and, furthermore, that all action and production are the result or consequence of contemplation.[22] These two claims are closely connected. Since everything desires the Good, each in its own way, and since the contemplation of the One by Intellect is the paradigm of achievement of the Good, it follows that each (intelligible) being contemplates insofar as possible. The paradigm of contemplation is cognitive identity with all that is intelligible. And since every instance of contemplation is the qualified achievement of the Good, and since the Good is essentially diffusive, all action and production can be said to be the result of contemplation. That is, by contemplation, the diffusiveness of the Good is emulated. Nature, in particular, produces the sensible shapes of bodies by means of contemplation.[23] It contemplates all that is intelligible within it, that is, the rational expressions (λόγοι) of Intellect. These are images of the Forms with which Intellect is eternally cognitively identical. Nature is itself an unmoved mover or producer. Were it not so, it would either need an unmoved mover of which it would be an instrument or else there would be some part of it that is the unmoved mover, in which case *that* would be nature.[24] That nature is unmoved and is still a producer is, for Plotinus, indicative of its genuine, not metaphorical, contemplation.

---

[22] See III 8 [30], 1.11–18, 4.39–43.   [23] See III 8 [30], 1.22–4.   [24] See III 8 [30], 2.13–19.

So, all animate bodies are produced by nature's contemplation.[25] This contemplation, Plotinus says, is a sort of understanding (σύνεσις) and self-awareness (συναίσθησις), like that of someone asleep.[26] Nature is aware of what it is, non-representationally and non-discursively.[27] This sort of unconscious awareness by nature of all that nature is is intended to account for the unity of nature. That is, it is intended to explain the fact that despite the multifarious variety of nature, there is an underlying unity. The variety is explained ultimately by the multiplicity of intelligible beings within Intellect manifested in a dispersed manner owing to matter. The unity is perhaps most easily appreciated if we compare what Plotinus is saying to the physical and chemical unity we now assume to underlie nature. More particularly, the physical and chemical laws underlying nature are conceptual expressions of what is extra mentally one. I mean that every law expressed in an equation of the form A = B, is *quoad nos*, what is in reality a unity. Thus, for example, temperature and pressure are different ways of representing one thing; so, too, water and H_2O.

It is tempting to view production and action as substitutions or surrogates for contemplation. I am more inclined to interpret Plotinus here in the light of Plato's *Symposium* and his claim that production is the function of or work (ἔργον) of the love of the beautiful which in fact is nothing but the desire for the Good.[28] Production and action are the natural outcome of the obverse of the diffusiveness of the Good, namely the desire to be united with that Good. This is, however, not to deny that production and even action can become substitutes for contemplation. This occurs when and only when rational souls are dislodged from their orientation to the Good. In such cases, production and action are markers or signposts on the road to evil which is dissolution into the unintelligible, that is, into matter.[29] Nature is, of course, immune from a diminution of its contemplation, although its contemplation is relatively weak in the first place.

When action is not a weakening of contemplation, it is for the sake of contemplation.[30] As Plotinus says, this is so because action is for the sake of a good. All things desire the real as opposed to the apparent good, even

---

[25] See III 8 [30], 4.7–10.   [26] See III 8 [30], 4.19–25.
[27] See III 8 [30], 1.22. Cf. III 6 [26], 4.21–3. Specifically, nature has no 'mental images' (φαντασίαι), the requisite for representation and discursive thinking.
[28] See Plato, *Symp.* 206B–C; Aristotle, *Meta.* Λ 7, 1072a27–8.
[29] At III 8 [30], 4.39–43 Plotinus says that production and action are *either* a weakening *or* a consequence of contemplation. I take it that the former is the substitute or surrogate and that the latter is not.
[30] See III 8 [30], 6.1–2.

though the real Good cannot be pursued except as it appears to anyone. One simply holds that what appears to be good is in fact so. The identity between the apparent and real Good is so only for the virtuous. So, action is for the sake of an apparent good that appears to be the real Good. And the real Good is achieved by contemplation. Hence, all action is really for the sake of contemplation.

An action is for the sake of an end. The end can be viewed as an external product, in which case it is really a production and not an action, or it can be viewed as an internal state of the agent. This internal state is precisely the cognition of an intentional object by the agent. But for embodied agents, this can only be done with 'internal λόγοι' or thoughts and images.[31] This representationalism found, say, in one contemplating the achievement of an action, is itself an image of Intellect's contemplation. For the necessary representationalism is a mediation between agent and object, only a qualified version of the cognitive identity belonging eternally to Intellect and, we should add, to the undescended intellects of all human beings.[32]

So, all action has as its end cognition (γνῶσις).[33] And cognition is gradable contemplation, the paradigm being that of intellects generally and the lowest being that of sense-perception in which the intentional object can only be qualifiedly identical with the subject.[34] But even nature, which has no sense-perception, has in a way cognition and so contemplation. One justification for attributing a sort of cognition to nature is that cognition is paradigmatically productive. The last intelligible productions are the shapes of things that exist in the sensible world. These shapes or anatomical features produce nothing further and so do not contemplate and are in no sense cognitive.

Prior to cognition is desire for cognition (ἔφεσις γνώσεως), that is, desire for contemplation.[35] Desire is the essential property of soul, including its lowest part. We should distinguish what I would call the 'horizontal' desire of all souls from the 'vertical' desire for the Good. The former is the desire which is the principle of all psychical motion or activity. For

---

[31] See III 8 [30] 6.21–6.
[32] See III 4 [15], 3.24; IV 3 [27], 5.6, 12.3–4; IV 7 [2], 10.32–3, 13.1–3; IV 8 [6], 4.31–5, 8.8; VI 4 [22], 14.16–22; VI 7 [38], 5.26–9, 17.26–7; VI 8 [39], 6.41–3 for Plotinus' claim that our intellects are 'undescended', a claim that most later Platonists rejected.
[33] See III 8 [30], 7.1–5.
[34] On Intellect as the paradigm of cognitive identity, see I 4 [46], 6.10; V 3 [49], 5.26–8; V 9 [5], 5.1–7; VI 7 [38], 41.18; VI 9 [9] 2.36–7. See Caluori 2015: 101–11.
[35] See III 8 [30], 1.5.

Plotinus, there is a divide between the desire of non-rational and rational souls. Non-rational souls, including the non-rational part of the soul of the cosmos, nature, cannot be self-reflexively aware of the identity or lack of identity between the object of desire – the apparent good – and the real Good. Such a recognition requires intellect and its ability to grasp universal propositions. Non-rational animals, plants, and nature itself 'horizontally' desire their own perpetuation. The drama of human life consists largely in the fact that we are enmeshed in nature to the extent that we possess living bodies. Our living bodies are the locus of bodily desires or appetites. When these arise, however, they do not arise as alien to us. Far from it, for when they arise a *subject* of desire also arises and our natural response, so to say, is to identify ourselves with that subject. We seldom say, for example, that our body is hungry or thirsty; rather, we say and think that we are hungry or thirsty. The drama revolves around how we respond to this ephemeral subjecthood. That it is even possible that we respond to these succession of subjects by distancing ourselves from them and by distinguishing what the real *we* wants from what those subjects want is, for Plotinus, sufficient evidence for the claim that rational living beings are really intellects.[36]

Another justification for attributing cognition to nature or to non-rational psychical functioning is that these are rational principles (λόγοι) expressive of that at a higher level which produced them.[37] So, these psychical functionings are manifestations of the intellection (νόησις) eternally engaged in by Intellect. This intellection is primary life.[38] A point to be stressed here, and that will be the central focus of the next section of this chapter, is that while Soul is the principle of embodied life, Intellect is the principle of life itself. And, we should add, the One is the principle of being, though it is not the principle of complex being, that is, essential being. Again, Intellect is the principle of this. So, there is a strict parallel between One and Intellect and Intellect and Soul in that in each case the latter is a principle of a restricted and limited and inferior version of the former.[39] By a sort of metaphysical transitivity, the One is to Intellect and Soul as Intellect is to Soul. This important distinction will allow Plotinus to say, on the one hand, that there is a radical break between the intellect or intellectual soul and the non-intellectual soul and its lowest part, and on the other hand, that there is continuity in all living things.

---

[36] See I 1 [53], 7.21–2, 13; IV 4 [28], 18.1–19.   [37] See III 8 [30], 8.16. See Horn 2012: 218–20.
[38] See I 4 [46], 3.33–4; V 4 [7], 2.44–5; VI 6 [21], 18.12–19; VI 7 [38], 17.10–11, 31.1–4; VI 9 [9], 2.24–5. Cf. Aristotle, *Meta.* Λ 7, 1072b26–7.
[39] Thus, the principle of being: the principle of essential being:: the principle of life: the principle of embodied life.

The continuity is provided by the One; the discontinuity is provided by the non-reducibility of the principle of embodied life, Soul, to the principle of life, of Intellect and of the non-reducibility of Intellect to the One. The One is the 'productive power of all things' (δύναμις τῶν πάντων).[40] It is what nature aspires to be insofar as it is able. The One as goal or end is the Good, the Good that all desire.

14.3   The Soul of the Cosmos

I have presented the above exposition of Plotinus's account of nature in such a way that those familiar with the philosophical position known as panpsychism will have noted certain striking similarities in what Plotinus says with what panpsychists – including contemporary panpsychists – have argued.[41] Panpsychism is the view that all things have *psyche*, where at least in contemporary terms, *psyche* is taken as equivalent to mind. What the proponent of panpsychism denies is that mind or cognition or higher cognition is unique to human beings or to things with a human brain. As we have already seen, Plotinus is quite eager to argue that even nature contemplates, and so has a type of cognition. The shadow of nature, that is, the shapes in bodies, has no cognition; neither, of course, does matter. Nevertheless, he attributes to the elements themselves souls, while denying them cognition.[42] So, if panpsychism is taken to be the view that absolutely everything that exists – including atoms, electrons, quarks and so on – has a mind or has cognition, then Plotinus does not share this view. But if we stick to nature, the lowest part of the soul of the cosmos, and all things insofar as they are alive and so exist by nature, then grounds for comparison seem possible. Or so I shall try to show. But what I also want to show is that the panpsychism of Plotinus is ultimately vastly different from the panpsychism of contemporary philosophers. Indeed, the cognition found in, say, an amoeba, although superficially recognised equally by Plotinus and the contemporary panpsychist, is explained in fundamentally irreconcilable ways by both.

---

[40] See III 8 [30], 10.1. Cf. V 1 [10], 7.9–10; V 3 [49], 15.32–5; V 4 [7], 1.36, 2.38; V 5 [32], 10.10–22; VI 8 [39], 1.10–11.

[41] See the useful collection which presents state-of-the-art discussions of panpsychism, Brüntrup and Jaskolla 2017. Also, Strawson and Freeman 2006, Skrbina 2005 and the Introduction to the present volume.

[42] See IV 4 [28], 27; VI 7 [38], 11. In the first passage, it is not clear if it is the entire Earth or any bit of earth that has a soul. Plato, *Tim.* 40C2–3, stipulates that Earth is a god, but that is owing to its comprehensive ensoulment. Plotinus endorses Plato's claim, IV 4 [28], 22.8–9, but does not draw any conclusions about bits of earth.

Contemporary panpsychism, at any rate, is almost entirely a product of materialism or naturalism. It diverges from the view of materialists who maintain that mind or consciousness is somehow or other reducible to the material. Thus, for example, eliminative materialism holds that what is called mind or consciousness is nothing but one or more brain states. The panpsychist, by contrast, while accepting the view that every real thing is material or physical, denies that the material world can be described in terms that makes it impossible to attribute mind or consciousness to them. So, if mind or consciousness is real, then it can be a feature or characteristic of all material things just insofar as they are material. If this is true, then the appearance on this planet of human beings with mind or consciousness is not the radical ingression of something entirely new, but rather a more complex version of what can be found in the material predecessors or elements of human beings down to the most minute. It is important to stress that panpsychism is motivated not by a claim for the ubiquity of life but by a claim for the ubiquity of cognitional experience in some sense. The panpsychist does not maintain that things usually deemed to be non-living are in fact alive. Rather, it maintains that non-living things, assumed to be different from living things, are nevertheless capable of having experiences that are not substantially different from cognitive experiences even though they may differ in degree. The experience of thinking that is occurring in the mind of the author of this chapter right now differs only in degree from the experience that every physical particle in the universe is now experiencing. And since physicalism or material-ism is true, there is no mind-body problem. There is no problem at least in principle with human minds evolving along with human bodies out of things that are inanimate. Here is a clear and concise statement of contemporary panpsychism:

> Mind is real. I know this because I experience it first hand, and I hold it as an indubitable feature of reality (against eliminativism). Body is real. Rationally, intuitively, and empirically I have reason to believe that my body is a physical, material thing, situated in a physical universe (against pure idealism). There is thus both a material and a mental aspect to my existence; at my deepest, most fundamental level of being, I am a 'thinking thing'. Some aspects of my physical being are clearly not widely spread in this world – aspects such as 'male', 'homo sapiens', or 'alive'. But my *material nature* seems to be universal. Similarly, some aspects of my mental being are unique to me, or to others of my kind. But this does not preclude the possibility that something like a *mental nature* is universal. For both rational and empirical reasons I am convinced that I am not ontologically unique. Since my mentality is fundamentally connected to, or related to,

my material body, I have good reason to believe that mentality, in some form, is connected to all material beings. Therefore panpsychism must be true. QED.[43]

Note in particular that 'mentality' is here taken to be a broader and more inclusive term than 'alive'. Therefore, it is supposed that being alive is not a necessary condition for mentality. Mentality cannot be derived from the nature of life. This surprising supposition is made on behalf of the claim that if mentality were not dispersed as widely as are the particles that make up the universe, then mentality would have to come from nowhere.

Just from the positing of a soul of the cosmos that animates the cosmic body, one would think that Plotinus could follow a good distance along these lines. For if nature contemplates, and, as we have seen, contemplation is a type of cognition, then all nature including the non-living elements can be said to have some sort of cognition, albeit to a minimal degree.

Furthermore, Plotinus says explicitly that the parts of the entire cosmos have shared experiences:

> So, first, we should say that this universe is 'one living being encompassing all the living beings inside itself',[44] having one soul extending to all its parts, in so far as each of them is a part of it; and each thing in the sensible universe is a part of it, as regards its body entirely so, but also to the extent that it partakes of the soul of the universe; to that extent it is a part of it in this way, too. And those that partake only of this soul are parts in all respects, but those that have a share in another soul[45] thereby also have the status of not being altogether parts, but nonetheless undergo affections from the other parts, in so far as they have something of the whole, and in accordance with what they have.
>
> This unified universe is actually in a condition of sympathy, and is one in the manner of a living being, and the distant parts of it are actually close together, just as in a single particular living being a nail, a horn, a finger or any other of the parts that are not contiguous, but have something in between which is not subject to affection, are affected by what is not near to them.[46]

---

[43] Skrbina 2005: 254. Cf. Nagel 1979: 'By panpsychism I mean the view that the basic physical constituents of the universe have mental properties, whether or not they are parts of living organisms' (181). Nagel argues somewhat halfheartedly for a form of panpsychism according to which the mental and the physical are themselves derived from some more basic constituent of the universe.

[44] See Plato, *Tim.* 30D3–31A1.

[45] A distinction between inanimate things which depend entirely on the soul of the universe or cosmos and things with their own souls (including plants and animals).

[46] IV 4 [28], 32.4–17. Cf. 35.8–17.

The term 'sympathy' (συμπάθεια), borrowed from the Stoics, is a fundamental term in Plotinus used to indicate the organic unity of the cosmos.[47]
It is also used, along with the term συναίσθησις (self-awareness), to
indicate the bipolar state of a cognitional agent. That is, one can be self-
aware of the state (πάθος) that one is in when, say, receiving the form of
a sensible. These are in fact two sides of the same coin. Sympathy is a
property of all individual souls, including the soul of the cosmos, in
relation to each other.[48] Indirectly, it is a property of that which souls
unify, namely bodies and their parts.[49]

What we might call the literal panpsychism of Plotinus stands in sharp
contrast to its contemporary version. For Plotinus, the experiences of
things that have experience are entirely a function of the presence of life
via soul. Only corpse-like matter is without experience. What appears to
be agreement between Plotinus and the contemporary panpsychist in their
mutual affirmation of experience for, say, the elements (whatever these
might be), is in fact explained by incompatible principles. For Plotinus,
experience is explained by the presence of soul whereas the contemporary
panpsychist derives his minimalist account of experience not from the
presence of life but from some putative property of mentality or mind.

It seems to me that computational science provides the contemporary
panpsychist with a powerful tool for eliminating life or soul from the
discussion. For if mind can be modelled computationally, then there is no
need to have life or soul intrude in the investigation of whether or not
minimal experience is possible for the elements. The functionality of mind
can be hypothesised as replicatable in, really, anything with a structure
capable of processing inputs of some sort and producing outputs.

Plotinus argues extensively for the immateriality both of Intellect and
Soul and so, *avant la lettre*, against the possibility of using a computational
model as a tool generating panpsychism along contemporary lines. We
have already encountered the argument for the immateriality of intellect
which is, in essence, that intellection is paradigmatically self-reflexive and
self-reflexivity cannot belong to a material entity which, by definition, is a
magnitude having parts outside of parts. So, the motivation for contemporary panpsychism, which is to give a materialistic non-reductive account
of the mental, is directly challenged.

But Plotinus also argues for the immateriality of soul, most extensively
in his refutation of the Stoic doctrine that the soul is a body.[50]

[47] See Gurtler 1988: 91–3.   [48] See IV 3 [27], 8.1–3.
[49] See IV 4 [28], 26.8–17; VI 4 [22], 3.17–23.   [50] See IV 7 [2], 2–8³.

The argument would be relevant to a version of contemporary panpsychism that instead of mentality makes life the common denominator of all material bodies. Plotinus actually produces an array of arguments against Stoic materialising of the soul. We may put aside for now those arguments which focus on embodied thinking, for these are really version of the argument for the immateriality of intellect. Instead, we should focus on the argument for the immateriality of souls that do not think, such as the souls of plants, and on the immateriality of the soul of the cosmos itself, the lowest part of which is, as we have seen, nature.

The principal argument is that if soul is a body, then things with souls would not move, not even in the way that plants move without locomotion.[51] Bodies are three-dimensional solids with parts outside of parts. The principle of motion of the body cannot be one part of the body or the sum of all the parts. If it were one part, which at least in a continuous body would have to be arbitrarily chosen, then there would be no explanation for the motion, since any part could either be mover or moved. If it were all the parts as a sum, then the same line of reasoning would apply unless the sum were really a whole, something over and above the sum. But in that case, the principle of motion would presumably be that which transforms the sum into a whole. That is, the principle of motion would not be another part and so not material or bodily.

Psychical motion or activity is, therefore, necessarily distinct from bodily motion.[52] By 'distinct' Plotinus does not mean numerically distinct, but something generically different from bodily motion.[53] In fact, he argues that, as Aristotle says, a motion should be considered to be an incomplete activity.[54] Hence, activity is logically prior to motion. The motion itself is an activity, which is incomplete relative to the result or goal sought. Thus, walking is an incomplete actuality because, though an actuality, it is incomplete with respect to its conclusion. This assimilation of motion to activity is on behalf of the argument that soul is immaterial. The principle of embodied motion cannot be a body. For what the body

---

[51] See III 6 [26], 4.38–42.
[52] See Plato, *Lg.* X, 896E8–897B5. Where Plato provides what is obviously not a complete list of psychical motions (willing, examining, counseling, considering, believing truly or falsely, being pleased or pained, hoping, fearing, hating, and loving) which are prior to bodily motions. The psychical motions are responsible for the bodily motions of growth and decay, separation and conjunction along with the accompanying properties of hot and cold, heaviness and lightness, roughness and smoothness, white and black, bitter and sweet. The soul of the cosmos uses Intellect as the model for the effects on bodies produced by psychical motion.
[53] See O'Meara 1985: 255–9.
[54] See VI 1 [42], 16.1–8; Aristotle, *Phys.* Γ 2, 201b31–2; *Meta.* K 9, 1066A20–21.

does as a result of the activity in it, is accidental to that activity. Indeed, embodied motion is a sort of side effect of the activity of the soul that produces the motion.[55] Bodily motion of a particular sort is a function of the psychical activity causing the motion. Different kinds of souls move their bodies and their parts according as these are capable of moving. Again, following Aristotle, Plotinus characterises the effect of the activity of soul as realised in the patient, that is, in the body.[56]

Nature, says Plotinus, must be the unmoved mover that explains the motion of ensouled bodies.[57] It is the analogue of the unmoved mover of the universe. Its perfect activity, as opposed to incomplete activity or motion, is its 'horizontal' desire. Two points should be made in anticipation of the objection that this is a non-solution to the problem of how immaterial entities can move bodies. First, immaterial nature explains the motion of bodies only instrumentally. The essential diffusiveness of the One must ultimately be brought in for a complete explanation. Second, the only thing that for Plotinus counts as body in the contemporary sense of body according to which there is a mind-body problem is matter. And matter is in fact bodiless and unalterable.[58] The manner of framing the mind-body problem as a problem of how an immaterial mind can move a material body is for Plotinus no more problematic than the existence of psychical functioning, the expression of which is the presumed body immovable by immaterial mind. Perhaps it is appropriate to understand Plotinus' position as a refinement of Aristotle's. That is, as Aristotle maintains, we can define anger as a desire for revenge or as the boiling of the blood around the heart. The first is a formal cause; the second a material cause. But for Plotinus, this Aristotelian matter is not matter strictly speaking. It is the expression of the soul (with its specific state of anger), that is, the natural manifestation of a desire of an embodied soul of a certain sort.

As previously discussed, the actuality of the psychical agent in the bodily patient is an 'external' actuality. But in the case of soul and body, this sort of external activity – bodily motions – only occur if there is a present an underlying substrate of a certain kind. Plotinus has frequent recourse to the analogies of light and fire which, while they themselves are unchanged, illuminate air and warm bodies so long as the recipients are present.

[55] See VI 1 [42], 16.14–35; VI 3 [44], 23.5–12. In the latter passage, Plotinus insists that walking is not the feet but the activity in the feet that comes from their potentiality.
[56] See VI 3 [44], 23.18–20; Aristotle, *Phys.* Γ 3, 202b7–8.   [57] See III 8 [30], 2.13–19.
[58] For bodiless, see II 4 [12], 8.2, 9.5, 12.35; for unalterable, see III 6 [26], 10.20.

So, since soul cannot be a body, entities like computers which, *ex hypothesi*, have no souls, cannot serve as a way of extending mentality throughout the material world. Souls can be everywhere there is body in the cosmos, but only if souls are immaterial principles of motion. But since panpsychism was advanced as a way of undermining the apparently anomalous presence of mentality in physical nature, Plotinus' arguments for the immateriality of intellect and soul stand as a challenge to contemporary panpsychism.

The truly profound difference between Plotinus' account of nature and any account which seeks to make all human properties different only in kind from the properties of everything else is in the assumption of the compositional homogeneity of the natural world. Ironically perhaps this was an assumption of the Pre-Socratic Milesian philosophers. Compositional homogeneity means that there is one and only one fundamental kind of stuff in the universe. Let that one stuff be variously called matter or energy, which except in details does not differ from calling it water or air or fire. By contrast, Plotinus follows Plato and Aristotle in insisting on the hypothesis that only with compositional *heterogeneity* are explanations of the natural world possible. This is dramatically evident, for example, in Plato's *Phaedo* where, in Socrates' 'autobiography', Anaxagorean explanations of natural phenomena are dismissed as 'exceedingly absurd'.[59] Instead, the real αἰτίαι of these phenomena are found within the intelligible world.[60] The compositional heterogeneity must also include a material principle of some sort, which in *Phaedo* is called a 'necessary condition' and in *Timaeus* is called an 'auxiliary to the true αἰτία'.[61] Aristotle, of course, argues extensively for the compositional heterogeneity of nature. Without hylomorphic composition the natural world, that is, the world of change, would be literally unintelligible. But for both Plato and Aristotle, compositional heterogeneity entails that the intelligibility that nature possesses must in principle be qualified. Hence, *gradable* intelligibility is introduced with the unqualifiedly intelligible transcending nature and so transcending materiality.

Nature, for Plotinus, is at the outermost reaches of intelligibility. That it intersects cosmology and biology by being the lowest manifestation of the soul of the cosmos insures the dependence of natural science on metaphysics. When Aristotle stated that 'heaven and nature depend on the first

[59] See *Phd.* 99A4–5.
[60] This general formulation is meant to cover Socrates' 'simple αἰτία', his cleverer αἰτία, and the τι ἱκανόν, the ultimate explanation which, as I argue elsewhere, must be identical with the Idea of the Good.
[61] See *Phd.* 99B3; *Tim.* 46C7.

principle of all', he was making a claim that concerns cosmology and
biology as much as it does metaphysics or theology.[62] The problem that
contemporary panpsychism seeks to solve is unsolvable if mere compositional homogeneity is retained such that all heterogeneity must be only
phenomenal. Insisting that mentality is real and irreducible to physica-
lity does not in fact amount to a concession to compositional heterogeneity
any more than does the recognition of sensory modalities irreducible
one to the other. What allows Plotinus to speculate that all nature
contemplates is his doctrine that the principles for understanding nature –
principles in the Aristotelian sense of the starting-points for scientific
understanding – must transcend the natural. Nature only explains
anatomy and physiology *instrumentally* because nature is a λόγος of Soul,
which is in turn a λόγος of Intellect, which is in turn a λόγος of the One or
the Good. So, from a Plotinian, that is to say, Platonic, perspective, any
form of naturalism does not in principle have the resources to do more
than describe the phenomena, where 'description' includes the positing of
physical laws. Such laws actually presume compositional homogeneity
thereby draining them of any explanatory force.[63]

---

[62] See *Meta.* Λ 7, 1072b13–14.
[63] See Wittgenstein 1922: 'the whole modern conception of the world is founded on the illusion that
the so-called laws of nature are the explanations of natural phenomena' (6.371).

CHAPTER 15

Is the Heaven an Animal?
Avicenna's Celestial Psychology between Cosmology and Biology

*Tommaso Alpina**

'It must be known that the proximate cause of the first movement is a soul, not an intellect, and that the heaven is an *animal* obedient to God' (*Ilāhiyyāt*, IX, 1, 381, 10–11). In the ninth treatise of *Ilāhiyyāt* ([*Book of*] *Divine Things* in English, henceforth *Ilāhiyyāt*)[1] Avicenna (Ibn Sīnā, d. 1037 CE) outlines the emanative process of all creation from the Necessary Existent, i.e. God (IX, 1–5), and tackles the issues of theodicy (IX, 6) and of the return (*ma'ād*) of the creation to its principle (IX, 7).

From the end of *Ilāhiyyāt*, IX, 1 quoted above we learn that the proximate cause of the first movement, namely the heavenly circular motion,[2] is a soul (*nafs*), not an intellect (*'aql*), and that the heaven (*al-samā'*)[3] is an animal (*ḥayawān*) which obeys God. Avicenna thus refers to the heaven by the term *ḥayawān*, namely by using the same term by which elsewhere he refers to any sublunary animal.

That the heaven as a whole is an animal is not a novelty. This statement traces back to Plato, who in the *Timaeus* considers the celestial bodies ζῷα (animals), even though elsewhere he expresses his position in a more

---

* This chapter has been written under the aegis of the project 'Animals in Philosophy of the Islamic World', which has received funding from the European Research Council (ERC) under the European Union's Horizon 2020 research and innovation programme (grant agreement No. 786762). I would like to thank Peter Adamson, Amos Bertolacci, and Damien Janos for their comments on a first draft of the present chapter. Unless otherwise indicated, translations from Arabic are mine. Translations of Aristotle's works are drawn from Barnes 1984 with minor modifications. Terminological clarification: I use the adjectives *celestial* and *sublunary* respectively to superlunary and terrestrial entities/realms, whereas I use the adjective *heavenly* to refer to the circular motion performed by the heavens.
[1] It is the metaphysical part (*ǧumla*) of the *Kitāb al-Šifāʾ* (*Book of the Cure* or *the Healing* in English, henceforth *Šifāʾ*), Avicenna's *magnum opus* composed approximately between 1020 and 1027.
[2] For the identification of the first movement with the heavenly circular motion, see *Ilāhiyyāt*, IX, 1, 373, 13–14.
[3] By *heaven* here Avicenna refers collectively to a mutiplicity of celestial realities having their own principles, not only planets and stars, but also concentric and eccentric orbs, and epicyclic spheres. Souls and intellects are respectively their proximate and remote causes. See Janos 2011: 176.

tentative way.[4] Aristotle, by contrast, never refers to the celestial bodies as ζῷα; however, he seems to ascribe a certain form of life to them, which seems to require a psychological principle capable of accounting for their motion (*De Caelo*, II, 2; 12, and *Metaphysics*, XII, 8).[5] Moreover, in the *Principles of the Cosmos* (*Fī Mabādi' al-kull*, henceforth *Mabādi'*), a work extant only in Arabic translation, Alexander of Aphrodisias accounts for celestial motion by referring to the concepts of soul and intellect, which he identifies with the nature of celestial bodies.[6] Unlike Alexander, Simplicius seems to distinguish between nature and soul in celestial bodies, and to assign to them a rational soul.[7] It should also be mentioned that, according to Plotinus, the eternal circular motion of the heaven is the result of the activity of the universal soul (ἡ ψυχὴ ὅλη).[8] Moreover, in the second book of the *Planetary Hypotheses*, which is extant only in Arabic and Hebrew, Ptolemy maintains that a psychic power is responsible for celestial motion.[9]

By saying that the heaven is a *ḥayawān*, that is, an animate living being similar to a sublunary animal and endowed with the same soul, i.e. the animal soul (*nafs ḥayawāniyya*), Avicenna seems, therefore, to conform to a philosophical tradition in which Platonic and Aristotelian teachings are combined, and some of their tentative or implicit assumptions are made final and explicit. In doing that, he aims to account for an observable, but remote phenomenon, which cannot be directly grasped, i.e. heavenly circular motion, through an analogous, but closer and thus more knowable phenomenon, i.e. animal locomotion, whose principle is a soul. Consequently, Avicenna refers to celestial entities and their principle by the very same terms used to refer to sublunary animals and their principle, namely *ḥayawān* and *nafs*. However, saying that the heaven is an animal is not free from implications, and raises some fundamental questions: can the heaven be said to be an animal in the very same way in which any other

---

[4] See, respectively, *Timaeus*, 39 a-b, and *Laws*, 899 a-b. See also *Timaeus*, 92 c for the discussion of the entire cosmos.
[5] For an evaluation of these texts, see Falcon 2005: 91, n. 10. However, in *De Caelo*, I, 2, 269 a2–9, and II, 1, 284 a27–35 Aristotle seems to believe that the circular motion of celestial bodies does not depend on a soul but on a nature.
[6] See *Mabādi'*, 94, 9–15. However, Alexander maintains that celestial soul is not specifically the same (*ġayr musāwiyatin fī l-nawʿ*) as any sublunary souls (*Mabādi'*, 48, 3–4). For these texts as Avicenna's background, see Janos 2011: 179, n. 42.
[7] See *In Aristotelis de caelo*, 388, 16–25. In this passage, in commenting upon *De Caelo*, II, 12, 292 a18–22, Simplicius argues in favour of celestial bodies' ensoulment against some philosophers revered by him (τινες τῶν ἐμοὶ προσκυνητῶν φιλοσόφων).
[8] See Plotinus, *Enneads*, II, 2 (14), §1. See also II, 1 (40), §§ 2–4.
[9] See Feke 2018: 187–200. On Ptolemy's use of the planet/animal analogy in the *Planetary Hypotheses* and its influence on Arabic thinkers, see Janos, forthcoming.

sublunary animal, e.g. a dog, is said to be an animal? Also, is the soul ascribed to the heaven the very same kind of soul that is the principle of sublunary animals, i.e. the animal soul?

Many contributions have been written on Avicenna's account of the heavens and the celestial world, all focusing chiefly, though not exclusively, on celestial kinematics, the nature of the heavenly motion, and its relation to the theories of causality and emanation.[10] None of them – as far as I know – directly tackles the issue of the way in which Avicenna applies the concepts of *ḥayawān*, *nafs*, and *ʿaql* to both celestial and sublunary realms, and of whether a common ground for their application in the two realms is detectable. The aim of this chapter is, therefore, to shed some more light on Avicenna's use of these terms – which he defines in psychology – in the cosmological and metaphysical discourse on the celestial realm, in order to ascertain whether they can be applied in the same manner and with the same meaning to entities belonging to different realms. The issue is particularly relevant since Avicenna's attitude towards this possibility seems not to be perfectly consistent: in psychology he seems to deny the possibility to assign to celestial entities the same soul that sublunary entities have except by equivocation, whereas in metaphysics he seems not to distinguish the sense in which *ḥayawān* and *nafs* are predicated of celestial entities from that in which they are predicated of sublunary animals. In this connection, this investigation might also contribute to better understand how Avicenna conceives the relationship between psychology and metaphysics: for, contrary to his general tenet according to which metaphysics provides the foundation of any particular inquiry conducted by any particular science (*Ilāhiyyāt*, I, 1–3), in this case metaphysics seems to assume the conclusions of psychology without founding them.[11]

Heavenly Motion, or Why Heavens Need an Animal Soul

Avicenna's celestial realm is structured after Ptolemy's astronomical theories, which are integrated into an Aristotelian and Neoplatonic framework.[12]

---

[10] See Davidson 1992; Janos 2011; Hasnaoui 2014; Hasnaoui 1990; Hasnaoui 1984; McGinnis 2006; Twetten 2016; Wisnovsky 2003a; Wisnovsky 2003b; Wisnovsky 2002. A noteworthy complement is represented by Cerami 2017, and Rashed 2004.

[11] On this aspect, see Alpina 2021: 60–64 and 86–95; and Alpina 2018b: 218–19. For a thorough study of *Ilāhiyyāt*, I, 1–3 and the foundational role of metaphysics in Avicenna's system of science, see Bertolacci 2006: 111–31.

[12] Here I do not want to delve into the details of Avicenna's model of the heaven and its sources. On this aspect, see the exhaustive account provided by Hasnaoui 1990, Janos 2011, and Janos, forthcoming.

According to this model, the heaven consists of matter, i.e. the celestial body, and form, i.e. the celestial soul, which is its proximate, formal and efficient cause, and has a celestial intellect, which is its remote, final cause. All these entities ultimately emanate from the Necessary Existent/First Cause, i.e. God, to which they tend to assimilate themselves either by contemplating it (celestial intellects) or by moving in circles (celestial animate bodies). The first entity to emanate from it is the first intellect, since there is no multiplicity in God and, thus, from what is one only what is one emanates (*ex uno non fit nisi unum*).[13] Then, from the first intellect, or to be precise from its intellectual activity, a multiplicity derives: insofar as it conceives (*ya'qilu*) the Necessary Existent, an inferior intellect necessarily follows from it, whereas insofar as it conceives itself, the first celestial sphere (*falak*),[14] which is composed of body and soul, necessarily follows from it. This process of emanation of intellects and celestial spheres through intellective acts is not infinite, but ends with the emanation of the last celestial intelligence, i.e. the Active Intellect or Giver of Forms: for, though conceiving both the Necessary Existent and itself, it originates neither a soul nor a body.[15]

The emanative framework of his metaphysics, together with his psychophysical model for animal locomotion, enables Avicenna to account for the circular motion of celestial bodies, as we shall see.[16]

As has been said at the beginning, already Aristotle seems to have ascribed a psychological principle to celestial bodies in virtue of which they are animate and move.[17] Even though he does not explicitly call this principle *soul*, his explanation of celestial motion seems to presuppose this

---

[13] On this tenet see D'Ancona 2007.

[14] According to Avicenna, in each sphere there is not only the main planet (or stars), but there are also other bodies like the concentric and eccentric orbs.

[15] It should be added that it is not clear whether, according to Avicenna, there are only ten celestial intelligences/intellects, namely one for each main planet (a position that might be ascribed, not without problems, either to Ptolemy or to a subsequent synthesis between the Ptolemaic and the Aristotelian model), or more than ten, namely one for each celestial body (Aristotle's position), even though Avicenna seems to incline towards the second model. Besides *Ilāhiyyāt*, a brief presentation of these two positions can be found in *Nafs*, I, 1, 13, 3–10. For a discussion of the two models of Avicenna's celestial kinematics, see Hasnaoui 1990, Janos 2011, and Janos, forthcoming.

[16] For the principle according to which the investigation of nature must proceed from what is clearer and more knowable to us to what is clearer and more knowable in itself, see *Phys.*, I, 1. The same idea is expressed by Avicenna in the preface to his *Nafs*. On the preface to Avicenna's *Nafs*, see Alpina 2018a; and Alpina 2021: 64–68.

[17] See, for instance, *Cael.*, II, 2, 285 a27–31: 'Since we have already determined that powers of this kind belong to things having a principle of movement, and that *the heaven is animate and possesses a principle of movement* (ὁ δ'οὐρανὸς ἔμψυχος καὶ ἔχει κινήσεως ἀρχήν), clearly the heaven must also exhibit above and below, right and left' (emphasis mine). For a discussion of Aristotle's attribution of biological concepts to the heavens, see Lennox in this volume.

kind of principle. For he claims that both stars (i.e. everything constituting the heavens) and sublunary living beings are moved by a sort of combination of thought (which stands for any form of cognition), and desire,[18] both representing the ultimate cause of their voluntary motion.[19] However, according to Aristotle, both thought and desire are faculties of the soul.[20] In this way, Aristotle manages to account for what is more obscure to us because of its remoteness (heavenly motion) through what is clearer and closer to us (animal motion, and its psychological principle). The celestial and sublunary souls cause, therefore, the motion of their respective bodies. What is more, in *Metaphysics*, XII, 7–8 the celestial motion is said to be brought about by final causation:[21] for it occurs because of the desire of the stars to approximate to the eternal life of the first unmoved mover as much as they can, by the continuous, unceasing, but seasonally varying, circular motion of their bodies.[22] What remains implicit in Aristotle's account of celestial motion is made explicit by Alexander of Aphrodisias, who in his *Mabādi'* explicitly attributes a soul to the celestial bodies,[23] and describes the stars' approximation to the kind of life enjoyed by the unmoved mover through their eternal, circular motion, in Platonic terms as a form of *imitation* (*tašabbuh*).

In Avicenna's account of heavenly motion the function of soul is crucial. It is said to be the proximate principle of the motion of the celestial sphere, because it is engaged in constantly renewed acts of imagination, estimation and volition, that is to say, it perceives particular changing things, and

---

[18] One of the major differences between stars and sublunary living beings is that the former have only rational desire.

[19] See *De an.*, III, 10, 433 a9–10: 'These two things appear to be sources of movement: *desire and thought* (ἤ ὄρεξις ἤ νοῦς) (if one may venture to regard imagination as a kind of thinking; for many men follow their imaginations contrary to knowledge, and in all animals other than man there is no thinking nor calculation but only imagination)'; *De motu an.*, 6, 700 b17–19: 'Now we see that the animal is moved by intellect, imagination, choice, wish, and appetite. All these things can be reduced to *thought and desire* (εἰς νοῦν καὶ ὄρεξιν)'. (emphasis mine). See also *Metaph.*, XII, 7, 1072 a21–7, where Aristotle refers not to desire and thought, but to their objects (τὸ ὀρεκτὸν καὶ τὸ νοητόν). It is noteworthy that Aristotle does not conceive cognition and desire as two independent sources of motion. Rather, desire, as principle of motion, depends on a form of (rational or irrational) cognition.

[20] See *De an.*, II, 3, 414 a29–32: 'Of the aforementioned psychic powers some living beings, as we have said, possess all, some less than all, others only one. The powers we have mentioned are the nutritive (θρεπτικόν), the sensitive (αἰσθητικόν), the desiderative (ὀρεκτικόν), the locomotive (κινητικὸν κατὰ τόπον), and the power of thinking (διανοητικόν)'.

[21] See, for instance, *Metaph.*, XII, 7, 1072 b1–4.   [22] See Cooper in this volume.

[23] See Alexander of Aphrodisias, *Mabādi'*, 52, 6–8: 'It (*sc.* the celestial body) necessarily moves with this (*sc.* circular) motion by means of the soul and the intellect (*bi-l-nafs wa-l-'aql*) because this soul is from the beginning a form of this body, and one must not believe that its nature is something different from the soul'.

desires them insofar as they are particular. For this reason, Avicenna excludes that an intellect is the proximate principle of celestial motion, because it is self-subsistent in every respect, does not change, nor undergoes transition from one thing to another, nor is mixed with what is in potentiality.[24]

The soul is thus more suitable than the intellect to be the proximate cause for the motion of the celestial sphere, because its characteristics comply with the nature of motion. In *Samāʿ ṭabīʿī*, II, 1 motion is said to have an obscure nature because it involves a connection with what does not endure and is, consequently, ephemeral.[25] In *Ilāhiyyāt*, IX, 2 Avicenna refers back to *Samāʿ ṭabīʿī*, and makes more explicit that motion has three main features: its relations to its portions are constantly renewed (*mutağaddid al-nisab*), it has no permanence (*lā ṯabāta lahū*), and it cannot derive at all from a permanent notion alone (*lā yağūzu an yakūna ʿan maʿnan ṯābit al-battata waḥdahū*).[26] Motion does not have stability, namely it is not in actuality as a whole, but consists of a multiplicity of relations that are constantly renewed. In particular, every portion of motion has its own relation to its subsequent portion, towards which it tends as its ending point, and which is in potentiality. However, this relation changes when that portion of motion is reached: for, then, the portion of motion that was previously in potentiality, comes into actuality and becomes the starting point of another motion towards the portion coming after it, which is in turn in potentiality. The proximate principle of motion cannot be an intellect because of the instability of motion depending on the constant renewal of the relations between its portions, the transition from one thing to another, and the relation to potentiality. Intellect, by contrast, enjoys a stable condition, does not change from one thing to another, and is not mixed with what is in potentiality. Avicenna can thus argue that the proximate principle of heavenly motion is a soul.[27]

---

[24] *Ilāhiyyāt*, IX, 2, 386, 14–387, 1.

[25] *Samāʿ ṭabīʿī*, II, 1, 83, 5–7: '[Motion] has been defined in different obscure ways because of the obscurity of its nature, since it is a nature whose states do not exist as actually enduring and [since] its existence consists in seeing that something [that existed] before it (*sc.* the motion) has ceased to exist, whereas something else begins to exist'.

[26] *Ilāhiyyāt*, IX, 2, 383, 15–17.

[27] Avicenna has already excluded that the celestial motion is caused by nature, and argued that it is voluntary (*Ilāhiyyāt*, IX, 2, 383, 12–13). It must therefore be caused by a soul or an intellect. However, he also excludes that the proximate principle of heavenly motion is an intellect (*Ilāhiyyāt*, IX, 2, 383, 14–15).

In order to explain how the soul imparts motion to the celestial body, Avicenna has to determine which kind of soul celestial soul is. The celestial soul is said to have intellectual perception, by means of which it conceives its remote principle, i.e. the intellect, and consequently longs for its assimilation to it (and, through its mediation, to the First Cause, i.e. the Good). However, intellectual perception alone does not explain how the soul actually imparts motion to the body of the celestial sphere, since intellectual activity by itself does not have an immediate relation to matter and motion.[28] Avicenna, therefore, adds that, as a consequence of its relation to the body, the celestial soul is also endowed with imagination, estimation and volition.[29] It is by means of these faculties that the soul imparts circular motion to the celestial sphere in order to fulfil its intellectual desire to assimilate with its remote principle and, ultimately, with the First Cause: for, through imagination and estimation the soul perceives particular things, i.e. the particular portions of which motion consists, and through the volition connected with these perceptive faculties, it desires the portions of motion it perceives.[30] Thus, the celestial soul establishes relations to the particular portions of motion, which are constantly renewed because of its transition from one object of perception and, consequently, of desire, to another.[31] Then, Avicenna accounts for the connection of the intellectual contemplation of what is above with the perception of and the desire for the particulars, and the way in which circular motion results from the perceptive activity of the celestial soul: 'The motion [of the celestial sphere] also follows the aforementioned

[28] On the fact that intellectual perception is performed with no need of a bodily organ, and therefore does not have an immediate connection with the body, see *Nafs*, I, 1, 15, 17–16, 17 (*Flying Man* experiment), I, 4, and V, 2. For a thorough analysis of these texts, see Alpina 2018b and Alpina 2021.

[29] *Ilāhiyyāt*, IX, 3, 401, 2–3: 'Therefore every celestial sphere has a motive soul that conceives (* taʿqilu*) the good and, because of the body (*bi-sabab al-ǧism*), it has imagination (*taḫayyul*), that is, the conceptualisation of particular things (*ay taṣawwur li-l-ǧuzʾiyyāt*), and volition of particular things (*irāda li-l-ǧuzʾiyyāt*)'. Late Ancient commentators on Aristotle disagree on whether celestial beings have external sensation or not but, as far as I know, none of them assign to celestial beings internal sensation.

[30] For the connection between desire and perception in Avicenna's account of motion, see *Nafs*, I, 5, 41, 4–16; and IV, 4, 194, 5–195, 23.

[31] *Ilāhiyyāt*, IX, 3, 401, 6–9: 'In general, it is inevitable that in each [celestial sphere] that moves for an intellectual goal there is an intellectual principle that conceives the First Good, and that is in itself separated (*wa-takūnu ḏātuhū mufāriqa*) [from matter] (you have already learned that everything that conceives [something] is in itself separate [from matter] sc. *Nafs*, V, 2). [It is also inevitable that in each celestial sphere] there is a corporeal (*ǧusmānī*), that is, continuous with the body (*ay muwāṣil li-l-ǧism*), principle for motion (for you have already learned that the heavenly motion is psychic (*nafsāniyya*), [that is] proceeding from a soul that makes choices, and [continuously] renews [its] choices (*muḫtāra mutaǧaddida al-iḫtiyārāt*) because of their particularity'.

(*sc.* intellectual) conceptualisation (*sc.* that of the ultimate good, the First Cause) in this manner, not because it is primarily intended, even though this single conceptualisation is followed by particular (*sc.* imaginative) conceptualisations (*taṣawwurāt ǧuz'iyya*), [(. . .)]. These particular conceptualisations are followed by motions (*al-ḥarakāt*) through which the transition from one place to another takes place' (*Ilāhiyyāt*, IX, 2, 391, 1–4).

The heaven as a whole can therefore be considered an animal, that is, an animate living being similar to a sublunary animal and endowed with the same soul. Avicenna's account of the animal nature of the heaven is based on three elements: (a) its relation to particulars (*ǧuz'iyyāt*), which are the object of its perception and desire; (b) the constant renewal (*taǧaddud*) of this relation; and (c) its consequent connection with potentiality (*quwwa*). Unlike the intellect, which is a remote, separate and unmixed principle, the (celestial) soul, due to its relation to the body, perceives and, consequently, desires the particulars. Moreover, the relation of the soul to the particulars constantly renews because the soul is not stable but, as a result of its multiple perceptive and motive activities, it moves from one thing to another, and is consequently mixed with what is in potentiality. Ultimately, the relation to potentiality makes the heaven similar to sublunary animals. For, though Avicenna maintains that the circular motion of the heaven does not abandon any portion of its orbit except to advance towards it again,[32] and that there is nothing in potentiality in the substance of the heaven, potentiality still occurs to it with respect to its position and place.[33]

Celestial Soul, or Why the Heaven Is an Animal Only by Equivocation

The heaven can be referred to as *animal* because, like any sublunary animal, it is engaged in voluntary motion originated by a psychological principle. What remains to be investigated is whether the celestial soul

---

[32] *Ilāhiyyāt*, IX, 2, 382, 13–15.

[33] *Ilāhiyyāt*, IX, 2, 389, 13–390, 1: 'It, namely the celestial body, is, concerning its substance, in its utmost perfection since nothing in potentiality remains in its substance; likewise in its quantity and quality, except, firstly, in its position and place (*illā fī waḍ'ihī aw aynihī awwalan*) and, secondly, in the things that follow their existence. Its being in one position or place is not more appropriate for its substance than its being in another position or place within its (*sc.* of the celestial body) range. For no part of the orbit of a celestial sphere or of a star has a greater claim than another part to encounter it or a part of it. Thus, when it is in actuality in one part, it is in potentiality in another part. Hence, there would occur to the substance of the celestial sphere what is in potentiality with respect to its position and place'. For the fact that the celestial body is in potentiality with respect to its position, but not with respect to its substance, see Arist., *Metaph.*, XII, 7, 1072 b4–7.

(*nafs falakiyya/samāwiyya*),[34] the faculties ensuing from it, and their activities can be accounted for in the very same terms in which the animal soul, and its faculties and activities are.

In *Ilāhiyyāt*, IX, 2 celestial soul is designated as perfection (*kamāl*) and form (*ṣūra*) of the celestial body,[35] and is characterised as corporeal (*ǧusmāniyya*), subject to alteration and change (*mustaḥīla wa-mutaġayyira*), and not abstracted from matter (*wa-laysat muǧarrada 'an al-mādda*).[36]

Perfection and form are technical terms that Avicenna uses to refer to the instances of sublunary soul in the *Kitāb al-Nafs* (*Book of the Soul* in English, henceforth *Nafs*), i.e. the sixth section (*fann*) of the part on natural philosophy of the *Šifā'*. However, if in *Ilāhiyyāt* they seem to be considered as synonyms, in *Nafs* they are sharply distinguished. In particular, in *Nafs*, I, 1, where Avicenna carefully reviews several terms by which his predecessors have referred to the soul, the notion of perfection is said to be broader than that of form: if form always inheres in matter, perfection can also exist independently of it. Perfection is, therefore, considered a better term to refer to the soul since it is capable of encompassing not only the inseparable souls (e.g. the vegetative and animal soul), which are *forms* of the body and cannot exist independently of it, but also the souls that are separable from the body (e.g. the human soul and, possibly, the celestial soul).[37] The difference between, respectively, the soul of plants and animals, and that of human beings emerges throughout the *Nafs*.[38]

The synonym use of *perfection* and *form* in connection with the celestial soul in *Ilāhiyyāt* seems to suggest that the celestial soul is an instance of inseparable perfection, which identifies with form, always inhering in the matter of the celestial body and incapable of subsisting independently of it. The strategy behind this account of the celestial soul might be that of strengthening its connection with the body, from which the soul acquires the capacity for perceiving and desiring the particulars, a capacity crucial to

---

[34] I consider *falakiyya* and *samāwiyya* as synonyms when they are used to qualify the superlunary souls. However, I translate them as *celestial* and *heavenly* respectively in order to keep the words distinct in the English translation. In *Nafs* Avicenna always uses *nafs falakiyya* to refer to the celestial soul (I, 1, 12, 10, 14; 13, 11), whereas in *Ilāhiyyāt* he uses twice *nafs samāwiyya* (IX, 4, 402, 3; X, 1, 437, 9) and, more frequently, the circumlocution *nafs al-falak* (soul of the celestial sphere).

[35] *Ilāhiyyāt*, IX, 2, 386, 16.   [36] *Ilāhiyyāt*, IX, 2, 387, 4–5.

[37] *Nafs*, I, 1, 8, 7–8: 'Both the separable soul and the soul that does not separate are perfection'. For the similarity between the human and the celestial soul, see *Nafs*, IV, 2, 178, 17–18: 'Human souls are more similar to those angelic substances (*li-tilka l-ǧawāhir al-malakiyya*) than they are to the sensible bodies'. On Avicenna's notion of *perfection* and its Greek and Arabic antecedents, see Wisnovsky 2003a: 21–141.

[38] More on this in Alpina 2018b; and Alpina 2021.

account for the way in which heavenly circular motion originates. Avicenna's aim here is not to investigate all instances of soul but, rather, to account exclusively for the celestial soul, and to distinguish it from the celestial intellect. The result is that of making the celestial soul more similar to the vegetative and animal soul than to the human rational soul. In this connection, it is noteworthy that Avicenna distinguishes the celestial soul from the celestial intellect by saying that, unlike the latter, the former is not capable of self-subsisting.[39] The 'isolated self-subsistence' (*al-infirād bi-qiwām al-ḏāt*) is precisely the criterion that Avicenna uses to account for the human soul considered in itself, which ultimately identifies with the intellect, in *Nafs*, I, 3 (and V, 2).[40]

The divisions of substance listed at the end of *Ilāhiyyāt*, II, 1, where a reference to the soul is contained, might cast some light on which kind of substance the celestial soul is according to Avicenna. There, two main divisions of substance are listed: (i) body, and (ii) what is other than body. Within the second group Avicenna distinguishes (ii.i) what is part of a body (*ǧuz' ǧismin*), and (ii.ii) what is not part of a body but is something altogether separate from bodies (*mufāriq li-l-aǧsām bi-l-ǧumla*). Form and matter belong to group (ii.i), since they are parts of the body. Soul and intellect, by contrast, belong to group (ii.ii) because they are separate from the body. Nonetheless, soul and intellect are not separate from the body in the same way: for the soul still has some connection (*'alāqa*) with the body because it is its principle of motion, whereas the intellect is free (*muta-barri'*) from matter in all respect.[41]

Two remarks are in order. Firstly, here *form* and *soul* are sharply distinguished, since they belong to two different divisions of substance. The former belongs to the division of substances that are parts of the body and, consequently, inseparable from it; the latter, by contrast, belongs to the division of substances that are separate from the body. However, though being separate from the body, soul is said to have some connection with it, being its principle of motion. Secondly, the soul that Avicenna

---

[39] *Ilāhiyyāt*, IX, 2, 386, 16–387, 1.
[40] More on the investigation of the human soul considered in itself, and not in connection with matter and motion, i.e. with the body, in Alpina 2018b, 202–18; and Alpina 2021: 68–74 and 77–85. Moreover, in *Ilāhiyyāt*, IX, 4, 408, 16–18 Avicenna establishes a parallel between the metaphysical treatment of celestial intellects and the psychological treatment of human intellect. In particular, he refers back to natural sciences (*fī l-'ulūm al-ṭabī'iyya*, sc. psychology) as the place in which it has been already shown that there are simple (*basīṭa*) and separate (*mufāriqa*) intellects that come into existence together with the human bodies (*taḥduṯu ma'a ḥudūṯ abdān al-nās*) and, unlike them, do not corrupt (*lā tafsudu*) but endure eternally (*bal tabqà*).
[41] *Ilāhiyyāt*, II, 1, 60, 9–14.

mentions here is not every soul, but the celestial soul, since he describes it as the principle of motion of the body, and in the *Ilāhiyyāt* the celestial soul is referred to as *motive* (*al-muḥarrika*, IX, 2, 387, 4) and, what is more, in this list Avicenna mentions only substances that are going to be treated in *Ilāhiyyāt*, and celestial soul is the only kind of soul to be treated *ex professo* in metaphysics.[42] Therefore, soul, or to be precise celestial soul, seems to be something completely different from form: for, unlike form, it is separate from the body, though having some connection with it (it cannot be self-subsistent in every respect, otherwise it will be identical with the intellect). Thus, the celestial soul appears (again) to be similar to the human soul that, as has been shown, does not subsist in a body either as a faculty in it or as a form belonging to it, but nonetheless has a relation to its own body.[43]

Here Avicenna seems to be at an impasse: either the celestial soul is not a form at all, and is therefore separate from the body, though being somehow connected with it (*Ilāhiyyāt*, II, 1), or it is perfection and form of the celestial body, and is therefore corporeal and unable to exist independently of it (*Ilāhiyyāt*, IX, 2). However, a passage from *Ilāhiyyāt*, IX, 4 seems to offer a solution to the conundrum. There, Avicenna distinguishes between (i) forms whose subsistence (*qiwām*) and the activities following from their subsistence are through the matters of bodies (*bi-mawādd al-aǧsām*) and (ii) forms subsisting by themselves, not by the matters of bodies (*qiwāmuhā bi-ḏātihā lā bi-mawādd al-aǧsām*). Then, he connects the second division to the soul, adding that every soul is made to be proper to a body, because its activity is by means of that body and in it (*bi-ḏālika l-ǧism wa-fīhi*). If it were separated in both essence and activity from that body, it would then be the soul of all things, not the soul of that specific body.[44]

---

[42] On the fact that the celestial soul is the only instance of soul to be explicitly treated in metaphysics, see Alpina 2021: 86–88. See also *Ilāhiyyāt*, I, 4, 27, 16–28, 2, where celestial souls are listed among the topics dealt with in the ninth treatise. Moreover, in *Ilāhiyyāt*, X, 1, 435, 8, Avicenna describes the celestial souls as operative angels (*al-malāʾika al-ʿamala*). This might be a reference to their motive activity.

[43] See *Nafs*, V, 2, 209, 17–210, 1. In *Nafs*, V, 4, 229, 3–5 Avicenna distinguishes the reception (*qubūl*) of something in something else, from a mere relation (*nisba*) of something to something else. An example of the first kind of relation can be that of a sublunary soul *qua* form to the body, whereas an example of the second kind of relation can be that of an independent substance, i.e. the human rational soul, to the body it governs. On this aspect, see Alpina 2018b: 195 n. 24, and Alpina 2021: 117–129.

[44] *Ilāhiyyāt*, IX, 4, 407, 18–408, 5. This is reminiscent of what Avicenna says about the human rational soul in *Nafs*, V, 3–4: though self-subsistent, the human soul needs its specific body to perform its own activities, to be individuated, and to exclude transmigration. On these texts, see Alpina 2018b: 220 and Alpina 2021: 86, n. 100 and n. 101.

This distinction within the category of form is pivotal to properly define the celestial soul by using the term *form*. Although form in the proper sense should be inseparable from matter,[45] here Avicenna introduces a subset of forms capable of self-subsistence, having nonetheless some connection with their specific body by means of which they perform their own activities (here the body-soul relation seems the one described by the term *nisba* in *Nafs*, V, 3–4). These forms are called *soul*. An interesting feature of this distinction are the examples chosen for each division: through them Avicenna seems to distinguish natural, but inorganic and lifeless entities (fire, sun), from natural, organic and ensouled entities. Nonetheless, the characterisation of the forms that identify with souls seems to exclude those souls essentially inhering in the bodies, i.e. the vegetative and animal soul, and to comply with the characterisation of soul provided at the end of *Ilāhiyyāt*, II, 1, which primarily applies to the celestial soul, and can be possibly extended to the human soul.

If Avicenna's insistence on the fact that the celestial soul is a corporeal form in *Ilāhiyyāt*, IX, 2 is considered a manner of highlighting its connection with the body, through which the exercise of perception and volition is guaranteed, the account of (celestial) soul provided respectively in *Ilāhiyyāt*, II, 1 and IX, 4 can be reconciled at some extent: ultimately, the soul in the proper and fullest sense is that which is capable of self-subsisting (though not in every respect).[46] The two accounts only diverge about the possibility that the soul can be somehow considered a form: this possibility seems to be excluded in *Ilāhiyyāt*, II, 1, whereas it is acknowledged in *Ilāhiyyāt*, IX, 4 thanks to the introduction of self-subsistent forms. Hence, celestial soul would be similar to the human soul, not to the animal soul. Nonetheless, the problem concerning the place of the vegetative and animal soul in the metaphysical account of the soul still remains: for in *Ilāhiyyāt* Avicenna seems to have a notion of *soul* that

---

[45] *Ilāhiyyāt*, IX, 4, 405, 1–7: 'In general, even though the material form is a cause that brings matter to actuality and perfects it, matter also has an influence on its (*sc.* of form) existence, that is, in rendering it specific and in determining it, even though [the form] is the principle of existence without matter, as you have already learned (*sc. Ilāhiyyāt*, II, 4). Then each of them (*sc.* form and matter) is unquestionably a cause for the other in something, but not in one single respect. Otherwise, it would be impossible for the material form to depend, in any manner whatsoever, on matter. For this reason, we have previously said that form alone is not sufficient for the existence of matter; rather, it is like a part of the cause (*sc. Ilāhiyyāt*, II, 4). If this is the case, then it is impossible to make form a cause for matter in all respects, having no need for other than itself'.

[46] This perspective seems to emerge also from *Nafs*, where the soul in itself, without qualification, is the human rational soul, which is capable of self-subsisting but makes use of the body to perform its activities. The Philoponian influence on Avicenna's position is highlighted in Alpina 2018b, 189, n. 6 and Alpina 2021: 59, n. 8 and 82, n. 83.

encompasses the celestial and human soul, and to exclude the vegetative and animal soul, which is a form subsisting in the body and performing its activities in and through it.[47]

The difficulty of reconciling the psychological and metaphysical discourse on the soul lies in the impossibility of providing a unitary account of the soul that is capable of encompassing its lower as well as its higher instances: they appear to be irreducibly different. This difficulty is even more evident when Avicenna attempts to account for the activities the heaven performs by using the same terms he uses to account for animal activities.

The celestial soul is said to be engaged in perception (imagination and estimation) and volition, both contributing to set the celestial sphere in motion. Avicenna describes the activities in which the celestial soul is engaged as follows: 'its (*sc.* of the celestial soul) relation to the celestial sphere is the same as the relation of our animal soul to us (*nisbatuhā ilà l-falak nisbatu l-nafs al-ḥayawāniyya allatī lanā ilaynā*), except that [(a)] it is capable of conceiving to a certain extent by means of an intellection mixed with matter (*illā anna lahā an taʿqila bi-waǧhin mā taʿaqqulan mašūban bi-l-mādda*) and, in general, [(b)] its acts of estimation (*awhāmuhā*), or what is similar to the acts of estimation, are veridical (*ṣādiqa*), and its imaginings (*taḫayyulātuhā*), or what is similar to the imaginings, are true (*ḥaqīqiyya*), just as the practical intellect in us (*ka-l-ʿaql al-ʿamalī finā*). In general, its acts of perception are by means of the body (*idrākātuhā bi-l-ǧism*)' (*Ilāhiyyāt*, IX, 2, 387, 5–7).

In order to explain the perceptive activity of the celestial soul Avicenna establishes a parallel between it and *our* animal soul. Here a note of caution is required. Strictly speaking, the human being does not have an animal soul (or any other form of soul) besides the human soul. Rather, being higher in rank than the other instances of sublunary souls, the human soul performs its most peculiar activity, i.e. intellection of universals, by which it is defined, together with the lower vital activities (nutrition, growth, reproduction etc.).[48] Therefore, this compressed parallel simply suggests that celestial soul shares with human soul the faculties (and the correlative activities) specifically distinguishing animals, i.e. the perception of particulars and voluntary motion, which are as crucial to account for the motion of heavens in the celestial realm as they are to account for the motion of animals in the sublunary realm. And this is the result of the fact that both celestial and sublunary 'animals' have a body.

---

[47] See *Nafs*, I, 3, 29, 6–8.
[48] For the Aristotelian background of this position, see *De an.*, II, 3, 414 b28–33.

However, two restrictions to this parallel are introduced in order to account for the intrinsic difference between celestial and sublunary 'animals'. Firstly, in addition to the faculties it shares with the animal soul, the celestial soul is said to have also a form of intellection mixed with matter, which animal soul does not have.[49] The ascription of a form of intellection to the celestial soul is essential to explain what triggers heavenly circular motion, that is, the intellectual desire of the celestial soul to assimilate to what it intellectually conceives of the loftier realities (celestial intellect and, through it, the First Cause). As has previously emerged, celestial soul perceives particulars and desire them as a consequence of its intellectual conceptualisation and desire of what is above.[50] Secondly, though Avicenna assigns to the celestial soul apparently the same (internal) perceptive faculties of the animal soul, i.e. imagination and estimation (or what is similar to them),[51] celestial imagination and estimation are distinguished from their animal counterpart with respect to the correctness and precision of the outcome of their activity. Since the heavenly circular motion, which is eternally the same, depends on celestial imagination and estimation, their acts cannot be deceptive or erroneous. Therefore, unlike the acts of animal imagination and estimation, which are based on the changing data of external senses and might contain errors,[52] those of celestial imagination and estimation are said to be veridical and true like those for which our practical intellect is responsible. This new parallel is meant to highlight the accuracy and precision of the activity of celestial imagination and estimation: just as the activity of our practical intellect is reliable because it is based on the universal, demonstrative knowledge provided by the theoretical intellect,[53] the activity of celestial imagination and estimation is reliable because it is not based on the data provided by external senses, with which the celestial soul is not endowed (as we shall

---

[49] On the basis of this passage Bertolacci argues that for Avicenna the celestial intellect and the celestial soul are not absolutely distinguished, see Le cose divine: 710, n. 72.

[50] See Ilāhiyyāt, IX, 2, 391, 1–4. This passage is quoted in full at pp. 267–8 above.

[51] The addition 'or what is similar to [. . .]' (aw mā yušbihu) leaves room for the possibility that, as we shall see, the heaven does not have exactly the same imagination and estimation that sublunary animals have.

[52] On the fact that animal imagination operates without considering whether the forms that it combines or separates exist or do not exist in the extramental world, and that judgments formulated by animal estimation can be incorrect, see Nafs, IV, 1, 165, 19–167, 3. On this chapter, see Alpina, forthcoming.

[53] See Nafs, V, 1, 207, 12–13, where the practical faculty is said to depend on the theoretical faculty: 'This faculty (sc. the practical intellect) takes support from the faculty that concerns universals (wa-takūnu hāḍihi l-quwwa istimdāduhā min al-quwwa allatī 'alà l-kulliyyāt): from here it grasps the major premises in what it deliberates upon, and it infers concerning particular matters'.

see, it does not have organs), but depends on the intellection of the stable, intellectual realities that are arranged above the celestial soul.[54]

This parallel, however, reveals an unavoidable problem concerning the account of the faculties (and the correlative activities) ensuing from the celestial soul. In metaphysics Avicenna seems to establish a sort of *continuity* between the psychic faculties belonging to the animal and celestial soul, the only difference being the degree of truth of the outcome of their perceptive activity. Therefore, he seems to assume that the perceptive faculties of both animal and celestial soul work in the very same way. In psychology, however, Avicenna seems to have another position: in *Nafs* the activity of imagination and estimation is said to depend on the data provided by external senses and gathered by the common sense (*ḥiss muštarak*). The celestial 'animals', by contrast, do not have external senses as a consequence of their lack of organs. Thus, one might wonder how celestial imagination and estimation actually work, and whether they can be considered the very same internal senses that belong to us as well as to other sublunary animals. In metaphysics, where the main focus is celestial life, the issue of the dissimilarity between celestial and sublunary perceptive activity is not explicitly addressed. Avicenna, by contrast, directly tackles this issue in *Nafs*.

In *Nafs*, I, 1 Avicenna presents two possible objections to the Aristotelian definition of the soul as 'the first perfection of a natural, organic body, having the capacity to perform the activities of life' (*kamāl awwal li-ğism ṭabīʿī ālī lahū an yafʿala afʿāl al-ḥayā*, 12, 7–8):[55] (1) the first objection concerns the fact that the Aristotelian definition of the soul does not include celestial soul; (2) the second objection concerns the possibility of substituting the notion of soul with that of life (*ḥayā*). Here I will concentrate on the first objection without discussing the second one. Avicenna immediately excludes that the Aristotelian definition of the soul applies also to the celestial soul (*al-nafs al-falakiyya*) because, unlike sublunary souls, it acts without organs (*tafʿalu bi lā ālāt*),[56] and this seems

[54] On the fact that celestial imagination and estimation are turned upwards, instead of downwards like animal imagination and estimation, see Janos 2011: 203 and n. 106 (here Janos tends to relate the difficulty of accounting for celestial imagination and estimation to the problematic aspects of the account of internal senses in human beings. This connection, however, does not seem effective); Michot 1986: 110–18; and Lizzini 2018 (here a parallel between prophetic and celestial imagination is established). In this connection, the interpretation of this passage advanced by Gutas should be partially revised (Gutas 2006: 344). Here Avicenna compares the function of the celestial soul with that of the animal soul/faculties belonging to humans. Then, he says that the celestial counterparts of the animal imagination and estimation in humans, not the celestial soul, are similar to our practical intellect in terms of precision of their cognitive activity.
[55] On Avicenna's retrieval of Aristotle's definition of the soul, see Alpina 2018b: 195–202; and Alpina 2021: 106–117.
[56] *Nafs*, I, 1, 12, 9–10.

to be sufficient to exclude that the celestial soul is engaged in the same kind of activities performed by sublunary souls. What is more, the impossibility of applying the same definition of soul to the celestial soul is more radically interpreted as a sign of an irreducible divide between celestial and sublunary souls: even though we remove any reference to organs, celestial and sublunary souls will still differ with respect to the kind of life they enjoy.[57]

The reason that prevents from applying the same notion of soul to both sublunary and celestial soul can be detected in the hiatus between sublunary and celestial realm.[58] There is no continuity between sublunary and celestial souls, because celestial souls are not engaged in any of the activities that are minimally constitutive of sublunary life (namely self-nutrition, growth, decay and even external perception).[59] Hence, the term *soul* as it is defined in psychology, can be referred to both celestial and sublunary entities only by equivocation (*bi-l-ištirāk*).[60] Besides, sublunary and celestial souls do not share the same meaning of the term *life*. As a consequence, the manifestations of their form of life can be referred to by the very same terms, e.g. *rationality* and *sensation*, however their meaning is hopelessly different.[61]

---

[57] *Nafs*, I, 1, 12, 11–13: 'Even if you abstain from mentioning the organs and limit yourself to mentioning 'life', that would be of no help to you: for the life belonging to the celestial soul does not consist of nutrition and growth, nor even of sensation. And this is what you mean by 'life' in the definition [of sublunary soul]'.

[58] For the hiatus between sublunary and celestial realm in Avicenna's cosmology, see Rashed 2005: 103 and 109. For the Aristotelian background of this hiatus, see *Metaph.*, XII, 1.

[59] Besides that, even if the reference to nutrition, growth, and reproduction in the account of life is removed, another problem will arise, that is, the vegetative soul would be excluded from the Aristotelian definition of the soul. See *Nafs*, I, 1, 12, 13–16: 'And if by 'life' you mean that which belongs to the celestial soul in terms of, for example, perception, intellectual conceptualisation, and the [capacity for] setting in motion for a voluntary goal, then you would exclude plants from the group of what has soul. Moreover, if nutrition constitutes life, why do you not call the plants animals?'

[60] Aristotle does not explicitly speak of equivocation/homonymy, though he seems to be conscious of the difficulty of referring the same definition of soul to both sublunary and celestial entities. See, for example, *De an.*, I, 1, 402 b2–9, where Aristotle wonders whether the definition of soul is univocal, like the definition of 'animal', or equivocal, like the definition of 'animal' if it is referred to heterogeneous kinds of animal like horse, dog, human being, and star. It is telling that in the latter case, Aristotle hints at the possible equivocation of the definition of 'animal' and, consequently, of 'soul', by gathering together three instances of sublunary life (horse, dog, and human being) and one instance of celestial life (star). By contrast, in his own *De anima*, Alexander of Aphrodisias pointed out that the same notion of soul can be predicated of both sublunary and celestial soul (ἡ γὰρ τῶν θεῶν ψυχή) only by equivocation (ὁμωνύμως); see *De anima* 28. 25–8. It is noteworthy that in the Aristotelian passage quoted above, equivocation is a problem that, in principle, might also concern the relationship among all sublunary souls.

[61] See *Nafs*, I, 1, 13, 10–14, 8, where Avicenna reports an opinion about the celestial bodies that he seems to endorse, as the two references to *Ilāhiyyāt*, IX, 2, and its qualification as 'validated' suggest: 'These (*sc.* the advocates of this view) must believe that, when it is applied to the celestial soul and to the vegetative soul, the term *soul* (*ism al-nafs*) applies [to them] only by equivocation (*bi-l-ištirāk*), that this definition pertains only to the soul existing in composed things, and that, when a stratagem

Unlike the stance expressed in *Ilāhiyyāt*, IX, 2, in *Nafs*, I, 1 Avicenna seems not to detect any common ground for referring to both celestial and sublunary soul by means of the very same notions. Here two considerations are in order. Firstly, the Aristotelian definition of the soul is said to pertain exclusively to the soul existing in composed things (*li-l-murakkabāt*, 13, 12). Therefore, Avicenna seems to exclude that celestial soul constitutes an authentic hylomorphic compound with its body (this seems to be in line with the distinction between form and soul in *Ilāhiyyāt*, II, 1). Secondly, Avicenna refers twice to *Ilāhiyyāt*, IX, 2 as the place in which the dissimilarity between sublunary and celestial soul concerning rationality and sensation is argued for.[62]

Thus, in metaphysics Avicenna seems to have a consistent account of the celestial soul: it is the perfection and form of the celestial body; however, it is not its form in the same sense in which the vegetative and animal souls are form of, respectively, plants and animals. Rather, it is a sui generis, self-subsistent form, which however performs its activity by means of the body. In this perspective, Avicenna's account of soul in metaphysics seems to fit the higher instances of soul, i.e. celestial and human soul, but not the lower ones, i.e. vegetative and animal soul. This aspect, however, seems to comply with the limited scope of metaphysical investigation of the soul. Moreover, there Avicenna ascribes to celestial souls the same perceptive faculties that in psychology are attributed to animals, but he assigns to them a higher degree of accuracy and truth. In psychology, by contrast, Avicenna excludes that the very same notions can be used to account for the principle and the activities of both sublunary and celestial life, and explicitly speaks of equivocation, because of the irreducible hiatus between celestial and sublunary realm. Therefore, the heaven can be called

---

is used so that animals and the celestial sphere share in the meaning of the term *soul* (*ma'nà ism al-nafs*), the notion of plant is excluded from that group. Even so this stratagem is difficult. For animals and the celestial sphere do not share in the meaning of the term *life* (*ma'nà ism al-ḥayā*) nor, likewise, the meaning of the term *rationality* (*ma'nà ism al-nuṭq*), because rationality here (*sc.* in the sublunary realm) applies to the existence of a soul having the two material intellects, and this is not among the things that it is correct [to apply] there (*sc.* in the celestial realm), as you will see (*'alà mā tarà, sc. Ilāhiyyāt*, IX, 2). For the intellect there is an intellect in actuality, and the intellect in actuality is not constitutive (*ġayr muqawwim*) of the soul that is part of the definition of *rational*. Likewise, sensation (*al-ḥiss*) here applies to the faculty by means of which sensible things are perceived by way of receiving their likeness and being affected by it. This also is not among the things that it is correct [to apply] there, as you will see (*'alà mā tarà, sc. Ilāhiyyāt*, IX, 2). Moreover, if by making an effort one renders the soul a first perfection for what among the bodies moves at will and perceives, so that animals and the celestial soul are included in it (*sc.* in the definition of soul as 'first perfection'), plants would be excluded from this group. This is the statement validated (*wa-hāḏā huwa l-qawl al-muḥaṣṣal*) [by this investigation]'.

[62] See the text quoted in n. 61.

animal so to reduce the cognitive gap between the investigating subject, i.e. us, and the remote subject-matter of investigation, i.e. the heaven, but only by equivocation: for, though sharing some similarities with sublunary animals, in the end heaven is radically different from them.

Conclusion

In metaphysics Avicenna attempts to reduce the distance between the celestial and sublunary realm by providing an account of the former that is moulded after the account of the latter. In particular, he establishes a parallel between two analogous phenomena, i.e. heavenly circular motion and animal locomotion, and consequently tries to explain the former, which is remote from us and not directly attainable, by using the same categories he uses to explain the latter, which is closer and thus more knowable to us. The heaven as a whole is, therefore, considered to be similar to sublunary animals: like them, it moves at will in virtue of a psychological principle (celestial soul), undergoes change and shares to some extent in potentiality, although its motion follows an eternally identical pattern. Nonetheless, the parallel suggested in metaphysics is not unproblematic. Though the notions used by Avicenna in metaphysics to account for the principle and the activities of celestial 'animals' are the same used to account for the principle and the activities of sublunary animals in psychology (soul, sensation, rationality), in psychology Avicenna explicitly excludes that the same notions with the same meanings can be also applied to celestial entities and their activities, except by equivocation. Equivocation in the predication of the same notions in the case of sublunary and celestial beings stems from an irreducible divide between the realms to which they belong, and between the kinds of life they enjoy. If the same notions are stretched downwards so as to include also plant life, or upwards so as to include also celestial (and, perhaps, divine) life, the highest or the lowest form of life inevitably escapes. Consequently, the metaphysical and the psychological account have to be conceived independently of one another, as investigating the sublunary and the celestial life respectively. Furthermore, an additional difficulty is represented by the treatment of the human rational soul in psychology: being in itself separable from the bodily matter, it transcends the boundaries of natural philosophy. It can be then considered the *trans*-physical (or *proto*-metaphysical) aspect of Avicenna's psychological investigation.[63]

---

[63] More on this aspect in Alpina 2021: chapter 3.

References

Akinpelu, J. 1967. 'The Stoic scala naturae'. *Phrontisterion* 5: 7–16.

Algra, K. 2009. 'Stoic Philosophical Theology and Graeco-Roman Religion' in R. Salles (ed.), *God and Cosmos in Stoicism*. Oxford: Oxford University Press, 224–51.

Alesse, F. 2011–12. 'Dio, anima e intelligibili nella Stoa'. *Χώρα: Revue d'Études Anciennes et Médiévales* 9–10: 365–81.

Alpina, T. 2018a. 'Knowing the Soul from Knowing Oneself: A Reading of the Prologue to Avicenna's *Kitāb al-Nafs* (*Book of the Soul*)'. *Atti e Memorie dell'Accademia Toscana di Scienze e Lettere 'La Colombaria'* 82.68: 443–58.

2018b. 'The Soul of, the Soul in Itself, and the *Flying Man* Experiment'. *Arabic Sciences and Philosophy* 28.2: 187–224.

2021. *Subject, Definition, Activity: Framing Avicenna's Science of the Soul*, Scientia Graeco-Arabica series 28, De Gruyter, Berlin: Boston.

Forthcoming. 'Retaining, Remembering, Recollecting. Avicenna's Account of Memory and Its Sources' in V. Decaix, C. Thomsen Thörnqvist (eds.), *Aristotle's De memoria et reminiscentia and Its Reception*, Studia Artistarum, Brepols Publishers.

Alt, K. 1973. 'Zum Satz des Anaximenes über die Seele: Untersuchung von Aëtios Περὶ ἀρχῶν'. *Hermes* 101: 129–64.

Alter, T. and Nagasawa, Y. 2015. *Consciousness in the Physical World: Perspectives on Russellian Monism*. New York: Oxford University Press.

Andral, G. 1829. *Grundriss der pathologischen Anatomie: Erster Theil: Allgemeine pathologische Anatomie*. Leipzig: Leopold Voss.

Archer-Hind, R. D. (ed.). 1888. *The Timaeus of Plato*. London: Macmillan.

Armstrong, A. H. 1966–88. *Plotinus Enneads*. 7 vols. Loeb Classical Library. Cambridge, MA: Harvard University Press.

Attfield, R. 1994. *Environmental Philosophy: Principles and Prospects*. Aldershot: Ashgate.

Baltes, M. 1976. *Die Weltentstehung des platonischen Timaios nach den antiken Interpreten*. Vol. 1. Leiden: Brill.

1997. 'Is the Idea of the Good in Plato's *Republic* beyond Being?' in M. Joyal (ed.), *Studies in Plato and the Platonic Tradition*. Aldershot: Ashgate, 3–23.

1999. '*Gegonen* (Platon, *Tim.* 28b7): Ist die Welt real enstanden oder nicht?' in M. Baltes (ed.), *DIANOHMATA Kleine Schriften zu Platon und zum Platonismus.* Stuttgart: De Gruyter, 301–25.

Balme, D. M. 1992. *Aristotle's* De Partibus Animalium I *and* De Generatione Animalium I (*with selections from* II. 1–3). Oxford: Oxford University Press.

Baltzly, D. 2007. *Proclus, Commentary on Plato's Timaeus: Vol. III, Book 3, Part 1. Proclus on the World's Body.* Cambridge: Cambridge University Press.

Barnes, J. 1982. *The Presocratic Philosophers.* Rev. ed. New York: Routledge.

Bénatouïl, T. 2009. 'How Industrious Can Zeus Be?' in R. Salles (ed.), *God and Cosmos in Stoicism.* Oxford: Oxford University Press, 23–45.

Berryman, S. 2002. 'Galen and the Mechanical Philosophy'. *Apeiron* 35: 235–54.

2003. 'Ancient Automata and Mechanical Explanation'. *Phronesis* 47: 344–69.

Berti, E. 2000. '*Metaphysics* Lambda 6' in M. Frede and D. Charles (eds.), *Aristotle's Metaphysics Lambda: Symposium Aristotelicum.* Oxford: Oxford University Press, 181–206.

2012. 'The Finality of Aristotle's Unmoved Mover in the Metaphysics Book 12, Chapters 7 and 10'. *Nova et Vetera* 10: 863–76.

Bertolacci, A. 2006. *The Reception of Aristotle's Metaphysics in Avicenna's Kitāb al-Šifā': A Milestone of Western Metaphysical Thought.* Leiden: Brill.

Betegh, G. 2007. 'On the Physical Aspect of Heraclitus' Psychology'. *Phronesis* 52: 3–32.

2013. 'On the Physical Aspect of Heraclitus' Psychology (with New Appendices)' in T. Sider and D. Obbink (eds.), *Doctrine and Doxography: Studies on Heraclitus and Pythagoras.* Berlin: De Gruyter, 225–61.

2018. 'Plato and Cosmology, Theology and Cognition' in J. E. Sisko (ed.), *Philosophy of Mind in Antiquity: The History of the Philosophy of Mind*, vol. 1. London: Taylor and Francis, 120–40.

Bobzien, S. 1998. *Determinism and Freedom in Stoic Philosophy.* Oxford: Oxford University Press.

Bien, C. G. 1997. *Erklärungen zur Entstehung von Missbildungen im physiologischen und medizinischen Schrifttum der Antike.* Stuttgart: Steiner.

1999. 'Chrysippus' Theory of Causes' in K. Ierodiakonou (ed.), *Topics in Stoic Philosophy.* Oxford: Oxford University Press, 196–242.

Boechat, E. 2016. 'Stoic Physics and the Aristotelianism of Posidonius'. *Ancient Philosophy* 36: 425–63.

2017. 'The Concept of the Sun as ἡγεμονικόν in the Stoa and in Manilius' Astronomica'. *Archai* 21: 79–125.

Bolton, R. 2009. 'Two Standards of Inquiry in Aristotle's De caelo' in A. C. Bowen and C. Wildberg (eds.), *New Perspectives on Aristotle's De Caelo.* Leiden: Brill, 51–82.

Bos, A. P. 2007. 'Aristotle on Dissection of Plants and Animals and His Concept of the Instrumental Soul-Body'. *Ancient Philosophy* 27: 95–106.

Boudon, V. 2000. *Galien, Exhortation à la médecine, Art médical.* Paris: Les Belles Lettres.

Boudon-Millot, V. 2007. *Galien, Sur l'ordre des ses propres livres, Sur ses propres livres, Que l'excéllent médecin est aussi philosophe.* Paris: Les Belles Lettres.

Boudon-Millot, V. and Pietrobelli, A. 2005. 'Galien résussicité: édition *princeps* du texte grec du *De propriis placitis*'. *Revue des Études grecques* 118: 168–213.

Boys-Stones, G. 2007. 'Physiognomy in Ancient Philosophy' in S. Swain et al. (eds.), *Seeing the Face, Seeing the Soul*. Oxford: Oxford University Press, 19–124.

    2016. 'Philosophy as Religion and the Meaning of "Providence" in Middle Platonism' in E. Eidenow, J. Kindt and R. Osborne (eds.), *Theologies of Ancient Greek Religion*. Cambridge: Cambridge University Press, 317–38.

    2018 [= BS]. *Platonist Philosophy 80 BC to 250 AD: An Introduction and Collection of Sources in Translation*. Cambridge: Cambridge University Press.

Bremmer, J. N. 1983. *The Early Greek Concept of the Soul*. Princeton, NJ: Princeton University Press.

Brisson, L. 1995 (repr. 2017). *Platon. Timée-Critias. Traduction, introduction, et notes*. Paris: GF-Flammarion.

    1998. *Le Même et l'Autre dans la Structure Ontologique du Timée de Platon. Un commentaire systématique du Timée de Platon*. Sankt Augustin: Academia Verlag.

    2006. 'The Intellect and the Cosmos'. *Methodos* 16. http://journals.openedition .org/methodos/4463.

Brittain, C. F. 2002. 'Non-Rational Perception in the Stoics and Augustine'. *Oxford Studies in Ancient Philosophy* 22: 253–308.

Broadie, S. 2009. 'Heavenly Bodies and First Causes' in G. Anagnostopoulos (ed.), *A Companion to Aristotle*. Oxford: Blackwell, 230–41.

    2012. *Nature and Divinity in Plato's* Timaeus, Cambridge: Cambridge University Press.

Brouwer, R. 2015. 'Stoic Sympathy' in E. Schliesser (ed.), *Sympathy: A History*. Oxford: Oxford University Press, 15–35.

Brunschwig, J. 1999. 'Stoic Metaphysics' in B. Inwood (ed.), *The Cambridge Companion to the Stoics*. Cambridge: Cambridge University Press, 206–32.

Brüntrup, G. and Jaskolla, L. (eds.). 2017. *Panpsychism: Contemporary Perspectives*. Oxford: Oxford University Press.

Burkhard, U. 1973. *Die angebliche Heraklit-Nachfolge des Skeptikers Aenesidem*. Bonn: Habelt.

Burkert, W. 1972. *Lore and Science in Ancient Pythagoreanism*. Cambridge, MA: Harvard University Press.

Caluori, D. 2015. *Plotinus on the Soul*. Cambridge: Cambridge University Press.

Campbell, G. 2000. 'Zoogony and Evolution in Plato's *Timaeus*: The Presocratics, Lucretius and Darwin' in M. R. Wright (ed.), *Reason and Necessity: Essays on Plato's* Timaeus. Swansea: The Classical Press of Wales, 145–80.

Carone, G. R. 1998. 'Plato and the Environment'. *Environmental Ethics* 20: 115–33.

    2005. *Plato's Cosmology and Its Ethical Dimensions*. Cambridge: Cambridge University Press.

Carpenter, A. 2010. 'Embodied Intelligent (?) Souls: Plants in Plato's *Timaeus*'. *Phronesis* 55: 281–3.

Caston, V. 2006. 'Aristotle's Psychology' in M. L. Gill and P. Pellegrin (eds.), *A Companion to Ancient Philosophy*. Oxford: Blackwell, 316–46.

Caveing, M. 1965–6. 'Quelques remarques sur le *Timée* et les mathématiques'. *Revue de l'Enseignement Philosophique* 15: 1–10.

Cerami, C. 2017. 'The *De Caelo et Mundo* of Avicenna's *Kitāb al-Šifāʾ*: An Overview of Its Structure, Its Goal and Its Polemical Background'. *Documenti e studi sulla tradizione filosofica medievale* 28: 273–329.

Cherniss, H. 1944. *Aristotle's Criticism of Plato and the Academy*. Baltimore: Johns Hopkins University Press.

Coates, C. F. and Lennox, J. G. 2020. 'Aristotle on the Unity of the Nutritive and Reproductive Function'. *Phronesis* 65: 1–53.

Colish, M. 1990. *The Stoic Tradition from Antiquity to the Early Middle Ages*. Leiden: Brill.

Coope, U. 2007. 'Aristotle on Action'. *Proceedings of the Aristotelian Society* 81: 109–38.

2020. 'Animal and Celestial Motion: The Role of an External Springboard: *De Motu Animalium* 2 and 3' in C. Rapp and O. Primavesi (eds.), *Aristotle's* De Motu Animalium (Symposium Aristotelicum) 240–72.

Cooper, J. M. 2003. 'Stoic Autonomy' repr. in his *Knowledge, Nature and the Good: Essays on Ancient Philosophy*. Princeton, NJ: Princeton University Press, 204–44.

2009. 'Chrysippus on Physical Elements' in R. Salles (ed.), *God and Cosmos in Stoicism*. Oxford: Oxford Univerity Press, 93–115.

2020. 'The Role of Thought in Animal Voluntary Self-Locomotion' in C. Rapp and O. Primavesi (eds.), *Aristotle's* De Motu Animalium (Symposium Aristotelicum) 345–86.

Cornford, F. M. 1937. *Plato's Cosmology: The Timaeus of Plato*. London: Taylor and Francis. Reprinted in Indianapolis by Hackett, 1997.

Craik, E. 1978–84. *Galen: On the Doctrines of Hippocrates and Plato*. 3 vols. *Corpus Medicorum Graecorum* V 4,1,2. Berlin: Akademie Verlag.

1992. *Galen: On Semen. Corpus Medicorum Graecorum* V 3,1. Berlin: Akademie Verlag.

2017. 'Teleology in Hippocratic Texts: Clues to the Future?' in J. Rocca (ed.), *Teleology in the Ancient World: Philosophical and Medical Approaches*. Cambridge: Cambridge University Press, 203–16.

D'Ancona, C. 2007. '*Ex uno non fit nisi unum* : storia e preistoria della dottrina avicenniana della Prima Intelligenza' in E. Canone (ed.), *Per una storia del concetto di mente*. Firenze: L. S. Olschki, 29–55.

Davidson, H. A. 1992. *Alfarabi, Avicenna, and Averroes on Intellect: Their Cosmologies, Theories of the Active Intellect, and Theories of Human Intellect*. New York: Oxford University Press.

De Lacy, P. 1980–4. *Galen, On the Doctrines of Hippocrates and Plato*. 3 vols. Berlin: Akademie Verlag.

Diehl, E. 1903–6. *Procli Diadochi in Platonis Timaeum Commentaria*. 3 vols. Leipzig.

Diels, H. and Kranz, W. 1952. *Die Fragmente der Vorsokratiker*. 9th ed. 3 vols. Berlin: Weidmannsche Verlagsbuchhandlung.

Dillon, J. 2003. *The Heirs of Plato*. Oxford: Oxford University Press.

Distelzweig, P. 2013. 'The Intersection of the Mathematical and Natural Sciences: The Subordinate Sciences in Aristotle'. *Apeiron* 46: 85–105.

Dixsaut, M. 1991. *Platon. Phédon. Introduction, traduction et notes*. Paris: GF-Flammarion.

Duminil, M. P. 1983. *Le sang, les vaisseaux, le cœur dans la collection hippocratique. Anatomie et physiologie*. Paris: Les Belles Lettres.

1998. *Hippocrate : Book VIII. Plaies, Nature des os, Cœur, Anatomie*. Paris: Les Belles Lettres.

Eddington, A. S. 1928. *The Nature of the Physical World*. Cambridge: Cambridge University Press.

Falcon, A. 2005. *Aristotle and the Science of Nature: Unity without Uniformity*. Cambridge: Cambridge University Press.

2016. 'The Subject Matter of Aristotle's *Physics*' in T. Buchheim, D. Meissner and N. Wachsmann (eds.), *Sōma : Körperkonzepte und körperliche Existenz in der antiken Philosophie und Literatur*. Hamburg: Felix Meiner, 423–36.

Falcon, A. and Leunissen, M. 2015. 'The Scientific Role of Eulogos in *Cael* II.12' in D. Ebrey (ed.), *Theory and Practice in Aristotle's Natural Science*. Cambridge: Cambridge University Press, 217–40.

Fazzo, S. 2012. *Il Libro Lambda della* Metafisica *di Aristotele*. Naples: Bibliopolis.

Feke, J. 2018. *Ptolemy's Philosophy: Mathematics as a Way of Life*. Princeton University Press, Oxford.

Festugière, A.-J. 1966–1968. *Proclus. Commentaire sur le Timée*. 5 vols. Paris: Vrin.

Finkelberg, A. 2013. 'Heraclitus, the Rival of Pythagoras' in D. Sider and D. Obbink (eds.), *Doctrine and Doxography: Studies on Heraclitus and Pythagoras*. Berlin: De Gruyter, 147–62.

2017. *Heraclitus and Thales' Conceptual Scheme: A Historical Study*. Leiden: Brill.

Frankfurt, H. 1969. 'Alternate Possibilities and Moral Responsibility'. *Journal of Philosophy* 66: 829–39.

Frampton, M. F. 1991. 'Aristotle's Cardiocentric Model of Animal Locomotion'. *Journal of the History of Biology* 24: 291–330.

Frede, D. 'Alexander of Aphrodisias' in E. N. Zalta (ed.), *The Stanford Encyclopedia of Philosophy*, Winter 2017 ed. https://plato.stanford.edu/archives/win2017/entries/alexander-aphrodisias/.

Frede, M. 1992. 'Doxographie, historiographie philosophique et historiographie historique de la philosophie'. *Revue de métaphysique et de morale* 97: 311–25.

2003. 'Galen's Theology' in *Entretiens sur l'Antiquité Classicque* 49 (*Galien et la Philosophie*). Geneva: Fondation Hardt, 73–126.

2011. *A Free Will: Origins of the Notion in Ancient Thought*. Sather Classical Lectures. Edited by A. A. Long with a foreword by David Sedley. Berkeley: University of California Press.

Gerson, L. P. 2005. *Aristotle and Other Platonists*. Ithaca, NY: Cornell University Press.

Gibson, J. J. 1977. 'The Theory of Affordances' in R. Shaw and J. Bransford (eds.), *Perceiving, Acting, and Knowing: Toward and Ecological Psychology*. Hillsdale, NJ: Lawrence Erlbaum Associates, 68–82.

Goold, G. P. 1977. *Manilius, Astronomica*. Cambridge, MA: Harvard University Press.

Gould, S. J. 1977. *Ontogeny and Phylogeny*. Cambridge, MA: Harvard University Press.

Graham, D. W. 1991. 'Socrates, the Craft Analogy, and Science'. *Apeiron: A Journal for Ancient Philosophy and Science* 24: 1–24.

Gregory, A. 2016. *Anaximander: A Re-assessment*. London: Bloomsbury.

Goff, P., Seager, W. and Hermanson, S. A. 2017. 'Panpsychism' in E. N. Zalta (ed.), *The Stanford Encyclopedia of Philosophy*. https://plato.stanford.edu/archives/win2017/entries/panpsychism/.

Grube, G. M. A. 1997 (origin. 1935). *Plato, Phaedo* in J. M. Cooper and D. S. Hutchinson (eds.), *Plato: Complete Works*. Cambridge: Cambridge University Press, 49–100.

Gurtler, G. 1988. *Plotinus: The Experience of Unity*. New York: P. Lang.

Gutas, D. 2006. 'Imagination and transcendental knowledge in Avicenna', in J. E. Montgomery (ed.), *Arabic Theology, Arabic Philosophy. From the Many to the One: Essays in Celebration of Richard M. Frank,*, Leuven – Paris – Dudley: Uitgeverij Peeters en Departement Oosterse Studies, 337–354.

Habinek, T. 2011. 'Manilius' Conflicted Stoicism' in S. J. Green and K. Volk (eds.), *Forgotten Stars: Rediscovering Manilius' Astronomica*. Oxford: Oxford University Press, 32–44.

Haeckel, E. 1866. *Generelle Morphologie der Organismen*. Vol. 2. Berlin: Georg Reimer. 1903. *Anthropogenie*. 5th ed. Leipzig: Verlag von Wilhelm Engelmann.

Hahm, D. E. 1977. *The Origins of Stoic Cosmology*. Columbus: Ohio State University Press.

1994. 'Self-Motion in Stoic Philosophy' in M. L. Gill and J. G. Lennox (eds.), *Self-Motion: From Aristotle to Newton*. Princeton, NJ: Princeton University Press, 175–226.

Hankinson, R. J. 1988. 'Galen Explains the Elephant'. *Canadian Journal of Philosophy* 14.Suppl.: 135–57.

1989. 'Galen and the Best of All Possible Worlds'. *Classical Quarterly* 39: 206–27.

2017. 'Teleology and Necessity in Greek Embryology' in J. Rocca (ed.), *Teleology in the Ancient World: Philosophical and Medical Approaches*. Cambridge: Cambridge University Press, 242–71.

Forthcoming. 'A Hymn to Nature: Structure, function, design and beauty in Galen's biology' in D. De Brasi and F. Fronterotta (eds.), *Poikile physis, Biological Literature in Greek during the Roman Empire: Genres, Scopes, and Problems*. Berlin/Boston: De Gruyter.

Harding, S. 2006. *Animate Earth: Science, Intuition and Gaia*. Cambridge: Green Books.

Harte, V. 2002. *Plato on Parts and Wholes: The Metaphysics of Structure*. Oxford: Oxford University Press.

Hasnaoui, A. 1984. 'La dynamique d'Ibn Sīnā. La notion d'inclination: mayl' in J. Jolivet and R. Rashed (eds.), *Études sur Avicenne*. Paris: Les Belles Lettres, 103–23.

1990. 'Fayḍ' in S. Auroux (ed.), *Encyclopédie philosophique universelle*. Paris: Presses Universitaires de France, 2:966–72.

2014. 'La théorie avicennienne de l'impetus. Ibn Sīnā entre Jean Philopon et Jean Buridan' in M. Arfa Mensia (ed.), *Views on the Philosophy of Ibn Sīnā and Mullā Ṣadrā al-Šīrāzī (Carthage, 22nd–24th Oct. 2013)*. Tunis: al-Maǧmaʿ al-Tūnisī li-l-ʿUlūm wa-l-ādāb wa-l-Funūn, 25–42.

Heath, D. L. 1913. *Aristarchos of Samos*. Oxford: Oxford University Press.

Henry, D. 2015. 'Aristotle on the Cosmological Significance of Biological Generation' in D. Ebrey (ed.), *Theory and Practice in Aristotle's Natural Science*. Cambridge: Cambridge University Press, 100–118.

2016. 'The Failure of Evolutionary Thinking in Antiquity' in G. L. Irby (ed.), *A Companion to Science, Technology, and Medicine in Ancient Greece and Rome*. West Sussex: Wiley Blackwell, 2:313–28.

Helle, R. 2018. 'Hierocles and the Stoic Theory of Blending'. *Phronesis* 63: 87–116.

Helmreich, G. 1893. *Galeni Scripa Minora*. Vol. 3. Leipzig: B. G. Teubner.

1907–9. *Galenus: de Usu Partium*. 2 vols. Leipzig: B. G. Teubner.

Hine, H. M. 2014. *Seneca, Natural Questions*. Chicago: University of Chicago Press.

Horn, C. 2012. 'Aspects of Biology in Plotinus' in J. Wilberding and C. Horn (eds.), *Neoplatonism and the Philosophy of Nature*. Oxford: Oxford University Press, 214–28.

Huffman, C. 1993. *Philolaus of Croton, Pythagorean and Presocratic*. Cambridge: Cambridge University Press.

Inwood, B. 1985. *Ethics and Human Action in Early Stoicism*. Oxford: Oxford University Press.

2001. *The Poem of Empedocles*. Toronto: University of Toronto Press.

Isnardi Parente, M. 1982. *Senocrate-Ermodoro, Frammenti*. Naples: Bibliopolis.

1991. 'Fra Stoa e media Stoa' in *Filosofia e scienza nel pensiero ellenistico*. Naples: Morano Editore, 231–63.

Jaskolla, L. J. and Buck, A. J. 2012. 'Does Panexperientialism Solve the Combination Problem?' *Journal of Consciousness Studies* 19: 190–99.

Janos, D. 2011. 'Moving the Orbs: Astronomy, Physics, and Metaphysics, and the Problem of Celestial Motion according to Ibn Sīnā'. *Arabic Sciences and Philosophy* 21: 165–214.

Forthcoming. *Ptolemy's Theory of the Psychic Powers of the Planets in Arabic Philosophy: Some Key Sources and Problems* in A. C. Bowen, E. Gannagé, H. Umut, *The Philosophy of Ptolemy and its Greek, Arabic, and Hebrew Reception*, Brill.

Jouanna J. 1987. 'Le souffle, la vie et le froid: remarques sur la famille de ψύχω d'Homère à Hippocrate'. *Revue des Etudes Grecques* 100: 203–24.

Johansen, T. K. 2004. *Plato's Natural Philosophy : A Study of the Timaeus-Critias*. Cambridge: Cambridge University Press.

2009. 'From Plato's *Timaeus* to Aristotle's *De caelo*' in A. C. Bowen and C. Wildberg (eds.), *New Perspectives on Aristotle's* De Caelo. Leiden: Brill, 9–28.

2012. *The Powers of Aristotle's Soul*. Oxford: Oxford University Press.

2014. 'Why the Cosmos Needs a Craftsman'. *Phronesis* 59: 297–320.

Johnson, M. R. 2008. *Aristotle on Teleology*. Oxford: Oxford University Press.
  2019. 'Aristotle on *Kosmos* and *Kosmoi*' in P. Horky (ed.), *Cosmos in the Ancient World*. Cambridge: Cambridge University Press, 74–107.
Joly, R. 1960. *Recherches sur le traité pseudo-hippocratique Du régime*. Paris: Les Belles Lettres.
  1967. *Hippocrate Du Régime*. Paris: Les Belles Lettres.
Joly, R. and Byl, S. 2003. *Hippocratis De diaeta. Corpus Medicorum Graecorum* I 2,4. Berlin: Akademie.
Jori, A. 2005. 'Blut und Leben bei Aristoteles' in M. Gadebusch Bondio (ed.), *Blood in History and Blood Histories*. Florence: Sismel–Edizioni del Galluzzo, 19–38.
Judson, L. 1994. 'Heavenly Motion and the Unmoved Mover' in M. L. Gill and J. G. Lennox (eds.), *Self-Movers from Aristotle to Newton*. Princeton, NJ: Princeton University Press, 155–71.
Karbowski, J. 2014. 'Empirical *Eulogōs* Argumentation in Aristotle's *Generation of Animals* III.10'. *British Journal for the History of Philosophy* 22: 25–38.
Karfík, F. 2014. 'L'âme du monde: Platon, Anaxagore, Empédocle'. *Études platoniciennes*. http://etudesplatoniciennes.revues.org/572.
Kepler, J. 1596. *Mysterium Cosmographicum*. Frankfurt: Erasmus Kempfer.
Kerschensteiner, J. 1962. *Kosmos: Quellenkritische Untersuchungen zu den Vorsokratikern*. Munich: Beck.
Keyt, D. 1971. 'The Mad Craftsman of the *Timaeus*'. *Philosophical Review* 80: 230–35.
Kielmeyer, C. F. 1793/1993. *Über die Verhältnisse der organischen Kräfte unter einander in der Reihe der verschiedenen Organisationen, die Gesetze und Folgen dieser Verhältnisse*. Faksimile der Ausgabe Stuttgart 1793. Marburg an der Lahn: Basilisken-Press.
Kidd, I. 1999. *Posidonius: The Translation of the Fragments*. Cambridge: Cambridge University Press.
Kohlbrugge, J. H. F. 1911. 'Das biogenetische Grundgesetz: Eine historische Studie'. *Zoologischer Anzeiger* 38: 447–53.
Kudlien, F. 1981. 'Galen's Religious Belief' in V. Nutton (ed.), *Galen: Problems and Prospects*. London: Wellcome Institute, 117–30.
Laks, A. 2008. *Diogène d'Apollonie: édition, traduction et commentaire des fragments et témoignages*. 2nd rev. ed. Sankt Augustin.
  2007. 'Les fonctions de l'intellect chez Anaxagore' in *Histoire, Doxographie, Vérité : Études sur Aristote, Théophraste et la philosophie présocratique*. Louvain: Editions Peeters, 132–48.
  2015. 'Sommeils Présocratiques' in V. Leroux, N. Palmieri and C. Pigné (eds.), *Le Sommeil: Approches philosophiques et médicales de l'Antiquité à la Renaissance*. Paris: Honoré Champion, 29–50.
  2020. 'Articulating the De Motu Animalium. The Place of the Treatise Within the Corpus Aristotelicum' in Ch. Rapp and O. Primavesi (eds.), *Aristotle's De Motu Animalium*, Symposium Aristotelicum, Oxford University Press, pp. 272–95.

Laks, A. and Most, G. W. (eds.). 2016. *Early Greek Philosophy*. 9 vols. Loeb Classical Library. Cambridge, MA: Harvard University Press.

2018. 'How Preplatonic Worlds Became Ensouled'. *Oxford Studies in Ancient Philosophy* 55: 1–34.

Lanza, D. and Vegetti, M. 1971. *Opere biologiche di Aristotele*. Turin: Unione Tipografico-Editrice Torinese.

Lapidge, M. 1989. 'Stoic Cosmology and the Roman Literature, First to Third Centuries A.D.' in W. Haase (ed.), *Aufstieg und Niedergang der römischen Welt*, II 36, 3. Berlin: De Gruyter, 1379–1429.

Le Blay, F. 2014. 'Pneumatism in Seneca: An Example of Interaction between Physics and Medicine' in B. Maire (ed.), *'Greek' and 'Roman' in Latin Medical Texts. Studies in Cultural Change and Exchange in Ancient Medicine*. Leiden: Brill, 63–76.

LeBlond, J.-M. 1938. *Eulogos et l'argument de convenance chez Aristote*. Paris: Les Belles Lettres.

Leboucq, J. B. G. 1944. 'Une anatomie du cœur humain. Philistion de Locres et le "Timée" de Platon'. *Revue des Études Grecques* 57: 7–40.

Lennox, J. G. 1985. 'Theophrastus on the Limits of Teleology' in W. W. Fortenbaugh (ed.), *Theophrastus of Eresus: On His Life and Works*. New Brunswick, NJ: Rutgers University Press, 143–51.

1986. 'Aristotle, Galileo, and the Mixed Sciences' in W. Wallace (ed.), *Reinterpreting Galileo*. Washington, DC: Catholic University of America Press, 29–51.

1994. 'The Disappearance of Aristotle's Biology: A Hellenistic Mystery'. *Apeiron* 27: 7–24.

1997. 'Nature Does Nothing in Vain. . .' in H.-C. Günther and A. Rengakos (eds.), *Beiträge zur antiken Philosophie*. Stuttgart: Franz Steiner Verlag, 199–214. Repr. in Lennox 2001b, 205–24.

2001a. *Aristotle on the Parts of Animals I–IV*. Oxford: Clarendon Press.

2001b. *Aristotle's Philosophy of Biology: Studies in the Origins of Life Science*. Cambridge: Cambridge University Press.

2009. '*De caelo* II.2 and Its Debt to *De incessu animalium*' in A. C. Bowen and C. Wildberg (eds.), *New Perspectives on Aristotle's De Caelo*. Leiden: Brill, 187–214.

Lernould, A. 2000. 'Mathématique et physique chez Proclus: l'interprétation proclienne de la notion de lien en *Timée* 31b-32c' in D. J. O'Meara and G. Bechtle (eds.), *La Philosophie des mathématiques de l'Antiquité tardive*. Fribourg: Éditions Universitaires, 129–47.

Leunissen, M. 2009. 'Why Stars Have No Feet: Teleological Explanations in Aristotle's Cosmology' in A. C. Bowen and C. Wildberg (eds.), *New Perspectives on Aristotle's* De Caelo. Leiden: Brill, 245–71.

2010. *Explanation and Teleology in Aristotle's Science of Nature*. Cambridge: Cambridge University Press.

Levi, I. 1997. *The Covenant of Reason: Rationality and the Commitments of Thought*. Cambridge: Cambridge University Press.

Lewis, O. 2017. *Praxagoras of Cos on Arteries, Pulse and Pneuma. Fragments and Interpretation.* Leiden: Brill.

Lizzini, O. 2018. 'Representation and Reality: On the Definition of Imaginative Prophecy in Avicenna' in B. Bydén and F. Radovic (eds.), *The Parva naturalia in Greek, Arabic and Latin Aristotelianism: Supplementing the Science of the Soul.* New York: Springer, 133–54.

Lloyd, G. E. R. 1971. *Early Greek Science: Thales to Aristotle.* New York: Norton.
   2005. 'Mathematics as a Model of Method in Galen' in R. W. Sharples (ed.), *Philosophy and the Sciences in Antiquity.* Aldershot: Ashgate, 110–30.

Loenen, J. H. 1954. 'Was Anaximander an Evolutionist?' *Mnemosyne* 4: 214–32.

Long, A. A. 2002. *Epictetus, a Stoic and Socratic Guide to Life.* Oxford: Oxford University Press.
   2003. 'Stoicism in the Philosophical Tradition: Spinoza, Lipsius, Butler' in J. Miller and B. Inwood (eds.), *Hellenistic and Early Modern Philosophy.* Cambridge: Cambridge University Press, 7–29.

Long, A. A. and Sedley, D. N. 1987. *The Hellenistic Philosophers.* 2 vols. Cambridge: Cambridge University Press.

Lovelock, J. E. 1972. 'Gaia as Seen through the Atmosphere'. *Atmospheric Environment* 6: 579–80.

Lovelock, J. E. 1976. 'The Quest for Gaia'. *New Scientist* 6: 304–6.
   2001. *Homage to Gaia: The Life of an Independent Scientist.* Oxford: Oxford University Press.

Lovelock, J. E. and Margulis, L. 1974. 'Atmospheric Homeostasis by and for the Biosphere: The Gaia Hypothesis'. *International Meteorological Institute* 26: 2–10.

McGinnis, J. 2006. 'Positioning Heaven: The Infidelity of a Faithful Aristotelian'. *Phronesis* 51: 140–61.

McKirahan, R. D., Jr. 1978. 'Aristotle's Subordinate Sciences'. *British Journal for the History of Science* 11.39: 197–220.
   1992. *Principles and Proofs: Aristotle's Theory of Demonstrative Science.* Princeton, NJ: Princeton University Press.

Mansfeld, J. 1990. 'Doxography and Dialectic: *The Sitz im Leben* of the "Placita"' in W. Haase (ed.), *Aufstieg und Niedergang der römischen Welt* II.36.4. Berlin: De Gruyter, 3056–3229.
   2014. 'Alcmaeon and Plato on Soul'. *Etudes platoniciennes* 11: 1–9.
   2015. 'Heraclitus on Soul and Super-Soul: With an Afterthought on the Afterlife'. *Rhizomata* 3: 62–93.

Mansfeld, J. and Runia, D. T. 1997. *Aëtiana: The Method and Intellectual Context of a Doxographer: Vol. I. The Sources.* Leiden: Brill.
   2009. *Aëtiana: The Method and Intellectual Context of a Doxographer: Vol. II: The Compendium.* Leiden: Brill.
   2020. *Aëtiana V.* An Edition of the Reconstructed Text of the Placita. With a Commentary and a Collection of Related Texts. Part 3 (Books 4 and 5), Leiden: Brill.

Manuli, P. and Vegetti, M. 1977. *Cuore, sangue, cervello: biologia e antropologia nel pensiero antico.* Milan: Episteme Editrice.

Marcovich, M. 2001. *Heraclitus: Greek Text with a Short Commentary*. 2nd ed. Sankt Augustin: Academia Verlag.

Margulis, L. 1999. *Symbiotic Planet: A New Look at Evolution*. Houston: Basic Books.

Marmodoro, A. 2017a. *Everything in Everything: Anaxagoras's Metaphysics*. Oxford: Oxford University Press.

2017b. 'Stoic Blends'. *Proceedings of the Boston Area Colloquium in Ancient Philosophy* 32: 1–24.

Mathews, F. 2011. 'Panpsychism as Paradigm?' in M. Blamauer (ed.), *The Mental as Fundamental*. Heusenstamm: Ontos Verlag, 141–56.

Maudlin, T. 2007. *The Metaphysics within Physics*. Oxford: Oxford University Press.

May, M. T. 1968. *Galen on the Usefulness of the Parts of the Body*. 2 vols. Baltimore: Johns Hopkins University Press.

Meijer, P. A. 2007. *Stoic Theology: Proofs for the Existence of the Cosmic God and of the Traditional Gods Including a Commentary on Cleanthes' Hymn on Zeus*. Delft: Eburon.

Menn, S. 1995. *Plato on God as Nous*. Carbondale: Southern Illinois University Press.

Michalewski, A. 2014. *La puissance de l'intelligible : La théorie plotinienne des Formes au miroir de l'héritage médioplatonicien*. Leuven: Leuven University Press.

Michot, J. 1986. *La destinée de l'homme selon Avicenne. Le retour à Dieu (ma'ād) et l'imagination*. Louvain: Aedibus Peeters, 110–18.

Morison, B. 2020. 'Completing the Argument that Locomotion Requires an External and Unmoved Mover. De Motu Animalium 4–5' in C. Rapp and O. Primavesi (eds.), *Aristotle's De Motu Animalium* (Symposium Aristotelicum), 273–98.

Mortley, R. 1969. 'Plato's Choice of the Sphere'. *Revue des Études Grecques* 82: 342–5.

Müller, J. 1891. *Galeni Scripta Minora*. Vol. 2. Leipzig: B. G. Teubner.

Nagasawa, Y. and Wager, K. 2016. 'Panpsychism and Priority Cosmopsychism' in G. Brüntrup and L. Jaskolla (eds.), *Panpsychism: Contemporary Perspectives*. Oxford: Oxford University Press, 113–29.

Nagel, T. 1979. 'Panpsychism' in *Mortal Questions*. Cambridge: Cambridge University Press, 181–95.

2012. *Mind and Cosmos: Why the Materialist Neo-Darwinian Conception of Nature Is Almost Certainly False*. Oxford: Oxford University Press.

Needham, J. 1959. *A History of Embryology*. 2nd ed. Cambridge: Cambridge University Press.

Nickel, D. 2001. *Galeni de Foetuum Formatione. Corpus Medicorum Graecorum* V 3, 3. Berlin: Akademie Verlag.

Norman, R. 1969. 'Aristotle's Philosopher God'. *Phronesis* 14: 63–74. Repr. in J. Barnes, M. Schofield and R. Sorabji (eds.), Articles on Aristotle*: Vol. 4. Psychology and Aesthetics*. London: Duckworth, 93–102.

Nutton, V. 1978. *Galeni de Praecognitione: Corpus Medicorum Graecorum* V 3,2. Berlin: Akademie Verlag.

1987. 'Galen's Philosophical Testament' in P. Moraux (ed.), *Aristoteles: Werk und Wirkung 2: Kommentierung, Überlieferung, Nachleben*. Berlin: De Gruyter, 27–51.

1999. *Galen: On My Own Opinions. Corpus Medicorum Graecorum* V 3,2. Berlin: Akademie Verlag.

Obbink, D. 1996. *Philodemus, On Piety. Part 1: Critical Text with Commentary*. Oxford: Oxford University Press.

O'Brien, C. 2012. 'The Middle Platonist Demiurge and Stoic Cosmobiology' *Horizons* 3: 19–39.

O'Brien, D. 1987. 'Problèmes d'établissement du texte' in P. Aubenque (ed.), *Études sur Parménide, II: Problèmes d'interprétation*. Paris: Vrin, 314–50.

1997. 'L'Empédocle de Platon'. *Revue des Études Grecques* 110: 381–98.

O'Meara, D. 1985. *Platonic Investigations*. Washington, DC: Catholic University of America Press.

2017. *Cosmology and Politics in Plato's Later Works*. Cambridge: Cambridge University Press.

Opsomer, J. 2005. 'Demiurges in Early Imperial Platonism' in R. Hirsch-Luipold (ed.), *Gott und die Götter bei Plutarch. Götterbilder, Gottesbilder, Weltbilder*. Berlin: De Gruyter, 51–99.

Osborn, H. F. 1929. *From the Greeks to Darwin*. New York: Scribner's.

Oser-Grote, C. M. 2004. *Aristoteles und das* Corpus Hippocraticum: *Die Anatomie und Physiologie des Menschen*. Stuttgart: Franz Steiner Verlag.

Parry, R. D. 1979. 'The Unique World of the *Timaeus*'. *Journal of the History of Philosophy* 17: 1–10.

1991. 'The Intelligible World-Animal in Plato's *Timaeus*'. *Journal of the History of Philosophy* 29: 13–32.

Patterson, R. 1981. 'The Unique Worlds of the *Timaeus*'. *Phoenix* 35: 105–19.

Peck, A. L. 1942. *Aristotle: Generation of Animals*. Loeb Classical Library. Cambridge, MA: Harvard University Press.

Pérez-Jean, B. 2005. *Dogmatisme et scepticisme: l'Héraclitisme d'Enésidème*. Villeneuve-d'Ascq: Presses universitaires du septentrion.

Polito, R. 2004. *The Sceptical Road: Aenesidemus' Appropriation of Heraclitus*. Leiden: Brill.

Potter, P. 2010. *Hippocrates*. Vol. IX. Loeb Classical Library. Cambridge, MA: Harvard University Press.

Pritchard, P. 1990. 'The Meaning of Δύναμις at *Timaeus* 31c'. *Phronesis* 35: 182–93.

Ramelli, I. 2008. *Stoici romani minori*. Milan: Bompiani.

2014. 'Manilius and Stoicism' in M. Garani and D. Konstan (eds.), *The Philosophizing Muse: The Influence of Greek Philosophy on Roman Poetry*. Cambridge: Cambridge Scholars Publishing, 161–86.

Ramelli, I. and Lucchetta, G. 2004. *Allegoria*, Vol. I: *L'età classica*, Introduction by R. Radice. Milan: Vita e Pensiero.

Rapp, C. and Primavesi, O. (eds.) 2020. *Aristotle's De Motu Animalium (Symposium Aristotelicum)*, Oxford: Oxford University Press.

Rashed, M. 2004. 'The Problem of the Composition of the Heavens (529–1610): A New Fragment of Philoponus and Its Readers'. *Bulletin of the Institute of*

Classical Studies 83.Suppl.: 35–56. French version: 'Le problème de la composition du ciel (529–1610): Un nouveau fragment de Philopon et ses lecteurs' in M. Rashed, *L'héritage aristotélicien: Textes inédits de l'Antiquité*. Paris: Les Belles Lettres, 649–89.

    2005. 'Imagination astrale et physique supralunaire selon Avicenne' in G. Federici-Vescovini, V. Sorge and C. Vinti (eds.), *Corpo e anima, sensi interni e intelletto dai secoli XIII-XV ai post-cartesiani e spinoziani*. Turnhout: Brepols, 103–17.

Reinhardt, K. 1926. *Kosmos und Sympathie: Neue Untersuchungen über Poseidonios*. Munich: Beck.

Reydams-Schils, G. 1999. *Demiurge and Providence: Stoic and Platonist Readings of Plato's Timaeus*. Turnhout: Brepols.

    2005. 'Le sage face à Zeus. Logique, éthique et physique dans le stoïcisme impérial'. *Revue de Métaphysique et de Morale* 4: 579–96.

    2006. 'The Roman Stoics on Divine Thinking and Human Knowledge' in S. Gersh and D. Moran (eds.), *Eriugena, Berkeley, and the Idealist Tradition*. Notre Dame: Notre Dame University Press, 81–94.

    2010. 'Seneca's Platonism: The Soul and Its Divine Origin' in A. Nightingale and D. N. Sedley (eds.), *Ancient Models of Mind: Studies in Human and Divine Rationality*. Cambridge: Cambridge University Press, 196–215.

    2013. 'The Academy, the Stoics, and Cicero on Plato's *Timaeus*' in A. G. Long (ed.), *Plato and the Stoics*. Cambridge: Cambridge University Press, 29–58.

Richards, R. J. 1992. *The Meaning of Evolution*. Chicago: University of Chicago Press.

Rivaud, A. 1925. *Platon. Timée. Texte et traduction*. Paris: Les Belles Lettres.

Robin, L. 1919. *Études sur la signification et la place de la physique dans la philosophie de Platon*. Paris: Alcan.

    1926. *Platon. Phédon. Texte et traduction*. Paris: Les Belles Lettres.

    1950. *Platon. Oeuvres complètes,. Traduction nouvelle et notes (avec la collaboration de M.-J. Moreau)*. Books I and II Paris: Gallimard.

Ross, W. D. 1922. *Aristotle: Metaphysics*. 2 vols. Oxford: Oxford University Press.

Rowe, C. 2010. Plato, *The Last Days of Socrates. Eutyphro, Apology, Crito, Phaedo*. Translation with introduction and notes. London: Penguin.

Rudberg, G. 1951. 'Empedocles and Evolution'. *Eranos* 49: 23–30.

Runia, D. T. and Share, M. 2008. *Proclus, Commentary on Plato's Timaeus: Vol. II, Book 2. Proclus on the Causes of the Cosmos and Its Creation*. Cambridge: Cambridge University Press.

Russell, B. 1927. *The Analysis of Matter*. London: George Allen and Unwin.

Salemme, C. 1983. *Introduzione agli* Astronomica *di Manilio*. Naples: Loffredo.

Salles, R. 2005. 'Ekpurosis and the Goodness of God in Cleanthes'. *Phronesis* 50: 56–78.

    2005. *The Stoics on Determinism and Compatibilism*. Aldershot: Ashgate.

    2003. 'Determinism and Recurrence in Early Stoic Thought'. *Oxford Studies in Ancient Philosophy* 24: 253–72.

    2009. 'Chrysippus on Conflagration and the Indestructibility of the Cosmos' in *God and Cosmos in Stoicism*. Oxford: Oxford University Press, 118–34.

2015. 'Two Early Stoic Theories of Cosmogony' in A. Marmodoro and B. D. Prince (eds.), *Causation and Creation in Late Antiquity*. Cambridge: Cambridge University Press, 11–30.

2018a. 'Why Is the Cosmos Intelligent? (1) Stoic Cosmology and Plato, *Philebus* 29a9–30a8'. *Rhizomata* 6.1: 40–64.

2018b. 'Two Classic Problems in the Stoic Theory of Time'. *Oxford Studies in Ancient Philosophy* 55: 133–83.

Sambursky, S. 1973. *Physics of the Stoics*. Westport: Greenwood Press. First ed. 1959 in Princeton, NJ: Princeton University Press.

1987. *The Physical World of the Greeks*. London: Routledge and Kegan Paul.

Sánchez Castro, L. C. 2016. *Traditio animae: la recepción aristotélica de las teorías presocráticas del alma*. Bogotá: Universidad Nacional de Colombia.

2021. 'The Aristotelian Reception of Heraclitus' Conception of the Soul' in C. Harry and J. Habash (eds.), *The Reception of Presocratic Natural Philosophy in Later Classical Thought*. Leiden: Brill, 377–403.

Sattler, B. M. 2012. 'A Likely Account of Necessity, Plato's Receptacle as a Physical and Metaphysical Basis of Space'. *Journal of the History of Philosophy* 50: 159–95.

In preparation. 'Thinking Makes the World Go Round - Intellection and Astronomy in Plato's *Timaeus*'.

Saunders, T. 2004. *Plato: The Laws*. London: Penguin.

Sauvé-Meyer, S. 2009. 'Chain of Causes: What Is Stoic Fate?' in R. Salles (ed.), *God and Cosmos in Stoicism*. Oxford: Oxford University Press, 71–92.

2014 'Aristotle on What Is Up to Us and What Is Contingent' in P. Destrée, R. Salles and M. Zingano (eds.), *What Is Up to Us? Studies on Agency and Responsibility in Ancient Philosophy*. Sankt Augustin: Academia Verlag, 75–89.

Schaffer, J. 2010. 'Monism: The Priority of the Whole'. *Philosophical Review* 119: 31–76.

2013. 'The Action of the Whole'. *Aristotelian Society* 87.Suppl.: 67–87.

Schofield, M. 1983. 'The Syllogisms of Zeno of Citium'. *Phronesis* 28: 31–58.

1999. *The Stoic Idea of the City*. With a foreword by Martha Nussbaum. Chicago: University of Chicago Press.

Schwartz, W. 1972. 'Praecordia mundi. Zur Grundlegung der Bedeutung des Zodiak bei Manilius'. *Hermes* 100: 601–14.

Sedley, D. N. 1989. 'Teleology and Myth in the *Phaedo*'. *Proceedings of the Boston Area Colloquium in Ancient Philosophy* 5: 359–83.

1997a. 'The Ideal of Godlikeness'. Repr. in G. Fine (ed.), *Plato 2: Ethics, Politics, Religion, and the Soul*. Oxford: Oxford University Press, 309–28.

1997b. '"Becoming Like God" in the *Timaeus* and Aristotle' in T. Calvo and L. Brisson (eds.), *Interpreting the* Timaeus-Critias. Sankt Augustin: Academia Verlag: 327–39.

1998. 'Platonic Causes'. *Phronesis* 43: 114–32.

2002. 'The Origins of Stoic God' in M. Frede and A. Laks (eds.), *Traditions of Theology: Studies in Hellenistic Theology, Its Background and Aftermath*. Leiden: Brill, 41–83.

2007. *Creationism and Its Critics*. Berkeley: University of California Press.

2009. 'Three Kinds of Platonic Immortality' in D. Frede and B. Reis (eds.), *Body and Soul in Ancient Philosophy*. Berlin: De Gruyter, 145–61.

2016. 'Empedoclean Superorganisms'. *Rhizomata* 4: 111–25.

2017. 'Socrates, Darwin, and Teleology' in J. Rocca (ed.), *Teleology in the Ancient World: Philosophical and Medical Approaches*. Cambridge: Cambridge University Press, 25–42.

Sedley, D. N. and Long, A. G. 2011. *Plato, Meno and Phaedo*. Cambridge: Cambridge University Press.

Shields, C. 2015. *Aristotle: De Anima*. Oxford: Clarendon Press.

Siegel, R. E. 1973. *Galen on Psychology, Psychopathology, and Function and Diseases of the Nervous System*. Basel: Karger.

Skrbina, D. 2005. *Panpsychism in the West*. Cambridge, MA: MIT Press.

Solmsen, F. 1961. *Cleanthes or Posidonius? The Basis of Stoic Physics*. Amsterdam: N.V. Noord-Hollandsche Uitgevers Maatschappij.

Shani, I. 2015. 'Cosmopsychism: A Holistic Approach to the Metaphysics of Experience'. *Philosophical Papers* 44: 389–417.

Steckerl, F. 1958. *The Fragments of Praxagoras of Cos and His School*. Leiden: Brill.

Steel, C. 2001. 'The Moral Purpose of the Human Body: A Reading of *Timaeus* 69–72'. *Phronesis* 46: 105–28.

Strange, S. K. 1985. 'The Double Explanation in the *Timaeus*'. *Ancient Philosophy* 5: 25–39. Repr. in G. Fine (ed.), *Plato 1: Metaphysics and Epistemology*. Oxford: Oxford University Press, 1999, 397–415.

Strawson, G. and Freeman, A. 2006. *Consciousness and Its Place in Nature: Does Physicalism Entail Panpsychism?* Exeter: Imprint Academic.

Tarán, L. 1975. *Academica: Plato, Philip of Opus, and the Pseudo-Platonic Epinomis*. Philadelphia: American Philosophical Society.

Taylor, A. E. 1928. *A Commentary on Plato's Timaeus*. Oxford: Clarendon Press.

Thein, K. 2006. 'The Life Forms and Their Model in Plato's *Timaeus*'. *Rhizai* 2: 241–73.

Tieleman, T. 1991. 'Diogenes of Babylon and Stoic Embryology. Ps.-Plutarch, Plac. V 15.4 Reconsidered'. *Mnemosyne* 44: 106–25.

1996. *Galen and Chrysippus on the Soul: Argument and Refutation in the* De Placitis *Books II–III*. Leiden: Brill.

2003. *Chrysippus' On Affections: Reconstruction and Interpretation*. Leiden: Brill.

Tirard, S., Morange, M. and Lazcano, A. 2010. 'The Definition of Life: A Brief History of an Elusive Scientific Endeavor'. *Astrobiology* 10: 1003–9.

Twetten, D. 2016. 'Aristotelian Cosmology and Causality in Classical Arabic Philosophy' in D. Janos (ed.), *Ideas in Motion in Baghdad and Beyond: Philosophical and Theological Exchanges between Christians and Muslims in the Third/Ninth and Fourth/Tenth Centuries*. Leiden: Brill, 312–434.

Tyrrell, T. 2013. *On Gaia: A Critical Investigation of the Relationship between Life and Earth*. Princeton, NJ: Princeton University Press.

Verbeke, G. 1945. *L'évolution de la doctrine du pneuma du Stoïcisme à S. Augustin*. Paris: Desclée De Brouwer/Éditions de l'Institut Supérieur de Philosophie.

Vicaire, P. 1983. *Platon. Phédon. Texte et traduction*. With an introduction by L. Robin. Paris: Les Belles Lettres.

Vlastos, G. 1939. 'The Disorderly Motion in the *Timaeus*'. *Classical Quarterly* 33: 71–83.

Vogt, K. M. 2008. *Law, Reason, and the Cosmic City: Political Philosophy in the Early Stoa*. New York: Oxford University Press.

2012. 'Michael Frede, a Free Will'. *Classical Philology* 107: 161–8.

2014. 'I Shall Do What I Did: Stoic Views on Action' in P. Destrée, R. Salles and M. Zingano (eds.), *What Is Up to Us? Studies on Agency and Responsibility in Ancient Philosophy*. Sankt Augustin: Academia Verlag, 107–20.

2018. 'A Unified Notion of Cause'. *Rhizomata: A Journal for Ancient Philosophy and Science* 6: 65–86.

Volk, K. 2009. *Manilius and His Intellectual Background*. Oxford: Oxford University Press.

Vorwerk, M. 2010. 'Maker or Father? The Demiurge from Plutarch to Plotinus' in R. D. Mohr and B. M. Sattler (eds.), *One Book, the Whole Universe: Plato's Timaeus Today*. Las Vegas: Parmenides, 79–100.

Vottero, D. 1989. *Questioni naturali di Lucio Anneo Seneca*. Turin: Unione Tipografico-Editrice Torinese.

Westra, L. and Robinson, T. (eds.), *The Greeks and the Environment*. Lanham: Rowman and Littlefield.

Wilberding, J. 2006. *Plotinus' Cosmology*. Oxford: Oxford University Press.

2011. 'Intelligible Kinds and Natural Kinds in Plotinus'. *Études Platoniciennes* 7: 53–73.

2014. 'Teratology in Neoplatonism'. *British Journal for the History of Philosophy* 22: 1021–42.

2015. 'Plato's Embryology'. *Early Science and Medicine* 20: 150–68.

2017. *Forms, Souls and Embryos: Neoplatonists on Human Reproduction*. London: Routledge.

Wildberger, J. 2006. *Seneca und die Stoa: Der Platz des Menschen in der Welt*. 2 vols. Berlin: De Gruyter.

Wilson, M. 2013. *Structure and Method in Aristotle's Meteorologica: A More Disorderly Nature*. Cambridge: Cambridge University Press.

Wisnovsky, R. 2002. 'Final and Efficient Causality in Avicenna's Cosmology and Theology'. *Quaestio* 2: 97–123.

2003a. *Avicenna's Metaphysics in Context*. Ithaca, NY: Cornell University Press.

2003b. 'Towards a History of Avicenna's Distinction between Immanent and Transcendent Causes' in D. Reisman and A. H. Al-Rahim (eds.), *Before and after Avicenna: Proceedings of the First Conference of the Avicenna Study Group*. Leiden: Brill, 49–68.

Wittgenstein, L. 1922. *Tractatus logico-philosophicus*. London: Kegan Paul, Trench, Trubner.

Zeyl, D. J. 2000. *Plato: Timaeus*. Indianapolis: Hackett.

Index

Index Locorum

The index only includes the main passages discussed in the chapters

Aetius

De Placita Philosophorum

1.3.4: 12
1.7.9: 200 n. 64
1.7.11: 10
1.7.13: 12
1.7.33: 215, 216 n. 28
1.18.6: 23
2.17.4: 16
4.2.1: 11
4.2.2: 24
4.2.3-4: 26
4.3.2: 12
4.3.12: 15
4.5.7: 193 n. 15
4.7.2: 15
4.17.1: 191 n. 3
4.21.2-4: 182 n. 18

Alcinous

Didaskalikos

12.1: 95 n. 19
14.3: 95 n. 20

Alcmeon

(Ed. Diels-Kranz / Laks-Most)

DK 24A5: 191 n. 3
DK 24A12 / LM 23D9 and R3-5: 24
DK 24B1 / LM 23D10: 24

Alexander of Aphrodisias

De Mixtione

216, 14-218, 6: 214 n. 23
225.1-2: 213

Principles of the Cosmos (Mabādi')

52, 6-8: 265 n. 23

Ammonius

In Porphyrii Isagogen Sive Quinque Voces

104, 32-105, 8: 151 n. 62

Anaximander

(Ed. Diels-Kranz)

DK 12A10-11: 132 n. 4
DK 12A30: 132 n. 4

Anaximenes

(Ed. Diels-Kranz / Laks-Most)

DK 13A10 / LM 7D5-6: 12
DK 13A23 / LM 7D30: 12
DK 13B2 / LM 7D31 and R5: 12

Apuleius

De Platone et eius dogmate

1.9 [199]: 91

Aristotle

Analytica Posteriora

72a15-24: 118
75b14-20: 112 n. 6
76a22-25: 112 n. 6
78b32-79a16: 112 n. 6

De Anima

Book 2: 137 n. 19
Book 2.2-3: 136

2.87-97: 152 n. 1
2.94-95: 153 n. 2
2.118: 154 n. 6
2.154-162: 178 n. 10
3.23: 185 n. 21

Clement of Alexandria
Protrepticus ad Graecos

66.2: 24

Stromata

4.26: 211 n. 12

Cornutus
Theologia Graecae Compendium

7: 171

Diogenes Laertius
Vitae Philosophorum

1.24: 10
1.27: 10
8.83: 24
7.88: 181 n. 17
7.121: 221
7.134: 212–13
7.135: 167 n. 33, 213 n. 20
7.136: 169–70
7-138-139: 170, 182 n. 18, 200 n. 61
7.139: 161 n. 18, 163
7.142: 166–7
7.143: 162–3, 169, 200 nn. 60 and 64
7.147: 163 n. 22, 210 nn. 7 and 9
7.154: 201 n. 69
7.157: 200 n. 59
9.7-11: 21

Diogenes of Apollonia
(ed. Diels-Kranz / Laks-Most)

DK 13A4 / LM D7: 20 n. 37

Empedocles
(Ed. Diels-Kranz / Laks-Most)

DK 31A97: 193 n. 19
DK 31A30: 192 fr. 31A97 and 11
DK 31A74: 194
DK 31A86: 191 n. 3, 194 n. 20,
 205 n. 98
DK 31B136 / LM R39: 22
DK 31B57-59: 133 n. 7
DK 31B57: 133 n. 9

DK 31B61: 133 n. 8, 134 n. 11
DK 31B63: 133 n. 9, 134 n. 10
DK 31B100: 194
DK 31B105: 193 n. 16

Epictetus
Dissertationes ab Ariano

1.6.7: 152 n. 1
1.6.18-22: 179
2.5.24-25: 179
2.6.8-10: 180 n. 12
2.10.5-6: 180 nn. 12 and 13
3.13.7: 154 n. 6, 168 n. 36

Eusebius
Praeparatio Evangelica

1.8.10: 192 n. 10
11.28.8-9: 24
15.14.2: 215 n. 26
15.20.2: 21 n. 44

Filósofos Estoicos [Boeri-Salles 2014 = BS]

12.11: 174 n. 6
12.13: 174, 182 n. 18
12.14: 175
12.16: 174, 182
13.13: 182 n. 18
13.14: 182 n. 18
19.9: 182
29.7: 179
30.45: 181 n. 17

Galen
De foetuum formatione libellus (ed. Nickel)

92, 16-21: 240

De Placitis Hippocratis et Platonis

2.5.8: 196 nn. 35 and 36
2.8.40-48: 192 n. 13
3.7.34-35: 196 n. 37
3.8: 198 n. 51

586, 7-590, 11 De Lacy: 226

De Propriis Placitis (ed. Nutton)

2.1-3; 56, 12-58, 16: 225
3.1; 58, 22-60, 6: 226
13.5; 106, 14-23: 243
15.1; 116,5-118, 10: 226

Platonist Philosophy [Boys-Stones 2018 = BS]

Plotinus

Enneads

Plutarch

De Animae Procreatione in Timaeo

De Communibus Notitiis

De Defectu Oraculorum

De Stoicorum Repugnantiis

Platonicae Quaestiones

For EU product safety concerns, contact us at Calle de José Abascal, 56–1°,
28003 Madrid, Spain or eugpsr@cambridge.org.

www.ingramcontent.com/pod-product-compliance
Ingram Content Group UK Ltd.
Pitfield, Milton Keynes, MK11 3LW, UK
UKHW020359140625

459647UK00020B/2553